I Looked and I Listened

Informal Recollections of Radio and TV

I Looked
and
I Listened

Informal Recollections of
Radio and TV

Ben Gross

Arlington House
New Rochelle, N.Y.

Library of Congress Catalog Card Number—78-115344

SBN 87000-095-0

MANUFACTURED IN THE UNITED STATES OF AMERICA

CONTENTS

(Illustrations Following Page 150)

v

Anyone presumptuous enough to write about his three decades in radio and TV should be able to come up with a weighty excuse for indulging himself in the delightful exercise of self-revelation.

But after a prolonged period of pondering, I have been able to fish from my subconscious only one plausible reason for writing this book: it has been great fun.

Although the chapters that follow have been committed to paper by a veteran observer of the radio-TV scene, this is *not* a formal or scholarly history of broadcasting. Those who seek detailed information in this field are urged to read such authoritative volumes as Francis Chase, Jr.'s *Sound and Fury*, Robert J. Landry's *This Fascinating Radio Business*, Abel Green and Joe Laurie, Jr.'s *Show Biz*, Orrin E. Dunlap, Jr.'s *The Story of Radio*, the historical brochure, "The First Twenty-Five Years of RCA," and Gleason L. Archer's monumental works on the early days of the industry. The serious student may consult any or all of these with profit.

The assembling of a story such as this involves reliance not only on memory, diaries and random notes but also on the co-operation of kind and generous friends. For their aid in checking data and in contributing other services, grateful acknowledgment is made to Sydney H. Eiges and George Crandall, press-relations chiefs of NBC and CBS, respectively; Mike Boscia and Hardin Callithan of the CBS press department; Ethel Kirsner and Sam Kaufman of the NBC publicity staff; Jack B. Perlis, TV-radio public-relations consultant; Kay Gardella and Matty Messina of the New York *News* TV-Radio Department, and Kathleen Cotter Gross for her criticisms and many suggestions.

For their help in contributing photographs for the revised edition, I have to thank Gene Walsh, Director of Program Publicity, NBC; Charles S. Steinberg, Vice President, Public Information, CBS-TV Network; Sid Garfield, Director of Special Projects, CBS-TV Network; Edward Reynolds, Associate Director, CBS-TV Press Information; and Larry Carr of Larry Carr Photos.

B. G.

NEW YORK
MARCH, 1970

To the memory of two good people,
my mother and father,
Sarah and Adolph Gross

Encore

In TV there are the reruns of programs already seen during the regular season. The world of publishing also has its repeats; so here is a new edition of *I Looked and I Listened.*

For some years after it had joined the vast legion of books listed as being "out of print," there was a continuing demand for it in public libraries and universities. This, primarily because the episodes and personalities that it highlights are part of the popular history, folk legends and traditions of broadcasting, the country's most powerful medium of communication—true Americana.

In this new edition there has been no tampering with the volume's nostalgic elements. These comprise the human interest appeal of the story of TV and radio. But so much has happened, so far–reaching have been the changes during the last 14 years, that I have added a new chapter briefly summarizing some of the most important of these developments.

Each one of these might be worthy of a full–length book. However, *I Looked and I Listened* does not pretend to be a formal or scholarly history of American broadcasting. Rather, it is a series of events and vignettes that some critics have been kind enough to praise as both "entertaining" and "informative."

Those seeking a more detailed treatment of the subject matter are referred to such authoritative works as Gleason L. Archer's monumental history of the early days of radio, Prof. Erik Barnouw's comprehensive *A Tower in Babel* and *The Golden Web,* Abel Green and Joe Laurie, Jr.'s *Show Biz* and Robert J. Landry's

This Fascinating Radio Business. The serious student may consult any of these with profit.

So here again are some personal recollections of one who for more than four decades, from the days of the crystal radio sets to the time of live telecasts from the moon, has had a down–front–center seat in the theatre of broadcasting. On its stage, the heroes and the knaves, the serious–minded and the clowns, the idealists and the crass commercialists have played their roles in the comedy and drama of radio and TV.

If anyone should ask why a collection of reminiscences should be reissued at a time when stirring events blot from the memory the happenings of even last week, there is this obvious answer: One cannot understand the present without knowledge of the past.

Anyway, it was great fun writing this book, and it will be an even more joyous experience to see it in print once more. Also, not to be lightly overlooked, there is the little matter of collecting royalties again.

NEW YORK
AUGUST, 1969

ONE

How I Became an "Expert"

I must have been all of ten years old when I read somewhere that Destiny is a protean artist, coming to us in many guises. Sometimes, the writer, never at a loss for large or small analogies, went on to say, it might manifest itself in a bloody battle on which hangs the fate of empire and, on other occasions, it might show itself in the favor of a beautiful woman.

But my destiny announced its presence in the guttural command of the world's toughest city editor on a baking, breathless afternoon in the summer of 1925.

I had just returned to the long and narrow city room of the New York *Daily News* in a dingy loft building on Park Place in downtown New York. That morning, a *crime passionelle* had taken me to Passaic, New Jersey, where a hot-blooded but methodical Magyar had used a butcher's knife to carve his initials on the brow of his fiancée, whose fidelity he had cause to doubt. The city editor, a fervent believer in newspaper mores as portrayed in Hollywood movies, had ordered: "Get her picture—or don't come back!"

A new and as yet somewhat uncertain member of the tabloid's staff, I deposited the pilfered photograph on his desk with a glow of triumph. But instead of rewarding me with a benevolent word, Colonel Frank J. Hause, one of the most dynamic and certainly the hardest-boiled newspaper executive of the 1920's, gave me only a baleful glare.

"Okay," he said. "Look, Gross . . ."

Not only I but at least one-half of those in the city room looked, for, although addressed as "Colonel," the boss, even in casual conversation, had the bellow of a top sergeant.

"Look," he repeated, "turn your stuff over to a rewrite man and go up to the radio room."

Thrusting a Yale key into my hand, the Colonel informed me that our radio editor was ill and I would have to replace him for the night. "Listen to the programs and write a column about it."

I knew, of course, that we had a radio room, but where it was or what it was like, I had not the slightest idea. He might as well have assigned me to the lost continent of Atlantis.

The Colonel's terse command changed my life. The brief climb up the rickety flight of stairs to a cubicle just off the advertising department was the first stage of a journey into a razzle-dazzle world. It led to a turbulent sphere in which brutal materialism, blatant fakery and corroding insincerity vied with high ideals, fantastic dreams and miraculous achievements.

Up to that day, radio to me, as to most "sophisticated" young newspapermen of that time, had been only an irritating although occasionally fascinating toy. It was kid stuff, a vogue, a passing craze, a mélange of jarring commercials and of raucous static.

This, although as far back as 1921, while I was visiting relatives in Pelham Manor, out in Westchester, a youngster had clamped on me the earphones of his homemade crystal set and over it had come the faint screech of a soprano singing "The End of a Perfect Day." This, although on that occasion the ancient Negro cook of the family, after hearing a saxophone solo on the same machine, had exclaimed in unbelieving tones: "Uh-huh! That sure is a box full of magic!" This, although with millions of others I had been stirred by the dramatic broadcasts of the 1924 Democratic National Convention, which, it is said, had a longer run than *Abie's Irish Rose* and *South Pacific* combined.

Going blithely up those *News* Building stairs, a youthful reporter did not have opportunity to reflect on the age in which he lived. That, however, might have been a profitable enterprise, for the tumultuous airwaves echoed every folly and every virtue of the times. . . .

Calvin Coolidge, the lean oracle from Vermont, meditated in the White House. Wall Street brokers in striped trousers watched the coiling ticker tape in ecstasy. Tin lizzies rolled off the assembly lines in Detroit and bobbed-haired flappers with jade earrings and in knee-length dresses paraded Fifth Avenue. Ivy Leaguers lolled beneath the Biltmore clock and big butter-and-egg men guzzled apple cider at twenty dollars a bottle in Manhattan speakeasies, while down in Dayton, Tennessee, Clarence Darrow and William Jennings Bryan debated evolution in the Scopes "monkey" trial.

Money, money, everywhere and many new things to buy. New things, fantastic things: tomato juice, sauerkraut juice, toasters, vacuum cleaners, jeweled hip flasks, improved safety razors, wondrous beautifying lotions and now that most amazing gadget of all—radio.

In cluttered electrical shops on New York's Cortlandt and Vesey Streets, on Chicago's State Street and on thoroughfares in towns clear across the continent, loud-speakers rasped through the daylight and the evening hours. High-school boys, in barns, back yards, and attics pored over diagrams in newspapers and built amazing contraptions which brought forth music from the air. Fathers smiled tolerantly and mothers shook bewildered heads at the breakfast-table chatter of their offspring.

"I got Kansas City last night."

"Aw, you couldn't!"

"Well, I'm sending 'em a log card, telling what program I heard. They'll mail me an acknowledgment."

And down in Washington, the Great Engineer pondered sagely the future of radio. Herbert Hoover, as Secretary of Commerce, had theoretical supervision of the nation's broadcasting and he uttered idealistic words, visualizing it as a medium of culture and of education. He saw it as "an instrument of beauty and of learning," untainted by blatant advertising. But others did not share his dream and he was powerless against them, for the Government's control was almost as invisible as the airwaves themselves. . . .

But all of this was of no concern to me on that hot afternoon when I entered the radio department of the *News* for the first time. In the center of an unkempt room, no bigger than a good-sized closet, stood a dusty pine table and on it was a boxlike contraption with a multitude of knobs and dials. Near by, on a broken chair, rested a gigantic goose-neck horn—the loud-speaker. On the splintered floor, four or five A-batteries oozed acid on the rotting planks. I could identify these foul-smelling objects, at least, and I had heard in a vague way that each battery had a positive and a negative pole, and there was also something about plus and minus.

From the battered set on the table dangled several wires attached to clamps. Something told me that these clamps were to be connected with the batteries. About that time my eyes wandered to the beaten-up roll-top desk in the corner with a dusty typewriter and a jumble of coils, switches, tubes and other mysterious gadgets, all merging into a futuristic nightmare scene straight out of *The Cabinet of Dr. Caligari*.

"Lemme see," I muttered, taking off my coat, "one clamp goes on plus, the other on minus." Somehow, I got them connected and then twirled the dials. Nothing happened. I pulled a switch and turned knobs. Still there was no sound. "You've got to be an electrical engineer to get this thing going," I thought.

A gray-haired advertising solicitor standing in the doorway of the cubicle watched me with a tolerant smile. "Know how to turn this thing on?" I asked.

"Nope," he said. "Don't like 'em. Too noisy." He strolled away, leaving me helpless and profane, with the deadline for the first edition drawing near.

"Why did Marconi have to think of radio?" I asked myself, giving up the struggle and starting for the city room again.

"I can't turn it on," I confessed sheepishly to the Colonel, who at that moment was absorbed in drawing black pencil lines through some unfortunate reporter's lurid prose.

"What!" His exclamation exploded with a force that must have shaken the foundations of the Woolworth Building across the street.

"I thought maybe you could tell me how to . . ." I stammered.

"How the hell would I be knowing anything about a radio?" he roared. "I haven't got one of the damned things and don't expect to have one!"

The Colonel squinted at the battery of rewrite men near by and pounded the desk with an enormous fist. "Anybody here who knows how to turn on a radio?" he thundered.

Typewriters ceased clicking; conversation faded into a ghost of sound. He shouted the question again.

Unbelievable as it may seem now, in that crowded editorial room of a great metropolitan newspaper there wasn't a man or woman who knew how to hook up a radio! Or at least no one admitted such knowledge.

"Try the composing room," said the Colonel, now in a mere whisper which could not be heard more than fifty yards away.

I did, but there was no help there either. Finally, a linotype operator suggested I see Pete, one of the building electricians. I found him a half hour later coming out of the restaurant adjoining the *News*. Just twenty minutes before the deadline, he lumbered into the radio room and with an air of boredom attached the clamps, plugged in the loud-speaker, pulled a switch and turned several dials. "Easy. Nuthin' to it," he said.

Before I could thank him a piercing rasp and a shrill whine shook the horn on the broken chair. I gave the dials another twirl and— wonder of wonders!—the voices of two men surged through the dust-flecked air. Billy Jones and Ernie Hare, "The Happiness Boys," were singing their theme song, "How do you do, everybody, how do you do?"

"It works!" I exclaimed exultantly, pumping the lethargic electrician's hand.

"Sure," said Pete with a shrug and then ambled out of the room.

A few days later, subbing in the press room of the Criminal Courts building, I remarked to a fellow reporter that I had spent several evenings listening to programs.

"Condolences," he said.

"Do you think radio is here to stay?" I quoted the popular gag of the day.

"God forbid!" he said.

Apparently the young man who functioned as radio editor of the *News* shared his sentiments. Convinced that there was no future either in broadcasting or in writing about it, he resigned his job and some time later I stood before the city editor again.

"Gross, you're it," said the Boss.

"I don't like radio," I said. "I want to be a drama critic."

"You'll be a radio critic," he insisted. "It's not a full-time job; you'll also cover other stories and continue writing that labor column you're doing."

"But I'm not qualified," I protested. "I don't know a thing about radio."

"Oh, yes you do!" There was ice in the Colonel's voice and a determined glint in his eyes. "From now on you're our expert—our great authority. And do you know why? Because you're the only guy around here who knows how to turn one of the damned things on!"

And that was the beginning of my adventures among the kilocycles.

This, however, was just one climactic moment in the story of a young newspaperman's romance with the metropolis.

With gray cinders beating against the Pullman window pane, the Southern Railway special curved through the green hills skirting Birmingham. The click-clack rhythm of the wheels became staccato words: "New-York-is-a-golden-town-New-York-is-a-golden-town."

Flat fields of young cotton stalks . . . sunshine and a distant haze . . . pines and oaks in springtime green . . . red clay roads and wooden shacks . . . an aged Negro behind a mule-drawn plow . . . mills with spinning wheels and hissing steam . . . scenes of childhood and signposts on a happy road which one traveler doubted he would ever tread again.

"New York is a cruel place," a friend had said. "You'll be walking its streets and not a friendly face in sight." And an old teacher had added: "New York has no heart. It drains young people and then casts them aside."

But that was not the New York I had come to know via so many books, short stories and newspaper columns. It was the dwelling place of adventure and of romance, of giant newspapers and of glamorous newspapermen whose ranks one day I intended to join.

I had remembered the words spoken by an Irish laborer on Tilbury Docks, London, the very words which now found utterance in the clacking of the wheels. Our regiment's transport, the 348th Infantry, 87th Division, had tied up there during World War One. And as we enlisted men stood with full packs ready to entrain for a camp in Winchester, this bent old man had asked if by any chance I lived in New York. It saddened him when I told him no. He shook his head and said, "Too bad . . . New York, 'tis a golden town."

And it was because I had believed him, and others, too, that there now streaked through my mind not only visions of the bright future but remembrances of the happy past. . . .

School days in Birmingham . . . a few childhood years on the mirage-haunted Hungarian plain . . . visits to Budapest and Vienna . . . enchanted afternoons in the studio of the noted Southern painter, Edna Smith, talking of the great artists and writers she had known . . . carefree semesters at Tulane and the law school of the University of Alabama . . . the thrill of getting and writing a story for the Birmingham *News* . . . time in a law office, looking up citations and composing dunning letters to unresponsive deadbeats . . . the years of war: Camps Sevier, Wadsworth, Pike and Dix . . . the sailing from Montreal on the *City of Poona,* a converted East Indian cattle ship . . . an attack on the convoy by submarines off the Scilly Islands . . . the stay in France and Armistice Day, November 11, 1918, in Bordeaux, where a group of doughboys paraded down the rue St. Catherine arm in arm with a French colonel, a gob and a drunken shopkeeper carrying a loaf of bread and an enormous fish . . . and, above all, that happy day the following March when our transport steamed past the Statue of Liberty up New York Harbor. . . .

These images whirred in a vivid kaleidoscope throughout the afternoon, the evening and the sleepless night. But by morning only the present remained and as the train plowed through the tunnel to Pennsylvania Station I stood impatiently in the sleeper vestibule, eager for battle with that ruthless and yet bountiful antagonist—New York.

With two suitcases and seventy-eight dollars, plus a few cents, in my pockets, I stepped expectantly into the turmoil of the concourse on an afternoon in late May, 1919. In front of me was a bulletin board on which a placard advertised a servicemen's and veterans' hotel in the lower Thirties. I scanned it carefully, intent on finding cheap lodging immediately and a job as soon as possible. A few minutes later, after I had displayed my honorable discharge to a grumpy desk clerk, a bellboy wearing an Army tunic showed me to a cell of a room.

The next morning proved discouraging. My rounds of the newspapers failed to net an interview with even one city editor. The receptionists greeted me with variations of: "Sorry. We've got to take care of our men coming back from the war." At the *World*, however, a reporter from Georgia remarked: "Don't worry, kid. Hang around; you'll find something."

And, indeed, I did. For within a few days, Nell Freeman, the wife of Isadore Shapiro, a lawyer friend from Birmingham, introduced me to the editor of a small community paper on Washington Heights, *The Sentinel*, and he hired me as a man of all work for twenty-five dollars a week.

My home was a cramped, dark room on West 168th Street, for which I paid $3.50 every seven days. But most of my non-working hours were spent downtown in the more glamorous environs of Broadway and Greenwich Village. Even on my small income, living in New York was no problem for a single young man. In drug stores there were fifteen-cent breakfasts of coffee, toast, bacon or ham with one egg. And a countless number of Italian and French restaurants served good table d'hôte dinners, some with wine, for a half dollar.

Maybe it was being young, maybe it was merely the exuberant spirit of the times but, whatever the reason, even to the poorest hallroom boy New York seemed a truly wonderful town. In the mild spring and the early summer air there was the glow of victory; returning troops with bands blaring and banners flying paraded down Fifth Avenue; beautiful girls, free and gay, strolled the sidewalks; at night, Broadway with its lobster palaces and theatres had an effulgent glow; hope and optimism were the heritage of all. Through the ferry slips and the rail terminals thousands of youth poured each day; hotels were filled; rooming houses burst at their seams and during the evening the tiniest restaurants, cabarets and cafés were carnivals of laughter, the revelers unmindful of the drought that might come with prohibition in January, 1920.

During the final year of this century's second decade there was also something else in the air, more important than hope, laughter or victory—a fervent conviction that we had seen the last of war.

The conflict just concluded had, after all, been "the war to end all wars," and those who doubted were cynics, crass men of little faith. Ahead stretched the long, long vistas of bountiful and peaceful years. One could step aside and think and plan for the time to come. "I'll be here, doing this until 1921 . . . then I'll go to Paris . . . in 1922 I'll return . . . I'll get a nest egg, marry and settle down." It was all neatly blueprinted in millions of minds . . . no shadow of Russia . . . no fear of the atom bomb.

The bobbed-hair flapper and the collegiate with the coonskin coat were on the verge of being born. They would soon join us all in the merry dance of life and, as an offset to the comforting certainties that prevailed, indulge in the youthful adventure of rebellion. It was not to be a political revolt, for the country was about to swing to the conservatism of the Harding regime, but an aesthetic and intellectual one. I wanted to be at the heart of that rebellion, in Greenwich Village, and soon removed myself from the small room on Washington Heights to a large chamber overlooking a garden on 11th Street between Fifth and Sixth Avenues, for which the landlady demanded what I regarded as an exorbitant sum, $5.50 a week.

It was a lucky move, for in a Village tearoom, Romany Marie's, I met one night a man who introduced me to the publisher of a monthly travel magazine which was distributed to the guests of a number of chain hotels. A dapper Spaniard, bald, mustachioed and jovial, he hired me as editor for thirty dollars a week. To earn this stipend, I had to write pontifical editorials on world issues, intimate gossip of New York society, not one of whose members I had ever met, and lengthy articles on faraway places I had never seen.

"Here are some good pictures of Ceylon from a travel bureau," the boss would say. "Do three thousand words on it."

With the aid of reference books and files of the *National Geographic* at the Public Library, this was no problem at all. I dashed off poetic pieces on the South Sea isles, vivid descriptions of gay life in Rio and purple prose about the beauties of the Taj Mahal. On one occasion the boss, whom the office staff fondly called the "Grand Señor," gave me some stunning pictures of the towering pagodas of Rangoon. "You can really go to town on these!" he said.

I did. And, months later, the publisher received a letter from a high government official of Burma praising the story for its "authentic" touches and expressing regret that "your writer while here did not make himself known."

But it wasn't my powers of description that made me a favorite of the Grand Señor. Rather it was my keen eye for unexpected visitors, among the most frequent of whom was the gentleman's wife. On my desk in the outer office was a buzzer which notified me that I was wanted in the inner sanctum. And beside me there was also a button which sounded a buzzer in the publisher's room. He had repeatedly admonished me, "When you see the Missus coming, don't fail to press that button!" That gave him a warning and enabled him to exit via a side door. I devoted myself with such exemplary devotion to this phase of my duty that one day the Grand Señor remarked: "You're the best editor I've ever had. You never fail to push that button!" Thereupon, he gave me a raise of $1.50 a week.

Not a great sum, but enough to provide me with a pleasure-filled evening on Broadway, with perhaps a few cents left over following the fling. Fifty or maybe seventy-five cents would buy a gallery theatre ticket at Joe Leblang's basement cut-rate emporium on Times Square. One simply stood in the crowd before the counters, behind which hawkers, shouting the names of current attractions, pointed to a gigantic board. On it were cards advertising the plays or musicals available that evening. If one waited long enough, say until five minutes before curtain time, he could pick up some bargains in admission to many of the hit shows.

But this all-too-brief carefree interlude soon came to an end. For one day the Grand Señor informed me that his magazine had been sold. "And, quite frankly, I must tell you that the new publisher refuses to employ a Jew."

This came as a shock and a deep hurt. I knew about anti-Semitism, of course, but in all my years in the South had never encountered it personally. I had only vaguely heard of the anti-Jewish prejudices of certain social circles. Yet, in all truth, it had not affected me either at Alabama or Tulane and certainly not in Birmingham.

Racial injustice against the Negroes had been an ever present tragedy, but no intelligent Southerner within my circle condoned it. As for outspoken hatred of the Catholics and the Jews, that was an evil festering only among a minute lunatic fringe. At least this was true as far as the Jews were concerned until after World War One when the revived Ku Klux Klan rose to power. The Catholics, however, had begun to bear the brunt of increasing discrimination some time before that.

Isadore Shapiro, my lawyer friend, despite his obviously Jewish name, had managed to be elected to the State Legislature by a big majority. But certain anti-Catholic elements had refused to support him, as not long before he had denounced religious bigotry of every type.

One of the leaders of this group on being asked why he was against Shapiro answered: "I'll tell you why. That Jew ain't nuthin' but a goddamned Catholic!"

The melancholy induced by this manifestation of religious intolerance in New York soon passed and I set out again in pursuit of work with renewed optimism. A reporter friend, Harry Klemfuss, whom I had met on the Heights, recommended me to the *Bronx Home News* and the city editor promised me a job "within the next few weeks."

But the weeks passed and still there were no vacancies either in the Bronx or on the Manhattan and Brooklyn dailies. There was a little money to be made by accepting temporary assignments from the City News Association but at this time I knew nothing of these opportunities. In the meantime, I was behind in my room rent and the few greenbacks hidden in an old shirt in the bottom bureau drawer approached the vanishing point.

I lived on thirty cents a day . . . but there was no cause for worry. Something surely would turn up. For it was a good time, a gay time, a time filled with hope and, as that Irish dock worker had told me, New York was a golden town.

TWO

Young Man in the Bronx

Most of us on the *Bronx Home News* staff in 1921 were eager out-of-towners drawn to the metropolis by gaudy visions of journalistic fame; but there was an enormous gap between the reality and the dream.

We were apprenticed to what was essentially a small-town routine on the northern edges of the city. Our daily contacts were not with those basking in the klieg light of celebrity but with merchants, doctors, lawyers, housewives, magistrates and bailiffs of mere neighborhood repute. We did not realize that we moved in a treasure cave gleaming with jewels of character and human interest; we could not see that a district reporter covering Washington Heights and Inwood, as I did, had closer communion with the heart of New York than the columnists and the critics of the downtown papers whom we regarded with such envy.

But it was not my New York—not the enchanted Gotham of O. Henry's Baghdad-on-the-Subway, the fabled city of Richard Harding Davis or the magical realm evoked by O. O. McIntyre.

To me New York was a wondrous razzle-dazzle land: a million human ants scurrying on Wall Street during the luncheon hour; skyscrapers rising through the mist from the deck of the Staten Island ferry; the dim garrets and the candlelit tearooms of Greenwich Village; experimental theatres producing masterpieces in converted stables; bands playing "The Stars and Stripes Forever," as victorious troops marched up Fifth Avenue; the white incandescence of Broadway at night, with the names of Daniel Frohman, Arthur Hopkins and David Belasco flaunted against the sky; the lobster palaces—Churchill's, Shanley's and Rector's; the round table at the Algonquin; Caruso sobbing out his heart at the Met; and, above all, a berth on one of the great newspapers of Manhattan.

Out of these was compounded an elixir which had buoyed the spirits of so many of us on the Birmingham *News* and on other provincial papers throughout the land. A police card from the *World,* the *Times,* the *Herald,* the *Tribune* or the *Sun* would have been the open sesame swinging wide the gates to endless adventure. Not that we wouldn't have been satisfied with employment on a lesser journal. Sometimes, when the *Home News* staff gathered for afternoon coffee at a little lunchroom on Third Avenue and 149th Street, some of us admitted that we'd settle for a job even on that new tabloid, the New York *Daily News,* which according to many soothsayers of those days did not have "the slightest chance in the world" to survive.

The proprietor of this gathering place, a loquacious Irishman, had no sympathy for our ambitions. "Whatya wanta go downtown for?" he would ask. "Why the whole world's right here in the Bronx! The trouble is all you guys want to be journalists. My old man used to be a district man for the *Herald.* He'd always say, 'A journalist is a guy who ain't good enough to be a reporter!' "

But these sardonic admonitions did not sway us. Our hearts were set on Park Row. We would become big-time reporters, talk on terms of intimacy with the Mayor, the Police Commissioner and the big-shot gangsters; and we would be privy to political secrets which only the most privileged could know. Eventually, a few of us might attain the highest summit of all, those rarefied heights on which the gods of journalism had their being—the columnists and the drama critics of New York.

Today, an eager lad may aspire to be a crime reporter, a Washington or foreign correspondent, an expert on economics, finance, labor, or even a pundit of the editorial page. During the 1920's and the early 1930's, however, those with stardust in their eyes had reverent glances only for the columnists and the critics. Certainly, to most of us who labored in the Bronx, these men were idols, the personification of metropolitan sophistication and wit, the elect whose scintillating comments would be echoed and re-echoed by the "intellectuals" of every college campus and by the "literary" coterie of every newspaper in the country.

With thousands of others during my early years in New York,

I read with exultation each morning the page opposite the editorial page of the *World*. The quips of F.P.A. in his Conning Tower, his Horatian odes, even his persistent campaign for visible house numbers, were as so many jewels to me. The verses and the wise-cracks of George S. Kaufman, Dorothy Parker, Newman Levy and other contributors seemed to be more brilliant than those of Whistler or Wilde. Only the scathing comments of Henry L. Mencken in the *Smart Set* scintillated with brighter hues. And, in the days that shortly followed, the whimsies, jests and critical discourses of Heywood Broun, Alexander Woollcott, Samuel Chotzinoff, Deems Taylor and William Bolitho gleamed like incandescent guide posts along the pathway of the arts.

Also, a reader could refresh himself in the high comedy of Don Marquis' "Old Soak" and "archie the cockroach" in the *Sun*; he could find sustenance in the tweedy, pipe-smoke-flavored essays of Christopher Morley in the *Post*; go adventuring among the literati of Burton Rascoe's "Daybook" in the *Tribune*, and immerse himself in the glamor of the Great White Way, accompanying S. Jay Kaufman "About the Town" in the *Globe*. And for those of tougher breed, there were prize-fight-specialist Damon Runyon's colorful prose and Grantland Rice's Kiplingesque verse in praise of sport.

We who were exiles in the Bronx worshipped these men. They, or most of them, were the avant-garde, the apostles of a fresh and freer age, the drum-beaters for the new writers—the only ones who mattered—Eugene O'Neill, Edna St. Vincent Millay, Sherwood Anderson, James Branch Cabell, Carl Sandburg, Vachel Lindsay, Edgar Lee Masters, F. Scott Fitzgerald and, of course, James Joyce. Out of their newspaper pieces rose a glowing vapor. And through this emerged a picture of New York so bright that it dimmed the brilliance of coffee-house London in Samuel Johnson's day.

The foolish fervor of youth? Perhaps. But there was some justification for it. The columnists of that era *did* have the literary touch; they were creative writers. Their output may have lacked the lasting qualities of great literature; yet from their pillars came numerous volumes of essays and witticisms and at least two successful comedies, *The Old Soak* and *Dulcy*.

The worldliness of these writings brought into clearer focus the picture of the *Bronx Home News:* a village newspaper published in the world's greatest city. We, however, chose to ignore that this was the keystone of its success.

Within its territories there was no activity so minute that it did not draw the interest of its astute editors. A bar mizvah on the Grand Concourse, a bridge party on West 165th Street, a kaffeeklatsch in Yorkville—you'd find a detailed account in the *Home News;* not only that, but at the end of the story would follow a full list of the fortunate ones who had attended.

There was no social affair, no fraternal meeting, however insignificant, which was not given ample space in its columns. The reporting encompassed the smallest details, down to the crepe-de-Chine gown of the hostess and the diamond-studded tie pin of the banquet speaker. Thousands of birth, confirmations, weddings and funerals which failed to win even an agate line in the downtown papers were the objects of as tender a reportorial solicitude as that bestowed by the *Times* on one of Mrs. Vanderbilt's elegant soirées.

Then there was the "local angle." Seldom was a story of national and sometimes of international importance published that was not in some way—however far-fetched—related to the *Home News'* community of readers. Woodrow Wilson's proclamation of his Fourteen Points might serve as a mere prelude to the intelligence that one of the doormen at the Versailles Peace Conference hailed from Fordham Road. And a speculation concerning a change in President Harding's cabinet might be tied in with a rumor that a peanut politician of Harlem was about to pluck a plum in the U.S. Marshal's office.

Such a policy won a body of readers almost fanatical in their devotion. There was, for example, the story of the Bronxite who is said to have made this deathbed request: "When you bury me, be sure to put in the coffin my obituary from the *Home News.*"

Sometimes this loyalty was carried to ludicrous extremes. A Bronx man was arrested for a murder in Brooklyn, and, for days, resisted all efforts to make him confess. But he did so eventually only after he had been approached by a 149th Street reporter.

"I'll tell everything," he said to the cops, "if the *Home News* gets the story first!"

But the editorial staff found no comfort in such a worthy senti-ment. It did not allay our wanderlust. The city room became the Grand Central Station of journalism, with the more ambitious using it as a mere stopover point on the way downtown.

Many of the city's most celebrated byliners at one time or the other enjoyed the hospitality and the sparse salaries of the venerable institution. Among them: Aben Kandel, novelist and screen writer; Edwin Justus Mayer, playwright; Eric Knight, novelist; Lee Morti-mer, author and columnist; Lowell Limpus, former chief of the UN Bureau of the *News*; H. Stuart Morrison, editor of an English-language newspaper in Rio de Janeiro; Charles Zerner, playwright and staff member of the *Times*; Leo Rasche of the *World-Telegram*; Georgette Carneal, novelist, and many others. Some of these passed through at the time or shortly after I was turning out "B & B's."

"B & B," it should be explained, stood for "Brickbats and Bou-quets." These were brief items about neighborhood celebrities, usu-ally with a "humorous" twist. There were such gems as: "Dr. Morris Eisenbahn, the chiropodist, was sporting a fancy red tie on West 181st Street yesterday. Some neckpiece, eh Doc?". . . or "Mollie Smith, ye courthouse stenographer, will vacation with Esther Rosen-blum on Cape Cod. They're embarking next Saturday on the Fall River Line. Don't get seasick, girls!"

Almost daily, Jim O'Connor, now of the *Journal-American*, who edited the Washington Heights section, would remind his slaves, "Don't forget those B & B's, boys." Each staff member pounded out from five to ten a day. Harry Goodwin, the managing editor, and Harry Parsons, city editor of the Bronx edition, were just as in-sistent.

Some of us wearied of the stint and, sad to confess, there were a few scoundrels among us who saved shoe leather by writing purely fictitious items about totally nonexistent persons. But Jim was a smart man and suspected such skulduggery. So one afternoon he decreed that thereafter every name mentioned in a B & B would have to be followed by an address. And, he added, frequent check-ups would be made to verify the existence of such persons!

This cruel edict not only stifled the creative urge but also in-creased the working hours of the staff. For in addition to gathering

"Brickbats and Bouquets," I, for one, had to cover magistrates' courts, police, schools, churches, chambers of commerce, fires and women's clubs in the West Side area extending from 135th Street to the Yonkers line. And just to consume any spare time that might remain, there was also the little task of reading proofs.

For this effort I was rewarded with a salary of thirty dollars a week —which, after a year, reached the unprecedented height of thirty-five dollars. At least I thought it was unprecedented, because O'Connor, informing me of the raise, whispered, "Don't tell anybody around here how much you're getting."

But despite this generous pay I still looked longingly toward Park Row. During off days, I became familiar with every facial feature and tempcramcntal quirk of the receptionists in the outer offices of the downtown papers. I could tell whether the genteel fellow at the *Times* had had a few words with his mother-in-law the preceding evening; or if the day seemed fair to the schoolteacherish lady guarding the *Tribune's* portals; or that all was well with the white-mustached little man who barred my entrance to the *News*.

Not once, however, did I come within scowling distance of a city editor. "Fill out this form . . . name . . . address . . . experience . . . sorry . . . nothing doing today . . . come back a few weeks from now."

It seemed I should be marooned in the Bronx forever. Before me stretched the dreary years. . . .

Then came a bright and blessed Sunday afternoon in the spring of 1922. On a crowded bench in Washington Square I was reading eagerly the want-ad section of the *Times*. Looking first—as always —at the column beginning with the letter "E" (for Editorial) I came across a miraculous advertisement. I read it over and over again to convince myself that it was real:

EDITOR WANTED . . . *If you are a brilliant young man with a love of the more fascinating aspects of New York, if you are interested in the world about you, maybe you and I should get together; I'm starting a unique magazine and want an ambitious young man to run it.*

What more could one wish for? "Young," "ambitious," "brilliant" —by my own admission I was all of these. And I certainly was "interested in the world about me." As for having "a love of the more fascinating aspects of New York," just show me someone who had more!

Hurrying across the Square to the rooming house on Grove Street, I was soon sitting at a typewriter. But now all the advice I had ever read on the art of writing a letter for a job rushed in a jumbled stream through my mind.

"Be brief . . . be factual . . . no fancy stuff . . . never mind brevity . . . tell all . . . be serious . . . be bright and chatty . . . avoid chattiness as you would the plague." My fingers were paralyzed . . . a veil descended before my eyes.

Then, shaking myself free from conscious thought, I began to write. Although at times I have an almost photographic memory for details, I can't remember what I wrote. But it must have been convincing, for, after a few anguished days of waiting, on my return from the Bronx one evening there was a letter on the marble-topped table of the room.

In the envelope was a sheet of heavy linen paper, and on its upper left-hand corner there were these daintily engraved words: "*The Wilderness Magazine*—Daniel A. Brentwood, Publisher."

"Come in to see me next Monday afternoon at four," the letter advised me. "I'm a tough man to please, but should we be able to get together, you'll have the greatest opportunity ever given to a man in the magazine field."

THREE

From the Bronx to Green Peas

The wire-cage elevator came to a halt on an upper floor of the imposing apartment building near Carnegie Hall. A rococo remnant of the Nineties, it housed many literary and theatrical celebrities.

In the foyer of a vast apartment, a fragrant blonde at a tiny desk glanced up from her copy of *Judge*, the comic magazine, and directed me to Mr. Brentwood's office. Passing through a narrow corridor, I noticed a spacious chamber crowded with girls busily typing and answering phones.

The paneled room at the end of the passage was furnished with antique English pieces; an ornate grandfather's clock ticked lazily beside a fireplace. The tall man with silver hair, who rose from behind an enormous desk, came forward to greet me and, extending a bony hand, he towered above me like a slender gray pillar. His suit was gray, also his shirt and tie; his eyes and his face were gray and so were his suède shoes.

In an almost reticent manner, he invited me to sit in a brown leather chair facing his desk. Brentwood appeared to be the perfect picture of a literary gentleman. At his request, I gave him a detailed account of myself and as I told the story, I noticed his smile—sincere, warm and understanding.

But, without warning, in the midst of the monologue, he frowned, half-closed his eyes and asked brusquely, "What do you think of modern civilization?"

I stammered in surprise but he did not wait for an answer. "We're all living in a wilderness, aren't we?" he said. "It's the law of the fang and the claw, isn't it? That's way I'm calling my magazine *The Wilderness*. I'm going to fight injustice."

Perhaps, I suggested, it would be like the *Nation* or the *New Republic*.

"No," he said, "that's highbrow stuff. And too radical. I want something people will read and nothing to do with Socialism or Communism, either. I'm going to make people think and at the same time entertain them. Humorous stuff like Will Rogers, short stories by big-name writers like good old Irvin Cobb, Arthur Train and this fellow who wrote the funniest story I ever read, 'Pigs Is Pigs,' Ellis Parker Butler."

Pointing to a pile of manuscripts on the desk, he informed me, "I've got stories by these writers already for the first issue. Yes, the biggest authors in New York. And you know what? Didn't cost me a cent."

I expressed surprise.

"It's like this," he explained. "These boys and their agents are good fellows. They're willing to play along with me until I can afford to pay them some real dough."

Brentwood chuckled almost to himself. "I've always been pretty good, getting people to play along with me. You know why? Because I do the right thing—and they know it."

Then, giving me a searching glance, he asked slowly, "Now, young man, what about you? Will you play, too?"

I explained haltingly that my income was not exactly equal to that of Irvin Cobb. . . . There were certain expenses. . . .

Brentwood's face darkened. I could see that I had disappointed him.

"I'm not asking you to work for nothing," he said. "Would you be willing to start at seventy-five dollars a week?"

I couldn't believe it! From thirty-five to seventy-five, a forty-dollar jump in pay! Just as I was on the point of uttering an enthusiastic yes, there flashed through my mind a recent "success story" in the *American Magazine* which cautioned against the too-hasty acceptance of any business offer.

After a moment of silence, managed with considerable difficulty, I finally stammered, "Well, Mr. Brentwood, I—I—like your idea. . . . It's an opportunity. . . ."

"Of a lifetime," he added.

"And—I'll—yes, I'll take it."

He shook my hand and suggested that I persuade the *Bronx*

Home News to release me from the customary two weeks' notice. "I'd like you to start next Monday. Got to work on that first issue immediately."

Then, smiling paternally, "And now, young fellow, how about a drink?"

Up in the Bronx and on Washington Heights I had patronized a few illicit joints run by swarthy men in shirt-sleeves and frequented by neighborhood merchants, cops and small-time politicians. But Tony's, the speakeasy in the Fifties to which we adjourned, personified to me the elegance of metropolitan New York. The two bartenders in crisp white jackets were casually jovial; the waiters wore tuxedos and the fashionably garbed patrons, Brentwood informed me, were the elite of the advertising, magazine and theatre crowd.

He introduced me to several men at the bar as "my new editor" and advised me to make this place my "hangout." After all, he remarked, it was part of my duty to "know the crowd."

With this I heartily agreed.

By the time we had consumed our third orange blossom, he was "Dan" and I was "Ben." Then, as he ordered the fourth serving, Brentwood observed gayly, "You know what? I think this is our lucky day. We'll both remember it."

That night, during a dinner at Bertolotti's in the Village, my wife, Kathleen, and several impractical but enthusiastic friends agreed this was an opportunity which might never come again. After all, they had my first-hand account of the afternoon's adventure: Brentwood's easy camaraderie with the bigwigs of the magazine world, his luxurious offices, that blonde receptionist and the clerical staff.

The next morning, Jim O'Connor consented graciously to waive the two weeks' notice. After all, he wasn't one to prevent a reporter from becoming the editor of "an important new national magazine."

"But, kid," he added wryly, "I hope you're not making a mistake."

I was certain I hadn't when, the following Monday, shortly after 9 A.M., Dan introduced me to his staff—all luscious-looking Howard Chandler Christy types of girls—and then ushered me into a cozy office next to his big room. This certainty was bolstered by a prim

English-lettered placard on the corridor door: "Mr. Gross—Editor-in-Chief."

It did seem odd, though, that of all that pulchritudinous staff not one was assigned as my assistant. The girls, I was informed, were clerical and secretarial workers devoting themselves to such prosaic pursuits as advertising and circulation. The editorial destiny of *The Wilderness* rested entirely in my hands, a thought which caused me to tackle with fervor the contents of three wire baskets on the desk—unsolicited manuscripts.

These had come in response to several notices inserted in amateur writers' magazines and included an old-maidish essay about the wild flowers of Montana, several almost illiterate World War One reminiscences and at least a dozen short stories with unsurprising O. Henry "surprise" endings. By the time I was asking myself, "Is this what they call the literary life?" Dan opened the door and said, "Let's have lunch at the Algonquin."

That was all I needed. Within two seconds I was beside him, ready to go.

It did not matter that Dan did not seem to be on cordial terms with the headwaiter or that we were seated in a far corner. At last, a *Bronx Home News* reporter had entered the inner shrine of New York's gastronomic-literary society! Even from our distant observation point we could peek at Woollcott, F.P.A. and the other great ones at the round table. Suddenly Dan sprang from his chair as a tall, homely man with friendly mouth and laughing eyes approached.

"Why, Irvin Cobb! It's damned nice to see you!"

He presented me, and after a casual inquiry about the progress of the magazine, Cobb went on.

"This is better than doing 'B & B's,'" I said to myself.

During our walk back to the office, Dan added several more drops to the cup of his editor's happiness, a receptacle which was already overflowing.

"You know what?" he said. "I think we should have a drama department. They tell me that Woollcott and George Jean Nathan draw lots of readers. It's extra work, but you wouldn't mind going to the theatre, would you?"

"Not at all," I said.

Somehow or other, I resisted the temptation to tell him that perhaps the Gross brand of criticism might not prove to be as popular as that of Woollcott or of Nathan. But I did suggest a novel form of play reviewing—although since then its format has been imitated on the radio. The idea was to present the reviews in the frame of a dialogue within a court setting. The Critic would be the prosecutor; the Author, the defendant; and the Judge would represent the public.

Dan was such an enthusiast that within ten days the newsstands of Broadway displayed placards advertising this "sensational new feature." Now I was not only an editor but also a drama critic who would see the shows from a comfortable orchestra seat, instead of from a hard balcony chair bought at Joe Leblang's cut-rate emporium.

There were probably a few others walking on air in New York at that time, but I doubt that anyone was treading the invisible roadways with a lighter and a gayer heart than the editor of *The Wilderness Magazine*. There had been blessed weeks of reading scripts, writing articles, attending dinners, cocktail parties and now —the theatres. Also, Dan and I had made a trip to Atlantic City to persuade Evelyn Nesbitt Thaw to write her life story. All this, and every Saturday morning a check for seventy-five dollars!

The weather was not merely fair; it was radiantly sunny. And during this time only the tiniest shadow of a cloud had fluffed across the skies. This happened during the fifth week, when Dan placed three neatly typed pages on my desk.

"Run this as an editorial," he said.

It was a fiery and somewhat incoherent denunciation of the treatment of patients in insane asylums. I suggested that perhaps he would permit me to make a few changes. He grumbled but finally consented.

The next day he dropped another lengthy editorial on the desk —on the same theme, but even more incoherent than the other one. He ordered that both appear in the first issue and refused to listen to my argument that it would not be proper to publish two pieces dealing with the same topic at one time.

"Let's get this straight: this is my magazine and what I say goes," he said in surprisingly velvety and yet menacing tones. But his eyes had contracted and there was the suggestion of a sneer. "This stuff is more important than anything in the book!"

I continued to argue with him, however, and at last he agreed that the editorials should appear in separate issues.

As he walked from the room with an air of impeccable dignity, several questions to which as yet there were no answers began to plague me. I recalled one afternoon at the speakeasy when I had asked Dan what he had done prior to becoming a publisher. He had immediately switched to another topic. And there was the time when his chauffeur, Joe, who drove the 1919 Packard limousine, had seemed to be unreasonably diffident in discussing the past activities of his employer. Also, I remembered the evening I had offered to come to the Brentwood apartment, less than a block away, to discuss an article.

"I don't discuss business in my home," Dan had said. "My wife . . . well, she isn't well. Visitors upset her."

Often, too, I had wondered about his wife, a mousy little woman who would sit beside his desk for hours. Like a pathetic wraith, her hands folded in resignation, she rarely broke her silence.

But there was no reason to dwell on these matters. Brentwood had made certain promises and so far he had been a man of his word.

So the cloud vanished as suddenly as it had come. But the following week there was a far heavier overcast. I noticed one morning that half of the desks in the big room across the hallway were deserted. The blonde receptionist explained that Mr. Brentwood had "laid off some of the help temporarily." And for several days there was no sign of him at the office.

By the beginning of the seventh week, all of the others, except the receptionist, were gone. Then Dan came in one afternoon and I found him slumped over his desk.

"We're in a hell of a jam," he told me. "The fellow who was backing me has walked out. But you know what?" He suddenly smiled again. "I'm not worried. I'll get a new backer. I'll get ten backers! They can't lick Dan Brentwood!"

The full impact of this development came a few days later. Kathleen phoned that my last week's salary check, which she had cashed at a grocery store on Fourth Street, had bounced. The merchant demanded that it be made good immediately or else—I had visions of being hailed into Jefferson Market Court. I could already see the headlines. So I rushed down to the Village grocer to assure him it all was a "mistake." He grudgingly promised to wait a few days.

"Our troubles are over!" Dan greeted me the next morning. His eyes were shining as he explained that for weeks he had been trying to interest a Hungarian inventor named Kanselman in *The Wilderness*. This very evening, this genius would demonstrate a world-shaking invention, a fantastically efficient new burglar alarm. If the demonstration were successful, Kanselman would be "in the big money" and he would pour a goodly portion of it into our magazine.

"Be at the Columbia Theatre Building tonight at eight—on the fifth floor. You'll see something wonderful!" he said.

A few minutes before that hour I found myself in a dim corridor of the old burlesque structure, which today houses the Mayfair Theatre. Clustered about the frosted glass door of a small-time talent agent's office were that gentleman himself, a dapper fellow with waxed mustache; Brentwood; Kanselman, who looked like a pudgy little symphony musician; and a tall angular fellow with nose glasses, as solemn as a deacon.

On the inside, there was a contraption attached to the wooden frame of the door, something resembling a cross between a fire extinguisher and a skyrocket. Kanselman was explaining to the man with the nose glasses that this was probably the greatest crime preventer ever envisioned by the mind of man. Tonight we should see that it was an absolutely safe gadget which could be used in an office building even in the heart of Times Square. It was "noiseless, fireproof and foolproof." It could not fail.

There was a tiny hole bored in the door frame. Through it a long key of wire thinness could be inserted into a lock on one side of the contraption. A person on a legitimate errand who desired to open a door or a window to which the device was attached had merely to give this key a turn and he could enter safely. But if one tried to do so without using such a wire key, a gas container would explode and spray the luckless intruder with an invisible and odorless vapor.

No real harm would be done, Kanselman assured us, for although the gas would render the burglar unconscious, its effects would not be fatal. The felon would be trapped as the explosion would immediately set off an electric alarm in the police station. The cops would arrive within a few minutes and find the helpless victim.

"All right, we'll begin now," the chubby little inventor announced. "But don't be alarmed, gentlemen. Tonight we're using a substitute for the real gas. We don't want anyone unconscious," he laughed.

All of us, except Kanselman and the man with the nose glasses, scurried gingerly in the direction of the elevators. The inventor shut the door, clicking the latch. Then, inserting a Yale key in the lock, he opened it and there was a hissing red-and-white flash, followed by an ear-shattering boom! We heard the crashing of glass and saw Kanselman and his companion sprawled on the floor, their eyes dilated and their arms wildly gesticulating.

Also, the solemn man's coat tails were afire. We rushed forward to smother the flames and glancing through the now paneless door, which had been blown off its hinges, we could see that an office desk and a wastebasket were burning. And what was more, gray smoke was billowing through one of the splintered windows overlooking Seventh Avenue.

There were cries from the street and soon clanging bells and screaming sirens. Just as we were making some headway with the burning office furniture, firemen, policemen and the emergency squad burst in on us from the corridor. While the nozzles of coiling hoses drenched the premises with cascades of sizzling water, a red-faced policeman was berating Kanselman furiously. Brentwood attempted to defend him.

"He's done nothing wrong," he said. "He's just trying to help you cops in your fight against lawbreakers. We came up here to take part in a scientific experiment."

"Oh, so you're in this, too!" the cop yelled. "All of you come down to the house!"

Dan, Kanselman, the agent, the man with the nose glasses and I, accompanied by a patrolman and a plain-clothes man, could scarcely wedge our way through the mob surrounding the downstairs entrance. At the height of the theatre rush hour, thousands of curious pedestrians and hundreds of squawking taxis had paralyzed traffic.

At the precinct house, after questioning, Dan, Kanselman and the agent were booked on charges of illegal possession and detonation of explosives within city limits. The story made front-page boxes in the papers the next morning. That afternoon, after a severe lecture by the magistrate, the three defendants were fined fifty dollars each and it was Kanselman who came up with the cash.

"I guess we didn't do so well," was Dan's only comment as we walked from the drab courtroom. But by the time we had arrived at our office he was in a light-hearted mood again.

"Tonight, I'm seeing another prospect," he informed me.

By now, having acquired a somewhat down-to-earth attitude, I reminded Dan that tomorrow morning we should have to be at the printing plant on Lafayette Street to make up the first issue of our magazine. He had told me that as yet he had passed no cash to the printer.

"I hope he'll be nice about it," I said. This irritated Dan. "You don't think that, after all my work, I'm going to let this go down the sewer? Sure, he'll be nice about it!"

Then, in a gesture of bravado, he drew a five-dollar bill from his wallet. "Buy yourself a good stiff drink!"

Instead of a drink, I spent the money on bread, meat and groceries. After all, my last salary check had bounced and there were no indications of another—even a rubber one.

The next morning, Daniel A. Brentwood was among the missing at the printing shop. I was already in the midst of making up when a galley boy informed me that I was wanted at the front office.

There, a wiry man with a pompadour haircut, who in his past dealings had always been most cordial, gave me an icy glance. He wanted to know why Mr. Brentwood wasn't there. If he didn't show up immediately with a certified check, he said, the page forms would be smashed and the type dumped into the "hellbox."

"I'm fed up with that faker's promises," he growled, "and you'd better tell him so right now!"

I picked up the phone but Dan was neither at home nor in his office.

"I thought so," the printing executive said. "Well, you got until twelve noon—not a minute more!"

It was a few minutes after 10:30 A.M. and I resumed work in a daze, directing the placement of type with robotlike gestures, scarcely uttering a word. There was a knotty lump in my stomach and the print on the galley proofs wavered crazily before my eyes. Eleven o'clock . . . 11:15 . . . 11:45. I lived in quarter-hour segments of time. Now the minute hands of the clock above the foreman's cubbyhole began to race as swiftly as the one ticking off the seconds. I watched it . . . watched it . . . watched it. . . .

The man with the pompadour was coming down the aisle. Twelve o'clock! The clicking of the linotypes in the far end of the room grew louder and louder.

"Please!"I said. "Hold it until two o'clock."

"No, sir," the man said.

"Let me call him just once more."

"Okay," he nodded.

Again, no luck. The man smiled.

"Look," I pleaded, "I know Mr. Brentwood must be on his way here now. Just a few more minutes!"

"Not even a half a minute!" he said. "I hate a faker!" The executive nodded to the shirt-sleeved foreman beside him. The latter cupped his hands and yelled with a piercing squawk, "All right, boys, tear her up!"

While my eyes widened and my chest tightened, bolts and nuts were loosened and hammers crashed against forms. Then there came a metallic tinkle as loose type cascaded into squirming mounds.

The work of weeks . . . Irvin Cobb . . . Will Rogers . . . Evelyn Nesbitt Thaw . . . the editorial about insane asylums . . . the comments on world affairs . . . the criticisms of Broadway plays . . . the bright prospect of becoming a big-time editor . . . all, now only a shapeless mass of metal!

I rode the subway uptown to the deserted office and sat there waiting. Shortly after 5 P.M., Dan entered with his wife, her eyes red from weeping.

"I've heard all about it," he said.

Mrs. Brentwood, now articulate for the first time since I had met her, turned to her husband. "I told you not to go into this. You knew you had no money."

Dan drew himself up proudly. "I had backing."

"He had no backing, believe me, just promises," she said to me pathetically. "Yes, there were a few thousands to pay the help for a while. All except the chauffeur—he'll get his when we sell the Packard."

Dan smashed his fist against the desk and looked at her scornfully.

Ignoring him, she continued hysterically. "This office, and even our furnished room down the block—it was all on credit!"

Dan, muttering to himself, turned his back on her and walked to the rear of the apartment.

It did not seem possible that a man could have set himself up in such an extravagant manner without considerable money. Certainly, it would require a fortune to attempt the launching of even the most insignificant general magazine today. The costs of paper, of rentals, and of labor are fantastically high and credit is not available to an unheeled beginner. But during the 1920's it was feasible for a publisher to start on the proverbial shoestring and many of them did.

"I just want you to understand," Mrs. Brentwood reduced her voice almost to a whisper. "Dan's an honest man. He wouldn't cheat anyone. Yes, I know you gave up a job to come with him and that you're broke. But you've got to realize this—he's not responsible."

Then she began an amazing story. It was that of a man who until two years before had been the owner of one of the largest wholesale grocery establishments in Connecticut.

"But Dan was never satisfied," she said. "He had always wanted to be a writer. He was a poor boy, with no schooling, but he had this hankering to see his name in print. Used to send stuff to newspapers and magazines and they always sent it back. Why, once he even wrote a book—a fine book—but no one would take it. He used to worry over that and then, one day, he had a—a—nervous breakdown and they took him to an institution. With him gone—well, you know how it is—the business went down, and when he came back home, we had nothing left. No money, only our house and some groceries.

"Not long ago, Dan sold the house for a few thousand dollars and with the cash he came to New York with his car and the chauffeur. He said that he would start a magazine and show up all the others. He'd print his own stuff and expose the conditions in asylums and sanitariums. I begged him not to do it; he didn't know anything about this business; but he just wouldn't listen.

"Dan splurged on this fancy office and hired all those girls—heaven knows why, he didn't need 'em. But he said he had to put up a 'front.'. . . Well, you yourself know how he could convince people. Mr. Gross, I just can't get over it! The way he's stalled them for rent, the way he was able to get all those big writers to give him things without one cent! Even some of the girls here accepted only half the salaries he promised them!"

"Ben! Come here!" Dan was calling me. With Mrs. Brentwood I walked back to a large room which had always been locked, one which I had not entered before. At the rear wall, Dan was pushing to one side an enormous rolling door, revealing gray wooden shelves which reached to the ceiling. On them were hundreds of cans.

"Know what these are?" he asked and then supplied the answer. "Green peas . . . the best goddamned green peas you ever ate!"

I looked closer and he was right.

"And you know what?" he continued. "I can't pay you off and you're out of a job, but I won't let you starve. You can have these damned peas . . . as many as you want. I'm tired of eating 'em!"

Suddenly, all the bitterness in my heart was gone. All the resentment over having been deceived, over the check that bounced, over being cast adrift in New York again, over the hard times that were sure to come—all the bitterness evaporated. Now, for the first time, I saw Daniel A. Brentwood as a tragic figure, one who had been victimized by an impossible dream. I felt pity for him—and I liked him.

"But, Dan, maybe Mr. Gross doesn't care for green peas," Mrs. Brentwood said.

"He's got to," said Dan, "because he's going to get 'em!"

Even though I knew that these tinned goods might save me from starvation, I protested mildly, but Dan cut off my words angrily. Far into the evening, the three of us lugged cans down the service elevator and piled them into the Packard limousine on Seventh Avenue. We made three trips between the office and the rooming house on Grove Street. In the furnished room, cans covered the floor, the table and the bureau; they piled high in the closets and filled the space beneath the bed.

The next day, I drew the last few dollars in my savings account and turned the money over to the grocer, along with the few dozen cans of green peas he had agreed to accept in partial payment of my debt. For days thereafter I made the rounds of other Village shops, trading peas for tinned asparagus, tomatoes and other edibles. I not only lived on but actually ate my salary.

And even today, entering a grocery store and glancing at the well-stocked shelves, I recall with a wry pang that, in all the history of publishing, I am probably the only editor who was ever paid off in green peas!

The Old Car Barn

Now I had to find a job again.

But during 1922 employment was scarce on Park Row, an effect of the minor depression which had swept the country the year before. Even so, a young newspaperman seeking work in New York had it far easier than one on a similar quest today.

At this time, only seven dailies of general circulation are published Manhattan. Then, there were the *Times*, the *News*, the *Herald*, the *Tribune*, the *World*, the *Sun*, the *American*, the *Evening World*, the *Evening Sun*, the *Telegram*, the *Journal*, the *Post*, the *Evening Mail* and the *Globe*, in Manhattan; and Brooklyn boasted of three newspapers, the *Eagle*, the *Standard-Union* and the *Citizen*. All these, in addition to the financial journals and the *Morning Telegraph*. Also, one must list those havens of temporary work—Hearst's Universal press service, the Standard News and, above all, the City News Association.

During the years immediately following World War One there still lingered some of the wanderlust of the "tramp" newspaperman. He had esteem only for those who had worked from coast to coast on at least a dozen sheets.

Now the higher average pay and the more secure working conditions won by the Newspaper Guild have soothed the itching feet of most editorial workers. It has been argued that much of the "romance" and individual initiative have gone from newspaper work as a result of this, with the lights of the few stars dimmed in favor of the uninspired plodders. But nine out of ten in the profession, although conceding some academic merit to the argument, emphasize that nowadays, regardless of political viewpoint, the great newspapers of the land are powerful corporations whose primary and justified aim is to make a profit.

This, of course, is necessary for survival, certainly a worthy motive. The time when many dailies were the mere organs of picturesque characters, when metropolitan newspaper employees had intimate personal relationships with their employers, has long ago gone. Economic necessity has made it imperative for editorial as well as mechanical workers to organize.

The movies to the contrary, today the average reporter is apt to be a businesslike fellow whose habits are as steady as those of a bookkeeper or bank teller. Concerned with his suburban garden and the problem of finding a reliable baby-sitter, he seeks a decent base salary and job security.

The current beginner in New York is usually a lad fresh from college who begins his journalistic career as a copy boy. He does not seem perturbed by the prospect of working a decade or even a lifetime in one shop. The *News* and the *Times*, for examples, abound in veteran employees; the former has a Twenty-Five-Year Club of more than four hundred men and women.

But in the 1920's a young man might start on a Manhattan sheet as a cub reporter, receiving his tutelage under a ruthless city editor. The lack of a college degree did not work to his disadvantage; on the other hand, if he were so unfortunate as to have attended a school of journalism, he was viewed with suspicion. Today, however, some exposure to college is almost a necessity for the would-be copy boy. Three decades ago, when a myopic copy reader yelled, "Boy! Get me a cup of coffee!" a freckle-faced, tousled-haired youngster, speaking in the accents of the lower East Side or Brooklyn, would respond to the call. Now the cry may bring on the run (verbal exaggeration) a Princeton graduate or a Vassar beauty of the daisy chain.

Even so, although in those primitive times youthful journalistic job-seekers were undoubtedly more favored than their brethren of today, I personally did not profit from these circumstances. Office after office turned me away. One day, however, Harry Klemfuss, the City News reporter, introduced me to his editor. The latter suggested that I return that evening, as sometimes outsiders were hired for assignments on a piece basis.

"Brother, take your turn on the mourners' bench," a friendly blonde behind a glass partition with a porthole opening greeted me some hours later in the City News anteroom.

Joining three others on the hard wooden bench, I noticed that one of them wore spats and carried a cane; the other was a stout man in tobacco-stained tweed, smoking a vile-smelling stogy. The third was not only ill-kempt but reeking of whiskey and snoring.

The young man with spats informed me he was a Bostonian and had heard about City News from a friend on the *Transcript*. The tweedy journalist confided that he hated New York.

"Now, you take Chicago, that's a helluva town," he said. "Know every cop and politician out there and the newspaper guys make these New Yawkers look like boy scouts."

"Why did you leave?" the Bostonian asked.

"Just happened to call my boss a sonofabitch," said our Chicago friend. "But I'm going back. We'll kiss and make up."

A few minutes after the man with the cane and the one with the stogy had entered the city room and then departed on their assignments, I was summoned to the city desk.

The man on the desk explained that hundreds of banquets are given in New York every night. The important ones were, of course, covered by the dailies. But City News made an attempt to report as many of these minor affairs as possible, just as it did hundreds of small accidents, fires, disorderly-conduct arrests and speakeasy brawls which seldom appeared in the metropolitan newspapers. The function of C.N. was to give its subscribers—these newspapers— a complete record of Manhattan around the clock. And that it did.

"I've got a dinner for you tonight," he said. "The Master Plumbers' Association of Yorkville, at the Martinique."

At the "press" table in the long banquet hall there was only one other reporter—from the ever-alert *Bronx Home News*. Among the bulgy artisans and their wives, all of them in tuxedos or evening gowns, our street clothes made a shabby sight, indeed. But the chairman of the dinner committee served us "Scotch—right off the boat" from a silver hip flask and we soon were unmindful of our sartorial inelegance. And, having lived rather economically for several weeks, I tackled with zest the olives and celery, the clear consommé, the broiled chicken with green peas and French-fried potatoes, the lettuce salad with Russian dressing, the biscuit tortoni or spumoni (choice) and the demitasse.

My colleague and I were in a jovial mood by the time the cigars were passed and the toastmaster threw away a few gags about Prohibition, William Jennings Bryan and Mayor "Red Mike" Hylan. Even the speaker of the evening, a state assemblyman who called for more economy in government, did not seem too tiresome. After I had written the story and collected my fee in the City News offices later that night, the dinner appeared in retrospect as not only a gainful but a highly enjoyable one. And the boss invited me to return the next evening.

I did—and it was a banquet again, a feast at the McAlpin given by a society of stamp collectors. The topics discussed were different —but not the menu. In fact, night after night, at all of these gatherings devoted to eating and to postprandial talk, the menu *never* changed! Sometimes the celery was a bit more crisp or the chicken a bit less leathery; occasionally, instead of green peas there was asparagus; but I always knew what I was going to get—and I got it.

One evening, being by now an old banquet hand, I asked the desk man plantively, "Don't they ever eat *anything* but chicken?"

"I've got a treat for you, boy," he said, taking a red cardboard invitation from his desk drawer. "I think you'll enjoy this."

He was a prophet. An hour later in a smoky, laugh-filled assembly room of a Tammany club on West 23rd Street, there was a delectable meal. None of this rubbery fowl for the crowd of well-fed small-time politicos and their wives. Instead there were great round platters heaped high with luscious slices of crimson corned beef, surrounded by mounds of firm green cabbage.

There are great dining places in New York, London, Paris, San Francisco and Hollywood. I have visited many of them. But neither the Stork, Twenty-One, the Colony, the Caprice, Fouquet's, Romanoff's, nor Omar Khayyam's, with all of their caviar, steak Diana, pheasant under glass, Dover sole or shish-kebab have ever served a dish half so succulent as those Tammany politicians did on that night, so many years ago!

After that, one simply could not return to regulation banquet menu B-699. Therefore, it was a relief when the next evening's assignment took me uptown, where the Reverend John Roach Straton, a fundamentalist Baptist pastor of the day, addressed a meeting of Sunday-school workers. He delivered a furious philippic against the morals of the younger generation, two of his main targets being bobbed hair and the hip flask. If anything, his scorn for the hairdo of the flappers was even more virulent than his anger at the scofflaws who flouted Prohibition.

On my way to the office, while waiting for a train on the Times Square subway platform, I approached two flappers and quoted the Reverend's statement: "Short-haired women are headed straight for the fiery furnace of damnation!" and then asked for their comments. One of the girls giggled and moved away. The other did comment: "Aw, go to hell!"

Interviewing six other girls on Sheridan Square the next day, I condensed their opinions into a brief feature. The *Evening Sun*, a wide-open market for free-lancers then, bought it for $3.50. Thus encouraged, I continued the bobbed-hair quiz among ministers, beauty-parlor operators and housewives. Out of the twelve persons quoted, seven opposed the abbreviated cut as either "unwomanly" or "immoral."

With this tonsorial anthology I made a trip to the office of the *Morning Telegraph*, at that time on Eighth Avenue and 50th Street. It loomed as a good prospect, as this paper was famous for its Sunday features.

Housed in a dingy, sprawling structure, the building had at one time been a streetcar barn and even in its remodeled condition its sallow walls seemed permeated with ghostly odors of scorched rubber and of humming electric motors. As one ascended the creaky wooden stairway, one could almost hear the clang of trolley bells and the shouts of lusty conductors and motormen calling to one another in the frosty dawn.

There was no receptionist and no one seemed to pay the slightest heed to me in the cavernous city room. The wooden floor sagged and here and there holes, like so many periods, punctuated the decaying planks. A grayish light filtered through dust-covered windows and enfolded in a dull pallor the desks piled high with copy paper and crumpled press releases.

Finally, a middle-aged man wearing a cap and a turtleneck sweater, who resembled Victor Moore as Kid Burns in *Forty-Five Minutes from Broadway*, directed me to the city editor. He pointed to a cubicle alongside a bare brick wall.

I knew, of course, that my wares should have been offered to the feature editor rather than to the lord of the city desk. But, I reasoned, should the latter be impressed with my masterpiece, he might give me a job. And that's exactly what happened.

After glancing lackadaisically through the contribution, the benign-looking old gentleman with gold-rimmed glasses suggested I take it upstairs to "Teddy" Bean, in charge of features. Somehow—very subtly, no doubt—I managed to channel the conversation to the topic of my reportorial prowess. He didn't seem to be impressed but remarked wearily that one of his staff—a destestable low-lifer—had abandoned newspaper work last week for the more profitable field of press agentry. If I could return tomorrow, he'd "try me out" for a week.

The salary? Forty dollars. A comedown from the seventy-five dollars of *The Wilderness*, but the pay check would not be dependent on the successful demonstration of a burglar alarm. So I accepted.

"Very well," said "Pop" Price, "as long as you're going to be with us, leave your story with me. We'll use it on the city side and consider it part of your job."

Then he began the indoctrination talk designed for all of his new employees.

"The *Morning Telegraph* isn't like any other newspaper," he said. "The only rules we have around here are: work hard and write interestingly. But there's one important thing to remember: I don't like a reporter who gets a big head. The trouble with so many of you young fellows is that you think you're geniuses. You want to become novelists and playwrights. Why? To my mind, there's nothing better than being a good newspaperman."

Referring to the reporter I was replacing, he said, "From now on I'll hire only men who'll stick. The next time I hear that any of you is scouting around for another job, out you'll go!"

From my first moment there as a reporter, I realized that Pop Price had not exaggerated when he had said that the old Telly "wasn't like any other newspaper." Today it's primarily a horse-players' sheet; but during the 1920's, although it had the best racing section in the country, it was also a great theatrical daily. It gave detailed and graphic coverage to the legitimate houses, to vaudeville, burlesque and the movies. And its feature section under stout Theodosia ("Teddy") Bean was one of the brightest in the land. Books, art and music were dealt with in expert fashion; its "Beau Broadway" column was widely quoted for its caustic comments; and its general news, although limited in quantity, was presented with a metropolitan flair.

Despite Pop's prejudice against the "arty," there was a literary tradition about the grimy shop. Staff members still spoke of Heywood Broun, one of the bright beacons of the *World*, who not long ago had labored in the old car barn. There were tales of "Two Gun" Bat Masterson, the legendary Western sheriff, one-time sports editor, and of Alfred Henry Lewis, the Western story writer, related to the two Lewises who served, respectively, as publisher and managing editor. And there were whispers that even the great O. Henry, in need of quick cash, had often written unsigned pieces for the hallowed sheet.

But for color and human interest one did not have to hark back to the past. For the staff at that time was comprised of men and women who, if nothing else, were highly individualistic. There was Louella Parsons who, long before she had transferred to Hearst, was working as motion-picture editor at a salary reputed to be a fabulous one hundred dollars a week. She presided over what was known as "the hen house," a flock of chattering girl movie reviewers, among whom was a daughter of Channing Pollock, the playwright. Even then Louella was celebrated as a "smart" reporter with an ability to get "exclusives."

Another staff celebrity was columnist Ashby Deering, a sour-expressioned gentleman in baggy trousers, who was known for his raging hatred of the typewriter.

"It's the enemy of all good writing!" he would proclaim. "Was the Bible written on the typewriter? Did Shakespeare use one of these mechanical abortions? No, by God! . . . And neither will Ashby Deering!"

He was a man of his word, for despite the anguished protests of the linotypers he wrote his copy with a pencil on long sheets of yellow paper.

The sports department, especially, was the home of colorful characters. One of them, Sammy Taub, spoke so rapidly that one had difficulty understanding him. Years later, however, he achieved fame as a sports announcer on the radio. The sartorial brilliance of another inhabitant of this bizarre world illumined the editorial room. In a tight-fitting blue suit, with white vest, red tie and white carnation, he would have been a technicolor cameraman's delight.

Then there was a Major Wheatley, an imposing Georgian who had been military governor of a Cuban province during the Spanish-American War. A six-footer with a majestic Roman head and an aquiline nose, he regaled all who would listen with tales of plantation life and of boyhood days down in Augusta. In languorous tones, he would hold forth on the grandeurs of fried chicken, black-eyed peas and other delights of Southern gastronomy.

In his late sixties, the Major had an aversion to old age.

"I want to be with the young," he would say. "Even if I live to be a hundred, I'll never be old."

True to his philosophy, the Major, with the dignity and polish of a prewar (Between the States) Senator, entertained groups of youthful artists, writers and newspapermen in his Greenwich Village apartment. They gathered around him for evenings of conversation about politics, literature and horses—and also to enjoy his home-cooked meals.

Often he would speak with longing of his home in Georgia, vowing that some day he would desert "contaminated" New York, for the soft pure beauty of the Southern countryside. But the lure of the city held him in its spell. Even after a lengthy illness, which resulted in the loss of his job, the Major stayed on. He maintained himself in proud dignity on a small income, augmented occasionally with a few dollars earned through temporary work in the sports department of some newspaper.

One day during the late Thirties, a mutual acquaintance informed me that the man who had hated old age had died a few days before during a race-horse auction at Saratoga.

"And I guess the old boy was a great reader to the very last," he said. "They found on the night table beside his bed, a copy of *Racing Form*, a New Orleans cookbook and a physical-culture magazine in which he had marked an article on 'How To Stay Young.'"

The direct opposite of the Major in volubility was one of his sports colleagues, "The Silent Armenian." Although neither I nor my fellow reporters ever learned his name, we knew it was something unpronounceable ending in "ian."

Day after day, he sat at his desk, poring over mysterious charts. He seldom looked up; the world around him seemed to hold no interest for him; and, being stone-deaf, he rarely spoke. Yet this man was looked on with awe by all of us. For he was reputed to be the greatest handicapper in the United States. It was said that he knew more about horses and their money-making potentials than any other person. I tried to engage him in conversation on a few occasions, but he merely smiled and grunted in a friendly fashion.

One night in Beefsteak Charlie's, a restaurant down the block on 50th Street, I told a race-track tout that I worked within a few feet of "The Silent Armenian." He looked at me in unbelief and, emitting an exclamatory whistle, said, "No kiddin'! Boy, I'd give a million dollars just to talk to him for five minutes!"

As for the city staff, it, too, was unlike any other in New York, being made up of only four reporters: Alfred ("Bishop") Harding, son of the Episcopal Bishop of Washington; a blond youth, Harlow Peters, nicknamed "Pete, the college boy"; a third colleague who seemed to be replaced by a newcomer every two weeks; and this writer.

The "Bishop," now public-relations man and editor of the Actors Equity Association, lived up to his ecclesiastical heritage by displaying a solemn mien; but he had one of the most robust senses of humor I've ever encountered. "Pete," a blond youth who later joined the United Press, looked like a typical Yale senior of the day, a fashion plate with a devil-may-care attitude. Whipping us into action during the daytime was Pop Price and, during the evenings, a jovial stout fellow, Tom Hanley, who eventually drifted to the *World*.

If we turned in a story before 6 P.M., we had to write our own heads. This gave us added experience and also saved the management money. But after that hour, a lugubrious, squint-eyed copy reader handled our output, for the greater part of the time muttering under his breath as he did so. This was not surprising, considering that his chief article of faith was: "Outside of Frank Ward O'Malley there ain't a New York reporter who can write."

This gentleman suffered severely from several stylistic allergies. He would detonate violently when a reporter used "stated" for "said." He would blow a fuse when some unfortunate typed "conflagration" for "fire." But his choicest expletives were reserved for those criminals who wrote "Reverend John Smith" instead of "the Reverend John Smith."

"You'll burn in hell for that!" he would cry. And that was only the beginning of his diatribe.

Apparently having no hope for our salvation, this disgruntled copy reader soon left us. He was succeeded by a placid silver-haired little man who corrected our crimes against grammar and syntax without outward signs of fury.

In fact, this guardian of our stylistic morals joined us enthusiastically in our weekly ritual of libation and song. On Saturday nights after the first edition had rolled off the presses and the opposition papers had been checked, a hunchbacked circulation department employee known as "Johnny the Dope" would appear in the city room with a cask of ethered beer. To the accompaniment of shouts but no murmurs, the reporters would hoist it atop Tom Hanley's desk.

Then, with the coins we had chipped in, Johnny would rush downstairs to the Telegraph Delicatessen and reappear a few minutes later with a brown paper bag filled with ham, cheese and caviar (twenty cents) sandwiches, pickles, sauerkraut and red peppers.

The city staff would gather around the desk and, with lager foaming over the edges of the Dixie cups, eat, drink, jest and break into song. Hanley's sonorous baritone rose above the voices of the others in "Sweet Adeline," "Rosie O'Grady," "The Sidewalks of New York" and sometimes "Auld Lang Syne."

Cask emptied, sandwiches eaten and larynxes aching, the ritual would at last come to an end. It marked the official closing of the week for Pop Price's four reporters.

It was a week which, among many other things, included the writing of at least half a dozen paragraphs a day for a famous column of that time known as "Beau Broadway." It was highlighted daily in the upper left-hand corner of the front page.

Some years before, it had been written by one man; now it was the joint product of the city staff. So when friends inquired concerning the identity of that "sophisticated" columnist who wrote such scathing and yet urbane comments on world affairs, each of us could take a modest bow.

With only a small number of reporters under his command, Pop naturally enough assigned us only to the most important stories. Because of our limited experience, if we had been on a major newspaper we should have been doomed to minor items. As *Telegraph* men, however, we found ourselves at political conventions, murder trials and press conferences at which first-page news was made. We were in direct competition with the top byliners of the giant dailies.

And we had fun—probably more than those on any other New York newspaper. One of the chief pleasures of any ambitious young reporter is to write—the lengthier the story the better. Many an eager cub has had his heart broken by some city editor's curt order: "Keep it down to fifty words." But there was no such problem on the *Morning Telegraph*.

If we asked, "How much, Pop?" the inevitable answer would be: "As much as you need to make it interesting; but not a word more."

Certainly there was one story on which neither I nor any other reporter was forced to stint on words. One afternoon—the calendar says it was September 16, 1922—I was at my desk discussing Sinclair Lewis' *Main Street* with the "Bishop" when Pop Price called from his office.

"Looks like this might be a good one," he said, handing me a sheet torn from the UP ticker.

It was a bulletin announcing that two bodies—that of the Reverend Edward W. Hall, rector of a fashionable New Brunswick, New Jersey, church, and that of a choir singer, Mrs. James Mills, had been found beneath a crab-apple tree on nearby DeRussey's Lane.

"Take a quick run out there, clean it up and get back in time for the first edition," he said.

Neither of us apparently realized what we were getting into. Anyway, that was my introduction to what proved to be one of the most headlined murder stories of all time. Only the Gray-Snyder homicide and the kidnap-murder of the Lindbergh baby equaled it in public impact or in the amount of space devoted by the newspapers.

I didn't return to the office that night. In fact, I didn't come back to New York for more than two weeks. After phoning Pop that "new angles were breaking every minute," I rented a room at a hotel and wired my story.

The Western Union office in New Brunswick that evening was more chaotic than any movie mob scene: reporters pounding typewriters and shouting at the clerks behind the counter; Morse operators tapping out copy in "takes"; policemen, detectives and curious passers-by pouring through the open door. Within a few hours, every available room in town was rented; more and more reporters, photographers and newsreel men were rushing in via car and train from Trenton, Philadelphia and New York. Restaurants and speakeasies vibrated with shrill talk and hysterical laughter; and dazed local residents watched in amazement the procession of newshawks who dashed in and out of the prosecutor's office in the courthouse, and then sped away in roaring motors to the nearby town of Somerville.

The people of New Brunswick were stunned and then resentful. For the invasion was like a mighty wave which inundated not only the town but the surrounding countryside for miles around.

As so many have said before, the Hall-Mills case had everything for a murder story: violence, sex, religion and brooding mystery. Gossip and rumors—one couldn't keep track of them. There was always someone who knew someone who could solve the puzzle. Did the rector's austere wife, consumed for years by a raging jealousy, finally give vent to her long-suppressed hatred that dark night in DeRussey's Lane? "I'm seeing a woman tomorrow who knows the truth." Was Mrs. Hall's brother, the fire-chasing and none-too-bright Willie Stevens, responsible for the outburst of sadism which resulted not only in the shooting but also in the slashed throats of the victims? "There's a short-order cook in Somerville who has the dope."

Of the millions of words written about this epic murder, many thousands have been used in the memoirs of newspapermen, some of whom had no more than the remotest connection with the case. It would, therefore, be mere repetition to rehash the colorful tale. For the record, however, I, too, fought the battles of New Brunswick and of Somerville; I, too, dodged the buckshot of that eerie character, "the pig woman"; I, too, tried to draw on the impressions of the late choir singer's daughter, Charlotte Mills—unsuccessfully, because her utterances, in lieu of a cash consideration, were reserved solely for another newspaper.

The *Times*, the *News*, and all of the other New York dailies had a corps of reporters, photographers, rewrite men, sob sisters, fixers, and even copy readers on the scene. They swarmed over the landscape "tying up" officials for exclusives and beating the bushes for tipsters. Stories broke simultaneously in two county seats, New Brunswick and Somerville, and in the territories between.

One lone-wolf reporter could not possibly handle the entire job. So I was fortunate to make an arrangement with Jim Haggerty, in charge of the *Times* crew. In return for feeding him my coverage, he permitted me to use some of his data. "After all, we're not competitors," he said. As a result, I was able to file at least 2,000 words a day which, with the UP story, gave the *Telegraph* as big a splash as most of the other Manhattan papers.

Although Pop Price said that we did not miss a single important development, his appreciation did not go so far as to grant me a by-line. I was always "Our Special Correspondent."

"The worst thing that could happen to a young fellow is to get a byline too quickly," he explained.

However, on my return to town there were five more dollars in the weekly pay envelope. Also there was another reward. He informed me that thereafter I should have the privilege of choosing my own assignments. He wanted interesting feature stories.

I told him that, above all, I wanted to be a drama critic.

Pop was disgusted. "Why should a man who can cover murders want to be a critic?"

He saw my disappointment and added: "A reporter writes about life as he sees it. A critic writes about life as *another* fellow sees it."

Among our most devoted readers, who saw life as neither the reporter nor anyone else ever saw it, were the horse players. But it would be impossible to estimate the amount of joy—and sorrow—gleaned from the pages of our paper by these picturesque scalawags. They lined up nightly at the Broadway newsstands for copies of the first edition in the same manner that many do now awaiting the arrival of the *Daily News*. Some of the more impatient ones stood in front of the plant on Eighth Avenue, eager to snatch their holy writ as it rolled from the presses. Still others made special efforts to cultivate members of the staff in the hope of gaining a tip which would make their fortunes the next day.

Referring to the sheet as their "holy writ" is not far-fetched. For, at that time, the management of the old Telly could see no incongruity in combining its sporting features with lavish doses of theology.

While the editorial pages of other dailies discussed the failures or the merits of the Harding administration, or discoursed learnedly on the evils of Prohibition, on many occasions the editorial pundit of the *Morning Telegraph* would hold forth on some passage of the Gospels. He would proceed to interpret it and, as he droned along, would take issue with some distinguished clergyman who had a different conception of that particular chapter and verse.

It no doubt made fascinating reading for ministers and seminarians but we reporters often wondered how many of them were subscribers to the *Morning Telegraph*. A considerable number of others were also puzzled, including the horse players.

One evening, "Johnny the Dope" introduced me to one of this gentry in an Eighth Avenue speakeasy. He offered to "make it worth while" if we could "reach a little understanding."

I asked what he had on his mind and he came right out with it. "I want to get the code."

"What code?" I asked.

"You know, all them editorials about the Bible. What's it about?"

"About the Bible," I said.

"That ain't what I mean," he said. "You cain't tell me that they'd do all this writin' about Matthew, Luke and Mark and all them other apostles unless they had something in mind. All the boys say it's a code, tellin' the winners of next day's race."

With "Johnny the Dope" taking no sides in the discussion, I tried my best to convince his friend that, so far as I knew, there was no code. But if he is still among the living, I'm certain he believes to this day that a selfish young reporter captiously refused to make him privy to a profitable secret. Muttering disgustedly, he turned away from the bar and made his way to the street.

"You know," said "Johnny the Dope," "I myself have been tryin' to find that code. But no use . . . ain't had no luck."

At that, he had more than I did; for about this time my own "luck" was running out on the *Morning Telegraph*. I had ignored Pop Price's warning and one day had permitted a friend to recommend me for a scenario writer's job at Paramount Pictures. I was summoned by the story editor for an interview and told that I should hear from him within a few days.

I did hear—but it was from Pop.

"You're a promising young fellow," he said. "I hate to do this. But a friend up at Paramount tells me you were up there talking about a job."

I tried to explain but he cut me short. "I'm going to write you a damned good letter of recommendation—and I'll be glad to help you—but two weeks from now you're no longer working for us."

On the Saturday evening of the second week following, I wrote my last story and cleaned out my desk. Then, at 11 P.M., I returned to the office for the weekly ritual.

"Johnny the Dope" rolled in the casket of ethered beer and it was hoisted to Tom Hanley's desk. We ate ham, cheese and caviar sandwiches and drank the Dixie cups filled with brew. The city staff sang "Sweet Adeline" and "Auld Lang Syne." I shook hands with Tom, Pete, "Bishop" Harding and the rest of the gang and walked down the creaky stairs into the cold night air of Eighth Avenue.

I did not return to the Old Car Barn again.

FIVE

How It All Began

The journeyman newspaper reporter ranges far and wide within the confines of one city. In quick succession I knew what it meant to go crusading under the Hearst banner in the rough and tumble of writing the news so that it would shriek from the page. Then, suddenly, as if I had entered another world, I found myself in the genteel surroundings of the Associated Press, where the atmosphere was that of an exclusive club and the pay that of a galley slave. Finally, emerging from the academic groves of AP, I was plunged headlong into the thunderous world of the *Daily News* when it was young and when it was creating new and still unsurpassed records in dramatic journalism. The fever of newsgathering was in my bloodstream.

A reporter accepts the comedy and the drama of his daily assignments as a matter of course. These are mere by-products of a calling whose devotees are often reminded that they "meet such interesting people." But to have been plunged suddenly from the comparatively sane atmosphere of the "city-side" into the maelstrom of radio was a dizzying experience.

"How long has this been going on?" and "What's behind it all?" These were questions which demanded answers.

Broadcasting was less than five years old and the men who had launched this far-reaching innovation were still—as some are today —at the height of their activities. Through personal interviews and correspondence it was possible to obtain their first-hand stories. What they told me comprises chapters in one of the most engrossing epics of human enterprise. And even though these memoirs make no pretense at being a complete history of radio, a brief account of some of the experiences of these pioneers deserves space here.

It is inconceivable that one could write a book about broadcasting without a glowing mention of Dr. Lee De Forest, who is rightfully hailed as "the father of radio." As far back as 1907, he had patented the grid tube, acknowledged by scientists as the "first practical three-electrode vacuum tube." Without this, neither radio nor television would have been possible.

It was Dr. De Forest who broadcast the first musical program in 1907, from a tiny laboratory on the top floor of the Parker Building on Fourth Avenue and 19th Street, New York. Earlier in the evening, he had dinner with an old friend, a Swedish concert singer, Madame Eugenia Farrar, and her companion, a young newspaperwoman.

"If you'll come up to my laboratory," the Doctor told them, "I'll show you a wireless set which transmits the human voice over the air. In fact, you can be the first one to sing into it."

An hour later, in the laboratory, she faced an old-fashioned phonograph horn and into it the Swedish artist sang "I Love You Truly." It was the first song ever broadcast. "Encore!" Dr. De Forest shouted, and the Madame sang "Just A-Wearyin' For You."

She had scarcely begun her first number, when in the Navy Yard in Brooklyn a young wireless operator sprang from his chair. "I hear a woman singing!" he exclaimed to the lieutenant in the room.

The officer, fearful of the enlisted man's sanity, clamped on the earphones. "I'll be damned!" he said, and then immediately phoned to the city desk of the New York *Hearld*. His call was transferred to a rewrite man, and the latter, convinced that the newspaper was the target of a practical joker, called back a few minutes later to check on the authenticity of the information.

The lieutenant assured him that both he and the sailor were of sound mind. The rewrite man dashed off a brief story which was buried on page 5 of next morning's *Herald*. One of the most significant developments of modern times was given the treatment usually accorded an item of no more importance than a street-corner brawl. As for the young newspaperwoman who had witnessed the history-making broadcast—she regarded it so lightly that she did not even trouble herself to write a story about it!

By the time I began comment about the radio, this event had already passed into the realm of legend. But partisans of a singer,

Vaughn de Leath, known as "the original radio girl," proclaimed that she was the first woman ever to have sung on the air. According to their version, Vaughn, who was the creator of the "crooning" style of vocalizing, had been invited to the De Forest laboratory by some of the Doctor's assistants the night before Madame Farrar's visit. There, after facing the phonograph horn, she is reported to have said, "Well, here goes something into nothing" just before singing "The Old Folks at Home." Recently, however, De Forest, in a letter to me, said that he had no knowledge of this incident.

On the many occasions I have chatted with David Sarnoff, chairman of the board of the Radio Corporation of America, I have had to remind myself: "This man is one of the great innovators of our age." Certainly there is nothing in the appearance of this heavy-set, balding son of poor Russian-Jewish immigrants to suggest it. And yet, just as De Forest must be credited with the first voice broadcast, so Sarnoff must be cited as the pioneer who had the first vision of radio as a medium of public enlightenment and entertainment.

An operator for the Marconi Wireless Telegraph Company of America, he eventually pounded the keys in New York. There, in 1912, at his post for seventy-two suspenseful hours, he received the list of survivors of the steamship *Titanic* after it had collided with an iceberg.

Just four years later, by then assistant traffic manager of the Marconi Company, he filed a memo with Edward J. Nally, its general manager. This 1916 document has become the Magna Carta of radio. For the twenty-five-year-old executive wrote, in part: "I have in mind a plan of development which would make radio a household utility in the same sense as the piano or phonograph. The idea is to bring music into the home by wireless.

"For example, a radio-telephone transmitter having a range of, say, twenty-five to fifty miles can be installed at a fixed point where instrumental or vocal music or both are produced. . . . The receiver can be designed in the form of a simple 'radio music box' and arranged for several different wave lengths, which should be changeable with the throwing of a single switch or pressing of a single button. . . . The same principle can be extended to numerous other fields, as for example receiving lectures at home, which can be made perfectly audible; also events of national importance can be simultaneously announced and received. Baseball scores can be transmitted in the air. . . . This proposition would be especially interesting to farmers and others living in outlying districts removed from cities. By the purchase of a 'radio music box' they could enjoy concerts, lectures, music, recitals, etc., which may be going on in the nearest city within their radius.

"Aside from the profit to be derived from this proposition, the possibilities . . . are tremendous; for its [the company's] name would ultimately be brought into the household and wireless would receive national and universal attention."

This blueprint by a mere youth, radical as it may have seemed at the time, was actually most conservative. Sarnoff had envisaged sales of approximately seventy-five million dollars' worth of radio sets during a three-year period; but RCA eventually reported that in a mere two-year span, from 1922 to 1924, its income from the sale of receivers totaled $83,500,000!

Aside from its financial foresight, however, this document had predicted with uncanny clairvoyance almost every phase of radio's program structure: music, entertainment, cultural features, sports, news and special events. But it did not foresee the day when broadcasting companies would make tremendous profits from the sale of time to sponsors. For it should be noticed that Sarnoff, like most of his fellow pioneers, looked on broadcasting, in its commercial sense, as primarily a means to induce the purchase of receiving sets.

It is difficult to realize today the revolutionary nature of Sarnoff's concept unless one remembers that at that period wireless was used solely for the transmission of messages. And even in this field there was much to be done. Words spoken over a radiophone lacked privacy; any "ham" equipped with a receiver could eavesdrop on the conversation. The next big step, it was believed, would be the perfection of radio as a medium of point-to-point commercial communication.

Not until a half a decade had passed did Sarnoff's dream become a reality. During World War One, the U.S. Navy Department had urged that an all-American communications company should be formed—after all, the Marconi Company was British-controlled. So, in 1919, the Radio Corporation of America was born, with Owen D.

Young as chairman of the board, Edward J. Nally as president and David Sarnoff as commercial manager. A corporation with great resources, it began the development, on a scale unheard of before, not only of commercial wireless but of the transmission and reception of voice and music.

It was during this period that another colorful radio pioneer, Dr. Frank Conrad, made his mark. As a direct result of his experiments, KDKA of Pittsburgh, hailed—inaccurately—by most historians as the "first regular American radio station," came to the air.

A wireless enthusiast since his high-school days, Conrad in 1912 had built a seventy-five-watt transmitter in the garage of his Pittsburgh suburban home. By the time RCA was born in 1919, he was assistant chief engineer of Westinghouse, devoting himself to the improvement of radio transmitters. Night after night he would enter his garage, turn on his mysterious machine and read from newspapers into the microphone. Men stationed at listening posts in nearby areas listened and reported on the quality of the reception.

Soon, however, these checkers tired of Dr. Conrad's monotonously spoken words. "How about playing some phonograph records?" one of them suggested, and the scientist obliged.

Within a few weeks, an odd kind of mail poured into the Westinghouse headquarters. These letters and post cards did not come from the official listeners but from "hams" who had built their own crystal sets and through chance had tuned in on Dr. Conrad's music. In no time at all, these uninvited fans became critics.

"Why do you play the same records over and over again? Give us some new ones," wrote one. "The music you select is too slow; for heaven's sake put on something lively!" commanded another. "I'd appreciate it if you would let me hear 'Silver Threads Among the Gold' and also 'My Old Kentucky Home,'" said a third one.

Soon most of the mail was made up of requests for selections. Dr. Conrad, desirous of gaining as large a checking audience as possible, informed his listeners one night that thereafter he would try to play the records they had asked for every Wednesday and Saturday evening at 7:30. Thus, without realizing it, he became the world's first disk jockey!

Now came an amazing development. "I know several persons who are picking up this music Dr. Conrad is broadcasting," said a head of a Pittsburgh department store to one of his executives. "Maybe it would be a good idea if we put on the market a few of these gadgets on which people could listen in. We might sell a lot of 'em."

The executive agreed that it was a "good idea," and shortly thereafter the Pittsburgh newspapers carried an advertisement announcing this wondrous new device. That day H. P. Davis, a Westinghouse vice-president, remarked to Conrad: "This advertisement proves that we can learn something from these department-store people."

Davis mentioned the fortune that had been spent fruitlessly in an effort to improve the radiotelephone, but as yet the big obstacle —lack of privacy—had not been overcome. "However, here we have something in which privacy isn't needed," he said. "In fact, the more people listening in the better."

Conrad saw the point immediately. From that moment on, their objective became the transformation of radio into a medium of home entertainment. This meant that companies would have to manufacture transmitters, tubes and receivers and that someone would have to provide programs which would encourage the purchase of such equipment.

The result was the birth of the Westinghouse station KDKA which came into national fame on Tuesday, November 2, 1920. That was the day of the Harding-Cox election.

Up to then, on election nights, in towns and cities throughout the land, thousands had gathered in front of newspaper offices to read the returns chalked on blackboards or written on signs in windows. But that evening an unprecedented scene occurred. In a small combination transmitting shack and studio atop a factory building in the Westinghouse Works of East Pittsburgh, Pennsylvania, before a small group of interested company officials, Dr. Conrad and an announcer took their turns before a primitive microphone. Into it they read the latest bulletins, their voices being carried to an antenna on the roof and from there wafted out on the air, propelled by a mere one hundred watts of power.

It is estimated that not more than five hundred "hams" or amateur operators tuned in on that broadcast. But it was a sensation of the first order. Reported by press associations from coast to coast, millions of Americans talked for weeks thereafter of this miracle which brought election returns right into one's home.

Ever since then, many newspapers, magazines and books have credited KDKA with having been the first American station on the air and the Harding-Cox summary as the first broadcast. They are wrong on both counts. WWJ, the radio outlet of the Detroit *News*, deserves this recognition, which was lost because, although the station was operated by a newspaper, it lacked the publicity flair of its Pittsburgh rival.

Under its original call letters of WBL, it actually went on the air some two and a half months before KDKA's celebrated election broadcast. Proof of this may be found in a story printed in the Detroit *News* of August 20, 1920, when this Michigan station began a series of regularly scheduled daily programs. Then on August 31st, readers of that newspaper were informed that WBL (WWJ) would air that evening the results of the day's primary elections. The headline read: "The News Radiophone to Give Vote Results." The story itself began: "Radio Operators! Attention!" It went on to say: "So far as is known, this is the first time in the history of radio development that a newspaper will use the radiophone in the transmission of news." And this "radiophone" also had an additional distinction—that of broadcasting the first dance band over the air, Paul Specht's, on September 14, 1920.

Westinghouse in 1921 opened three new stations—WJZ, Newark; WBZ, Springfield, Massachusetts; and KYW, Chicago. In short order WOR, Newark; WGY, Schenectady; and WEAF began to operate. Within a few years, the number of outlets approached the one-thousand mark, their transmitters churning the air-waves, interfering with, distorting and drowning out one another's signals.

One epoch-making broadcast followed another. Major J. Andrew White phoned his thrilling description of the Dempsey-Carpentier heavyweight championship fight from Boyle's Thirty Acres in New Jersey to a special RCA station in Hoboken, where it was read into a mike by J. O. Smith, an engineer, on July 12, 1921. Then, for the first time, a show went out over two stations simultaneously— WEAF, New York, and WNAC, Boston, which on January 4, 1923, were linked with telephone wires. And the following June, listeners tuned in the President of the United States for the first time, when Warren G. Harding spoke over WEAR, Baltimore, and later on WEAF and KSD, St. Louis. Then again, on November 11th of that year, radio brought them within earshot of another historic figure, former President Woodrow Wilson, by then an ill and broken man, as he delivered an Armistice Day address over WEAF.

These were just a few among the many landmark broadcasts of that period. The new wonders came with increasing frequency. People were still discussing the first religious program on the air-waves, which the Reverend Dr. E. J. Van Etten inaugurated on KDKA, January 2, 1921; they were repeating the songs and the "snappy" patter of the Happiness Boys on WEAF; and in December, 1923, political conservatives shook their heads in amazement over the first airing, over six stations, of a Presidential message to Congress —that of Calvin Coolidge.

The year of 1924, just before the one in which I became a professional listener, was crowded with red-letter events for the radio fan. On February 8th, the A.T.&T. Company demonstrated the first hookup of stations coast to coast via telephone wires. And both the Republican National Convention in Cleveland (the first ever broadcast) and that memorable Democratic powwow in Madison Square Garden, New York, were heard by millions.

Such significant programs as those I have already mentioned were the desserts, the special treats of the infant years. The main courses were dolorous servings of dull talks, screechy songs and ear-shattering instrumental numbers. Considering the economic setup of the average station, it could not have been any other way.

WOR, now a key outlet of the Mutual Broadcasting System, was a representative studio of that period. It went on the air February 22, 1922, from a cramped room in a corner of the sports goods and radio department of the Bamberger & Co. department store in Newark. There were only a piano, a battered desk, walls hung with oriental rugs to deaden the echoes, and one microphone, which in reality was only a converted telephone transmitter with a large phonograph horn at the end. This was connected with a 250-watt transmitter built by Dr. Lee De Forest. Its signals were aimed at crystal sets and large battery receivers with three or four dials. A historical pamphlet issued by WOR reminds us that the machines were advertised as selling from fifty to seven hundred dollars each, and that these public notices attracted far more attention than real-estate ads offering fashionable East Side apartments for sixty-five dollars a month or eight-room suburban houses at $6,500.

All the station equipment in those days was on the uncertain side, so neither the management nor the public was too concerned over occasional breakdowns. A story in the Newark *Ledger*, July 10, 1922, recorded: "WOR was as silent last night as a Thanksgiving gobbler with a slit gullet. A puncture in the armature of the generating set put a quietus on the new station. Jack Poppele, WOR operator, said: 'We'll be back on the air in a week.' "

Although WOR was intended primarily to exploit its parent department store, just like all other broadcasters of the time it was extremely "DX conscious." It had pride in being heard at "distant" points. So after a number of listeners had reported that they had picked up its programs in such faraway places as Brooklyn, Staten Island and Asbury Park, the station proclaimed this news to the world in large newspaper advertisements. And in 1923, persuaded by Estella Karn, at that time Paul Whiteman's manager, the station actually announced that it would attempt to transmit a program to Japan. Nightly, for two weeks, Paul Whiteman's band played jazz intended for Nipponese ears. And strangely enough, the final program brought an acknowledgment card from a Tokyo fan saying that he had heard the music!

A perfect cross-section of American radio programming of that period could be found in WOR's listings for 1922–1924. Reading its logs, you would discover that there was no such thing as a continuous schedule, with the broadcasting periods divided into segments of 10:30 A.M. to 12 Noon, 1 to 1:30 P.M., 2:30 to 4 P.M. and 6:15 to 10 P.M. The station went silent during the lunch hour, so that its staff might have a bite to eat and there were no broadcasts on Sundays and holidays.

During the Christmas season of 1922, however, the Bamberger store sold so many radio receivers that John Poppele, WOR's engineer—or "operator," as he was called then—decided the purchasers should have some kind of Yuletide entertainment. So he sacrificed his Christmas dinner at home and put the station on the air, playing an assortment of holiday records. The next morning, newspapers praised WOR enthusiastically for "this display of initiative."

Even in those days, Poppele, who later became WOR's vice-president in charge of engineering and then president of the Television Broadcasters Association, was a fervent believer in broadcasting. His boss, the chief engineer, remarked to him one day, "I'm going into a better field; there's no future in radio," and promptly resigned.

"You're wrong," said John, and hung on.

What he hung on for was to make it possible for listeners to hear as odd a collection of performers as you could imagine. One of the most persistent of these was the "studio pianist." It was her job to fill in when scheduled artists failed to show up. Often these hard-working keyboard artists appeared five or six times a day, introduced on each occasion under a different name. Sopranos abounded; so did Irish tenors and bassos, too, with their inevitable "Rocked in the Cradle of the Deep," and it was a rare evening which did not bring forth at least two or three male quartets harmonizing "Sweet Adeline" or "My Old Kentucky Home."

Almost every artist was billed with a descriptive phrase intended to snare the listener's interest. For example, at 6:45 P.M. there were "Haunting solos by Alice Naomi Thomas, dramatic soprano of Hoboken"; at 8:02 P.M. "Princess Waukomis, contralto, full-blooded Indian princess"; and then at 9:50 you could hear "solos by G. Paladino, mandolin player, recently arrived from Russia."

There were talks galore, most of them of the how-to-do-it school, delivered in the orotund style of the oldtime Chautauqua or lyceum orators. Alfred G. Butler gave instruction on "The Art of Billiards"; Belle Bart, the astrologer, revealed the connection between "The Stars and You." Richard D. Judge entranced his fans with a "poetic reading" of "The Soul of the Violin," followed by Horace Dennis, who explained "Why I'm a Patriot." Then there was Mrs. Elvira McPherson, who held the listeners with her pointers on "How to Raise Bees."

Some fascinating stories of the beginnings of radio were given

to me by Thomas H. (Tommy) Cowan, the first announcer in the
New York metropolitan area, and, at this writing, the oldest practitioner of his art on a major station in this country. He put Westinghouse's WJZ on the air in September, 1921. This is a fact of
historic significance, considering that WJZ later became the key
outlet of RCA-NBC's Blue Network and now, under the call letters
of WABC, is the flag station of the American Broadcasting Company.

"Because I had knowledge of the theatre, Colonel E. F. Harder,
Newark plant manager of our company, selected me to talk over
its new 'radio-telephone broadcaster,' " said Cowan. "The first words
I spoke were: 'This is the radio-telephone broadcasting station of the
Westinghouse Electric and Manufacturing Company located in
Newark, New Jersey. We are talking now with the idea that some
of you out there can pick up our remarks. If you do, will you please
let us know. Remember, it's Newark, New Jersey . . . WJZ . . .
WJZ . . . WJZ . . .'

"After a few nights of this aimless chatter, I thought we should
have some music. So I borrowed a phonograph and some records
from Thomas A. Edison himself, whom I happened to know. I'd
say: 'We will now play records. . . . Will you please stand by to
tune your sets? . . . This is announcer Cowan, Newark.'

"Eventually, I got tired of saying 'Announcer Cowan, Newark'
and abbreviated it to 'A.C.N.' Announcers on other stations adopted
this custom and for some time thereafter they identified themselves
by their initials instead of their names.

"After only about ten days on the air, we received a trunkful of
mail, some from as far west as the Mississippi. Then, Sandy Hunt,
sports editor of the Newark *Sunday Call*, came to me with a startling proposal. He suggested that we should broadcast the World
Series. We approached the telephone company but they refused
to lease us a line. However, this did not discourage us; we arranged
for Sandy to buy a box at the Polo Grounds in New York and, after
much argument, had a telephone installed there.

"So on the day of the opening game between the Giants and the
Yankees, October 5, 1921, Sandy was in that box and we began the
first broadcast of a World Series. I sat in our studio in Newark with

earphones clamped on as my colleague called the plays into the telephone. I would repeat each word before the mike but the strain was so great that I did not have the slightest idea of what I was saying. In fact, at the conclusion of the game, I did not even know which team had won!

"Colonel Harder was skeptical about the whole stunt, but he ceased grumbling after our mail count showed that we had received more than four thousand letters commenting on the Series broadcasts."

Despite the sensation created by this stunt there were still many persons who had only a hearsay knowledge of radio. In fact, a week or so before the Series, Cowan received a phone call from Joseph P. Tumulty, the New Jersey man who had served as secretary to President Woodrow Wilson. As Cowan recalled it, Tumulty said, "What are you people doing over there in Newark?"

"We have a radio station here," Tommy explained.

"My kids came home late the other evening," said Tumulty, "and when I questioned them, they told me that they had been over at a friend's house where they were listening to music out of the air. I was about to send for a doctor and then I remembered about this radio, but it still puzzles me."

Cowan invited the former White House secretary to visit the Westinghouse plant. He did and went on the air as a guest speaker.

"It was in October of that year, 1921, that we broadcast what was probably the first children's program, 'The Man in the Moon,' " Cowan said. "It had its birth under most unusual circumstances.

"A woman was running a series of juvenile stories in the Newark *Sunday Call*. So we asked her to read these over the air. Our studio was situated on the top of one of the factory buildings and to reach it one had to climb a fifteen-foot iron ladder which led through a hole in the roof. Well, it so happened that this lady was afraid to make the climb and we had to drag her up forcibly. She was so frightened that she fainted. Bill McNeery, a reporter on her paper asked, 'Now what do we do?'

" 'It's your paper; so you do it,' I said to Bill, giving to him a sheet on which several of her stories were pasted.

" 'Yeah,' said Bill, 'but what do we call it?'

"Just then through a window, we saw a big moon in the sky. 'I'll give you a name—The Man in the Moon,' I said. So McNeery read the story and became 'The Man in the Moon,' one of the most beloved characters of the early days of radio."

Less than a year later, one of the most famous announcers of the country joined Cowan at WJZ as his assistant. He had made his debut as a tenor soloist and was shocked when Cowan had suggested that he become an announcer. "I'm a student of serious music," said Milton Cross, "and if I went into radio, I'd lose all of my musical contacts."

Milton permitted himself to be persuaded, however, and not only did he not lose his musical contacts but eventually became the commentator for countless symphony and Metropolitan Opera broadcasts—the country's Number One announcer of music programs. On WJZ, just like most other mike men of that day, including Graham McNamee at WEAF, Cross divided his time between talking and singing.

Despite the favorable reactions of WJZ's fans, Colonel Harder, the boss of the Westinghouse plant, had a sour view of the broadcasting setup. Pointing to the loud-speaker in his office one day, he remarked to Cowan, "I continue to ask myself why anyone would bring this thing into his home to destroy its peace."

It was then that Tommy informed him of a master stroke. He had met one of the world's greatest opera stars, Madame Johanna Gadski, at Aeolian Hall and had won her promise to broadcast over WJZ. The Colonel, being a lover of the opera, expressed astonishment and also doubt that an artist of her reputation would consent to sing on the roof of a factory building. But Madame Gadski did just that, and a few nights later, sitting on a camp chair in the studio, was Harder himself beaming in contentment.

Not long thereafter in 1922, Cowan brought to the station the Gallo Opera Company for a full-length performance of *Aïda* and again the Colonel showed some interest in radio. But not for long. One morning he called Tommy to his office and said decisively, "I want this fantastic thing out of here! It's too demoralizing. Why, we open an envelope expecting to find a big order for electric fans —and what do we get? A letter from a silly woman telling us how well some nincompoop sang last night!"

So the station moved its headquarters to Aeolian Hall, on West 42nd Street, in New York. Cowan went along with it. The Radio Corporation of America acquired WJZ in 1923 and, with WJY, operated it as "Radio Central." Tommy, working there with such noted figures as Norman Brokenshire and Ted Husing, remained until July, 1924, when as chief announcer he opened WNYC, the municipal station of New York. There he has been ever since, winning fame as the man who has broadcast the ticker tape parades and the official receptions to visiting celebrities from Colonel Charles A. Lindbergh and Queen Marie of Romania to King George and Queen Elizabeth of Great Britain and General Dwight D. Eisenhower.

It was during this hectic time that radio ignited the imaginations of the American people with one of the most dramatic broadcasts of history—a suspenseful account of the runaway flight of the U.S. dirigible *Shenandoah*.

It had broken away from its moorings at the naval air station in Lakehurst, New Jersey, and Jack Poppele, WOR's chief engineer, put his station on the air to meet the emergency. "If this ship should pass over you, please call us here!" he announced again and again, and soon hundreds of messages from New Jersey towns and villages flooded the switchboard.

In staccato fashion, Poppele repeated the names of the communities where the craft had been sighted. His words, picked up by the *Shenandoah* radio operator, gave the crew information regarding its position as the ship was buffeted by a gale above the windswept countryside. At last, as it swept over Newark, whose thousands of lights gleamed through the murky clouds, Joe Barnett, one of the station's announcers, rushed to the studio roof with a microphone.

"*Shenandoah! Shenandoah!*" he shouted. "This is WOR. You are now directly over the Prudential Building in Newark!"

Within a few moments through Poppele's earphones came the crackle of code, which he translated into words: "Thanks, WOR."

More and more reports of the ship's position surged over the loud-speakers, as the dirigible lurched and swayed in the storm. Millions of listeners held their breaths and then—a few hours later—Poppele announced, "The *Shenandoah* is safe! It is moored in Lakehurst again!"

Radio had played a major role, for the first time, in the report of a stirring real-life drama. It had guided the *Shenandoah* home. There would be many such eyewitness accounts of fateful events of history in the years to come—and most of these this reporter was privileged to hear.

Scarcely two years before this incident, while the industry was still in its toddling stages, a startling development took place: advertising came to the air-waves. For the first time in the history of radio, a commercial was broadcast over the American Telegraph and Telephone Co. station WEAF, at 5:15 P.M., August 28, 1922. It is a significant date because today, for good or ill, the huckster is the most potent figure in broadcasting.

This first commercial was a stodgy ten-minute talk delivered by a "Mr. Blackwell" on behalf of the Queensboro Corporation's new apartment building, Hawthorne Court, in Jackson Heights. The sponsor paid the station one hundred dollars for this privilege.

A copy of this talk, which I still have in my files, covers two single-spaced typewritten pages. It dwells in detail on the views of Nathaniel Hawthorne, who had advocated "a home removed from the congested part of the city, right at the boundaries of God's great outdoors." Blackwell emphasized that the great writer had "analyzed with charming keenness the social spirit of those who had thus happily selected their homes," and added that Hawthorne Court would have met with the approval of the author of *The Scarlet Letter*.

Nowhere in this discourse was there any direct appeal to the listener to visit Jackson Heights and not once was price mentioned. The series of commercials continued until September 21st and although the Queensboro Company admitted that as a result of Mr. Blackwell's radio efforts "several thousand dollars of sales had been made," it was not overenthusiastic. And neither, as a matter of fact, was WEAF, which during two months succeeded in selling only three hours of time, bringing in a gross income of $550.

Within a few months, however, there were better results after straight talk gave way to advertising programs with music. The Browning, King & Co. clothing firm and the Gimbel Brothers department store, for example, both aired orchestras. By the end of 1922, WEAF alone boasted fourteen sponsors.

I had not been on the new job more than a month when I heard of a Colonel William H. Rankin, head of the important William H. Rankin advertising agency. And with good reason. For he and James M. Mathes, of J. M. Mathes, Inc., another agency, had as profound an influence on radio programming as any men in this country. Acting on behalf of big business, they proved the power of broadcasting as a sales medium and played major roles in establishing the sponsor as the dominant figure in radio.

On December 22, 1922, Rankin's was the first advertising agency to go on the air. He bought fifteen minutes of time on WEAF to deliver a talk on "Advertising and Its Relation to the Public" for the purpose of testing the "pull" of broadcasting. The results revolutionized the entire structure of radio, bringing the giant industries of America to the microphones as sponsors of programs.

Here is how he told me this significant story:

"My boy, Bill, Jr., in his teens at the time, had built himself a crystal set. In December, 1922, he had me listen in on this strange gadget and, to my surprise, I heard Roxy introducing the Capitol Theatre Orchestra.

"I was so impressed that I visited my friend, George McClelland, sales manager for A.T.&T., which operated station WEAF at 165 Broadway. With his assistant, George Podyn, we discussed this new miracle and then Mac, one of the most far-sighted of all the radio pioneers, suggested that I sell a series of commercial talks, at the rate of one hundred dollars for ten minutes, to my clients, among whom were the American Tobacco Co., Union Carbide and the B. F. Goodrich Co.

"Well, I asked myself, just how good is this radio? I told Mac that before I'd approach any of my clients, I'd buy the first ten minutes myself, merely to see how it worked.

"The next thing, there I was before WEAF's mike and, as a consequence, the following day I received twenty-five letters and phone calls. One of these resulted in a $500,000 contract with a company to advertise its product, Mineralava. I needed no additional proof of what radio could do. So I talked this company into going on the air, with the motion-picture star Marion Davies in a thirteen-week series of ten-minute talks. The Mineralava people's business increased to such an extent that I had no difficulty in also bringing the Union Carbide Co. and the makers of Columbia and Eveready Batteries to radio.

"Not only I but McClelland and Podyn were amazed at what broadcasting could do for business. Shortly thereafter, we had the Goodrich Company on twice a week for an hour over a special hookup of eight stations at a cost of $1,600. The artists were Joseph Knecht and his Waldorf-Astoria Orchestra and the results were so good that within three months we had created the Goodrich Silvertown Orchestra, with its Silver Masked Tenor (Joe White), who was one of the song sensations of his time.

"Knecht received $300 an hour for his ten-piece orchestra and White got $50. But just a few years later, competition among sponsors had upped Knecht's pay to $2,500 and the Silver Masked Tenor's to $250. This was big money at that time; but if Joe White were in his prime today, he'd be earning thousands of dollars a week on the air."

The Goodrich program was broadcast on a network basis three years before the first network (NBC) was officially established in 1926. This had apparently escaped the notice of Mathes, whose agency was responsible for one of the most noteworthy programs in the history of radio—the Eveready Hour. For in 1924 he made what he believed to be a "revolutionary" suggestion to McClelland, the creation of a hookup of eleven stations for his show. This was done and the feature was heard as far west as Chicago.

But Rankin was the first one to see the possibilities of network broadcasting—indeed of any kind of broadcasting at all—for the major business and industrial enterprises of America. He, Mathes and a few others were responsible for channeling untold millions of dollars into the coffers of radio and then of television. Their actions helped to make these media instruments of private enterprise rather than of government, as in most foreign countries.

Odd as it may seem now, not only a portion of the listening public but a considerable segment of the broadcasting industry was shocked by this commercial intrusion! For it must be remembered that the original objectives of radio were to boost the sales of receiving sets and to publicize in an institutional way the businesses of their owners. That is why so many of the early outlets were operated by set manufacturers, department stores selling radios, and newspapers.

And Secretary of Commerce Herbert Hoover, himself, had made this statement at a conference of the radio industry in 1922: "It is inconceivable that we should allow so great a possibility for service, for news, for entertainment, for education to be drowned out in advertising chatter!"

This sentiment, uttered more than thirty years ago by the eminent conservative, would probably be regarded by some today as visionary idealism. Certainly Hoover's brave words have an ironic ring at a time when commercialism dominates television and radio.

Not that most Americans would prefer noncommercial broadcasting. It is obvious that someone must pay the bill—and that "someone" is either the sponsor or the Government. The latter alternative would eliminate the abuses of advertising and many other defects, but would also give birth to a host of evils inevitably associated with official control of a medium of expression.

And yet, some of the most ardent partisans of free enterprise have been forced to protest the excesses of the hucksters on the air. Their cries finally became so loud that the National Association of Radio and Television Producers was forced to adopt a code limiting the time devoted to plugs. Now the rule calls for the following: Before 6 P.M.: three minutes during a fifteen-minute program; four minutes and fifteen seconds in a half-hour show; and seven minutes for an hour. After 6 P.M.: two minutes and thirty seconds may be devoted to advertising in a fifteen-minute broadcast or telecast; three minutes during a thirty-minute one, and six minutes out of an hour program. However, on "participation" periods—that is, those with multiple sponsorship—one minute out of every five is allotted to commercials.

This may seem to be reasonable enough, considering the cost of some TV offerings—more than $200,000 a show. But too many local stations and, sometimes, networks, flagrantly violate their code. Not content with plugs at the beginning, the middle and the end of programs, they intrude commercials even between shows. I have heard fifteen-minute periods out of which eight or nine minutes were devoted to sales chatter, usually delivered in the loudest and most clamorous of tones. Even on programs featuring commentators discussing such problems as Communism, the dignity of man, or world peace, the defenseless listener must at times save his eardrums by tuning down the stentorian exhortations of the commercial announcer. Why advertising men confuse salesmanship with high decibels is one of the mysteries of this age. No door-to-door canvasser entering one's front hall would deliver his "message" in such a manner; and a man plugging a product over the air-waves is exactly that—a salesman entering one's home.

Even though the Madison Avenue magnificos argue that this shrill technique *does* sell goods, it is difficult to find anyone in the listening audience who approves of this loud-mouthed advertising. Recently, Edward L. Bernays, the public-relations counselor, supervised two studies on the reactions of viewers to television commercials. In the first, a cross-section of educators, businessmen and officials of trade associations said that they found the sales plugs highly "irritating." But the comment of the industry was that this group was "too intellectual," "too longhair" to be representative of the "average" fan. Therefore, in the second survey the interviewees were limited to bar and tavern keepers, barbers, beauticians and butchers. There was not an "egghead" among them. These men and women, responding to questionnaires mailed to thirteen cities in the East, the Midwest, the Southwest and on the Pacific Coast expressed, on the whole, the most emphatic dissatisfaction with TV commercials. In fact, their words, far more violent than those of the "intellectuals," included such scorching ones as "big-mouthed and low," "cheap," "noisy," "boring," "lying," "unscrupulous," "too much bunk" and "too much yak-yak about nothing." Bernays also cited the responses of N.Y. *Journal-American* readers to the query of Jack O'Brian, its TV-radio editor, "What do you do during commercials?" Some said they left the room or tuned to other stations. Others, that they read, served food and drinks or "rested their eyes."

Only 12 replies out of 400 received during a week indicated even a mild tolerance of the plugs!

In view of this, it may amuse you to read a story which Bruce Reynolds, a popular actor and lecturer, told in my column. One morning in 1922, he saw an ad in the New York *Times* announcing that A.T.&T. was "considering" the acceptance of advertising on its radio station WEAF.

"I rushed downtown to the station and made them an audacious proposal," Bruce said. "I offered to buy all of WEAF's commercial time. They said they would consider it and, in the meanwhile, they'd be willing to sell me some fifteen-minute segments for one hundred dollars each. So I raced about the city trying to interest manufacturers and merchants in going on the radio but most of them laughed at me.

"Finally, however, I succeeded in signing Coty's Perfume, United Cigar Stores, Bossert Houses and several others. I made many thousands on the resale of time and broadcast four or five different products every night. It was a real bonanza."

Then A.T.&T. complained. Its officials said Reynolds' straight sales talks were too blatant. "Be more subtle," they suggested, "so that the listeners won't realize it's advertising."

"As a result," Bruce continued, "I hired people with names, such as Texas Guinan, to deliver the talks and to be more 'subtle' about it. But again the WEAF management said too many listeners were protesting and they finally put me off the air."

Now Bruce made the rounds of other stations, among them WOR. The Bamberger executives were horrified at his proposal. "Never!" one of them exclaimed. "We wouldn't prostitute our station by accepting outside advertising!"

"Next, I met a manufacturer of electrical machinery who owned station WAAM, also in Newark," said Reynolds. "I offered to bring my former WEAF advertising to him. The mere mention of this caused him to frown. He said he feared that using his outlet for commercial purposes might cause him to lose his license."

Then with considerable trepidation the WAAM owner asked that Bruce "sound out" one of the U.S. Department of Commerce radio inspectors who had his headquarters at the Customs House. The eager salesman met this official; they became friendly and one day Reynolds invited him to lunch at the Lambs Club.

"If you tune in WAAM and heard advertising on it, would the station lose its license?" he asked the inspector.

"Well," said that gentleman with a smile, "I may not always be listening."

A few days later, Bruce Reynolds' commercials became profitable features on WAAM. But for a considerable time thereafter the station owner refused to accept his pay in checks.

"He insisted on cash," Bruce said. "Once a week, as if we were two shady characters, we met secretly in the lobby of the Hotel McAlpin. There, in a secluded corner, first making sure that no one observed us, I passed to him an envelope filled with greenbacks. You see, he did not want any written evidence that he was selling time on his station!"

SIX

Gold Rush in a Crazy House

Shortly after I had begun to write about broadcasting, I encountered Will Rogers in the lobby of the Hotel Astor and asked what he thought about radio. Chewing relentlessly on his wad of gum, the cowboy comedian drawled: "Well, all I can say is some mighty funny things happen on it."

Radio during the middle years of the 1920's merged robust slapstick, idealistic foresight and cutthroat competition into a picture that was truly fantastic; the air was heady with the essence of corn and the studios vibrated with excitement.

Without precedents or traditions, the stations announced program schedules on which almost any item was subject to change at air time. Scripts were a rarity and even commercials were ad-libbed. From one wild moment to another, the station directors zig-zagged in a state of agitated expectancy.

The networks, with their richly carpeted corridors inhabited by tweedy, pipe-smoking executives and Powers-model receptionists, had not yet entered the fray. Broadcasting, ignorant of Brooks Brothers flannels, was still in its dungarees, with an occasional attempt to garb itself in the flashy habiliments of a sideshow spieler.

Tailors, preachers, loan sharks, swamis and physical-culture men, merchants, nostrum dispensers and frenzied advocates of odd ideas, such as Colonel Henderson of Shreveport, Louisiana, who combined primitive theology with hatred of chain stores, indulged in a saturnalia of "free speech." Dr. J. Romulus Brinkley, the Kansas goat-gland charlatan, and a host of imitators won millions of devotees. In a steady procession, there came before the microphones newscasters who merely read word-for-word items from the daily papers, owners of diploma mills, crystal-gazing fortunetellers, in-

68

stallment furniture men, conductors of matrimonial bureaus, fakers, nuts and dreamers making merry carnival.

The New York *World*, commenting on the frantic invasion of broadcasting by adventurers and entrepreneurs, called it "the gold rush of 1925." It was that and more; for, as some observers of that day pointed out, the locale of this search for precious metal had been transferred from California and the Yukon to a Coney Island "crazy house" lined with distorting mirrors and equipped with loudspeakers.

But fairness demands even of the most informal historian that he record the existence of a number of noteworthy programs during those formative years. There were some shows conceived with imagination and presented with artistic integrity; there were numerous performers of outstanding talent. For example, no just account of those times would be complete without a mention of the world's radio première of *Peer Gynt* over WGBS, New York, in 1925, a production adapted and staged by the actor, Arvid Paulson, who portrayed the title role. It won and merited high critical acclaim.

The delightfully haphazard operation of the independent radio stations of the land was exemplified on WHN, atop a theatre building on Broadway. One evening about seven, I recall, a Hoboken soprano phoned the gentleman who served as combination announcer, sportscaster, disk jockey, comedian and time salesman.

"Got a heavy date tonight," she said. "How about singing tomorrow instead?"

"Okay," replied the program director, sportscaster, time salesman, etc. "I'll get someone else this evening."

Today, with program schedules arranged weeks in advance, such a message would send a studio executive right up into the ionosphere. But then these last-minute cancellations drew no more comment than a sour note in a baritone's "On the Road to Mandalay."

After all, this quavering soprano was just one of the thousands of sustaining performers contributing their efforts without fee. Anyone who failed to put in an appearance could usually be replaced with some other eager volunteer, equally untalented. If not, there was always the studio pianist who could favor the listeners with a few Victor Herbert selections or a staff announcer who could sing "The End of a Perfect Day."

In the company of the late Mark Hellinger, the Broadway columnist, and Bill Bessette, day foreman of the *News* composing room, a humorous gentleman with a fondness for odd folkways, I made frequent visits to this station during the late night hours. What went on in this enchanting madhouse (now known as WMGM) was duplicated at WEAF, WJZ, WOR, WMCA, WGBS and almost every other radio central of the United States.

In charge as program man and also doubling as a star entertainer was a flamboyant press agent and talent discoverer of the period, Nils T. Grandlund, who later became a noted night-club producer on Broadway and in Hollywood. With a sob in his voice and emphatic gestures, N.T.G. would stand before the carbon mike four or five times during an evening and, in response to telephoned requests, recite Kipling's "Boots." On WHN you could always hear him "movin' up and down again" and the audience never tired of it, just as it never wearied of what was probably the first "feud" of radio history—the "insults" exchanged between N.T.G. and a smiling piano player known as Harry Richman. The phones usually were freighted with requests for a ditty Richman sang over and over again, "There's No Hot Water in the Bronx."

Although studio audiences were not as yet officially encouraged, Broadway columnists, reporters, printers, prize fighters, out-of-work actors, assorted amateur entertainers and, occasionally, a representative listener would pass in through the unguarded station portals. Often he would be welcomed cordially by an announcer faced with the problem of filling a half-hour of time.

If the caller confessed to knowing a few good clean jokes or admitted that he sang in the morning shower, he might find himself before a microphone giving a truly "impromptu and unrehearsed" performance.

"Our talented friend, Jake Schwarzkopf of the Bronx, is here tonight and he will tell us some of his excruciatingly funny stories," listeners would hear. Jake, then, would be on his own, usually with some variation of what Pat said to Mike or with a slightly laundered version of the one about the traveling salesman and the farmer's daughter.

Now and then, Francis X. Shanahan, "that sterling Irish tenor" from Jersey City, would oblige with "Mother Machree," and if the time-filler were a woman, it was almost certain that the selection she would "execute" would be either "At Dawning" or "I Hear You Calling Me."

A surprisingly large number of famous radio professionals learned about the mike in this informal manner. For example, one of the most persistent on-the-cuff jesters was a shoe salesman, Charlie Cantor. During the day he would test his dialect stories on his customers. If they not only laughed but also ordered footwear, he would tell these jokes over WHN that evening. Some years later, Charlie became the highest-paid stooge in radio on the Fred Allen show and on the coast-to-coast broadcasts of "Duffy's Tavern."

Soon, however, N.T.G. abandoned radio, and then came the dizzy era of Perry Charles. A small wiry fellow with twinkling gray eyes, a crew haircut and a pugnacious chin, he was three-fourths out of Kaufman and Hart and one-fourth out of Lewis Carroll—a jester whose uninhibited exploits are still recounted when oldtimers gather to tell of broadcasting's early years.

Today, when, as Fred Allen says, the industry is so highly departmentalized that there is even a vice-president-in-charge-of-"Ah! . . . Ah!-You-mustn't-raise-that-window!" Charles would be the despair of any personnel manager. He functioned as a one-man broadcasting studio: program chief, talent auditioner, press agent, football and prize-fight sportscaster and, now and then, if the porter failed to put in an appearance, as a wielder of broom and mop. Being by nature a gregarious fellow, during the late hours he held open house in the studio above Broadway. While he was on the air, his friends, sitting or reclining a few feet away, consumed hamburgers and, occasionally, home brew donated by one Joe, the friendly owner of a speakeasy an 45th Street. Annoyed by the constant sound of his visitors' chatter, Perry would now and then make an anguished plea: "For cryin' out loud, why don't you bums pipe down?" One night, while our host was interviewing me before the mike, Joe rushed in waving a bottle. "Look!" he shouted at Charles and into the open microphone. "Scotch—right offa the boat!"

When twitted about his unconventional antics, Charles would give a wry but logical explanation: "It's a crazy business and you gotta to be crazy to be in it."

His "craziness" took the form of ridiculing the solemn commercial announcements of his sponsors long before the orchestra leader Ben Bernie, supposedly the pioneer in this field, did so. Also, at the suggestion of Cliff Clifton, known as The Nut Club's "King Solomon, the Wise Guy," he emceed a show, the Amateur Hour, which had a predecessor on WRNY. It became so popular that the managing director of WHN, Major Edward Bowes, eventually took it over. According to the announcement, he did so in order to "lighten the burden of Mr. Charles' work." Shortly after this the entertainment became known as "Major Bowes' Amateur Hour." Although Charles did not receive a cent extra in pay for his efforts, the Major won both fame and an estimated income of twenty-five thousand dollars a week out of this apotheosis of the hillbilly and the musical saw.

It was for his highly original manner of broadcasting prize fights that Perry Charles gained a special kind of distinction during the early days of radio. Unlike Major J. Andrew White, Graham McNamee and Ted Husing, this bantam of the microphone eschewed the dramatic; he refused to depict two comparatively inert pugilists as enraged titans battling for the supremacy of the world. If the action in the ring were dull or nonexistent, he'd say so. "These here stumble-bums ain't fighting, they're just waltzin' around," he would comment in injured tones. "Aw, what's the use of boring you with this stuff! Maybe, instead, you'd like to hear some jokes?"

He would tell a few and then suddenly: "Well, they've come alive again. One of 'em actually struck a blow just now! Let's get on with the fight."

During a broadcast of one of these minor bouts from a small-time uptown New York fight club, Perry created a furor with an unprecedented act of lese majesty: He "told off" his sponsor while on the air!

To assure himself that his temperamental hireling would not short-change him on the number of commercials, the bankroller, owner of a men's clothing store, seated himself directly beside Perry at the ringside. The gentleman, weighing a conservative 250, with a shining bald dome and continuously puffing an enormous black cigar, towered over his wage slave like Vesuvius beside an ant hill. At the conclusion of every round, and sometimes before, he would tug at the sportscaster's sleeve and whisper pantingly, "How about another plug?"

Waving the choking clouds of cigar smoke from his nostrils, Perry would dutifully request his listeners to rush immediately down to 14th Street for the bargain sale of the century. But the sponsor's demand for blood was still not satisfied. He continued his pleas for "another plug" and finally Charles could stand it no longer.

With a sadistic smile, Perry drew close to the mike and said: "My sponsor ain't contented. All evening he's been blinding me with fumes from his vile Pittsburgh stogy and he's pulled at my elbow so hard I myself am in need of a new coat. And each time he keeps asking me for 'just one more plug.' Okay, boys and gals, I'll give him one:

"As I've told you for the one thousandth and umpteenth time, down at his place on 14th Street, there's a sale going on. It's gigantic, colossal and stupendous! For just $18.95, you can get yourself a wonderful suit, with two pair of pants. You never saw such suits . . . amazing suits . . . eye-filling suits . . . stunning suits . . . unbelievable suits! . . . but between you and me, kiddies, there's just one little thing you ought to know about 'em: *I wouldn't be caught dead in one!*"

The sponsor had a spasm. Restraining himself from committing assault and battery on the slight Mr. Charles, which might have provided a better spectacle than the one in the ring, he rushed, instead, from the arena to phone his lawyer. The next day, this gentleman served notice that both the station and its announcer could consider themselves to be defendants in a two-million-dollar libel and slander action.

Unfortunately, the case did not come to trial. A few days later, during a luncheon at an illicit taproom, WHN agreed to make due amends for the mortal sin of its employee. Over glasses of prime New Jersey Scotch and Manhattan soda, the outraged feelings of the clothing-store merchant were deftly soothed. Sacrificing the two million he had demanded, he gratefully accepted the settlement so generously offered by the radio station: Six free fight broadcasts—with Perry Charles at the mike!

And while such fantastic goings-on provided rousing slapstick for professional viewers of the scene, broadcasting recorded a steady series of significant technical improvements. In 1925, for example, RCA introduced the all-electric receiving set and a year later it came forth with startling news, the perfection of a radio tube which operated on alternating current. This was a revolutionary advance; it did away with the need for those cumbersome acid-seeping batteries which had disfigured millions of American living rooms. Radio now was so simple that even a child could tune it in without fuss, mess or bother.

By now, too, broadcasting had become commercial with a capital C. Forgotten were the idealists who, less than five years before, were still visualizing it as a medium in which even entertainment programs were to be without taint of the marketplace. Radio was openly and unashamedly a gigantic cash register of the air.

Even so, some programs were still being presented, according to the announcers, "through the courtesy of So-and-So." And on many stations sponsors were not permitted to make mention of specific prices of their wares.

With more and more programs becoming mere come-ons for products, the sopranos, the tenors and the saxophone players who had heretofore contributed their services gratis now insisted on being paid. But their stipends were ridiculously meager by current standards. For example, I commented in my column during 1926 that "The Radio Franks," appearing on WOR "have become radio's highest paid artists. They receive $10 a minute or $150 a broadcast! I wonder how many sponsors would be willing to pay for an hour's program at this rate."

About this time, the availability of radio reception became a matter of prime concern to the average American family in the metropolitan centers. Almost every mail brought to me inquiries from readers who wished to know whether they could get good DX (long distance) in certain communities of Long Island or Westchester. Alton C. Brickman a real-estate salesman, told the New York *Trib-*

une during the summer of 1925: "The first thing the prospective purchaser of a suburban home asks me is, 'Can we get WEAF, WJZ and WOR out there?'"

Although twirling the dials had become a national mania, it still was news when some celebrated citizen announced himself as a radio fan. A Princeton professor, for example, received a box on the front page of the New York *World* because he let it be known that he approved of some programs. Harry Houdini, the famous escape artist and magician, also made the front pages, but for slightly different reasons. He had told friends that he was so enamored of this new medium that he would purchase the most expensive set he could obtain. After the elaborate and highly complicated super-heterodyne job had been installed in his home, he found that he could get nothing on it save static. This so enraged Harry that he invaded the store which had sold him the contraption and proceeded to vent his fury by smashing several radios.

The indignant proprietor swore out a warrant for his arrest. Hearing of this, Alfred H. (Hollywood) McCosker, the almost legendary press agent who later became chairman of the board of the Mutual Broadcasting System, invited Houdini to explain his actions before the microphones of WOR. Harry accepted the offer and Mac tipped off the police. The cops arrested the escape virtuoso in the midst of his broadcast and the press associations sent the story from coast to coast.

Although their protests were not quite so violent as Houdini's, static—the bane of early radio—also enraged millions of other fans and caused great concern to sponsors. The already-mentioned Hollywood McCosker took recognition of this by utilizing that perpetual friend of the press agent—Lloyd's of London. After WOR had booked a popular singer of the day, Ernie Young, Mac applied for a fifty-thousand-dollar policy to compensate the station in the event his broadcast should be "ruined by electrical interference." Lloyd's turned McCosker down—but it made a story.

Such zany episodes marked the course of radio during the 1920's not only in New York but throughout the land. I recall several which occurred on WGN, the broadcasting outlet of the Chicago *Tribune*.

The transmission of police calls on short waves to patrol cars is a routine matter today. But WGN created a nationwide stir in those years by installing radio receivers in squad automobiles and volunteering, as a public service, to relay urgent messages to cruising patrolmen. These instructions were phoned directly from headquarters to the station. There an announcer clanged an enormous bell before the microphone and cried: "Attention! Squad 48! Pawnshop held up . . . Dearborn Street!"

Not only did the listeners fail to object to such interruptions of entertainment programs, but many of them became police "buffs." They rushed to the scenes of crimes in such numbers that the cops often had difficulty in forcing their way into the premises mentioned on the radio.

One night, during a musical show, there were many such intrusions: reports of assaults, robberies, hold-ups and attempted murders. In each instance the patrolmen were told that the criminals were fleeing in specified directions in certain makes of cars.

Before the half-hour program was over, Ford, Packard and Buick had received no fewer than seven free and unsolicited plugs. This was embarrassing, considering that the show was being sponsored by the makers of Elcar, a rival automobile manufacturer!

It wasn't even considered unusual that Chicago, the second city of the country, and other communities, too, should enjoy the blessings of "silent nights." Local stations would shut down at 7 o'clock every Monday evening, so that listeners could indulge in their favorite pastime of "DX-ing," that is, listening to distant radio stations on their living-room sets.

Broadcasting, despite its progress, was still in its formative stages; even the "experts" frankly admitted they did not know "what it was all about." The simplest new program became an adventure. Did a performer or a technician have an idea? No matter how farfetched it may have seemed, there was always someone to say, "Let's try it." There were no stuffy boards of directors to appease; no hair-splitting vice-presidents to pacify. "You want to do something different? Okay, Bud, try it!"

Perhaps one of the wackiest incidents resulting from this spirit of uninhibited experiment was a quaint production on a now-defunct New York station of what the press releases described as a "thrilling melodrama of life in Czarist Russia."

During one scene, the cast was supposed to have been assembled around a table drinking vodka. Although, of course, the listeners could not see the hearty revelers of the steppes, the director, a David Belasco stickler for realism, insisted on a literal interpretation of the script.

"Real vodka shall be drunk by all of you," he told his players in a thick German accent. "This will give an air of absolute authenticity."

As these instructions were uttered during one of the most arid periods of Prohibition, none of the players made any frantic objections. In a laudable effort to induce the proper mood, the director obtained two bottles of the Muscovite distillation from a Second Avenue restaurant and displayed them proudly to a studio executive.

The latter seemed doubtful. "This is only a radio play," he said. "Why is it necessary to drink anything at all—even water?"

"Because I cannot compromise with reality," said the director.

An eager member of the cast who had never tasted vodka suggested that, in order to accustom the players to the Russian potion, it wouldn't hurt to serve a little of it during the dress rehearsal. The director acceded grudgingly and became impatient when the cast found it necessary to devote an extraordinary amount of time to the drinking scene. It required four readings. And the master of realism would have been even more perturbed had he noticed several members of his "Art Players" pouring themselves secret slugs in Dixie cups.

The artists were still trying to master the more subtle nuances of their portrayals when the announcer put them on the air. The Muzhik Ivan uttered the opening line of the drama and immediately the bored technician in the control room knew it wasn't Stanislavsky. And he was even more certain of this when the St. Petersburg droshky driver, to whom Ivan had addressed his remarks, suddenly lost his Russian accent and began to hold forth in a refined version of Brooklynese. Then, a few minutes later, matters became more confused when the heroine, a fugitive from the Okrana, the Czarist secret police, instead of reading her own lines, began to spout those of her mother.

At this point the director gave one of the most "realistic" impersonations of a madman ever seen in a studio. Tearing his hair, he stamped, gurgled and choked for breath, as his "artists" sank to the lowest depths of the Thespian pit. One stammered; another seemed to be in a coma. Plainly, they were cockeyed! Finally, the control engineer, a gentleman with the emotional range of a cucumber, flicked a dial and cut the "Art Players" off the air.

"Ladies and gentlemen," he announced with icy matter-of-factness, "because of technical difficulties we are forced to discontinue this program. Please stand by for a piano solo."

There was an equally ardent paladin of realism on another New York radio station of that time. A director of hillbilly shows, he argued that his barnyard sound effects were not what they should be. And he was eminently correct.

Today, sound experts are trained technicians who work with cleverly contrived mechanical devices and comprehensive libraries of recorded noises. On their platters and tapes are imprisoned a vast variety of aural agitations, from the buzz of a mosquito to the roar of a lion, from the creaking of an oxcart to the whoosh of a Thunderjet. There are still a few of the old-time mimics of animals, fowls and reptiles around but, save for these outstanding exceptions, they are waging a losing battle against electronics. In the 1920's, however, this gentry practically had a monopoly in the production of barks, chirps, howls and hisses. Some of these "artists" were excellent, but many of them wouldn't have deceived a five-year-old.

The hillbilly director, as eager as the genius of the "Art Players" to invest his show with "reality," phoned one of his friends who was in the wholesale poultry business downtown near Washington Market. "Send up a couple of crates of birds to make some sound effects," he said, "and we'll mention your name on the air."

The poultryman obliged but, unfortunately, the truck bearing the assorted fowl to the station on West 57th Street was delayed in a traffic jam. The crates were brought into the studio a few minutes after the broadcast had begun and the director, lacking time for any detailed instructions, merely told the truckman, "Turn 'em loose!"

As the crates were opened, the hens, roosters, ducks and geese, panic-stricken by the lights, the music and the singing, sprang in alarm onto the studio floor. The "realist" had demanded true-to-life sound effects—and now he had them!

Roosters flew about the studio and an angry goose, furiously hissing, nipped an ankle of the Bronx "farm girl" singing into the mike. She screamed and dashed for the nearest door and a score of barnyard fowl followed her through the open exit and then made their way to the adjoining stairs. One of the roosters, gaining a ledge, jumped onto a fire escape and, becoming air-borne, flew through a window of a nearby building. It landed on a grand piano, where a music student was practicing her next day's lesson. The girl, unaccustomed to such intrusion, sprang in fright from the stool, tripped on a rug and fractured an ankle. Some of the other birds had by this time made the street via an open lobby door, with studio employees, policemen and passers-by in pursuit.

The sponsor canceled the show; the nipped girl hillbilly gave up her job; the music student collected damages and the unhappy director developed an allergy for fowl of every kind.

Such shenanigans disappeared from the air within a few years after radio had become a formalized institution. But in at least one instance the joyous madness of the 1920's came to life again in the 1950's. For it was only a few years ago that one Maurice Dreicer, the millionaire gourmet and radio producer, broadcast probably the oddest series of programs over to emanate from a microphone.

"Did you ever stop to think of the thousands of dogs in New York City who can't sleep at night?" he asked me one afternoon. "Well, I have, and I'm going to cure their insomnia."

The following Monday he went on WOR at midnight, reading sentimental poetry in somnolent tones and occasionally crunching beefsteak bones for "sound effects." A few days later, I wrote in the column that although it was understandable that his reading of verses might induce slumber among the canine audience, it seemed that the crunching of bones would have just the opposite effect.

"Ah, my boy, you are wrong," Dreicer assured me. "First, my poetry puts 'em to sleep; then, my bones bring 'em dreams of luscious steaks!"

Maury's unusual program ran for many weeks. But, sad to confess, this reporter missed one of the scoops of all time, when he failed to check on whether any New York dogs had actually been cured of insomnia.

Because radio during the third decade of this century was an even greater novelty than television during the 1940's, the mass enthusiasm generated by its stars can scarcely be imagined. A singer with a new style or a comedian with a catchy tag line became the overnight vogue of millions.

In later years, the bobby-soxers and teen-agers went wild over Frank Sinatra and Johnnie Ray, but even their adolescent frenzy failed to approach the fervor of the Rudy Vallee maniacs. During the span between 1928 and 1933, the "king of crooners" won a degree of feminine adulation surpassed only by that given to that other Rudy, the movie star Valentino. The Vallee fans were the original fanatics of radio. As someone has said, they had love in their eyes and murder in their hearts, with the homicide reserved for those unappreciative radio critics who did not prostrate themselves in worship at the Maine minnesinger's shrine.

One day, I remarked casually in the News column: "After all, Rudy Vallee is not the only great singer the world has known. What about Enrico Caruso?"

Scores of letters on ruled tablet pages and on scented stationery gave me the answer: "You can have Caruso; I'll take Rudy!" There were also such sweet admonitions as "Go out and drown yourself!" and such gentle comments as "I'd like to tie you to a post and turn loose a million man-eating ants on you!"

Seeking to strike back, in a moment of mental lapse, I next published a letter from an indignant Brooklyn husband who lamented that his wife, instead of devoting her evenings to pleasant social conversation—about the Dodgers, no doubt—insisted on tuning in Rudy Vallee.

"I want to make a sporting proposition," he wrote. "I've got an old hound dog from Virginia. Well, sir, if my beast can't yowl better than this nasal crooner, I'll not only eat my hat but do the consuming in Macy's most prominent window."

A few days later, the column ran another letter, from a woman in Jersey City who insisted that my Brooklyn correspondent was not only jealous but plain dumb. His hound, she said, was not anything special; she had a Boston bull terrier which "cannot only yowl as well as Rudy, but do it to piano accompaniment. You ought to hear him carry a tune."

Now scores of letters came from every section of the metropolitan area. For weeks, the "Great Rudy Vallee Hound Dawg Controversy" raged in the column. Each correspondent espoused the merits of his or her musical canine. Wearying of this, I made a tragic error. "It's ridiculous," I wrote. "I don't believe that there is such a thing as a singing dog. If there is, let's have proof: Bring your animal to my office Friday at 3 P.M. and I'll give him an audition for the Ziegfeld Follies."

Now I was taught a lesson that sooner or later every columnist learns: It is fatal to jest in print. Two days later, fom Manhattan, Brooklyn, Bronx, Queens, Staten Island and the nearby communities of New Jersey, a snarling, yipping procession converged on our Park Place plant. Men, women and children carrying and leading poodles, bulldogs, hounds, fox terriers, wirehairs, cockers, pointers, setters and canines of questionable ancestry poured through the narrow front entrance. Guards tried to halt them, but up they came via elevator and stairs, right into my tiny office, overflowing into the aisles of the adjacent advertising department.

"Where's this fellow Gross?" they demanded. "Whatya mean my dog can't sing? Trixie can do 'Rosie O'Grady'!"

"It's all a joke," I protested. "I was just having a little fun."

That really made the visitors furious. But their vituperations were drowned in a noisy fight between a wirehair and a cocker spaniel. Soon others joined the fray and their barks, growls, yelps and whines spiraled high above the clacking of the advertising-office typewriters. All activity there came to a halt and clerks and typists crowded about the door of the radio room while their bosses raged. Guards pleaded and pushed, and from the floors below, the composing and the editorial rooms, employees rushed in to watch the fray.

There were no more stunts like that, at least not in my column, even in that fantastic era of broadcasting. And what's more, never again did I question that Rudy Vallee was the world's greatest crooner or that some dogs could sing!

SEVEN

When Radio Was Young

Vincent Lopez' band was playing "Yes, We Have No Bananas," but it had gone no more than ten bars when the music faded, to be replaced by a talk about the Mexican jumping bean. It, in turn, was drowned by the stentorian tones of a laxative salesman demanding, "Are you regular?"

It was often like that on the radio of the middle Twenties. You took it for granted that while you were listening to the merry sleigh-bells of Harry Reser and his "Eskimos," you might suddenly find yourself an unwilling auditor of a swami revealing the secrets of successful love.

One of the popular anecdotes of the period told of a sermon delivered by the evangelist Billy Sunday over a New York radio station. In the midst of his hellfire-and-brimstone talk he shouted, "Brothers and sisters! I ask you what did Jonah say to that whale?" And then, immediately, listeners heard the announcer of another studio come in: "Take Carter's Little Liver Pills!"

For that was the most chaotic and raucous time of American broadcasting. A multitude of neighboring stations operated on the same wave band, clashing, jumbling and blanketing one another's signals. Over the loud-speakers poured words and music mixed with staccato crackles, shrill whistles and deafening roars.

There was a law on the statute books to control broadcasting, but it was a tenuous one. Whatever order prevailed on the air-waves had its source in a "gentlemen's agreement" made by the station owners themselves. This provided for the sharing of time on an "equitable basis."

In 1912 Congress had enacted a communications act which gave the Department of Commerce the power to regulate commercial wireless by the issuance of licenses and the assignment of wave lengths. Therefore, it was this arm of the government, headed by Secretary Herbert Hoover, which was charged with the policing of radio. But by the end of 1921, when there were only sixty stations and only 600,000 receiving sets in the country, it was already apparent that some modifications of the law were necessary.

In 1922, therefore, Secretary Hoover called a conference of the radio industry, attended by what he describes as "about one thousand agitated men and women." This assembly adopted certain statements of principle, among the most important of which were that broadcasting should be a private, not a government enterprise; that the air channels should be public property, and that, above all, there must be regulation of traffic to prevent interference.

But a short while thereafter, with more than a thousand stations churning the air all on the same wave band, the problem of interference had become a titanic one. Hoover took recognition of it by assigning the more important outlets to the 400-meter channels and the lesser broadcasters to the 300-meter band. Actually, however, this had little effect, for the Department of Commerce lacked the means of enforcing its edicts.

The Secretary urged again that the station operators do all in their power to eliminate interference by living up to their time-sharing agreements. But his words went unheeded.

Advertisers insisted that their programs be broadcast during the most profitable listening hours, from 8 to 11 P.M. If Station A had been so foolish as to agree to be off the air at that time, the sponsors would take their business to Station B, which had been wise enough to pre-empt this desirable period.

Occasionally, Station A might be able to "work out a deal" with Station B, whereby the former would be permitted to break into the latter's schedule in order to broadcast a commercial program. But not often. Not all studio managers were as accommodating as Tommy Cowan, who, in 1922, took his station, WJZ, off the air in order to permit WOR to broadcast its formal inaugural. He did this without even having obtained the permission of his employers!

In a frantic effort to scoop in the sponsorial dollars, the station men thumbed their noses at pacts. If rival broadcasters would not give up valuable time segments, they would go on the air despite that. The result would be two or more programs coming in on the loud-speaker at the same moment!

This did not exactly delight the sponsors. So the broadcasters tried a new tack. Without permission of the Department of Commerce, they blithely changed their wave lengths!

Thus, Station A, operating tonight on 316 meters, might be heard tomorrow at 374 on the dial! But no sooner would it be snugly ensconced in its new home than another poacher would invade its territory and again you would hear two programs simultaneously, the merger sounding like a dialogue between Donald Duck and Pluto the Pup.

Aimee Semple McPherson, the Los Angeles evangelist, took full advantage of this situation. She drove the listeners of Southern California mildly insane by repeatedly changing the wave length of her Temple's broadcasting station. Department of Commerce inspectors pleaded, cajoled and threatened, but she ignored them. Finally, one of the exasperated officials sealed her transmitting apparatus and thereby put an end to the interference.

The next morning, Secretary Hoover received a telegram from Aimee. It called on him to order his "minions of Satan" to "leave my station alone." And it added that he could "not expect the Almighty to abide by your wave-length nonsense!"

Was her license revoked? Was her transmitter banished from the air? Certainly not. Hoover's diplomatic inspector had another talk with the lady and, after persuading her to employ a friend of his as engineer, permitted Aimee to resume her broadcasts!

Some outlets, such as WEAF, WOR and KDKA, of course, did not engage in such freebooting. After all, they could not afford to jeopardize the prestige of the great corporate enterprises backing them.

By 1925, as a result of the various industry conferences called by Secretary Hoover, some semblance of order had been restored. Then the dikes broke again. A Federal judge in Chicago decided that year that the Communications Act of 1912, under which the Department of Commerce exercised its scant authority, did not cover radio broadcasting. He held, as a matter of fact, that the Government lacked the right even to insist that a station operate on any one wave length!

Now it really became a game of every man for himself. But in this instance the devil could not take the hindmost, for not even Satan could locate a victim in the confusion. What had been bedlam before became multiplied by a thousand. Hoover and the heads of powerful corporations engaged in broadcasting—who, a decade later, were to cry out against government interference with private enterprise—now all but fell to their knees praying for some legal power to put an end to the chaos. Their supplications were not answered until two years later, in 1927, with the creation of a national regulatory agency, the Federal Radio Commission, which in 1934 became the Federal Communications Commission.

Judged by current critical standards most of the programs were crude, naïve or downright nonsensical. And yet, many of the personalities and shows had a profound influence on the development of radio and were worthy of the acclaim accorded them.

First and foremost, there were the announcers. Today these men, save for Milton Cross, Ben Grauer and a few others, have ceased to exist as personalities. Their job is to deliver the commercials and to get the show on and off the air as expeditiously as possible. On the major programs they are, for the most part, unctuous technicians, working efficiently and smoothly as so many well-oiled talking machines. No longer stars in themselves, they merely parrot the words of the hack script-writers and are easier to replace than the tires of an automobile.

But it was not like that when radio was young. Mike men such as Major J. Andrew White, Graham McNamee, Milton Cross, Tommy Cowan, Ted Husing, Norman Brokenshire, Phillips Carlin, Alois Havrilla, Marley Sherris, Lewis Reid, Perry Charles, Walter Neff, David Ross, Norman Pearce, Ted Nelson, A. L. Alexander and Basil Ruysdael were top-flight names. They handled sports, news, special events, variety shows and broadcasts from night clubs with equal facility. Completely independent of script, they could and did hold forth for hours at a time, if necessary, masters of the ad lib and of impromptu chatter. The day of the specialist, exemplified by the colorful Clem McCarthy of horse-racing fame, had not yet arrived.

Sponsors today spend millions on stars and shows which have only momentary vogues, but those who rose to fame during radio's formative span retained the loyalty of their fans for years. One need only recall Billy Jones and Ernie Hare, Vaughn de Leath, Wendell Hall, May Singhi Breen and Peter de Rose, Whispering Jack Smith, Jessica Dragonette, Madame Ernestine Schumann-Heink, Reinald Werrenrath, James Melton, Roxy and his Gang, Gladys Rice, Beatrice Belkin, Wee Willy Robyn, Carolyn Andrews, Joe White (The Silver Masked Tenor) and Major Edward Bowes' Capitol Theatre Entertainers.

Even now old-timers speak fondly of Harry Horlick's A. & P. Gypsies, the Ipana Troubadours, Harry Reser's Eskimos, Joseph Knecht's, Joseph Bonime's and Cesare Sodero's concert ensembles. They doted on the Revellers, the Lone Star Rangers, the Sylvania Foresters and other male quartets, and gave long-enduring allegiance to Will Rogers, Moran and Mack (The Two Black Crows), Weber and Fields, the Atwater Kent Concerts and Auditions and the Eveready Hour.

Veteran listeners still reminisce about vaudevillians Van and Schenck, comedians Joe Laurie, Jr., and "Senator" Ed Ford, just as they recall the operetta prima donna Evelyn Herbert. And as vivid in their memories are those ridiculously named musical groups: The Royal Stenographers, the Dodge Brothers Fast Four, and Red Nichols' Ginger Mint Julipers. There are graybeards who have fond recollections even of the Bromo Seltzer Blue Bottles, led by the same Don Voorhees who is now the dignified conductor of the symphonic Telephone Hour.

Many a youth today never heard of "Myrt and Marge," the serial of backstage life enacted by Myrtle Vail and her daughter, Donna Damerel. But the mention of their names brings a glow to their parents who can't forget that during 1932 and 1933 this radio show was among the "top ten" attractions of the air and eventually attained such popularity that it was broadcast twice a day, five times a week. And to a generation weaned on television, their seniors could tell of the melodic glories of Lanny Ross, the romantic tenor, and the robust comedy of Charles Winninger in the old "Maxwell House Showboat." Likewise, the Old Guard would be happy to enlighten them concerning the joys of the "Lady Esther" show, the tall tales of Jack Pearl's Baron Munchausen, the dialect stories of Henry Burbig. And without being pressed at all, they would dwell on the throbbing love songs of the "Street Singer," the ditties of "Singing Sam" and the sharp sallies of Phil Baker, the accordion-playing funny man.

The *News* issued on September 16, 1928, a special supplement in honor of the fifth annual Radio World's Fair at Madison Square Garden. It featured the year's "blue-ribbon list" of artists and shows, probably the first such compilation made by a metropolitan newspaper in the history of broadcasting.

Some of those included on this honor roll, in addition to most of the names already mentioned, were: Walter Damrosch's New York Symphony and young people's concerts, the Philco comic-opera presentations, the "Great Moments of History" sketches, the Jewish Hour, the New York Philharmonic musicales, the popular song duos of Prince Piotti and Madeline Hardy and of Artie Dunn and Sammy Fain, comedians Henry Burbig, Frank Moulan and Phil Cook. Also, the Edwin Franko Goldman concert band, studio pianists Marjorie Harding, Lolita Cabrera Gainsborg and Herman Neuman, violinists Arcadie Birkenholz and Godfrey Ludlow, saxophonists Merle Johnston and Clyde Doerr, cymbalomist Joseph Moskowitz and organists Emil Velazco and Lew White.

The personalities and programs mentioned in the "blue-ribbon list" of the following year, 1929, included many who had become nationally famous during the preceding twelve months.

Thus one found such newcomers as Rudy Vallee, "Amos 'n' Andy," Raymond Knight, of "Kuku Hour" fame, and Ludwig Laurier's Slumber Hour Ensemble, of which Milton Cross was the tenor soloist. There were also the "Bible Dramas," George Frame Brown's "Main Street Sketches," "Empire Builders," Don (Uncle Don) Carney, the Radio Guild Plays and the dance orchestras of Ben Pollack, Duke Ellington, Phil Spitalny, Paul Tremaine, Gene Ingraham, W. C. Polla, Larry Funk and George Olsen (featuring singer Ethel Shutta).

Among the others in this choice group, were the sea dramas of the "Forty Fathom Trawlers," the song duo of Scrappy Lambert and Billy Hillpot ("The Smith Brothers"), Katherine Tift-Jones' "Cabin Door Sketches," sports announcers Buck O'Neill and Sam Taub, the dumb blonde comedy team of Marcella Shields and Helen Handin, Erminie Calloway, the "baby vamp singer," ukelele soloist Roy Smeck, Andy Sanella, the guitarist, hillbilly vocalists Carson Robinson and Dad Pickard's Family and the unbelievably riotous broadcasts of the Village Grove Nut Club.

At least one veteran listener looks back with fond nostalgia on many of these pioneers. One of them, Joe White, the Silver Masked Tenor, was the target of thousands of mash notes from lovesick maidens. The silver mask he wore during his public appearances made him a man of mystery and caused much speculation as to his identity. Some letter writers to newspapers guessed he was John McCormack, the great Irish tenor, and a few women even accused him of being their long-lost husbands.

By 1925, Joe drew such crowds that police escorts were required to sneak him through the stage doors of theatres where he made personal appearances. His income from these probably did not average more than four or five hundred dollars a week; today a singer of equal reputation would draw from five to fifteen thousand dollars.

But Joe considered himself a lucky fellow. Just a few years before, he had sung on as many as four stations a night without pay. "And even when I became a regular on WJZ, I didn't collect a cent," he told me. "As a matter of fact, it cost me twenty-five dollars a week out of my own pocket to pay my accompanist."

I shall always remember his performance on a night in 1933, when NBC moved from 711 Fifth Avenue to its studios in Radio City. Joe sat atop a heap of chairs and desks on the last van-load of furniture leaving the old quarters, broadcasting via short wave over a portable microphone. He sang "Kathleen Mavourneen," the beginning of the song going out on the air from the Fifth Avenue building and its end from the towering RCA structure in Rockefeller Center.

But my most vivid memories of those days are of a man who was

Joe's intimate friend, the legendary Graham McNamee. He had often told me of how one day he had visited station WEAF on downtown Broadway while doing jury duty in the old Federal Court and Post Office Building near by. As a result, he was engaged as a baritone soloist-announcer.

By the time I met Graham, three years later, he was already a nationally famous figure, although the station still had only two cramped rooms as studios. McNamee was "Mr. Radio" during these early times. As far as WEAF was concerned, he was its vocal symbol, just as Lamdin Day, "The Little Colonel" of Atlanta, Ty Tyson of Detroit and George Hay (The Solemn Judge) of Nashville were the idols of their communities.

Millions of fans were still discussing his memorable coverage, with Phil Carlin, of the Democratic National Convention of 1924. As for his description of the 1925 World Series, the most revealing comment on it is that he received fifty thousand personal letters from those who had heard it. But regardless of what event Graham described, he made it one of overwhelming drama to his listeners.

Once I sat beside McNamee as he broadcast a third-rate bout in an uptown boxing club. Those present saw only a slow-moving, slovenly exhibition of gentle taps, awkward feints and repeated clinches, but that was not the way Graham depicted it for his radio audience. From the opening bell to the last tepid blow, it was a fast-paced furious action.

Graham was not faking; he did not mean to deceive his listeners. But he was such an enthusiast, such an instinctive showman, that before his eyes any action became per se a thrilling, spine-tingling drama.

"Why do you make it seem so exciting, when you know very well it isn't?" I asked him one day.

"I only tell it the way it looks to me," he said.

Among the older generation of listeners there are many who recall what was probably the most hectic and purplest description of a football game ever heard on the radio—the first broadcast of a Rose Bowl contest between Alabama and Stanford in 1927. I couldn't for the life of me tell you what the score was, but Graham's word pictures over NBC of the blue skies above Pasadena, the fragrance of the roses and the gentle caress of Southern California's balmy breezes will not pass from my memory.

Shortly thereafter, I inquired of Merlin H. Aylesworth, the first president of NBC, "What does McNamee actually know about football?"

"Damned little," said Aylesworth, "but he certainly puts on a great show."

And that he did, a circumstance which finally unhorsed him. For although McNamee knew more about various games, having played them as a boy, than Aylesworth admitted, he did sacrifice accuracy to showmanship. Yet, that's what the public of the 1920's demanded. Given a choice between an expert who knew the fine points of boxing or football, but who gave a colorless account of a contest, and one who had only scant knowledge, but infused his words with glowing drama, the listeners preferred the latter every time.

With the passing of the years, however, the fans began to demand accuracy above everything else. Graham, who loved description more than what he described, could not adjust himself to this less colorful but more factual method of reporting.

During his later years, I visited him one evening in his apartment. A tall and by now balding man, he sat in a room crowded with trophies, countless scrolls, loving cups and medals bestowed on him by athletic, civic and patriotic organizations. He spoke with affection of some of his famous broadcasts, especially of his stirring account of Lindbergh's 1927 reception in New York.

Suddenly he banged a fist into a palm and frowned. "They don't want me any more," he said sadly.

Nevertheless, in a day when such factual sports announcers as Red Barber, Jimmy Powers, Mel Allen and Russ Hodges rule the roost, when there are specialists for every game and for politics, music and special events, the name of Graham McNamee lives on as a legend.

Vying with Graham and the other announcers of that period in popularity, but on a different level, were Billy Jones and Ernie Hare, "The Happiness Boys," the first act I reviewed in my newly assigned job as radio editor. When they came to the air via WJZ in

1921, they were already among the most popular recording artists of the country. By 1925, their song and patter act was a "must" for listeners. For some eight years more they rode high on the air-waves and then faded temporarily from the scene.

The duo returned later via local station WMCA of New York, but their vogue had passed. Ernie died and his daughter Marilyn teamed up with Billy to continue the old Jones and Hare act until 1940, when Billy, too, passed away.

It is with the same affectionate feeling that I look back on the performances of May Singhi Breen and Peter de Rose and of Larry Funk and his "Band of a Thousand Melodies." They were on the air so often it was impossible not to become familiar with them during the 1920's.

May and Peter, who were known as WEAF's "Sweethearts of the Air," were the first of the popular song and instrumental duos. They were famous not only for their sweet singing of sentimental numbers but for May's ukulele playing. She was in fact greatly responsible for the ukulele craze that swept the country at that time. As for Larry Funk, his "Band of a Thousand Melodies," also on WEAF, was heard four or five times a day. Listeners regarded them as "pretty hot stuff," but what they didn't know was that this impressively named group numbered only four musicians who were adept at the art of doubling, tripling or quadrupling on instruments!

Equally enthusiastic was the fan reaction to John B. Gambling, still one of the prize personalities of New York's WOR. His morning programs, inspirational in tone, had fervid followers, and he created the husband-and-wife chatter format which, years later, all but swamped radio in a sea of sweet talk and other gooey chatter. But as the actress who faced the mike with him was not married to John, the credit for being the truly first husband-and-wife team (one certified by a marriage license) must go to Ed and Pegeen Fitzgerald, who did not come to the air until 1940. They, unlike so many of their imitators, did not hesitate to omit the "dears" and the "darlings." Occasionally Ed violates all broadcasting mores by even daring to speak sharply to his mate.

Although the column's fan mail contained numerous expressions of opinion about many performers, the artist of those days responsible for more written comment than any of them was "the little angel of radio," Jessica Dragonette. She was as much worshipped by the listeners of that period as that other "sweetheart of America," Mary Pickford, was by the movie addicts.

A frail little girl with golden blonde hair and delicately etched features, her soprano voice had a clear pure sweetness and a touch of sincere emotion that enraptured millions. Her performances in "The Philco Theatre of Memories," a series of operetta adaptations directed by Harold Sanford, were among the memorable attractions of this century's third decade.

She eventually became one of the biggest money-makers in radio. Reports had it that she was paid $1,300 a week as the soloist of the Cities Service broadcasts, and that when she became the star of the Palmolive Hour her salary had jumped to $2,500 or more.

Unlike other stars of radio, Jessica lived an aloof and sheltered life with her manager-sister, Nadia, in a richly furnished apartment in the Sutton Place sector of East 57th Street. There, in an atmosphere of monastic calm, she moved among candlelit old silver, exquisitely woven tapestries, antique furniture and religious art. Sitting before a fireplace on gray winter afternoons, sipping tea from a cup of transparent china and discussing books and Oriental philosophy with her friends, she seemed like a golden princess out of a fantasy by Maeterlinck.

Her millions of admirers were shocked and then infuriated when, after many years, Jessica suddenly disappeared from the air. There were all kinds of rumors. Some said her "price was too high," which she emphatically denied; others that she was the victim of a "conspiracy" which kept her from employment. But whatever the truth may have been, Jessica did not remain idle.

Year after year she has toured America in concert recitals, breaking box-office records and winning critical acclaim. And when the Cities Service program celebrated its twenty-fifth anniversary on the air, she made a guest appearance and received the ovation of the evening. Her fans had not forgotten.

One of the men appearing on the "blue list" of 1929, Don Carney, under the name of "Uncle Don," became the favorite of millions of children. Singing doggerel, playing the piano and admonishing youngsters to brush their teeth and to eat their spinach, he wished them happy birthdays and announced that there were gifts for them in the bedroom closet or beneath the sofa pillow. Probably the most popular entertainer of toddlers in the history of radio, he helped to mold the characters of several generations of juveniles. But, eventually, his form of song and patter became too naïve even for the three- and four-year-olds; they preferred cowboys, Indians and space cadets.

A widely circulated story of those days told of how Uncle Don, mistakenly believing that he was off the air following his sign-off song, remarked to his announcer one evening, "There! That ought to hold the little bastards for a while!" His words, according to the tale, were picked up by the still-live microphone and broadcast to a multitude of outraged listeners.

A good yarn, but Don insisted there was no truth in it. However, the veteran Ted Husing maintains that such an incident did occur on a Philadelphia radio station where, under similar circumstances, an "Uncle WIP" said, "I'm a bastard if this isn't one hell of a job for a he-man!"

Whether he did or did not, the good Uncle's behavior certainly could not have been more odd than that of some of his contemporary broadcasters. For example, that of the mysterious bearded old man who bought a minute of time daily for a week over WLTH of Brooklyn to say, "I love you! . . . I love you! . . . I love you!" Whom, what or why he loved, he did not explain and the station did not care. And Uncle WIP's words could not have surprised radio folk more than the voice of a 250-pound setting-up-exercise man on WMSG in Manhattan. It was almost that of a soprano, but he solved his problem by hiring a microphone ghost, an anemic 130-pounder with the tones of a basso profundo.

By contrast, such shenanigans as these made the dignified Eveready Hour on WEAF and a number of connected stations all the more noteworthy. Its variety and cultural content caused it to stand out among the programs of early radio. Immediately after its première in 1923, it became the most important program in broadcasting. Offering drama, music, comedy, poetry and factual material, it appealed not only to the mass desire for easy entertainment, but also to the adult intelligence.

Sponsored by the National Carbon Company, makers of Eveready Batteries, among its supervisors were Douglas Coulter, a pioneer producer, and George Furness, father of actress Betty Furness, the nation's "Number One ice-box opener" during the political conventions of 1952. The hour presented among its stars Julia Marlowe, Eddie Cantor, George Gershwin, Moran and Mack ("The Two Black Crows") John Drew, Weber and Fields, Walter C. Kelly ("The Virginia Judge"), Irvin S. Cobb, Van and Schenck, Will Rogers, the Flonzaley String Quartet, Elsie Janis and David Wark Griffith.

Out of the thousands of programs I have heard during the last twenty-nine years, one of those that remains most vividly in my memory is the Eveready Hour's oft-repeated production of *Joan of Arc*. Rosalind Greene, "the girl with the most beautiful speaking voice on the air," played the role of the Maid. Then there was Wendell Hall, "the Red-headed Music Maker," singing over and over again his ditty, "It Ain't Gonna Rain No Mo'." Also, there was the show's annual feature, Edgar Rice Burrill's eloquent reading of Ida Tarbell's *I Knew Lincoln*. And, topping even this in popularity, the tales of the Galapagos Islands, related by Red Christianson, the adventurous Manhattan taxicab driver. His accounts were so dramatic, his descriptions so colorful, that millions sat spellbound beside their receiving sets. His was the art of the Arabian Nights story-teller magnified via the loud-speaker. Since then there have been no such weavers of word magic on the radio.

During the 1920's radio began to mint the fortunes and the reputations of the "big name" bands. The primitive carbon microphone, ensconced on the bandstands of hotel dining rooms, garish night clubs, inns, taverns and honky-tonks from coast to coast, transformed dance rhythms from a minor appendage of the entertainment world into a sprawling cacophonous industry given space in the *Wall Street Journal*.

The early fans sent thousands of letters to Leo J. Fitzpatrick, the "Merry Old Chief," and the Coon-Sanders Nighthawks, blasting

away at the Hotel Muelbach in Kansas City, and then in Chicago's
Blackhawk Restaurant, where Ted Weems' crew also achieved
fame. Beginning in the century's third decade, on through the
1930's and into the 1940's, shining groups of instrumentalists made
their raucous bows. Vincent Lopez, Paul Whiteman, Guy Lombardo, Ben Bernie, Kay Kyser and Ben Pollack were magnets drawing millions of late-hour listeners. Freddie Martin, Fred Waring,
Ernie Golden, Ozzie Nelson, Eddy Duchin and Phil Harris were as
celebrated as any of the Hollywood stars. Tommy and Jimmy Dorsey, Glenn Miller and Duke Ellington, shared acclaim with Cab
Calloway, Hal Kemp, Larry Clinton and Glen Gray—all members
of the new nobility of popular music created by radio. Any high-
school freshman could have identified Paul Specht, Gene Goldkette,
Louis Prima or Stuff Smith. And as for the lustrous Bix Beiderbecke, Louis Armstrong, Fletcher Henderson or Earl Hines, even
the mention of their names brought fervent salaams from those
who were "sent." The syrupy waltzes of Wayne King, Ted Lewis'
"Is Everybody Happy?," the sentimental sighings of Sammy Kaye,
the torrid swing of Benny Goodman and of Gene Krupa and the
"modernistic" forays of Artie Shaw and of Raymond Scott evoked
adulation throughout the land. Even the boycott of the networks
against ASCAP, the songwriters' organization, in 1940–41, when
about the only number heard on the air was "Jeannie with the Light
Brown Hair," could not halt the triumphant march of the bands-
men. And the net result of all these Tin Pan Alley stray notes,
churned over the air-waves by thousands of slick "sidemen," was
that by the 1940's the box-office "take" of the dance musicians had
reached a total of $125,000,000 a year!

Although "commercial" jazz, neatly set down on paper and arranged with due consideration of those on the dance floor, was the
staple of broadcasting, radio also brought into prominence that
earthy and improvised brand of music known as "pure" jazz or
swing. The "Original Dixieland Band," holding forth at the long-
defunct Reisenweber's in New York, had set the vogue. So from
Manhattan's Hickory House and the Famous Door, from dives in
Chicago, Kansas City and San Francisco and from hole-in-wall
joints of New Orleans' French Quarter, this truly native expression

of the folk soul throbbed over the loud-speakers in millions of homes. But not for long. The powers-that-be deemed it "uncommercial."

Jelly Roll Morton, King Oliver, Jimmy Noone, Jimmy Blythe, Blind Willie Johnson, Bessie Smith and Ma Rainey, among many others, continued to be prized by the connoisseurs and the record collectors of this country and of Europe. These aficionados gave them stature, but for the small contribution early radio made to their success the disk jockeys deserve the major credit. Today, these platter spinners, the Martin Blocks and the Art Fords, "make" the "commercial" bands. Live broadcasts no longer establish either dance orchestras or singers.

At this time, however, the words "disk jockey" need clarification. Now the term is applied not only to those whose prime function is the playing of records but also to the gentry holding forth during the late hours, pontificating on the state of the world.

It was a press-agent-author, Ed Weiner, who, some years ago introduced the first "controversial" post-midnight disk-jockey program in a New York restaurant. He was quickly followed in other cafés, and finally in studios, by Barry Gray, George Hamilton Combs and others. In contrast with such purely entertainment discoursers as Henry Morgan and Maxine Keith, they, in addition to interviewing guests, editorialized on local, national and international problems. Occasionally they aired a recording but during the lengthy stretch between a song by Rosemary Clooney and one by Eddie Fisher, they argued, debated and exhorted on topics ranging from Communism and income taxes to Senator McCarthy and the hydrogen bomb. Although the periods featuring music still draw more listeners, these pundits have large followings among those who, even in the early hours of the morning, prefer a torrid argument to the tunes of Tin Pan Alley.

Sharing the air-waves with the music makers of the Twenties, but worlds apart in its appeal, was the maddest and rowdiest series of broadcasts ever to split the eardrums of listeners, those of the Village Grove Nut Club. Typifying the slapstick spirit of the 1920's, it was a mélange of insane abandon which, if aired today, would bring thousands of complaints to the Federal Communications Commission.

In the rear of the Village Grove Restaurant on Sheridan Square in Greenwich Village, the younger proprietor, one Meyer Horowitz, staged these entertainments which were heard Mondays and Thursdays from 11 P.M. to 2 A.M. via WAAT, WHN and WMCA. Among the first and most popular of regularly scheduled late-hour café broadcasts, these shows drew such hordes of visitors, including Broadway celebrities, that Horowitz was forced to open another establishment next door, the Nut Club, in order to accommodate the cash-bearing customers.

The programs featured a stock company of comics and emcees: Lou Dolgoff, "Nutsy" Fagan, Buddy Walker and Cliff Clifton, who billed himself as "King Solomon the Wise Guy." Taking part in the proceedings were a waiter known as "Albert, the Pancake Juggler," who delivered impassioned diatribes on any and all topics, a dim-witted amateur advertised as "Lehigh Vallee, distant brother of Rudy," and the star—a Scottish female impersonator, "La Belle Rose." Singing in a screechy, off-pitch soprano, he would snap the upper plate from his mouth every time he attempted to hit a high C.

With Paul Whiteman, Mildred Bailey, Bing Crosby, Graham McNamee, Ted Husing and other "big names" of uptown at the ringside tables, this crew would indulge in scathing insults, flippant wisecracks and knock-'em-down-drag-'em-out sketches. During the proceedings performers hurled pots, pans and pies and the club's cry of "Cuckoo! Horsefeathers!" assaulted the microphones. Thousands throughout the New York area echoed those senseless words on the slightest provocation.

Occasionally, members of the notorious "Hudson Dusters" gang, or their cousins, crashed the premises during a broadcast. They would be attacked by Horowitz and a flying wedge of husky waiters and hurled into the street. While mayhem was being committed and horrendous cries split the air, the program would continue as if such intrusions were all part of a normal evening's entertainment. These riotous sounds reached thousands of radio listeners, but if there were any protests the stations did not act on them.

One evening while I chatted with Horowitz in his café, he remarked, "I'd like to open another night club that wouldn't be so noisy. Got any ideas?"

Without knowing why, I said: "Some Broadway boobs call this kind of stuff 'sophisticated.' So why don't you go to the other extreme and offer a country type of entertainment, something that would be in contrast to anything now in New York."

"I don't get you," said Meyer.

"Well, you know," I said, "maybe a place fixed up like a barn, with milk cans, wagon wheels and things like that. And for your show, put on some hillbillies and square dances."

"What are square dances?" Meyer wanted to know.

I told him.

"How about a name like—like The Village Barn?" he asked.

And that was the origin of one of the most popular and profitable night club restaurants in this country. There, Horowitz has made several fortunes and, as those who have listened to the coast-to-coast broadcasts from this spot remember, he introduced as budding young performers Judy Canova, Joe E. Lewis, the Pickens Sisters, and the Hartmans, as well as Gene Krupa's, Will Osborne's, and Enoch Light's orchestras and Larry Funk's "Band of a Thousand Melodies."

But through the years, the Barn has primarily been the national showcase for the nasal-singing and guitar-twanging hillbillies of radio. It is the Number One stopover for the cowhands and mountaineers of Texas, Tennessee and Brooklyn, some of whose recordings coin money faster than the far more famous Perry Comos and Eddie Fishers of the upper levels of popular song.

Shortly after his radio broadcasts had made the Barn one of the most widely known night clubs in America, I asked Horowitz, who is now dubbed "the Billy Rose of the hayseeds," how he accounted for his success.

"Easy," he said. "As you well know, the most popular songs on radio aren't the Tin Pan Alley numbers, but the hillbilly tunes."

"But after all," I said, "this is hokum. Why should a supposedly sophisticated city like New York go for it?"

"Haven't you heard what thousands of others have said before me?" he laughed. "This is still the biggest hick town of 'em all!"

The Networks Are Born

The old Waldorf-Astoria's marble corridors and its elegant Peacock Alley echoed with tense chatter that evening. Crowds, eager for a glimpse of celebrities, surged behind the police lines before the hotel on the corner of Fifth Avenue and 34th Street, the present site of the Empire State Building. They applauded as famous political figures, giants of industry and stars of the entertainment world emerged from their limousines to witness the birth of network broadcasting on the night of November 15, 1926.

The word had spread that those in attendance would behold "the inauguration of a new epoch in American life," an innovation that might eventually "affect the thoughts and the habits of millions of Americans."

Even the cynical among the reporters present had premonitions of great events to come. One of them sitting beside me remarked: "Maybe our stories tonight might turn into history. You know, like the stuff of the guys who covered Morse's first telegram, or the Wright brothers at Kitty Hawk."

Perhaps he, too, had been impressed by an advertisement in New York newspapers during the preceding September, which announced that the Radio Corporation of America had purchased WEAF, New York, from the American Telephone and Telegraph Company for one million dollars and that the station would be incorporated as The National Broadcasting Company. The latter, it was explained, would broadcast programs not only through WEAF but also would make these available to outlets throughout the country. The ad emphasized that the time was ripe for such a venture as already five million homes in the United States were equipped with radios and some twenty-one million homes "remain to be supplied."

RCA at that time was the largest distributor of radio receivers in the world, handling the entire output of General Electric and Westinghouse. It, of course, also was engaged in broadcasting on a limited scale. As for WEAF, it had served A.T.&T. well in its efforts to develop programming; but this gigantic corporation soon found that such activities placed it in the entertainment field. Its sedate executives resented this; they wanted to get on with their essential business, which was communications. So they were more than happy to conclude this deal with RCA, under the provisions of which NBC leased A.T.&T. long lines exclusively for the transmission of programs from city to city.

RCA shared with General Electric and Westinghouse the ownership of the new network and its most important stations were those owned and operated by these corporations.

NBC's first president, Merlin H. Aylesworth, was even more widely known by his nickname of Deac. Just before he had assumed his fifty-thousand-dollar-a-year job, he had been so little interested in radio that he did not even have a receiving set. But as managing director of the National Electric Light Association, he had proved himself to be a first-rate executive and had gained the friendship of political and financial leaders throughout the country. George McClelland, the corporation's executive vice-president, Mark Woods, its treasurer (later president of ABC), and O. B. Hanson (later vice-president in charge of NBC engineering) were all ardent broadcasting enthusiasts.

These facts, in disorderly array, were flashing through my mind when, suddenly, all of us in the Grand Ballroom were called to attention by a blare of trumpets. The clock on the balcony indicated exactly 8:05 P.M. and a few moments later Aylesworth began to speak. Tall, suave and with smiling eyes, he told his guests that this inaugural program would be carried by twenty-four stations. "Think of it!" he said. "Ten or maybe even twelve million persons may be hearing what takes place in this ballroom tonight!" A murmur swept the audience.

Then, the entertainment went on the air. Even today, when the public is accustomed to "million-dollar shows," it would be difficult to equal that première program. It was a four-and-a-half-hour presentation offering among its all-star acts two "remote control" features which created sensations. Mary Garden, the glamorous diva of the opera, was heard singing from Chicago a group of numbers including "Annie Laurie," "Open Thy Blue Eyes" and "Little Gray Home in the West." Will Rogers faced a microphone in Independence, Kansas, drawling a humorous monologue, "Fifteen Minutes with a Diplomat," during the course of which he mimicked President Calvin Coolidge. It was such a perfect mimicry that many listeners believed they were hearing Cal himself.

Among the other items on that gala inaugural were the New York Symphony Orchestra, conducted by Dr. Walter Damrosch; the New York Oratorio Society; Harold Bauer, concert pianist; Cesare Sodero's grand- and light-opera ensembles; Edwin Franko Goldman's band; Tito Ruffo, Metropolitan Opera star; the comedy team of Weber and Fields and the dance orchestras of Vincent Lopez, Ben Bernie from the Roosevelt Hotel Grill, George Olsen from the Hotel Pennsylvania, and Ben A. Rolfe from the Palais d'Or on Broadway.

By the time the program signed off at 12:35 A.M., the Waldorf-Astoria audience was not only weary but amazed. I can still hear a stout dowager's remark to her dignified husband as we filed from the ballroom: "My dear, I had no idea! We simply must get one of these radios the first thing tomorrow!"

Even so, the professional critics, suspecting that tomorrow's programs would not be quite so good, had some reservations. Although they were properly enthusiastic in their comments, they could not resist the temptation to prove they were knowing fellows. I, for example, remarked in my column that Mary Garden's songs were occasionally marred by a "whistling sound," and some erudite fellow writing in the New York *Times* doubted that "even the most advanced type of engineering could surmount every obstacle to perfect rendition from a distance."

According to some newspapers, the show had cost NBC fifty thousand dollars, but President Aylesworth told me that the program had set his company back "hardly a cent," as the stars had offered their services gratis. "Hereafter, however, advertising will pay for the elaborate broadcasts we plan to present," he said. And he added that these "elaborate broadcasts" would achieve one of the main objectives of network operation—the sale of more receiving sets. With David Sarnoff, Aylesworth shared the belief that the quality of the programs would insure the success of radio in America and quoted the former's remark, "The richest man cannot buy for himself what the poorest man gets free by radio."

But there were still a goodly number of doubting Thomases in the theatrical profession. Joe Weber, whom I met shortly after the first night near the Palace Theatre, said: "A great show, all right, but I don't know if it can last. Who'd take radio against the theatre or the movies, even if it is free?"

The listening public, however, had no such doubts. Within less than two months, network broadcasting had gained such popularity that NBC opened a second chain, "The Blue Network," with WJZ of New York as its key outlet. (WEAF was the flag station of "The Red Network.") And even before that, during the first week following the Waldorf-Astoria première, David Sarnoff was already looking forward to television! A release brought to my office by G. W. (Johnny) Johnstone, NBC's first press-relations director, began:

" 'Television is just around the corner,' stated David Sarnoff today in an announcement following his first conference with Merlin Hall Aylesworth, president of NBC."

The ever smiling Johnny Johnstone needed no such assurances from the brass to convince him of the rosy future of broadcasting. While at WEAF, before it became a network operation, he had functioned not only as that station's press agent but also as a control engineer and as a "hot" piano player. But now he had an assistant publicity man working under his direction and soon his department expanded into a gargantuan operation, numbering among its employees William B. ("Skeets") Miller, the reporter who, a few years before, had won fame through his interviews with the trapped Floyd Collins in a Kentucky cave.

Fans were still dwelling on the glories of that epochal NBC opening program, when on January 1, 1927, they had the thrill of hearing Graham McNamee's account of the Rose Bowl Game between

Alabama and Stanford at Pasadena, California. This, too, was a historic event, for that day the telephone lines carrying programs from both coasts had been joined at Denver. My office at the *News* was crowded with visitors from the editorial floor during that broadcast. To them and to me, it seemed just another proof of the magical times in which we lived that, while the street lamps of New York blinked through the cold of a winter's evening we should be hearing Graham describing the brilliant sunshine of a California afternoon.

Just twenty days later, NBC, over its combined Red and Blue Networks, broadcast another history-making program—the garden scene from *Faust* sung at the Chicago Civic Auditorium. It was the first time opera had been aired from coast to coast; but what was even more important, a sponsor picked up the tab.

This was a fact of the greatest significance. Just as Aylesworth had said, advertisers were now beginning to pay for the "elaborate" broadcasts. If they had not, it is doubtful that radio could have survived without government subsidy. For NBC had been on the air no more than two weeks when it became plain that the original idea of broadcasting merely to increase the sale of receivers was no longer feasible. The network was losing money at an astounding rate—$800,000 during its first year. It would have to depend on the advertiser's dollar.

Aylesworth was among the first to realize this. Although he had a fund of three million dollars placed aside by General Electric and Westinghouse who, with RCA, were co-owners of NBC, he decided to get out of the red as soon as possible.

Deac was not only an executive with a sense of public services but one of the greatest salesmen this country has ever produced. If there is one man who may be said to have "put over" broadcasting with both the public and the sponsors, it is this first president of NBC. I can still recall the elation with which he informed me that he had just sold time to the Cities Service and the American Tobacco Company, two of his networks' most profitable advertisers. But he was just as enthusiastic when he spoke of the cultural and educational programs for which he was responsible: Dr. Walter

Damrosch's "Music Appreciation Hour," "The National Farm and Home Hour" (the first great agricultural series of radio) and the broadcasts of the Metropolitan Opera Company.

One of the first fruits of Deac's efforts was the gala opening at Carnegie Hall, on the night of February 18, 1927, of the Cities Service program, which is now radio's oldest sponsored network show. There were a great deal of hullabaloo, pretentious formality and more uniformed flunkies than in the palace of a Latin-American dictator. But a full-dress audience gave an ovation to Edwin Franko Goldman's band, which was starred in the series.

The program included such old warhorses as Liszt's "Second Hungarian Rhapsody," and the *William Tell* overture and also excerpts from *Faust* and the overture to *Mignon*. Goldman had played these numbers repeatedly during his New York concerts, but certain NBC executives wondered if his selections weren't "pretty highbrow" for a popular type of sponsored program. One of the network's vice-presidents remarked to me: "I sure hope this music isn't above their heads!" What would he have said if someone had told him that there would be a time when even on sponsored concerts one might hear compositions of Igor Stravinsky, Arnold Schoenberg and Darius Milhaud?

Two events of 1927 powerfully influenced the growth of radio: the triumphant return of Charles A. Lindbergh from his non-stop flight to Paris and the Dempsey-Tunney "battle of the century." During the hysterical receptions which greeted "Lucky Lindy" in both Washington and New York, NBC used, for the first time, a multiple pickup. That is, the broadcasts originated from several widely scattered points.

This was such a novelty that thousands of non-radio families rushed to buy receiving sets. Then, during the following September, when NBC aired the fight between the "Manassa Mauler" and his challenger, the interest of the public rose to an even higher pitch. For here was not only a contest in which seemingly every man, woman and child in the land had become interested, but one which was broadcast over sixty-eight stations, the largest network ever joined together up to that time.

Programs such as these called for the expenditure of larger sums than NBC had anticipated. It became more essential than ever to bring new sponsors into the fold and to hold those who were already in. The mortal sin of radio was any act of omission or commission displeasing to an advertiser.

That is why the president of NBC had to dance for his salary! It was the president himself, Deac Aylesworth, who told me the story.

He had succeeded in persuading George Washington Hill, president of the American Tobacco Company, to broadcast a sponsored hour of Saturday-night dance music on behalf of Lucky Strike cigarettes. Anyone who has read the novel, *The Hucksters*, in which that eccentric genius of business, thinly disguised, played a leading role, may realize what a formidable task that was. But he became NBC's most profitable advertiser and Aylesworth guarded his account with the tender care a movie actor bestows on his thinning locks.

One hot Saturday afternoon I called his office about an important story and was informed that Deac could not be disturbed. I ventured up to NBC at 711 Fifth Avenue and a typist in the president's anteroom told me that the boss had gone to the board of directors' suite.

"But it won't do you any good to go there," she added, "because he won't see anyone."

Nevertheless, I did go there and found the door locked. I knocked repeatedly but my pounding was ignored. And yet the room was obviously occupied, as from it came loud sounds of fast-paced dance music. Just then an executive strolled along the corridor, gave me the facts I needed and, still wondering about the mystery of Deac's behavior, I left.

Later, I learned that a few Saturdays before, Aylesworth had come to his office to pick up some golf clubs, en route to an afternoon of relaxation on Long Island. As he was about to leave, he was surprised by the entrance of George Washington Hill, accompanied by a strikingly beautiful blonde. She was the famous Lucky Strike Billboard Girl, whose features were familiar to millions throughout the United States, a glamorous creature who had been denounced in many sermons, as her picture was the first one of a woman ever used in cigarette advertising.

Hill, as was his wont, got down to business immediately. "Deac," he said, "the Lucky Strike Orchestra is costing us a lot of money. It's supposed to give the people good dance music; but how do I know it's really good?"

Aylesworth pointed out that Ben A. Rolfe, the moon-faced musician who led the band, was one of the greatest cornet players of his day. Also that the listeners obviously liked his tunes.

But Hill was not convinced. "There's only one way to tell whether Rolfe's music is danceable," he said, "and that's to dance to it."

The NBC president could find no flaw in this logic and agreed.

"Very well," said Hill. "Your board room has a good loud-speaker. B. A. is in the studio now rehearsing his band. We'll tune in his music and this young lady and I will dance to it."

Deac, who always addressed Hill as "Chief," opined that was an excellent idea. But his face fell when Hill added, "Of course, Deac, you'll join us?"

"Yes, certainly," said Aylesworth.

"Send for Bertha Brainard!" Hill snapped.

Deac did and Bertha joined them. An attractive and exceptionally able program executive, she took Aylesworth's arm and was one of the foursome who marched into the board of directors' sanctum.

There, in that stately paneled chamber, Deac turned on the loud-speaker and to the rapid-fire, rivet-hammer rhythms of Rolfe's music the quartet danced and danced around the enormous director's table. The president of NBC and his program assistant soon showed signs of weariness but not the tobacco tycoon and the beautiful bill-board girl. In fact, at the conclusion of the rehearsal, Hill announced that he and his partner would return the following Saturday!

"And do you know," Deac said to me mournfully, "Hill and that girl came back not only the following Saturday but for several Saturdays after that. Bertha and I had to join them and it ruined my week-ends!"

"Couldn't you have found an excuse for staying away?" I asked.

"I wouldn't have dared," Deac said. "We couldn't afford to lose that account. So even though I was president of NBC, I had to dance for my salary!"

But, despite the vagaries of such sponsors as George Washington Hill, and despite the losses incurred by NBC during its first year, more and more broadcasters became certain of radio's financial future. It was taken for granted that soon there would be another network to compete for the listening audience.

In fact, no more than two months after NBC had gone on the air, Major J. Andrew White, the pioneer announcer, told me that he was engaged in organizing a new chain. And early in 1927, the newspapers reported the formation of the United Independent Broadcasters.

That might not have happened if a certain road-materials salesman, George A. Coats, had not passed through the lobby of New York's Hotel Astor one day during the fall of 1926. He was attracted by a jovial group of men who obviously were delegates to a convention. Among them he encountered a friend and soon discovered that this enthusiastic, boisterously laughing crew had something to do with that odd business—radio.

Coats joined them and attended their meetings. Before the day had ended, he turned to his friend and remarked, "You know, this radio seems to be a pretty good proposition. I'd like to get into it."

This led to a conference with Arthur Judson, a leading manager of concert and opera stars and his associate, Major White. It seems they were planning a new network and were looking for a man with money. Coats not only had enthusiasm but was a top-notch salesman. So he teamed up with them, and with Frank Marsh, a music publisher, Edward Ervin, assistant manager of the New York Philharmonic, and a Mrs. Harold Yarnell, to incorporate the United company. And aiding this crew of bold adventurers was an ambitious young radio announcer with a resonant voice who served as assistant to Major White. His name was Ted Husing.

Coats took to the road to sign up affiliate stations and soon had sixteen of them. But in his enthusiasm he outsold himself. For he had agreed to pay each station fifty dollars an hour for ten hours a week to carry the United programs. This meant a weekly expenditure of eight thousand dollars, and the new network as yet had no assurance that it could recoup that amount from sponsors.

Therefore, it made a deal with the Columbia Phonograph Company whereby the latter bought the operating rights of United and changed its name to the Columbia Phonograph Broadcasting System. The new network came to the air on the night of September 18, 1927, less than a year after NBC's gala opening.

Those of us who listened to that inaugural broadcast were impressed by its artistic merit, for it was the Metropolitan Opera Company's production of the Edna St. Vincent Millay–Deems Taylor *The Kings Henchman*. And also we were annoyed by the fact that the program continued far beyond its scheduled time.

Now, at last, we had another network—but a quaint one. It did have programs, yes; these were supplied principally by Judson's artists bureau. It had offices, yes; a few small rooms in a Times Square building. But, unlike NBC or even the smallest of independent stations, it did not have a single studio!

Columbia leased air facilities from WOR in New York. Its programs originated there and during certain hours of the evening this station's own offerings were replaced by CPBS entertainment.

Only a few weeks had passed before radio editors heard, "Columbia's losing its shirt. It's going to fold any minute."

And we had every reason to believe this when, after three months, it came to light that the Columbia Phonograph Company had decided that it had made a poor investment and sold its operating rights back to the United Independent Broadcasters for a mere ten thousand dollars, plus thirty hours of free air time! But now fate took a hand in the person of a Dr. Leon Levy, a Philadelphia dentist who had an interest in a local radio station, WCAU. Major White, Coats and Judson knew him and persuaded Levy to interest a millionaire fellow Philadelphian, Jerome Louchheim, in their network venture. As a result, the latter put in $150,000, with more to follow, and Dr. Levy and his brother, Isaac, also came up with considerable sums for the chain, now known as the Columbia Broadcasting System.

But the patient continued ill and might have even died had it not been for the cigar known as La Palina.

Dr. Levy's in-laws, the wealthy Paley family, were the owners of one of Philadelphia's most famous enterprises, the Congress Cigar Company. But, because of the rising popularity of cigarettes, its La Palinas had come upon parlous days, with a drop in sales from

600,000 to 400,000 a day. The young son of the family and the firm's sales manager, William S. Paley, had advertised his product on WCAU and found the results to be so encouraging that he also bought time on the new broadcasting system.

Paley created a stir with his sponsored show, "La Palina Smoker." It was a dramatic program featuring stories of adventure. Critics hailed it as "novel," "gripping" and "exciting." The series became so popular that two programs, one a musical version, were aired each week, and it was here that Kate Smith made her first commercial success as a singing star.

Even the enthusiastic Paley was amazed. Within a brief time the sale of his company's cigars had jumped from a mere 400,000 to almost 1,000,000 a day. Being a young man of both enterprise and imagination, he said to himself, in effect: "This radio is an astounding business. I should get into it."

And that is what he did. Only twenty-seven years old at the time, he bought a controlling amount of stock in the new and as yet unsuccessful network and became its president on September 26, 1928. Moving to New York, he took immediate charge and injected a spirit of competition into network broadcasting.

On my first meeting with him, a few weeks later, I remarked that some persons were doubtful one so young and inexperienced in broadcasting could buck the powerful combination of interests represented in NBC: RCA, General Electric and Westinghouse. The tall, dark-complexioned man, completely at ease behind his desk, smiled.

"This is a young industry," he said casually. "Even its pioneers have been in it only eight years."

Within a brief time, Paley proved what he could do. In less than two years, his venture showed a profit; but at that time, of course, all of radio was experiencing a boom. NBC, for example, which had suffered heavy losses during its initial year, reported for 1929 a net profit of almost $800,000.

But the state of CBS' ledgers did not concern the listeners. What mattered were the enthusiasm, the verve and the willingness to take a risk which marked the activities of the network. It gave the public such new performers as Bing Crosby and Kate Smith; such trail-blazing programs as the New York Philharmonic concerts from Carnegie Hall and the "American School of the Air"; and it created a strikingly efficient worldwide news organization which produced such commentator-reporters as Edward R. Murrow, Eric Sevareid and Howard K. Smith. Also, it eventually brought forth one of broadcasting's most far-sighted executives, Dr. Frank Stanton, a recruit from the academic world, who succeeded Paley as president when the latter became chairman of the board.

Columbia was less than six years old when, in 1934, I asked the ten-year-old son of a fellow newspaperman: "How do you like it in New York?"

"Okay," said the lad who had recently come from Michigan, "but I'd rather be in Detroit. They got the 'Lone Ranger' out there."

Millions of kids in the Midwest within hearing range of WXYZ, Detroit, shared his enthusiasm for this Western series which continues even today both on TV and on radio. And it was because the Kunsky-Trendle Corporation, which operated the station and created the show, believed that boys and girls throughout the country would welcome "The Lone Ranger" that the Mutual Broadcasting System was born.

The owners of the show had sought outlets for it on both NBC and CBS without success. So WXYZ made arrangements for it to be carried by WGN, Chicago, WOR, New York, and WLW, Cincinnati. The result of this move was the integration of these four high-powered stations, each with an audience covering many states, into the "Quality Group." This quartet of major broadcasters became the base of the Mutual Broadcasting System, during the closing months of 1934.

The fourth major radio chain, the American Broadcasting Company, however, had its inception under far more prosaic circumstances. Originally a part of NBC as the Blue Network, in 1942 it became an RCA subsidiary. But on July 30, 1943, in conformance with a ruling of the FCC that no company could operate more than one network, it was sold to the American Broadcasting Co., Inc., with Edward J. Noble, the Life Savers candy millionaire, in control. Recently, ABC was merged with the United Paramount Theatres, Incorporated.

NBC, CBS, MBS and ABC—these initials are as familiar to Americans as Arthur Godfrey's drawl or Jack Benny's "stinginess." But mention ABS—short for the Amalgamated Broadcasting System —and not one out of ten thousand will remember that such a chain ever existed.

Yet this short-lived network, organized by the comedian Ed Wynn, wrote one of the most fabulous chapters in the history of radio. Those who attended its opening night will never forget it: a combination of a Marx Brothers movie and a rush-hour riot at Times Square. It is still recalled as "the great pastrami and salami opening."

Wynn, as he had explained to me in 1933, sank his savings into it because "acting is such an uncertain profession, and I want to establish a business for my actor son, Keenan, which will be sane and secure and bring in plenty of profits." Unfortunately, Ed, who was riding high on the air-waves at the time as the famous Texaco "Fire Chief," left the organizational details to others, and as the time for opening drew near he was out in Hollywood making a motion picture.

That there was something awry became evident during the press luncheon at ABS headquarters on Madison Avenue a few days before the première. Billie Gould, the young press agent, introduced our host, the network's spokesman, a lordly functionary who had made a reputation as a fiery and temperamental theatrical performer.

It seemed odd that such a picturesque and volatile personality should make his bow in the role of a practical executive. He opened his address to the newspapermen by blithely announcing: "I hope we'll get a good press. But let me make myself plain, gentlemen, I'm not concerned about what the tabloids think of us, I only care about the New York *Times!*"

More in a spirit of disbelief than of indignation I rose from the table and strode from the room. The man from the *Times* also rose and followed me into the corridor. So did the others. The beauteous press agent pleaded and shed tears. We finally accepted her explanation that what the indiscreet official meant to say was that he was fond of the *Times!*

That was a warning of what was to follow. But none of us could anticipate the events of that memorable opening night, September 25, 1933.

It was a hot, muggy evening. Before the building housing station WBNX, at that time the key outlet of the Amalgamated Broadcasting System, a crowd swirled up and down fashionable Madison Avenue. Thousands of men, women and children, some in formal dress, others in shirt-sleeves and sports clothes, were pushing, shoving, screaming. Policemen cursed and sweated, trying to maintain a clear lane to the doorway.

After a half-hour, a group of radio editors insistently waving their engraved invitations made it as far as the lobby entrance. Through some legerdemain, Kate Smith and her manager, Ted Collins, entered the lobby. It was so hot that Kate almost fainted. And a few feet away, in a packed elevator, Vaughn de Leath, a singer who was well in the 250-pound range, actually did pass out!

We newspapermen were pushed off the elevator and into a long oblong room adjoining the main studio. In a space that would have been crowded with five hundred, there must have been at least two thousand specimens of gyrating humanity.

We were met, not by page boys, but by scowling attendants who rudely shoved us to the right and yelled: "Get in line for the eats!" But refusing to be commanded, we broke ranks and were swept to the whirlpool in the center of the room.

Angry men, women and bawling children made frantic efforts to wedge their way toward long tables piled high with succulent hot dogs, pastrami and salami sandwiches. And an even more boisterous mob swirled about two stands where beer was being *sold!* Referring to the innovation of selling refreshments at a network opening, the New York *Journal's* radio scribe, "Aircaster," commented the next day: "This was ABS's first commercial." He added: "It seemed to me that, for the first time in history, the entire audience of a radio station was inside the studio."

This phenomenon had come about, we learned later, because some promotional-minded genius of the company, intent on interesting the public in ABS stock, had sent out more than five thousand invitations. The telephone book, not the *Social Register* or the *Directory of Directors*, had been his guide. The butchers, bakers, candy-store owners and housewives who were thus flattered accepted the summons eagerly. Some even asked their assorted relatives and friends to accompany them and many also brought along their off-spring. After all, it wasn't every day that one had the chance to see in person Kate Smith, Vaughn de Leath, Taylor Holmes, the actor, and Rudy Wiedoeft, the greatest saxophonist of his time.

A few minutes after our arrival, above the din of a fist fight between two guards and several hungry guests, we began plowing our way toward a glass door through which seeped the faint sounds of a jazz band. Suddenly there was a shriek, the glass pane splintered and tinkled to the floor. We were hurled forward into an L-shaped studio. On a dais a harassed mustachioed man was leading a group of sweating musicians while Wiedoft tootled on his sax. Norman Brokenshire, the guest announcer, frantically waved his arms for quiet but the talking, laughing, pastrami-consuming audience paid him no heed.

Suddenly we saw George Hall, the orchestra leader, while conducting the band with his right hand, making emphatic gestures with his left toward the floor. Now he was kicking, first with one foot and then the other, in a restrained imitation of a restless bronco. We looked down and beheld a four-year-old boy, his face smeared with mustard and a hot-dog sandwich in his hand, crawling blithely between Hall's legs.

"Get away! Get away!" George whispered as an obese housewife sitting in the front row yelled, her voice going over the air-waves: "Chester! Come away from there! . . . Chester! Don't do that!" The boy ignored her; mounting the dais, she caught Chester by the seat of his pants and gave him a furious whack. He let out a terrific yelp that had more decibels than all the brass, woodwind and percussion in the band.

In the midst of the commotion, we saw a distraught brunette beauty propelling herself toward us.

"Where have you been?" she asked. "Why aren't you on the executive floor?"

After an outraged group of radio editors had told Billie Gould why, we found ourselves in an impressive suite of offices with comfortable leather chairs and tables set with china, crystal and vases of fragrant flowers. Immaculately garbed waiters served us solicitously with breast of turkey, Virginia ham, and caviar resting in a bowl of crushed ice. Champagne, sauterne and burgundy, all of good vintage, flowed from tall bottles as over a wall amplifier came the raucous noises of the inaugural program in the studio downstairs. It was impossible to understand a word, as the hundreds of phone calls from indignant listeners to newspaper offices that night testified.

While we were still feasting, an excited young man rushed in and announced that one of the elevators had become stuck between floors. In it was a Federal Commissioner, who, as "Aircaster" put it, "unfortunately for ABS happened to do his commissioning on the Federal Radio Commission!"

In white tie and tails, with a broad red sash across his snowy shirt front, our host of the evening greeted us. The turmoil on the studio floor had not ruffled one hair of his shiny locks, although he had spent arduous hours greeting Postmaster General James J. Farley, Congressman Sol Bloom and other dignitaries.

"Gentlemen, I welcome you," he said with courtly grace. "What do you think of our opening?"

"Lousy!" someone blurted out.

"What's that?" The executive's face turned the deepest scarlet. "Who said that?"

Burning over the indignities that had been inflicted on us, the newspapermen said: "This opening's a disgrace . . . Run-around . . . Treated like bums . . . Who do you think we are?"

The gentleman's hands trembled; his eyes blazed and for a moment he stared at us in vengeful silence. He turned his fury on me. "How dare you! You have insulted me! In my country when one is insulted, he demands satisfaction!" And now, addressing himself to the others, he said: "And this goes for every one of you!"

We couldn't believe it. Was he actually challenging us to a duel?

"Please, gentlemen, please!" Billie Gould cried and began ushering us from the room.

"Shall it be swords or guns in Central Park?" one of the retiring radio editors taunted.

The following day, the News and several other New York newspapers discontinued the program listings of the Amalgamated Broadcasting System. And in its next issue, Variety, the authoritative trade journal of show business, summed up the fiasco by saying that "although the invitees to the opening didn't get within hearing distance of what it was all about, there was at least plenty of beer, pastrami and salami."

A little more than a month later, Ed Wynn's dream network expired. My column of November 3, 1933, recorded: "All day its offices were besieged by insistent employees demanding their salaries. They were ordered to go home . . . but refused to budge . . . During the afternoon the lights were extinguished in the deserted studios and reception rooms of the headquarters at 501 Madison Avenue . . . and in the deep gloom of the entrance just one thing was visible, a sign of one word in big black letters: 'Silence.'"

Not long thereafter, Wynn, just in from Hollywood, held a conference to apologize to the press in a private dining room of the Hotel Berkshire.

"If I hadn't been detained on the Coast, this wouldn't have happened," the comedian said. "Maybe I made a mistake in the choice of my executives."

His eyes blinking behind his horn-rimmed glasses, the melancholy clown told us that he had a premonition something would go wrong at the opening. "That very afternoon, as we were shooting a scene for my picture, I was wrestling with a trained bear. Suddenly, he did something he had never done before in all of his professional career. He misbehaved. And as I left the stage for my dressing room to change my costume, I just knew that things weren't going to be right in New York."

"Gentlemen," he added mournfully, "I not only lost my shirt in this venture; I also almost lost my show on NBC."

Wynn explained that, unknown to him, the musicians used on the première broadcast had not been paid. And, one night, just before he went on the air as "The Fire Chief," a walking delegate representing the union appeared and informed him: "Either you pay now—in cash—or you won't have any musicians on your program."

With banks, advertising and network executive offices closed, the comedian had the greatest difficulty in raising the required sum.

"We barely made it—two minutes before air time," Ed said. Then smiling sadly, "That's what I get for trying to be a businessman."

There was not a radio editor there who did not agree that Wynn was a grand guy, one who deserved our sympathy, not our anger.

"Too bad," one of us said, "but you're still a great comedian."

NINE

Big Bold Type

Radio, no longer a passing fancy, was now on its way. With the networks flourishing, broadcasting, in spite of the gagster, was definitely here to stay.

By this time the notebooks of one professional listener were already bulging with anecdotes and comments concerning some of the vivid personalities of the air. Even now their names stand out in big bold type.

There is the blond Vermonter, Hubert Prior (Rudy) Vallee, for instance. At this late date, there is no point in retelling the story of how he won the adulation of millions of females, from teen-agers to grandmothers. But all too often his role as an innovator in American radio has been ignored. Although Vaughn de Leath had introduced the style of singing known as crooning at least seven years before Rudy's advent, it was he who made it a national epidemic. In a sense, he exerted a greater influence on the art of the popular song than all of the opera and musical-comedy stars and voice teachers combined.

When I first heard and saw Rudy singing through a megaphone in New York's Heigh-Ho Club, in 1928, he looked like a carefree college boy. But even then this recent Yale graduate was effecting a revolution on the air-waves. The bandstand was so small that it could accommodate only a few musicians; so perforce his orchestra was a small one which played in an intimate manner. The club couldn't afford to pay for an announcer; so Rudy undertook that stint himself, talking with casual informality, and thereby making himself a personality. Vallee did not have enough money to hire a vocalist; therefore he did the singing, delivering his songs in cold, nasal tones. Although the formalists of the day ridiculed him,

Rudy's vocals had a novel quality: a person-to-person appeal which made it seem as if he were addressing his love songs to one girl rather than to a million.

Ted Husing, the sports announcer, had something to do with bringing Vallee to national attention. During 1928, when WOR of New York was broadcasting Columbia programs, one of the latter's shows was unable to go on one night because of an emergency. So Ted suggested that a substitute program be aired from the Heigh-Ho Club instead of the studio, with Rudy providing the music. This was done and his performance that evening, plus his later appearances on WABC and WMCA of New York, established him.

By this time even those New York radio executives who had sneered at Vallee began to admit that he "had something." Just how much was shown during the following year, when the man who introduced "Vagabond Lover," "My Time Is Your Time," and popularized the "Maine Stein Song," became the star of his own nightspot, the Villa Vallee. But Rudy carved his most important niche in radio with the "Fleischman Yeast Hour" on NBC. This variety show brought to the microphones not only leading figures of the screen, journalism and sports, but such stars of the stage as John and Ethel Barrymore, Eva Le Gallienne and Helen Hayes, and also it served as a showcase for radio top-notchers such as Edgar Bergen and Charlie McCarthy. The old "Eveready Hour" had introduced "big names" on a regional basis some years before, but it was Vallee, on a coast-to-coast hookup, who first did so nationally. Since then practically every variety show on radio or TV has followed his format.

During his heyday, including a period before high taxes, Rudy made more than $300,000 a year. And from my knowledge of him, I am certain not one cent of his savings has been spent foolishly. For this Vermonter of French-Canadian extraction, who was reared in Maine, is a most thrifty fellow.

Some years ago, after his radio vogue had passed and he had made a notable "comeback" during a personal appearance at the Latin Quarter night club, I interviewed him in a chop house off Times Square.

"Rudy," I said, "for years the story has gone around that you're a tightwad. If that's a libel, say something about it and I'll publish it."

"Oh, I've heard that, too," he answered without the slightest embarrassment. "The truth is, I'm just thrifty. Take food, for example. I have money to pay for the best and I like the best. That's why I often eat at the Automat; good vegetables and wonderful coffee."

Well, that's Rudy for you. But in fairness to him I must also record that I have often heard that, without publicity, he has paid thousands of dollars for the medical treatment of impoverished friends; and during the years, many other acts of kindness on the part of this "thrifty" fellow have come to my attention.

As important in her own field as Rudy was to popular music is a former Missouri farm girl with one of the kindliest personalities I have ever known. Frankly, I am prejudiced when I write of Mary Margaret McBride, who, after an unbroken run of twenty years on the air, recently gave up her five-times-a-week series of radio programs to enter television. For during my association with broadcasting she has been a generous and loyal friend; and I should have to work overtime to detect any flaws in her. Other critics have also attested to her pre-eminence. Those who assay the virtues and the defects of radio in a coldly analytical manner say that she has contributed more than any other individual to the quality of programs for housewives. Today she continues to be the best human-interest interviewer (male or female) of the United States.

I did not have such a high regard for her, however, when she came to the air via WOR-Mutual in the 1930's, after a career as a star newspaperwoman and magazine writer. Sharing an apartment at the time with Estella Karn, former newspaperwoman and circus press agent, and also manager for Paul Whiteman, Mary Margaret had been desperately in need of a job. She could have continued her successful work as a writer, but was determined to break into broadcasting. At last Estella, appointing herself guide and mentor, persuaded the New York station to give her protégé an opportunity.

Without scripts, without even a clear idea of what radio was about, Mary Margaret, under the studio-owned pseudonym of "Martha Deane," took her stance before the microphone and began to talk. And, for a woman's program, it was about the oddest kind of chatter heard on the air—comments on art, literature, politics and human relations; but not a single household hint or recipe in the entire hour. Mary Margaret, furthermore, was not a smooth talker. In a day when speakers were judged by the standards of announcers who had what was known as "diction," the Missouri girl held forth in a high-pitched rural twang; at times she stumbled over words; occasionally she giggled and, now and then, would begin a sentence without taking the trouble to end it.

After having heard her on one occasion, I told my readers that Mary Margaret McBride was, without question, the worst speaker I had ever come across on the radio. Her material was adequate, I deigned to admit, but "oh, what idiosyncracies!" A week later, impelled no doubt by masochism, I tuned her in again—and, much to my surprise, had not the slightest desire to dial immediately to another station. Her words fascinated me! It became obvious that here was no ordinary female gabber; that she had a rich background of experience; that during her interviews she revealed hidden facets of her guests; that she had a store of amusing and entertaining anecdotes about the great and the humble and, above all, that she loved people. The next day I listened again and by the time another week had passed the Mary Margaret hour had become an addiction.

So I wrote another paragraph, completely reversing the first verdict. Here is a great reporter, one who must be a first-rate newspaperwoman, I said (although, at the time, I did not know the identity of "Martha Deane"), and advised my readers to tune in.

Years later, Mary Margaret's interesting book about her radio career revealed that those few vagrant sentences tossed off between editions had proved to be a turning point in her life. For she wrote that, at the time, WOR's executives had decided to fire her because she did not have a "good radio personality." But the appearance of the complimentary paragraph in the *News* had given them pause. "Maybe she is a good reporter," they said; "maybe the gal has something." So they retained her for another trial period. Within a few days sponsors began arriving in droves—and it has been that way ever since. On Mutual, CBS, NBC, and later on ABC, there were times when between forty and fifty prospective advertisers stood in line impatiently awaiting their turns to buy time on her programs.

The mistake made in judging Mary Margaret is one that is common even today in broadcasting. Too often, a speaker is graded for his "pear-shaped" tones rather than for what he says. This, despite the obvious fact that radio and TV abound in poorly paid staff announcers whose speech is technically superior to that of a Walter Winchell, an H. V. Kaltenborn, a Quincy Howe or an Elmer Davis. But it is these commentators who win and hold millions of followers—not through elegant diction or perfect enunciation, but because of what they impart to their listeners. There are a few famous newsmen such as Lowell Thomas, Ed Murrow and John Daly whose graces of diction and voice are well enough developed to enable them to pass even the highly difficult tests given to applicants for network announcers' jobs. Yet it is significant that some of these fortunate ones do not attract so large an air audience to their news periods as some of their less polished but more opinionated competitors.

There is hardly a famous political, literary, scientific, military, naval or diplomatic figure living in or visiting New York who does not appear on Mary Margaret's ABC program. Starting her interviews in what seems to be an offhand, almost naïve manner, she turns a guest painlessly "inside out," eliciting information he or she would not ordinarily reveal to any other reporter. That is why schools of journalism in the metropolitan area have made her broadcasts required listening.

These interviews have behind them hours spent in "boning up" on guests. Calling on her for a story one evening in her duplex apartment overlooking Central Park, I found her in a rich silken robe sitting on a couch piled high with a score of books. In her hand was a Pearl Buck novel on China; she was marking passages in it. The other volumes contained biographical references to the author and accounts of peasant life in that country.

"Just getting ready for tomorrow," she explained.

The result of this research is that by the time she faces an author across a microphone, Mary Margaret often knows his book in greater detail than its writer. For the latter may very well have forgotten some of the paragraphs which are fresh in Mary Margaret's mind.

"I try to learn everything I possibly can about a person I interview," she told me. "Before I had Mrs. Theodore Roosevelt, Jr., as my guest, for instance, I read five big volumes by or about the members of her family. Then, my leg woman, Janice Devine, talks to these people and digs up more facts.

"I work all evening, sometimes until 2 or 3 in the morning, and am up promptly at 7:30. After breakfast, I put on a sheet of paper certain catch words, each of which reminds me of a portion of my notes. This is the sheet to which I refer during my broadcasts. There is no formal script."

Mary Margaret gained this almost fanatical devotion to facts when she was only sixteen. It was then that she began covering stories for her hometown weekly, the Paris, Missouri, *Mercury*. Her boss was an old-time country editor who set his copy in type by hand.

"And he made me rewrite and then rewrite again. Also, he insisted that I walk a mile if necessary to get some minute fact that I had missed. I covered everything, fires, church socials, sermons, lodge meetings and arrivals at the railroad station. He helped me to understand people and to see what made them click. My salary was nothing a week, but I should have paid him for what he taught me."

Mary Margaret worked her way through the University of Missouri as a ten-dollar-a-week reporter on the Columbia *Times*. Then more newspaper experience in the town of New Mexico, Missouri, in Cleveland and finally on the New York *Evening Mail*. This led her eventually to the *Saturday Evening Post* and other major magazines.

"All I pretend to be is a reporter—and I hope a good one," is the way she sums it up. "There are too many newscasters, commentators and interviewers on the air these days who lack newspaper experience. Even in television, it's more valuable than a Paris gown."

Knowing this, one is not surprised that she has been able to influence countless lives throughout the country to an extent achieved by no other woman broadcaster. I take it as a matter of course that Mary Margaret McBride has received more local, state, national and foreign honors than any of her competitors. And it did not at all amaze me that, when she celebrated one of her many anniversaries on the air, several hundred of the most illustrious personalities in the United States, led by Eleanor Roosevelt, paid tribute to her before a vast assemblage of her fans in the Yankee Stadium.

Gertrude Berg, creator of "The Goldbergs" and portrayer of its beloved Molly, is another broadcasting personality I met during the early years. One day in the 1930's, I encountered her on the lower East Side, among the pushcarts of Allen Street. Knowing that she was living at the time with her husband, a successful mechanical engineer, and her two children in a Park Avenue apartment, I jokingly inquired if she were saving money by doing her shopping down here.

"No," she said seriously. "I know it may sound patronizing, although I don't mean it that way, but I can't write about these people unless I renew my contacts with them. And, please believe me, I'm not here as a slummer, either. I love and feel at home with them and never stay away too long."

It has always seemed a cause of wonder to me that this buxom dark-haired woman with the kindly Semitic face and the flashing eyes should have been able to achieve success not only as a writer but also as a character actress on both radio and television. After all, she had not the slightest training as a performer and came to broadcasting as an amateur.

It all started back in 1929, when Mrs. Berg read a few Jewish character monologues to Ben Bernie, the orchestra leader. He sent her to station WMCA, but there her scripts were turned down. However, Hyman Brown, the director, who was doing a show on that outlet, smoothed the way for her at NBC.

An executive there could not decipher Mrs. Berg's handwriting —her scripts were not typed—and asked her to read them aloud. Although she had not even pretended to be a performer, he was so impressed with her reading that he promised to produce her series, but only on the condition that she would portray the role of Molly.

She consented reluctantly, and on November 20, 1929, went on NBC for the first time with "The Rise of the Goldbergs," as the show was then called. For this she received a fee of seventy-five dollars a performance, out of which she paid her entire cast. Then, after a few broadcasts, illness forced her off the air for a brief period. During this time the network received more than eleven thousand phone calls from listeners asking what had become of Gertrude Berg. That convinced her that she was an actress as well as a writer, and since then she has been on radio or television as a star performer.

One night, while dining with her in the Barberry Room, I asked her how many words she had written about her Bronx Jewish family and their friends. "Oh," she said casually, "about thirteen million, and all in longhand. Let me see, that's about 130 long novels of 100,000 words each. You know, it doesn't seem possible that there could be that many words in the world." She told me that she devoted about three days to the writing of each half-hour television script and that she rehearses with her company approximately 27½ hours a week.

"The Goldbergs" have made Mrs. Berg one of the wealthiest authors of the air-waves. She has reaped fortunes not only as a script writer but as a performer in four media—radio, TV, the movies and the Broadway stage.

This, however, is not what gives her work significance. Rather, it is that "The Goldbergs," along with "Amos 'n' Andy," was the first program to prove that a series devoted to a minority people, treated in a sympathetic manner, could become popular on the radio. In the Twenties and the Thirties there were many broadcasters who argued that a mass audience would not give serious consideration to a group of characters unless they were Anglo-Saxon, of the upper middle-class and preferably of some Protestant religious denomination. A Jew, Italian or Negro could very well be presented as a "character" but certainly not as a hero or even in a "straight" role.

Today, however, we have sympathetic series devoted not only to Jews but to Italians and other national elements. It is only a question of time before some network discovers that the public will accept, just as enthusiastically, a program portraying the American Negro without caricature or stereotype.

Perhaps the most telling commentary on this topic I have heard came from Gertrude Berg herself.

"Some years ago," she said, "I received a letter from a group of nuns. They told me they couldn't listen to the radio during Lent. So, would I please send them those scripts of 'The Goldbergs' that they had missed? I certainly did!"

And equally revealing of "The Goldbergs' " appeal to all races and creeds was the response of station owners when, during 1954, the Berg show was chosen as the summer replacement for Bishop Fulton Sheen on the DuMont Network. The latter's executives were doubtful of the reception it would be accorded in this time segment; so they wrote to the 164 stations carrying the eloquent cleric and asked whether the substitution of the series of Jewish family life would be agreeable to them. Within a week, 160 had answered in the affirmative.

As much of a trail-blazer as Mrs. Berg, but in a different sphere, was Ed Wynn, "The Perfect Fool." During what is now known as the "golden era" of radio, he was one of the giants who contributed to its phenomenal growth. Wynn, Joe Penner ("Wanna buy a duck?"), Will Rogers, Eddie Cantor, Al Jolson, Amos 'n' Andy, Edgar Bergen and Charlie McCarthy, Jack Benny, Fred Allen and George Jessel were among the laugh-makers who held sway over the nation at the time.

Ed Wynn, who during the 1930's was at his peak as "The Fire Chief," made history one night on the roof of the New Amsterdam Theatre, used then by NBC as a broadcasting studio. The "regulars" who were there on that evening in April, 1932, observed that something was missing. "Where is the glass curtain?" they asked, referring to the enormous transparent pane which up to then had been lowered between the performers on the stage and the audience out front. The latter had heard the dialogue and the music of a broadcast only through loud-speakers installed in the auditorium. The purpose was to exclude any sounds of applause or laughter from the microphones!

We soon had the answer. Studio attachés announced that, for the first time during a comedy show, this barrier would be eliminated. It had been decided to send over the air the reactions of the visible audience.

This, however, was not the only occasion on which Wynn, a melancholy fellow with blinking eyes, had served as an innovator. The "august clown," as he calls himself, was the first big-time comic to have a studio audience, back in 1932; and also he was the first performer to inject comedy into a radio commercial.

Almost every time I'd meet with him he would dwell with pride on his collection of "funny" hats and his grotesque stage shoes, which serve as his trademarks.

"I have more than eight hundred hats and four hundred 'outlandish' coats," he once told me.

As for his floppy shoes, Ed would not think of giving a performance without wearing them.

"But that's just superstition," I said.

"Sure, it is," said Wynn. "Just the same I have spent more than three thousand dollars on those shoes for repairs and, after I go, you'll see them on display in the Smithsonian Institution."

Ed is one of the kindliest men I know. He waxes enthusiastic when discussing all fellow comedians, save one.

"I'll never discuss Milton Berle's talents with you," he told me. "I dislike him, so I couldn't be fair in my judgment of him."

"Why?"

"Well, let's not go into that," he said.

As for Milton Berle, he has kept me laughing for hours while sharing a table with him at Lindy's or Toots Shor's. But I can't recall even one gag he has told me; his comedy is for the eye and the ear rather than for the memory.

Unlike Jack Benny, Wynn or Fred Allen, "Uncle Miltie" is always on stage, even when he is off. He is in the midst of a perpetual act and insists on being the center of attraction. One seldom sees him at Lindy's without a retinue of assorted hangers-on who laugh every time he utters a syllable.

During one of these post-midnight kaffeeklatsches, he remarked to me, "I wish my mother was a sponsor." I thought most of those at the table would collapse from merriment!

Early one morning, I saw him in a 52nd Street night club. As soon as the comedian—a minor one—came on the floor, Miltie began to fidget, tap his fingers on the table and twist in his chair. The club comic made a casual remark about Berle; the latter answered and, before you could say NBC, he was out on the floor. "Uncle Miltie" took over and for some forty minutes panicked the audience with laughter. Just a few days before (this was in 1946) he had refused to play several night clubs for a mere $18,500 week. And now he was giving a show on the cuff!

His reason for abandoning temporarily the night-spot circuit was his desire to make good on the air. For although he had been broad-casting since the 1920's, Berle up to that time had been a failure on radio. His rapid-fire, wise-guy gags, some of them off-color, of-fended many listeners, and his mugging was wasted on the micro-phones.

Shortly thereafter, while we were dining at Toots Shor's one night, Milton informed me that he was "going to lick this radio business. Hereafter, I'll devote all of my time to it. I'm going to make myself over."

Berle may be an arch-egotist but he does not deceive himself. To implement this determination, he canceled a total of $350,000 worth of club and theatre engagements and hired Nat Hiken, a writer for Fred Allen, to create for him a type of comedy that em-phasized character and situation rather than gags.

Even if his sponsor eventually did drop him, Berle's next radio series was by far his most successful one. The "wise crowd" at Lindy's, however, did not appreciate the change. But the comedian refused to be affected by their comments, just as he has ignored criticism, professional and amateur, during his entire career. For years he was accused of stealing material; columnists panned him; fellow comedians reviled him; but Berle acted as if he had not heard a word.

He is one of the few stars of radio and TV I have known who seemingly does not attribute base personal motives to the profes-sional critics who have scorned him. "What's the use?" he said to me one day. "Sometimes you fellows don't know what you're talk-ing about; but it doesn't matter. Because if I'm good—and I know I am—I'll come out on top anyway."

And he has. For when he came to TV he was its first big and most important attraction. He was dubbed "Mr. Television Him-self" and his hour-long variety show was responsible for the sale of more sets than any other feature since the development of video.

By the season of 1952–53, Berle's TV format of gags and broad skits—some of these adapted from burlesque—had begun to wear out its welcome. He faced a crisis. But again the comedian made a bold move, just as he did during his radio days, by hiring Good-man Ace, one of the wittiest writers in broadcasting, to create a show for him. In this series, he was transformed from the brash guy into a sympathetic "patsy" (à la Jack Benny), on the receiving instead of the giving end of gags. Many among the viewers preferred the old and more blatant Berle; but the change evidently worked wonders, for the new Berle program soon took its place among the top-rated attractions of television.

The chances are that, with the coming of other trends, Berle will continue to change his format. For although he has not entirely succeeded in "remaking" himself—after all, who could remake Milton Berle?—he has enough resiliency to bound back to the front of the procession.

Jack Benny stands in contrast to "Uncle Miltie." The latter is a lusty extrovert; the former, when away from cameras and microphones, is reserved, almost shy, and one of the chronic worriers of show business. Internationally renowned and now in his fifty-ninth year, he still awaits the reactions to his shows with as much concern as any beginner on the verge of his first appearance.

Tall, gray and handsomer than most fun-makers, Jack usually greets his newspaper friends with "How was I?" Tell him that his last telecast was not up to his usual standard and he will furrow his brow and ponder in silence. You can see the deep hurt in his eyes and are certain that he is on the point of uttering a violent dissent. But he confines himself to a mild "I thought I was pretty good; but, you know, you may be right."

Like all performers, Jack sometimes has the habit of forgetting the scores of favorable reviews given to him by a critic and remembering only the disapproving ones. I, for example, have been one of his boosters since he made his radio debut on an Ed Sullivan show in 1932. But on a recent trip to New York, when my name was mentioned in conversation, Benny, with a sense of injury, dwelt at considerable length on my lack of appreciation of his latest television effort.

Find a success in radio and TV and nine times out of ten you will also find a performer who has contributed something new either in material or in terms of personality. This Benny has done with his portrayal of the lovable boob or patsy, the stingy would-be smart-aleck, who always gets it in the neck. At the time of its introduction, it was not by any means a novel character in drama or literature, but certainly something different on the air.

Shortly after he began to exploit Jello in 1934, the comedian took hold of the public imagination to an extent equaled only by "Amos 'n' Andy." Sunday 7 P.M. on NBC became Jack Benny time for the nation, just as today, to a lesser extent because of the inroads of television, it is that on CBS Radio. Yet, despite the laughter he has created, one may fine-comb Jack's scripts of the last two decades and not find him uttering a single joke. He needs no gags. His simple "Is that so?" or "Hm-m-m-pf," uttered ever so casually, win a greater response than some other comic's smart retort. Benny is essentially a character actor placed in well-contrived situations which enable him to create merriment, not by what he says, but because of the circumstances in which he says it. Also, with Bob Hope and Berle, he is one of the top masters of timing.

Once, while he was headlining at the Roxy Theatre in New York, where he made box-office history, I visited him backstage for a chat. "Let's get this straight," he said. "I may not be the world's greatest comedian, but I am one of its most successful performers. And I have an explanation for this success. In the first place, I work closely with my writers, who are good ones. For example, they created the idea of the comic male quartet on my shows. I, on the other hand, had the notion of bringing the Ronald Colmans to the program. But the one factor which has been even more important is that I'm a damned good editor.

"Most persons don't realize that the star of a weekly comedy series is like the editor of a newspaper or magazine. He has to assign writers to produce certain material and then he must have enough knowledge to order rewrites and to know what to expand and what to cut. At least sixty percent of a show's effectiveness depends on this."

Benny, like most big-time radio-TV comedians, is in reality the captain of a close-knit team. Often I have known less successful stars to speak disparagingly of their staffs. But at no time have I ever heard him utter anything but praise for his associates. And his writers—Sam Perrin, Milt Josefsberg, George Balzer and John Tackaberry—and the regular members of his acting company—Roch-

ester, Don Wilson, Dennis Day and Artie Auerbach—always refer
to him in the most complimentary terms.

One of the most astute critics of Jack's shows is his wife and partner, Mary Livingstone. Although she began her career as a sales-
girl in May's Los Angeles department store, during her years in
the profession Mary has developed an almost instinctive sense of
what is right and what is wrong about a routine.

Like so many stars of the entertainment world, Benny was for
years a confirmed hypochondriac. At one time, he carried with him
on his travels a leather case containing forty different varieties of
pills! But one day during World War Two, Sydney Eiges, vice-
president of NBC in charge of press relations, visiting him at the
Savoy-Plaza in New York, noticed that the familiar leather case
reposed on a desk, covered with dust.

"I don't need pills any more," Jack explained. "I've just returned
from Europe entertaining our soldiers. When I saw what those fellows endured in the front lines—well, that cured me for good."

On no occasion that I have been with Benny socially have I
heard him say anything that was truly funny. That's because, unlike
Fred Allen, he is not a wit and, unlike Milton Berle, not a teller
of jokes. Speaking of Allen, his friend and professional "feudist,"
he once told me, "I'd never go up against that guy unless I had
my writers with me." But on his shows Jack does have his writers;
also his character, his situations and his ability as an editor. And
until he should decide to retire as a performer to devote himself
solely to the production end of the business, he will undoubtedly
hold his place as one of America's foremost comedians.

Fred Allen differs from Benny as greatly off-stage as on. He utters
one devastating crack after another. With bags beneath his eyes
and a sad expression on his wry countenance, he can wax scathingly
sarcastic about broadcasting and those who labor in its vineyards.
Some of his witticisms are far more amusing than many of those
heard on his shows. That is why someone once said, "Fred would
be the Number One man in television if only he could be as funny
on it as he is in talking about it!"

Shortly after that lavish giveaway show, "Stop the Music," had
lured away many of his listeners and caused him to retire tempo-

rarily from the air, he told me: "There's only one thing left to be done now. Some guy will have to put on a program in which a refrigerator gives away people!"

And discussing one of his pet abominations, advertising-agency executives, he remarked: "An agency vice-president is a fellow who went to Princeton, comes to his office at 9 in the morning, finds on his desk a pile of molehills and has until 5 P.M. to make a mountain out of them."

During the years I have known him, Fred has been one of the country's most incisive critics of both radio and television. "Broadcasting started off on the wrong foot," he once told me. "Instead of showmen, it had inexperienced, pipe-smoking collegians in tweeds running its programs. Unwilling to experiment, it offered no encouragement to imaginative talent and now it seems to me that television is following the same path.

"The big difficulty is this: No one is interested in the only people who count—the writer and the actor. The sponsors are concerned solely with selling their products; the advertising agencies with retaining the sponsors as clients, and networks with selling their time."

Of course, Allen said this before such an experimental program as "Omnibus" had come to the air and at a time when it was inconceivable that a network should sign writers of the stature of Robert Sherwood, William Saroyan and Ben Hecht to create their own dramatic series without interference from the top. In the main, however, Fred's criticism is still valid.

Allen's sour opinions of radio and TV are, of course, the products of some of his experiences in these media. In 1932, after having written a one-hour show with Helen Morgan as one of the features, he offered a recording of it to a sponsor, who immediately bought it. After having submitted his script for the première broadcast, however, he was told by an advertising-agency executive, "I can't see anything funny in it. Where are the jokes?"

Then he added: "But, Mr. Allen, I have a great suggestion for pepping up your show. Why don't you and your cast dress up like Keystone cops and bop people over their heads? That'll make 'em laugh."

Fred turned down the suggestion; but on the opening night he discovered that the agency man had taken another step to insure laughter. He had seated in the front row of the studio thirty boys from a local orphan asylum who had been instructed to guffaw whenever the announcer gave them a signal!

On one of his series, the sponsor's wife had a fondness for organ music. So Fred was forced to halt his fast-paced show in the middle and stand by while the program picked up Ann Leaf's organ solos from the Paramount Theatre. Also, he was encumbered with society women as guest announcers. Most of them became tongue-tied, so eventually they were placed behind a screen while they delivered the commercials!

Then there was the day when the head of an advertising agency sent for Fred. "You have a most interesting show," he told the comedian. "It's not only very funny but the first one in radio to have a definite locale. Now, frankly, we are trying to copy your stuff; but somehow or other, it just doesn't seem to work. We'd appreciate it if you could tell us why."

"Well," said the astounded Allen, "maybe you don't have the satirical humorous style that my scripts have. Why don't you hire me to write your stuff?"

"Oh, no," said the executive, "I don't think you'd do. I'm hiring someone else."

And he did!

The limited knowledge of some agency executives is another source of annoyance to Fred. In one of his shows there was a restaurant skit during which the comedian complained of poor food. "Trying to poison me?" he asked. "Who's the chef here? Lucrezia Borgia?"

It is the general practice, whenever the name of a living person is used in a script, to have it "cleared"—that is, to obtain that person's permission, in order to avoid a suit for invasion of privacy. The pipe-smoking magnifico in charge of "clearing" Allen's references, on coming across this mention, immediately ordered his assistant to "Call Miss Borgia." But the latter, not finding the lady listed in the Manhattan telephone directory, settled for the voice studio of Lucrezia Bori, the Metropolitan Opera star.

"Will you permit your name to be used on the Fred Allen show?" she asked. "He's mentioning you as a chef."

"Chef? Chef? But I am a singer," said the puzzled soprano.

"This is just a joke . . . Fred Allen, you know," the girl explained.

"Oh, Fred Allen! I like him so much!" said Lucrezia Bori and, an hour later, she signed the "clearance."

Network vice-presidents who wield the censor's blue pencil are also among Allen's pet hates. He still becomes choleric on recalling the NBC v.p. who killed a joke about ham. "The Hormel Company, one of our clients, might not like it," was the explanation. On one occasion this ogre permitted Fred to indulge in a crack about the small size of a hotel room he had occupied in Philadelphia. As a result, there was a protest by the hotel association of the Quaker City. And, eventually, any and all comic references to boarding-house prunes were ruthlessly eliminated from Allen's scripts, following dire threats made by the organized prune packers of California.

"Well," said Fred, "this just gives you an idea of what I've had to endure. Now maybe you understand why my health hasn't been so good."

Despite his scorn for the climate that prevails in broadcasting, the comedian did attain national popularity during the 1930's and 1940's. During that period the core of his shows was a humorous commentary on the American scene. This had elements of Josh Billings, Mark Twain and Will Rogers, superimposed on robust comedy of, at times, a cartoonlike broadness. But although his shows were always among the top ten, he did not equal Jack Benny in popularity. His observations were too dry and, at times, too intellectual. In some ways, he is a major-league and much more successful Henry Morgan; for the latter, a younger man, is also a comedian with a keen mind and a tongue of scalpel sharpness who has not achieved the acclaim he deserves.

And yet a man of Allen's school of humor, Herb Shriner, the rural philosopher, has during the last few years won an enthusiastic reception from the television audience. Fred's early ventures in this medium were disastrous, primarily because he was surrounded with dancing girls, spectacular sets and other appurtenances of a "production." His subsequent series, unfortunately, also failed to provide a proper frame for his sharp wit. The Boston-born Irishman, whose real name is John Florence Sullivan, and who started in show business as a mediocre juggler, requires a simple showcase, one devoid of elaborate doodads, in which he can indulge his talent for ad-lib remarks and comment on current events. Given such a setup, Fred might very well become the "new" sensation of video, an opinion evidently shared by NBC, which has him under a long-term exclusive contract.

To achieve as great a renown in television as he has on radio is a matter of artistic pride with him. As far as finances are concerned, he could have retired years ago, for Allen has been one of the big money-makers of the air-waves. Although he has lived comfortably, Fred has never been one of those ostentatious spendthrifts in which show business abounds. For example, he is the only star I know who does not own an automobile. "Too much of a bother to have one in New York and, when one is in the country, a car offers too much temptation to leave one's home," he once explained to me. "And besides," he said, "you meet a better class of people in the subway."

He has not visited a night club in years, as he dislikes music and floor shows while dining.

"But don't you occasionally want to catch some good act playing a night spot?" I asked.

"When I go out for an evening I like to talk and you can't do much schmoozing in a place like that," he said. "Night clubs and TV will kill the art of conversation in this country. The next generation, I tell you, will be born with four eyes and no tongue."

Save for visits to a few friends such as H. Allen Smith, the humorist, and Alton Cook, the motion-picture critic of the New York *World-Telegram and Sun*, Allen spends most of his time in the spacious yet simple apartment he shares with his wife, the comedienne Portland Hoffa, near Carnegie Hall. Its most important room is the library containing more than 3,500 volumes devoted, for the most part, to humor, history, philosophy and religion.

Years ago, I visited the celebrated tenor and night-club impresario,

Will Oakland, in a palatial home on Long Island, which he had rented furnished from a Broadway star. It also had an enormous library; but a close inspection revealed that its shelves were filled with cardboard prop books, plus a number of real volumes with uncut pages. In Allen's apartment, however, you may depend on it, the library is not for show; reading is his big interest. But, strangely enough, I did not find among his collection a single work on politics or economics.

"I read newspapers and magazines for things like that," Fred said. "Frankly, I just am not politically minded. And, anyway, if I ever give up performing, I want to write humorous stuff, perhaps for the theatre."

If he does, I should certainly like to be among the first-night audience. For his Admiral Byrd monologue, which he wrote for a Broadway revue many years ago, was one of the wittiest ever heard on that street, and his radio-character creations—"Titus Moody," "Mrs. Nussbaum," "Senator Claghorn," "Falstaff Openshaw" and other denizens of "Allen's Alley"—although mere caricatures, had a robust, almost Dickensian flavor. The American theatre could use such a talent.

Like Allen, Berle and Wynn, when Eddie Cantor came to radio in 1931, he already had attained fame as a star of the stage. The offspring of a poverty-stricken lower East Side family, who was orphaned at an early age, he had been, with Will Rogers and W. C. Fields, one of the big names of musical shows, including the *Ziegfeld Follies*. He has also played stellar roles in many movies and is now one of the important comedy attractions of television.

Cantor belongs to the school of the late Al Jolson, George Jessel, Ted Lewis and Sophie Tucker—a school which, although lacking in subtlety, is rich in sentimental corn, broad strokes of comedy and vitality. The latter attribute is especially important. For despite the changes in styles of performing, nothing as yet has been invented to replace it. Such old-timers—Bert Lahr is one of them—take possession of a stage in an emphatic manner. They do not creep up on an audience as some of the younger actors and singers do; they almost literally bang their listeners over their heads with a dynamic outburst of patter or song. From the first moment, there is no question of who is the master; they grip their audiences and do not let them go until the final bow. Often—and with considerable justice —the newer critics refer to the work of this tribe as being "hammy"; but the fact is that old-school mimes could impart many valuable lessons in showmanship to the more recent crop of performers.

I met Eddie during the 1930's when, as one of the pioneers of radio comedy, he had attained the height of his fame. That was when the cry of "We want Cantor" was chanted by school kids throughout the land, much as they pestered their parents with comedian Joe Penner's trademark, "Wanna buy a duck?"

Cantor brought to radio for the first time many features which are now commonplaces of broadcasting. Along with Wynn, he introduced funny costumes and indulged in mugging in order to win the laughter of the studio audience. He did this although he realized that such antics meant nothing to millions of outside listeners as yet without the benefit of television. But, strangely enough, Cantor at one time actually protested against the presence of studio visitors. He argued that visible spectators tempted a performer to play to them rather than to the microphone.

In this he was correct. But soon enough Eddie, like every other radio comedian, came to realize that sponsors had an annoying habit of judging the effectiveness of comedy by the reactions of the studio audience. So he went along with the trend.

After Cantor's early successes on radio, I did not have a conversation with him for almost twenty years. An aggressive fellow, the pop-eyed comedian was engaged in almost never-ending feuds with critics who dared to pan his shows. In one instance, it led to a suit for libel against Eddie by my assistant on the *News* radio column, Abe Greenberg (now a Hollywood publicity man) and me.

Cantor, riled by the comments of the metropolitan newspaper pundits, struck back, in an interview published in a fan magazine, by saying that every New York radio critic "except one" was either a chiseler or a log-roller. Naturally, many in the trade wondered about the identity of this journalistic pillar of virtue. Their doubts were soon dispelled when Nick Kenny, poet, songwriter and radio columnist of the New York *Daily Mirror*, modestly took a bow by writing, "Thanks, Eddie, for the compliment!"

"Well," said "Colonel" Frank Hause, the saturnine managing editor of the *News*, "I see that Nick admits he is the honest one. Cantor's certainly not going to dispute that; if he does, it'll give Nick a damned good case. And if Cantor keeps quiet, he is merely adding to the insult he has already given to the rest of you fellows. You and Greenberg gotta sue him!"

We did, for $100,000 each—and without actually coming to trial the case was fought on legal points up to the Court of Appeals of New York State. This august tribunal, in a precedent-setting decision which was deemed important enough to be published on the front page of the *New York Law Journal*, held that because at the time there were only a limited number of radio critics in New York City each could suffer injury through the comedian's blanket accusation. In other words, a group, if small enough, could be libeled, and all that remained was for a jury to determine the amount of damages.

Eddie settled for a nominal sum, paid the court costs and the considerable legal expenses for both sides. He has the satisfaction, however, of knowing that this decision, with due publicity to him, is still being cited in practically every action for group libel brought in the United States. But the newspapers of this country sometimes regret that our managing editor was so eager to go to law. For the case of Gross and Greenberg vs. Cantor *et al* has been used on several occasions to extract coin from the exchequers of various publications.

I did not meet Eddie again until one day in the summer of 1950, when, much to my surprise, he appeared at a luncheon given by NBC at Twenty-One in celebration of my 25th year on the *News*. During the broadcast, which was presided over by Mary Margaret McBride, he stepped forward, shook my hand and said: "Ben and I had a slight misunderstanding some years ago. But I must tell you that you never would have guessed it from reading his comments on my shows. I may not always agree with him; but he has been a fair-minded and honest reporter." No one could have given a newspaperman a more welcome compliment.

Cantor later told me that before he retires from show business he hopes, in co-operation with the networks and some universities, to establish a foundation for the training of young comedians. "My contemporaries and I gained our experience in burlesque, vaudeville and stock companies which are practically extinct today," he said. "Something will have to replace these."

I then asked him to comment on some widespread criticism of his playing so many benefits. His enemies had charged that such activities were motivated primarily by a desire for publicity.

"That, of course, is untrue," said Eddie. "Any name performer can get plenty of publicity through his professional work.

"But suppose a star had no other motive than to get his picture into the papers? If, at the same time, he can help to build a Catholic school in Las Vegas, or help rescue two thousand refugee children, or bring millions of dollars to the fight against cancer or polio, does the feeding of his vanity in any way lessen the value of his contribution? And, remember this, every time an actor is pictured handing over a check for some good cause, that picture may inspire another performer to do likewise."

I had not thought of this angle before. As for Eddie Cantor, any publicity he may have received for his philanthropic efforts is more than justified by this fact: During his long career he has raised more than $250,000,000 for charitable and civic enterprises.

Another performer who, after having attained fame on radio, has been able to make a successful switch to television is Kate Smith. But, regardless of her achievements in the new medium, she will continue to be remembered as one of the great popular personalities of broadcasting's early days. She belongs to that legendary time of the 1930's when radio built its own singing stars; a period when, through the spotting of young talent night after night at the same hour, Bing Crosby, Russ Columbo, the Street Singer and Morton Downey were turned into national celebrities. Neither radio nor television gives such buildups today to promising performers. Available sustaining periods are far too costly and the trend, unfortunately, is for broadcasting to cash in on personalities already developed by other media.

During her early years on radio, as a singer, variety-show emcee and human-interest commentator, Kate Smith had impressed herself on the mass mind as the embodiment of the homey American virtues. She had done this to such an extent that when King George VI and Queen Elizabeth visited this country, and President Roosevelt, sponsoring an entertainment in their honor, asked which typically American performers they wished to hear, both mentioned Kate Smith first.

Since she came to the air in 1932 on behalf of William S. Paley's La Palina cigars, she has grossed some forty million dollars out of radio, TV, recordings and other related entertainment ventures. Her full-throated singing and hearty, forthright manner of talking, with the emphasis on home, mother, family, patriotism, charity and other sure-fire topics, established her within a few years as the personality having most in common with the great American middle class. To millions, especially among the women, she was the indispensable purveyor of common sense and sentimentality—a kind of female Arthur Godfrey without, however, the latter's roguish impudence and occasional unorthodoxy. Kate's nighttime variety show, like Rudy Vallee's, was for years one of the major attractions of radio, and later her five-day-a-week afternoon show had a long run on television.

Yet, with all her success, of the thousands of stories which have been published about Kate Smith only a few have been in the form of interviews. Almost inaccessible to newspapermen, she draws a heavy veil over her private life. I am one of the few radio-TV editors with whom she has dined in a public restaurant; but during a period when I wrote "human interest" stories and background material for her daily commentary sessions, I did not once have a conversation with her.

Kate is basically an extremely shy person and for years was supersensitive about her weight. Even the most casual reference to it in print would bring violent protests from her manager-partner Ted Collins. Above everything, she feared ridicule. But, one day Kate decided to face reality; she wrote a magazine article telling how she had turned what might have been a handicap into a great asset. She realized at last that the public accepted her for what she was; and that might not have been the case had she been a sylphlike creature.

Her manager, Collins, is one of the remarkable personalities of the broadcasting industry. He has an almost fanatical devotion to his client which causes him to show fury at the slightest hint of criticism. His professional relationship to her is much like that of Estella Karn to Mary Margaret McBride and Anna Sosenko to Hildegarde. There is no written contract between them; theirs is a fifty-fifty agreement which has proved immensely profitable to both since that day, long ago, when he took Kate, then a comedienne in a Broadway musical, under his wing.

One night while Kate, Ted and I were having dinner at the Hotel Vanderbilt, an establishment rarely patronized by the broadcasting crowd, the astute manager told me that if there were a formula for a Kate Smith show, it probably would be this: "Make 'em laugh . . . make 'em cry . . . make 'em feel good."

On that occasion Kate revealed that she planned to retire from the air in 1960, on her fiftieth birthday. "And then I'm going to devote myself to what I've always had my heart set on—social service. I'm going to help the Sister Kenny Foundation, cancer research, the tuberculosis groups and organizations which fight for justice for minorities."

Kate lives quietly in a luxurious Manhattan apartment filled with early American furniture, rare glass and china. She seldom goes out during the evenings and has visited only one night club in twenty-three years. Neither a smoker nor a drinker, she spends most of her spare time reading her fan mail, which is so heavy that the cost of answering it runs to more than fifteen thousand dollars a year. Her hobby is the collection of cookbooks and when she is at her country place in Lake Placid, New York, Kate plays golf, tennis, swims or skates.

She is cynical about most persons in show business. "I've had some pretty bitter experiences," she told me. "That's why I consider myself lucky, finding a man like Ted Collins. He is more than a business partner; he's a friend."

One incident involving them has remained in my memory for years. I was going to do a story about Kate, so Ted invited me to attend her broadcast on November 11, 1938. He informed me that she would sing for the first time a song written in 1918 by Irving Berlin.

"Berlin himself played the number over for Kate," Ted said, "and she thinks it's a great song. But she argues it should have more of a martial air. Irving disagrees."

Well, Kate sang it that night and it failed to make much of an impression. But the following week I heard her singing it again, over the air; and this time, because of the change in tempo, it was a tremendous, stirring number. Thereafter, it was featured on every Kate Smith variety show for four successive years—and that is how "God Bless America" became a patriotic classic.

Speaking of popular classics, the man who introduced more of them to American listeners than any other bandleader is Paul Whiteman. G. W. (Johnnie) Johnstone, publicity director of NBC, and I were talking to him casually one day during the 1920's. Arguing with Whiteman concerning another bandleader, Johnnie said jokingly, "Aw, Pops, you don't know anything about jazz!" The double chins of the "King of Jazz" vibrated with laughter and his tiny mustache quivered in appreciation of a familiar joke. For the press agent was merely repeating what the leader of a dance band in Tate's Café, San Francisco, had told Paul just before firing him in 1916.

It is impossible to exaggerate the impact of the early Whiteman band on American popular music. There has been no other ensemble which, for so long a time, tinctured the blood stream of commercial dance rhythms. His "symphonic jazz," although denounced by the purists, gave this form of native music an established position such as it had not enjoyed before.

"Jazz men get together in what we call a jam session," he explained to me. "They produce some wonderful stuff, but the trouble is that, like gypsies, they never play a number the same way twice. I think this is a waste of talent; these improvisations are too good to lose. So all I do is to have them written down and then give them symphonic arrangements."

And what arrangements these were! They were made, for the most part, by Ferde Grofé, who composed the "Grand Canyon" and the "Mississippi" suites. And what players "Pops" had in his band—the brilliant Roy Bargy at the piano, and such jazz immortals as Bix Beiderbecke, Tommy and Jimmy Dorsey, Jack Teagarden,

Henry Busse and Miff Mole and also little Mike Pingiatore, the banjoist, the first instrumentalist hired for his orchestra in 1919. It wasn't surprising that this crew broke records in Broadway night clubs and on the Continent or that it was so popular in London that the Prince of Wales had engaged it to play for fifty of his parties.

The mention of Grofé reminds me that Whiteman was directly responsible for the birth of George Gershwin's "Rhapsody in Blue." In the early days of broadcasting, one of the major rivals of the Whiteman aggregation was Vincent Lopez' dance band. On the air since 1921 and reputed to be the first jazz crew with a regular radio period, Vince's trade mark, "Lopez speaking," and his piano solo, "Nola," were known throughout the land. So when a story appeared in the papers announcing that he was planning an all-jazz concert in Carnegie Hall, this was taken merely as another indication of Lopez' soaring ambition. It was also regarded as an affront by certain highbrows. To them it was sacrilege that this "lowdown" American music should be played in precincts devoted to the Three B's.

Whiteman was also affronted—and shocked—but for a different reason.

"You see," he told me, "the idea of giving a serious jazz concert had been on my mind for years. But what I needed—and didn't have—was a composer. I was looking for someone who could think symphonically and at the same time had his feet in Tin Pan Alley. Well, one afternoon I found him, a young fellow who was working as a staff pianist at the Remick Music Company. His name was George Gershwin and we became friends.

"We had a lot of bull sessions, talking about the future of jazz. George agreed with me that, musically speaking, it was still unexplored territory. So we talked about a jazz concert—but that's all we did—talked.

"When this Lopez item appeared, I tried to get in touch with George immediately, but couldn't. I was so aroused that, without even saying a word to him about it, I sent an announcement to the papers that I'd also be giving an all-jazz concert and that Gershwin would write a number for me. I had to describe it; so, on the spur of the moment, I said it would be a rhapsody based on the blues.

"The minute after George had read my announcement, he got on the phone and asked what it was all about. I explained and he protested.

" 'Why, it would take me at least six months just to collect the thematic material for a piece like that,' he said.

"I laughed and said, 'Look here, George, aren't you talking a little highbrow to another highbrow? You're going to start on it this moment; because we're giving this concert just a few weeks from now.'

"I wouldn't want to go through such a strain again. It was a backbreaking job. I made George lock himself in a room and work, work, work. He delivered the piano part of the 'Rhapsody' page by page and as soon as one arrived, it was turned over to Grofé so that he could dash off the orchestration. We barely made it—but look what we had after we did!"

On that historic night, when the "Rhapsody in Blue" was performed for the first time in New York's sedate Aeolian Hall, February 12, 1924, jazz at last stepped forth from the barrooms, bordellos and cabarets into the chambers of the musically elect. It was such a sensation that the concert was repeated in the much bigger Carnegie Hall, the first time a jazz band had ever performed in its sacrosanct surroundings. It went far beyond Lopez' original plan.

Whiteman also has to his credit the introduction of another American institution—Bing Crosby. And he takes almost as much pride in the fact that he helped to make famous the girl who, in his opinion, was "the greatest jazz stylist who ever lived," Mildred Bailey.

"Just to prove how wrong even the so-called experts can be, I recall that both of these great singers got the thumbs-down treatment during their struggling days. Mildred was dismissed by the cigarette sponsor of my band with the remark, 'That girl can't sing.' And when we played our first engagement in the New York Paramount Theatre, the manager raised hell because I gave Bing, who was a member of our vocal group, The Three Rhythm Boys, a chance to do a solo. As soon as he finished, the boss sent word backstage.

" 'Don't ever let that fellow Crosby sing alone again. He stinks!' "

Pops, who long ago retired from the dance-band business to become an executive of the American Broadcasting Company and a TV producer-performer, is gratefully hailed by dance musicians as their social "liberator." He has done as much for his profession in this field as union leader James Caesar Petrillo has done for it financially.

Up to the time Whiteman began to dominate the jazz world, band leaders and "sidemen," or instrumentalists, were regarded by society as on a par with waiters and busboys. But during the 1920's, the dowager Mrs. Astor had engaged Paul and his band to play for a party in her Fifth Avenue mansion. When Whiteman and his boys, most of whom were from substantial families, many of them college graduates, appeared at the front door, the butler referred them haughtily to the servants' entrance.

Paul informed the flunky, "Either we go in the front door or we don't go in at all!"

Mrs. Astor's social secretary, who had been summoned by the befuddled butler, was shocked. "Mr. Whiteman, do you mean to tell me you'd rather lose your five-thousand-dollar fee than to enter by the back way?"

"Madame," said Paul, "mighty right I would!"

Pops and his musicians went in by the front door and a great how-de-do followed among what still remained of the Four Hundred. Paul's entrance was as meaningful to the mores of that day as was Nora's exit in *A Doll's House*, many years before.

Without realizing it, Whiteman had demolished another barrier of society. Thereafter the kings of jazz could consort as equals with the kings of automobiles, steel or smoked hams.

TEN

I Remember—

Not long ago I did a little exercise in arithmetic and learned that during twenty-nine years of professional listening and viewing I must have heard or seen, in whole or in part, more than 69,600 radio and TV programs!

This is a conservative estimate, based on a five-day-a-week, forty-eight-week-a-year working schedule. The fact is, however, that there was a considerable period when I labored six days a week, fifty weeks a year and tuned in many more than the ten programs a day used for this estimate.

If, under such a regime, one's aesthetic taste buds have not atrophied or if one's mind has not become a mere catalogue of trivia, it is only by virtue of this precaution: One makes of his memory a sieve through which all but the most important or interesting items drain off into the void of forgetfulness. Those events and personalities which remain live vividly in one's consciousness.

For example, I can see even now a tall, slender man with a golden voice sitting beside me in the *News* office, more than a quarter of a century ago. He was a young announcer at WHN who had dropped in for a brief chat.

"You know," said Ted Husing, "this Graham McNamee is a god to me. I'll be happy if I can be only half as good as he is." (More than two decades later, Mel Allen, the famous announcer of the New York Yankee ball games, said to me: "If only I could be half as good as Ted Husing! He's the father of all of us sportscasters.")

In a sense this is true. The baseball and football announcers of today are descendants of Husing rather than of McNamee, as Ted was far more factual in his reports than Graham. But even so, he is regarded as too florid by some current listeners; and, although he knows sports as few men on the air, he is now primarily a top disk jockey. And in this endeavor he has a six-figure annual income, far more than he earned in his heyday as a sports ace of the air-waves.

After snaring a job on WJZ during the 1920's, Ted aided Major J. Andrew White in the establishment of what is now the Columbia Broadcasting System. By 1929, he was specializing in sports and along with Clem McCarthy, the beloved racing expert, and Sigmund Spaeth, "The Tune Detective," was one of the few devoting most of his air time to athletic competitions.

Edward B. Husing had McNamee's flair for drama and almost as resonant a voice; he knew the fine points of the games he described and was more accurate in conveying what was happening in the arena or on the field. But from his earliest days before the microphone, his career was a love affair with the dictionary. He was and still is enamored of words, a circumstance not entirely to his discredit, considering the colorless and limited vocabularies of some of his successors. Occasionally, his use of what to him seemed to be a fancy adjective landed him in hot water. This happened when referring to Harvard during a football game, he used the word "putrid," which caused that august institution to excommunicate him from its radio premises.

Husing once wrote a book in which he expressed contempt for most critics, including this one. Many of the tribe repaid him in kind when, after a long absence from the air as a sportscaster, he returned in this role on television. Because his wordage was as lavish on TV as it had been on radio, his detractors doused him in arsenic and vitriol. I, however, could not go to such extremes, recalling, as some of my colleagues failed to do, that Ted has contributed immeasurably to the development of broadcasting in this country. There is not one successful practitioner of the art today who is not his debtor.

This is especially true of Mel Allen, who, perhaps by no coincidence, has frequently been castigated for talking too much during his baseball telecasts. Like so many others, he often seems unwilling to permit the camera to tell the story and, at times, attempts to gild the picture on the tube with excessive verbiage. This undoubtedly annoys some viewers; but, despite this, in most of the recent popularity polls Mel has emerged as the Number One favorite among sportscasters.

Although Husing's career abounded in highlights, for unalloyed drama it could not approach that of another old-timer, Norman Brokenshire. Still very much in the broadcasting picture, "Broke" was one of that legendary company of announcers during the first decade of radio. He came to WJZ in 1924 in response to a New York *Times* ad which read: "Wanted—College graduate with knowledge of musical terminology."

After the station manager had asked whether he had such knowledge, Norman replied, "I don't even know what musical terminology is."

"Damned if I know, either," said the manager. "But our musical director, Keith McLeod, who'll give your test, sure does."

Brokenshire told me that he was given a copy of the *Musical Courier* and instructed to read therefrom a list of composers. "I couldn't even pronounce them; but I asked for ten minutes to practice and then I finally got them right and landed the job. Of course, today the tests given to would-be announcers by the networks are much more difficult. In fact, they're so stiff that I doubt even such great ones as McNamee, Husing or Cross could pass them, if they were beginners!"

But if you would like to know what applicants for microphone jobs had to face during the 1920's, here is an excerpt from a test forwarded to me by Phillips Carlin, who was famous at the time as Graham McNamee's co-announcer:

"Penelope Cholmondely raised her azure eyes from the crabbed scenario. She meandered among the congeries of her memoirs. There was the Kinetic Algernon, a choleric artificer of icons and triptychs, who wanted to write a trilogy. For years she had stifled her risibilities with dour moods. His asthma caused him to sough like the zephyrs among the tamarack."

No wonder mike men of those days boasted of their "diction" and took pride in the utterances of their verbal trademarks. Brokenshire's in those days was and still is: "How do you do, ladies and gentlemen, how DO you do?"

A tall, handsome man with a high forehead, keen eyes and a dapper mustache, he impressed me during our first meeting twenty-eight years ago as a jovial man of the world with a storehouse of good stories. One of these concerned a day when he broadcast the arrival of some around-the-world fliers at Roosevelt Field, Long Island.

In those times, an announcer on a "remote control," or out-of-the-studio assignment, was forbidden to permit any unscheduled persons to speak into the microphone.

"While waiting to go on the air, I got into a conversation with a slender young Englishman who had been watching me intently," said Norman. "He inquired what I was doing and I explained that I was a radio broadcaster. He examined the mike and I could see he was just dying to say a few words. In fact, he hinted as much."

Brokenshire asked, "What's your name?"

"I'm the Prince of Wales," said the young man.

And he was—but Norman still would not put him on the air. "I would have got hell," he said.

Try to visualize an announcer turning a crown prince away from a microphone today!

What I recall, however, most vividly about Norman Brokenshire are not his entertaining stories, but his tragic and then, eventually, his triumphant battle against strong drink. During the 1930's, one of the most sought-after "name" announcers in radio, he was earning for a considerable period well over $100,000 a year. Then, gradually, the gossip chamber which is the world of broadcasting began to echo with whispers, growing louder and louder. "Broke's hitting the bottle.". . . "He was unsteady when he came to the studio tonight.". . . "You can't rely on him."

Old friends shook their heads, sponsors shied away, he appeared on fewer and fewer programs. Finally, he was without a job. And then . . .

"I stayed drunk for a year and two months," Norman told me years later during an interview for the *News*.

As a matter of fact, during World War Two, I had seen him one afternoon on a subway train, bleary-eyed, in shabby, wrinkled clothes; but before I could speak to him he had got off at Times

Square. He was working at that time as a common laborer in an airplane factory on Long Island, unhappy and desolate away from the microphone. Then he turned up in Washington and begged an old friend to give him another chance. As a result, he became an announcer again over WWDC; but the man whose income had been two thousand dollars and more a week was now drawing only fifty dollars every payday.

"Then I started drinking again. I just couldn't resist it." Broken-shire said. "One night I was so tight that I collapsed and my friend, the boss, gave me a shot in the arm. The next day I awoke in an institute for alcoholics. There they gave me the cure—but it didn't work.

"So I left Washington and returned to New York. I was determined to start all over again in the town where so many had known me both as a great success and a miserable failure. I walked Broadway, Madison Avenue and the streets of Radio City for months. I haunted the offices of networks, stations, advertising agencies and talent men. I begged and I pleaded. But no one—no, not one—would give me a job. They said they couldn't trust me and, to tell you the truth, I couldn't blame them.

"Then, one evening, I ran into another old friend. He told me that he was radio director of Alcoholics Anonymous and invited me to go to a meeting with him out in Forest Hills. I did and found there every type of person, from truck drivers to college professors.

"While sitting there, listening to the speakers, something inside of me started whispering: 'Norman, just try! You can be a great guy again.'

"And, do you know, right there I made what to me was a great discovery: As an alcoholic, I was a sick person, and there was only one way to combat this illness—Don't taper off; don't do it gradually; just quit drinking completely. Don't touch the stuff at all.

"Well, I decided to try it for just twenty-four hours. It was tough, but I kept reminding myself it was just for twenty-four hours. And now, I'll tell you how I succeeded in living through that first night and day without a drink. I did it by creating and focusing my mind on two mental pictures. In one I was a dirty bum, drunk, in jail. My wife and family were in tears; my friends disgusted. In the other,

I was the guy I had been and knew that I could be again, successful, respected, with money, a fellow who could do some good in this world.

"When the craving for a drink became strong, almost unbearable, I concentrated harder and harder on these pictures. I wouldn't let go of them. Finally, the twenty-four hour period was up and I said to myself that I'd try it for another twenty-four. Then the next day, I did it all over again. And it worked, taking it step by step, just one day at a time.

"Of course, I couldn't have done it by myself. The A.A.'s helped me; encouraged me; stayed with me. With their aid, I licked this thing, and in the years that have passed since then I haven't had a single drink.

"My friends drink socially and I don't mind it one bit. My desire for it is gone. You see, it's okay to drink socially, if one isn't an alcoholic. But if one is—then even one sip is fatal. Now I'm giving my spare time to straightening out others who are in the same fix I was. I've done that with several hundred—and today I'm really a happy guy."

This is the story as Norman Brokenshire himself told it to me one night during dinner in New York's Chambord restaurant, an establishment not usually frequented by non-imbibers. The next time you tune him in you will realize that you are listening not only to one of the pioneers of radio but to a man who fought a great battle with himself—and won it.

During the first years of broadcasting, I also knew another celebrated figure, Dr. Walter Damrosch, who did more than any other American to bring about a mass love of good music. At the urging of President Aylesworth of NBC the good doctor brought to radio in October, 1928, a series of concerts which made Beethoven and Wagner fans of millions of youngsters and grownups, too. Known as "The Music Appreciation Hour," this program reached a weekly audience of more than five million schoolchildren.

Doctor Damrosch sat at a piano to explain and illustrate themes of symphonies and operas, excerpts of which were played by the men of his New York Symphony Orchestra. He had such a casual, friendly and unpatronizing manner that the doors to the works of the masters were unlocked for the first time for multitudes who had scorned anything with the slightest taint of the "highbrow." NBC issued manuals covering each season's concerts for classroom use and soon these weekly musicales became part of the curricula of schools throughout the country.

During the many years this feature remained on the air, it proved not only that broadcasting is an ideal medium for educational purposes, but also that educational programs can be entertaining. As a direct result of "The Music Appreciation Hour," local symphony orchestras throughout the land are today giving concerts for children.

One afternoon I chatted with him in his office at NBC; the imposing-looking man with the gentle face and the twinkling eyes was beaming as he showed me some of his fan mail. During his first year on the air, he told me, he had received more than a million letters. "And 95 percent of them are not from highbrows," he said.

I copied one written by a farm wife, near Des Moines, Iowa. It read:

I'm miles from the nearest village. During the winter days it gets mighty cold and lonesome out here. Months go by without my leaving this place and the only contact I have with the outside world is the little radio my nephew put together.

One day, by accident, I heard your program. What you said about Beethoven being deaf interested me because I'm kinda hard of hearing, too. At first I didn't understand some of the music you and your orchestra played, but I listened just the same. Now, I always tune in, because I like it. All those famous composers like Beethoven, Mozart, Brahms and Chailkolsky [sic] were names I hardly ever heard before. I mean I heard them but didn't know anything about them. But now I do know; and I also love the pieces they wrote. You see, Dr. Damrosch, they're really beautiful and when you explain it they're not so hard to understand, after all.

The famous conductor handed me another letter. It was from a man in Boston at a Beacon Hill address and was signed with initials:

Discriminating listeners will condemn rather than approve of your efforts to improve the musical tastes of the "people." Music, like painting, has always been an aristocratic art, tenderly nurtured by nobility,

Thomas Alva Edison was 79 years old when he appeared on radio in 1926.

NBC photo

On February 22, 1929, an NBC radio mobile unit made contact with an airplane, bringing the pilot's voice into the homes of listeners around the country.

NBC photo

Eddie Cantor, one of radio's earliest stars, feuded endlessly with critics. His acute sensitivity once led to a group libel suit, a landmark of jurisprudence. (See p. 135.)

NBC photo

Some of Red Skelton's characters have been Junior, the Mean Widdle
Kid, Clem Kadiddlehopper, Willy Lump-Lump, Bolivar Shagnasty,
J. Newton Numskull, and Deadeye. Here he is in 1939, 26 years old
and already a national personality.

NBC photo

The gifted Fanny Brice played Baby Snooks.

NBC photo

Arturo Toscanini was signed by NBC to conduct its symphony orchestra
in 1937. For his weekly concerts, the maestro rehearsed the orchestra
three afternoons, usually from 3:30 to 5:30—a rugged schedule for a
man in his eighties.

NBC photo

Bob Crosby in 1935. On his radio show he featured such up-and-coming girl singers as Jo Stafford, Kay Starr, and Peggy Lee.

NBC photo

The banjo-playing Harry Reser led the Clicquot Club Eskimos.

NBC photo

Will Rogers and Charles Winninger, January, 1935.

CBS photo

Captain Henry (Charles Winninger, right), used to say, "It's only the beginning, folks!" on "The Maxwell House Show Boat," one of radio's first variety shows. Other stars included Pat Padgett and Pick Malone as Molasses 'n' January, Aunt Maria, Irene Hubbard, and Annette Hanshaw.

NBC photo

Paul Whiteman, seated. From left to right, arranger Ferde Grofé, musi-
cologist Deems Taylor, entertainer Blossom Seeley and composer
George Gershwin.

Courtesy Larry Carr

Eddy Duchin, one of the country's top piano-playing bandleaders,
starred in several radio series.

NBC photo

Fred Waring and His Pennsylvanians were heard on "The Fred Waring Show." Some of the acts included Priscilla and Rosemary Lane, Les Paul, and Kay Thompson.

NBC photo

Arthur Godfrey broke into radio in 1929, over the next 12 years perfected his personal mike style, and in 1941 was a CBS network personality.

CBS photo

These two young men played the elderly codgers, Lum 'n' Abner. Photographed in November, 1933; Chester Lauck (Lum) and, on the right, Norris Goff (Abner).

NBC photo

Richard Widmark played David Farrell in "Front Page Farrell."

NBC photo

Orson Welles's most memorable radio show was his dramatization of *The War of the Worlds.* (See chapter 12.)

CBS photo

"My Friend Irma" starred Marie Wilson as Irma Peterson, John Brown as Al. In the center, Cy Howard, the director. The situation comedy moved to TV in 1952.

CBS photo

Nila Mack originated the children's radio program, "Let's Pretend."
CBS photo

A frequent guest star, radio comic George Jessel also had his own "George Jessel Show."

Dick Powell started as a sweet singer, then made a dramatic change to hardboiled private eye in the series, "Richard Diamond, Private Detective."

Frank Crummit and Julia Sanderson first broke into radio in 1929, as probably the first husband and wife team on the air. In the 40s they emceed the quiz show, "The Battle of the Sexes."

Cast of "The Aldrich Family" in 1939: (left to right) Ann Lincoln (Mary Aldrich, Henry's sister); House Jameson (Sam Aldrich, Henry's father); Katharine Raht (Alice Aldrich, Henry's mother); and Ezra Stone (Henry).

Freeman Gosden (top) and Charles Correll were familiar to millions as "Amos 'n' Andy."

NBC photo

Ted Husing reported sports bouts or gala movie premieres with equal aplomb. Here he is in May, 1937, reporting on the Hindenburg disaster.

CBS photo

A candid photo in the CBS newsrooms on V-E Day, May 7, 1945.
Robert Trout holds the mike for Quincy Howe.

CBS photo

Commentator Boake Carter, on the scene at the trial of Bruno Hauptmann, Flemington, N.J., 1935.

CBS photo

Elmer Davis, 1942. The Hoosier reporter was a tart-tongued analyst of the national scene.

Bert Gordon played the Mad Russian on "The Eddie Cantor Show."

The first feud on radio was probably between N.T.G. (Nils T. Grand-lund) and Broadway entertainer Harry Richman (seen here). They kept up a barrage of insults over New York radio station WHN.

Courtesy Larry Carr

Bob Burns and his "bazooka" were often heard on NBC in the late 30s. The military weapon was named after Bob's musical contraption.

NBC photo

Comic Al Pearce played Elmer Blurt, a very low-pressure salesman.
CBS *photo*

Jack Pearl was the beloved Baron Munchausen, whose question, "Vas you dere, Sharlie?" swept the country as a catchphrase.
NBC *photo*

Another catchphrase, "Wanna buy a duck?" was the theme of comic
Joe Penner.

Al Jolson made his radio debut very early. Here he is before a huge
NBC mike, November, 1932.

A very young Bing Crosby crooning into a primitive microphone of
the early 30s.

Courtesy Larry Carr

Russ Columbo was Bing Crosby's biggest rival in the 30s. He sang
on NBC while Bing was on CBS.

Courtesy Larry Carr

Kate Smith has grossed over 40 million dollars since her radio debut
in 1932.

CBS photo

Helen Morgan, the sultry torch singer, made frequent guest appearances on radio.

Courtesy Larry Carr

Joan Edwards and Frank Sinatra were the stars of "Your Hit Parade" in 1943.

CBS *photo*

Singer Tony Martin was featured on Glenn Miller's big Air Force radio show in 1943–44.

The songstress with one name, Hildegarde, was a radio favorite during World War II.

In his heyday, Rudy Vallee earned more than $300,000 a year. His "Rudy Vallee Show" was one of the most popular on the air. Seen in an August, 1936, airing: (left to right) Charles Butterworth, Helen Vinson, Fred Perry, and Rudy.

NBC photo

"And now smile a while with Lorenzo Jones and his wife Belle." Karl Swenson and Betty Garrett played Lorenzo and Belle.

NBC photo

Longtime radio favorites George Burns and Gracie Allen, May 20, 1949.
CBS photo

The cast of "Pepper Young's Family," 1938.

NBC photo

Jack Benny, Eddie "Rochester" Anderson, and the Maxwell—one of radio's oldest running gags.

CBS photo

Jack Benny and Mary Livingston in 1933, one year after Jack's radio debut on the Ed Sullivan Show.

NBC *photo*

One of the most delightful "feuds" on radio was the one between Jack
Benny and Fred Allen.

NBC photo

Kenny Delmar, the voice of Senator Claghorn ("that's a joke, son!"),
and Fred Allen.

NBC photo

Minerva Pious played Mrs. Nussbaum on "The Fred Allen Show."
NBC photo

Dorothy Lamour, Charlie McCarthy, and Edgar Bergen, May, 1937.
NBC photo

Ed Wynn, 1936. The comedian also owned a short-lived radio network, the Amalgamated Broadcasting System. The flag station of the ABS still exists, as radio station WNEW, New York. The EW in the call letters stand for Ed Wynn.

NBC photo

Kay Kyser usually wore the academic robes, but Bob Hope turned the tables on the Old Professor in this November, 1944, photo.

NBC photo

Entertaining the troops: Bob Hope and Bing Crosby at Santa Ana Army Air Base, March, 1944.

NBC photo

In April, 1939, David Sarnoff, President of RCA, dedicated the RCA Building at the New York World's Fair. Note the heavy headset worn by the assistant director behind the cameraman, who is aiming a cumbersome television camera.

NBC photo

This was the first televised sporting event—a baseball game in Manhattan between Columbia and Princeton, May 17, 1939.

NBC photo

Ed Sullivan's television show debuted as "Toast of the Town," June, 1948. Here he's seen with composer Irving Berlin, at a special 90-minute edition of "The Ed Sullivan Show," celebrating Berlin's 80th birthday in 1968.

CBS photo

Lawrence Welk's long-running ABC show began in 1955. The bandleader-accordionist (left) has led a band since 1925.

ABC photo

Milton Berle was the first major entertainer to head his own TV show—
"The Texaco Star Theater" in 1948. His popularity was so great that
Tuesday night was known as "Berle Night."

NBC photo

"Your Show of Shows," which starred Sid Caesar, first hit television as "Admiral Broadway Revue" in 1949. Its 90-minute productions starred (left to right) Imogene Coca, Howard Morris (tending bar), Sid, and Carl Reiner (in the double-breasted suit).

NBC *photo*

"Your Hit Parade" ran from 1950 through 1959. It starred (left to right) Russell Arms, Gisele MacKenzie, Dorothy Collins, and Snooky Lanson. Other singers featured through the years included June Valli, Eileen Wilson, Tommy Leonetti, Jill Corey, and Johnny Desmond.

NBC *photo*

Howdy Doody and his live partner, Buffalo Bob Smith. The children's show ran from 1947 to 1960.

"Lassie" first wagged its tail in 1955.

Dean Martin split with madcap comic Jerry Lewis in 1956, and went on to become one of TV's biggest stars.

NBC photo

Jack Webb played Sergeant Joe Friday on "Dragnet."

NBC photo

Raymond Burr (left) was the unflappable criminal lawyer on "Perry Mason," the popular show based on Erle Stanley Gardner's novels.

CBS photo

Rod Serling's program, "The Twilight Zone," was an offbeat dramatic series. Here, Ruta Lee and Patrick O'Neal co-star in "A Short Drink From a Certain Fountain," a story about an aging man who takes a shot of youth serum.

CBS photo

"Alfred Hitchcock Presents" was produced and hosted by the famous
movie director from October 2, 1955, through Sept. 25, 1960. The
mystery drama series returned to CBS as "The Alfred Hitchcock
Hour" on Sept. 20, 1962, and ran until Sept. 18, 1964.

CBS photo

Host Bud Collyer (standing) with panelists Tom Poston, Peggy Cass, Orson Bean and Kittie Carlisle (left to right), on "To Tell the Truth." The panel·show was a CBS feature from Dec. 18, 1956, through May 22, 1967.

CBS photo

E. G. Marshall questions a witness on "The Defenders." This prize-winning series was originally a two-part drama on "Studio One."

CBS photo

All regular programming stopped for three days, as the nation mourned
the death of President John F. Kennedy, November 22, 1963. Mrs.
Kennedy waits for the car in front of the White House which will take
her and her children to the Capitol rotunda, where her husband lies
in state.   *CBS* photo

"Face the Nation" interviewed Nikita Khrushchev, during his visit to
the United Nations, June 2, 1957.

CBS photo

The American flag has been planted on the moon and Astronaut Neil Armstrong goes about his duties on this epochal telecast. The Luna Module can be seen in the background.

CBS photo

"The Andy Griffith Show" ran for eight seasons, from October 3, 1960, through Sept. 16, 1968. Don Knotts, left, played deputy Barney Fife, and Andy Griffith was Sheriff Taylor of Mayberry.

CBS photo

Irene Ryan as Granny, Donna Douglas as Elly May (center), and Buddy Ebsen as Jed Clampett starred in "The Beverly Hillbillies." It began its eighth season on Sept. 24, 1969.

CBS photo

Mary Tyler Moore was Laura Petrie and Dick Van Dyke was her husband, TV writer Rob Petrie, on "The Dick Van Dyke Show," which ran from October 3, 1961, through September 7, 1966.

CBS photo

Jackie Gleason, Art Carney, Sheila MacRae (lower left) and Jane Kean in "The Honeymooners" on "The Jackie Gleason Show." "The Honeymooners" feature was introduced on "The Cavalcade of Stars," with Pert Kelton as Gleason's "Alice."

CBS photo

"The Lucy Show" succeeded "I Love Lucy," perhaps TV's most popular show. Both starred Lucille Ball, seen here with Vivian Vance and Gale Gordon.

CBS photo

Satirizing the espionage stories which flourished in the 60s, "Get Smart" featured Don Adams and Barbara Feldon.

CBS photo

"Hogan's Heroes," premiered on September 17, 1965, and made stars of Bob Crane as Colonel Hogan and Werner Klemperer as Colonel Klink.

CBS photo

Peter Pan (Mary Martin) soars into space before an awed audience of Wendy (Maureen Bailey), Michael (Kent Fletcher), and John (Joey Trent), in "Peter Pan," the perennially popular musical version of Sir James M. Barrie's fantasy.

NBC photo

"The Hallmark Hall of Fame" set high standards for television adaptations of important dramas. Starring in the April 28, 1959, production of Eugene O'Neill's "Ah, Wilderness," were Lloyd Nolan, Helen Hayes, Burgess Meredith, and Betty Field.

NBC photo

"Playhouse 90's" second presentation was "Requiem for a Heavyweight," starring Keenan Wynn, Jack Palance and Ed Wynn, on October 11, 1956.

CBS photo

the church and the upper levels of society who patronized the great
composers and interpreters. Opera, symphony and chamber music have
been, and still are, the pleasures of ladies and gentlemen of high stand-
ards and of impeccable tastes. They alone are responsible for the crea-
tion of masterpieces. Inviting the rabble into this fold will inevitably
result in a fatal lowering of standards. You and others who encourage
this are sinning against the very spirit of music. Let the hoi polloi revel
in the trash of Tin Pan Alley; but, for heaven's sake, keep them out of
Symphony Hall.

Damrosch smiled and shook his head. "There are people who
think like this. I have about fifty letters of this kind; they do represent a minority view. But I happen to believe in democracy and I'm
convinced that eventually the musical level of this country will not
be lowered but lifted to an undreamt-of degree."

More than twenty years later, James B. Conkling, president of
Columbia Records, told me that more than 40 percent of all records
sold during the last few years were "classical"—operas, symphonies,
etc.

"There are thousands of school symphony orchestras in the
United States," Conkling said. "Also many stations such as WQXR
in New York which devote most of their air time to good music.
And despite the success of the Johnnie Rays and other popular singers among the teen-agers, there is a regular Mozart craze sweeping
the high schools and college students of the country."

Also, in addition to the young folk, there are millions of the older
generation who "grew up" on the classics. They were the pupils of
Dr. Damrosch's "Music Appreciation Hour."

The harvest of the seeds sown three decades ago are being reaped
today. *Billboard,* the entertainment-world weekly, reported on April
10, 1954, that during the preceding year classical music had grossed
"an estimated $125,000,000, mostly from record sales and concert
attendance." Furthermore, to the amazement of its readers, the
story continued: "Americans last year spent more money attending
concerts than baseball games!" The figures, given by Marks Levine,
president of the National Concert and Artists Corporation, were
$50,000,000 for concerts and $40,000,000 for the so-called national
pastime.

Although the "classics" were regarded as a necessary evil rather than a joy by most broadcasters of Damrosch's time, there were some first-rate interpreters of great music on the air in those days: John McCormack, Lucrezia Bori, Ernestine Schumann-Heink, Emilio di Gorgoza, Reinald Werrenrath, Reed Miller, Frances Alda, among the vocalists; and such instrumentalists as John Powell, pianist; Albert Spalding, violinist and Georges Barrere, flutist. But, even more important were the series of symphonic concerts which were beginning to be broadcast on a regular schedule—those of the New York Philharmonic, New York Symphony, and the Boston and Philadelphia orchestras.

It was on October 5, 1930, that CBS started its Sunday afternoon New York Philharmonic airings from Carnegie Hall, with Erich Kleiber as the conductor. Carried by only sixteen stations, the venture was regarded as daring in those days. In fact, when young William Paley, president of the network, suggested to his board an entire season of the famous orchestra, fellow directors of the company told him: "You're crazy. There isn't an audience for good music." Paley answered that he would "make an audience," and proceeded to close the deal with the Philharmonic, providing for a fee of only fifteen thousand dollars for the entire season of 1930!

Today, these Sunday concerts are heard by millions over almost two hundred stations in the United States, and many in Canada, Hawaii and Alaska. And the popularity of serious music led eventually to the creation of a great network concert orchestra, the NBC Symphony, conducted by that titan of music, Arturo Toscanini.

With broadcasters groping for new formats throughout the 1920's, that phenomenon, the quiz show, came into being. The original intent of these parlor games played before microphones was to test the knowledge of contestants. Soon, however, these periods degenerated into carnivals of slapstick, with the ability to plop a custard pie into someone's face considered of more importance than memorizing an encyclopedia. "Truth or Consequences" and "People Are Funny" blossomed into the finest flowers of this ilk.

No wonder that in 1938 the literate "Information Please," with Clifton Fadiman as emcee, and Franklin P. Adams, John Kieran and Oscar Levant on the panel, was hailed as a veritable sensation.

Along with "Quiz Kids," it is still recalled as the quiz show which placed a premium on intelligence.

But the few exceptions could not stem the tide of childish hokum which inundated the air-waves. Having exhausted the available supply of horseplay, during the 1940's these shows became transformed into a major calamity—the "giveaways." Most of these operated on the premise that jackpot prizes are more important than talent. "Stop the Music," the undisputed champion of these raucous revels, in 1948 and 1949 was distributing gifts valued at $150,000 weekly to its listeners. No other program—not even Fred Allen's—could compete against it. The lure of a free refrigerator, plus a car, a mortgage-free house, an all-expense-paid trip to Paris, and a score of other prizes, was mightier than that of the comedian's astringent wit. Even though a recent U.S. Supreme Court decision held that such shows are legal, these offerings are not entertainment but incitements to human cupidity.

Although the popularity of the quiz has carried right over into television, only two giveaways—"Strike It Rich" and "Break the Bank"—have achieved high ratings in the new medium. Other types of question-and-answer programs and games now constitute more than 20 percent of regular season items, with a marked increase during the summer months. This is much too much and the result is boredom.

Of the guessing games, CBS' "What's My Line?" is by far the most entertaining. With a simple but amusing format and about the most appealing panel on the air—John Daly, emcee, plus Dorothy Kilgallen, Arlene Francis, Steve Allen and Bennett Cerf—it is also the most imitated program in television. And among the imitators, its own producers, the king of panel showmen, Goodson and Todman, are the worst offenders. All of these attempts—unsuccessful—to foist carbon copies on the public only demonstrate the lack of new ideas in broadcasting.

The formative years of radio developed not only new types of air entertainment, but also brought startling changes in blackface comedy. As evidence of this, there were Amos 'n' Andy. The first time I heard of them was in 1926, when a friend in Chicago reported that two vaudevillians, Freeman Gosden (Amos) and

Charles Correll (Andy), had created a sensation on WGN under the team name of Sam 'n' Henry. Two years later they were on WMAQ, billed as Amos 'n' Andy, because they were unable to use their former names, the property of the Chicago *Tribune* outlet.

During the early months of 1929, President Aylesworth of NBC used to tell me, "These boys are different from any other comedians you ever heard. They're great; but there's one thing odd about them: they don't have many jokes."

At that time, the Chicago offices of the network were in charge of an enthusiastic young man named Niles Trammell, who had the reputation of being the greatest time salesman in radio. He also knew programs, a combination of factors which eventually led him to the presidency and to the board chairmanship of NBC. Niles was so enthusiastic about Amos 'n' Andy that Deac Aylesworth, after long consideration, agreed to audition them for a network booking. The result was that they were spotted in a five-day-a-week fifteen-minute series under the sponsorship of a toothpaste manufacturer and made their national network debut from Chicago on August 19, 1929.

Theirs was a radical departure from the blackface comedy of the time.

Throughout the fifteen minutes the listeners failed to hear even one joke. Gags and wisecracks, such as marked the routines of the two most popular blackface comedians of that day, Moran and Mack, were completely missing. This evidently disappointed some critics. One, writing in a New York paper, said: "Amos 'n' Andy are the biggest fiascos in radio. If they're funny, I have no sense of humor."

Exactly twenty-one years later, during a party given at the Waldorf-Astoria by CBS to celebrate Amos 'n' Andy's coming to television, Gosden said to me: "I still remember that only you and a few others among the professional critics saw anything in our first skit. Most of them did not realize that we were after the creation of character, not gags. We believed then and believe now that once you establish your characters, if they're likeable, the public will become fond of them. All you have to do then is to put them into recognizable situations. You don't have to have a laugh in every line to be funny. This, I think, applies not only to radio and TV but to the theatre and books."

How right Correll and Gosden were in their ideas of radio comedy was demonstrated in less than a year, by which time almost every teen-ager in the country was repeating Andy's "I'se regusted" and Amos' "agh-wah-agh-wah!" "The Kingfish," "Brother Crawford" and "Madame Queen" became as well known as the President. Their series, the first fifteen-minute across-the-board strip in radio, attained such popularity that movie houses were forced to install receivers in their lobbies so that their patrons might not miss Amos 'n' Andy. And in Atlantic City, merchants and concessionaires, to combat the desertion of the famed Boardwalk by thousands at 7 P.M., placed loud-speakers in the street intersections, thereby enabling their patrons to hear their favorite comedy show. Prior to this, when NBC changed the broadcast time of the blackface pair, the state legislature of Colorado and scores of city councils passed resolutions protesting the sacrilege!

Correll and Gosden received their ultimate recognition when Herbert Hoover, President of the United States, requested Aylesworth to bring them down to Washington for a visit.

I asked Deac to tell me about this session and he said, "We spent a long time with the President and the boys told some of their best stories. But the payoff was that, before it was over, the usually aloof Mr. Hoover was reeling off some of *his* jokes, and he kept it up for more than an hour!"

From 1928 until 1943, Amos 'n' Andy were on the air without a vacation, save during the summer of 1934. In '43 they switched to a half-hour program. The TV version of the series with an all-Negro cast attracted more than sixteen million viewers a week; but neither it nor the thirty-minute weekly radio broadcast has ever equaled the impact of the original fifteen-minute program. That little five-a-week show drew 2,400,000 letters from listeners who had been asked to suggest a name for Amos 'n' Ruby's "first child." (Arabella, by the way, was the winner.) And many years ago, when this same Ruby became ill (in the script), sixty-five thousand fans wrote to express hopes for her early recovery. Then, after her condition took a turn for the worse, eighteen thousand indignant Amos 'n' Andy addicts threatened that, if she died, they would boycott the sponsor's product. Needless to say, she soon regained her health! But all of this was mild to the commotion created by Madame Queen's "breach of promise" suit against Andy, in 1933. The suspense became so intense that a dozen cases of nervous breakdowns were reported among housewives who were worried over the outcome. And on the evening of the denouement, thousands of calls tied up the switchboards of radio stations and newspaper offices from callers who had missed the broadcast and demanded to know whether "Andy got hooked."

Now past its ten-thousandth airing, Amos 'n' Andy is still a top attraction, a hallowed bit of Americana. Audiences become satiated and styles in comedy change; and yet it is perhaps of some significance that the program's satiation point was reached only after its format had been changed, placing a greater emphasis on bright retorts and "snappy" dialogue than on characterization.

While Correll and Gosden were riding high during the 1930's, the drama written specifically for the microphone began to achieve a respectable status. Arch Oboler, Norman Corwin and Archibald McLeish were primarily responsible, the first two products of radio and the third a distinguished poet.

Oboler, now a Hollywood picture producer, wrote the first air dramas employing the stream-of-consciousness technique. Corwin, today with the United Nations, pioneered in the documentary form and created a number of plays in verse—among them *Untitled* and *On a Note of Triumph* which won applause in the literary supplements. Along with the playwrights of CBS' experimental "Workshop," they brought an adult approach to a field when it was still in its one-syllable stage.

The plays of these men, however, were microscopic islands in the seas of sentimentality which swamped American radio. For that was the heyday of the soap opera.

As far back as 1925, Marian and Jim Jordan, a husband-and-wife vaudeville team, who later became famous as "Fibber McGee and Molly," had presented over a Chicago station a series of sketches concerned with "The Smith Family." An "average" American

household, it was the ancestor of all the thousands of such con-
coctions which have since cluttered the American air-waves.

But long before that, the raindrop had turned into a cloudburst.
For "Amos 'n' Andy," "The Goldbergs" and "Pepper Young's Family"—among the few stressing the comic note—had to come to the
air. Also "Ma Perkins," "Just Plain Bill," "Stella Dallas," "Myrt
and Marge," "Life Can Be Beautiful," "Front-Page Farrell," "The
Road of Life" and their likes already had or were about to make
their debuts before the microphone. And by the time the 1940's
had arrived, a husband-and-wife team, Frank and Anne Hummert,
of the Blackett-Sample-Hummert agency, were reigning as king and
queen of the country's most gargantuan soap-opera factory.

Earning a combined income of more than $150,000 a year, they
knew exactly what they wanted. And that was a deft merger of
soothing syrup, folksiness and heartbreak. They directed a corps of
hack writers whose millions of sentimental words produced enough
tears among the housewives of the land to create tidal waves in both
the Atlantic and the Pacific.

Critics raged and learned professors wrote scholarly tomes prov-
ing that this form of entertainment was a menace. A prolonged diet
of such pap, they warned, would surely undermine the mental
health of the American female. The soap opera, even the minor
crises of which involved bigamy, wife desertion or brain surgery,
would produce, they said, a race of neurotic women. Their afflic-
tions would include advanced hypochondria and an irresistible impulse to escape from reality. But deaf to such voices of doom, the
housewife continued her daily immersion in tears, and just before
World War Two, two major sponsors of such serials, Procter and
Gamble and Lever Brothers (both, appropriately enough, soap
manufacturers), were the biggest time-buyers in radio.

But the product of the continued-in-our-next-installment school
was not all dross. Some, such as Carlton Morse's "One Man's Family," finally attained enough stature to become weekly nighttime
shows on both radio and TV. The popularity of the dramatic form
led to the whodunits—"Sherlock Holmes," "The First Man," "Mr.
and Mrs. North," etc. Hundreds of these came to the air which, for

a long time, seemed to be inhabited solely by sophisticated private eyes who could solve any crime the dumb coppers couldn't. The soap opera and whodunit have now found new homes on television —a statement which will not come under the heading of news to any viewer. Neither has changed its format, however. This is especially true of the teary "cliff-hangers." "Valiant Lady," "Guiding Light" and "Love of Life" bring before the cameras the same collection of woes which benumbed the radio listener of two or three decades ago.

Another type of dramatic offering—superior in literacy to the soap opera, but still no more than a clever form of hack writing— won the largest audiences of all. These were the "situation comedy" series, well represented by the long-running "Aldrich Family," and the shows employing countless variations of the boy-meets-girl formula. By far the most popular of the latter was "The Lux Radio Theatre" (now on TV), which featured the stars of Hollywood in adaptations of their motion pictures. Cecil B. de Mille, famed for his movie spectacles, was its most celebrated producer and "host."

He became the central figure of one of the most violent controversies in the history of radio—a *cause célèbre* demonstrating the power of the entertainment craft and talent unions. In August, 1944, the American Federation of Radio Artists (AFRA) levied a one-dollar assessment on its members to fight a proposed open-shop law in California—an assessment which de Mille, a political conservative, refused to pay. Although he argued that the levy violated his rights as an individual, the union suspended him. This made it impossible for him to perform on any station; but the producer obtained a temporary injunction and, while the matter was under consideration, continued to appear on the air. The California courts, however, ruled against him and the U.S. Supreme Court finally refused to review the case. As a result, de Mille disappeared from radio (and TV) on April 19, 1948. Since then, as a matter of principle, neither AFRA (now the American Federation of Radio and Television Artists) nor the producer has receded from their respective positions. So, because of a dispute over the payment of a dollar, one of the world's most famous movie-makers is barred from broadcasting.

During the period in which the unions—especially James Caesar Petrillo's American Federation of Musicians—became dominant factors in the broadcasting picture, radio already had nurtured a group of microphone giants. But it had done little as yet to develop one of the greatest sources of its strength—its ability to disseminate news, both factual and interpretative. Almost a decade passed before the famous reporters and commentators of the air-waves came into their own.

During the 1930's, with Roosevelt, Hitler, Mussolini and Stalin, the New Deal, Fascism, National Socialism, the Anschluss, Munich and finally World War Two on the front pages, the men of the newsroom shared the top ratings with comedians and singers. Those years and the years of the next decade brought to their full heights Floyd Gibbons, spouting stories at the rate of 217 words a minute, H. V. Kaltenborn, Walter Winchell, William Shirer, Max Jordan, Edward R. Murrow, George Hicks, Eric Sevareid, Bill Downs, John Daly, John B. Kennedy, Elmer Davis, Boake Carter and Gabriel Heatter. Directors of news and special events Abe Schechter of NBC and Paul White of CBS were suddenly transformed from minor functionaries into magnificos of aerial journalism. Commanding dozens of foreign correspondents, they deployed their microphone minions to all quarters of the globe and issued their commands via short wave over far-flung seas and continents.

At home and abroad, the reporter at the microphone became a fixture wherever the headlines of history were being made. Radio extracted the full drama out of that never-to-be-forgotten first inaugural of President Franklin Delano Roosevelt in 1933. It highlighted every detail of the most sensational legal process of the century, the trial in Flemington, New Jersey, of the kidnapper-murderer of the Lindbergh child, Bruno Richard Hauptmann, in 1935. And on the night of Hauptmann's death in Trenton's electric chair, radio stirred countless millions with Gabriel Heatter's marathon ad-lib broadcast, a feat which propelled him from the ranks of minor newsmen into a $3,500-a-week commentator.

Is there anyone who sat beside a loud-speaker at the time who can not recall that tragic morning of September 1, 1939, when the air-waves crackled with news of Hitler's invasion of Poland? Who can erase from memory that first radio flash about the Japanese attack on Pearl Harbor, on the afternoon of December 7, 1941? And what of the rumors, reports and finally the confirming bulletin announcing the arrival of D-Day, June 6, 1944? Or the broadcasts telling the world of the death of President Roosevelt on April 12, 1945, and the haunting descriptions of his funeral procession in Washington? And even today, with the last world war already classified as ancient history, there are some aerial eavesdroppers who live again those suspenseful moments—the agonizing false alarms, the premature celebrations, and, finally, the outburst of uninhibited joy—which marked that conflict's end.

Of this group of celebrated newsmen, H. V. Kaltenborn was the first whom I met in the course of my work. The "dean of commentators" deserves his title, for by the time I began writing of radio in 1925 he already had a loyal following over WEAF, New York. This Wisconsin-born, Harvard-educated scion of German nobility was editor of the Brooklyn *Eagle* at the time. Thus, as the first man on radio who attempted an analytical interpretation of the news, he brought to his task a background of knowledge and experience which amazed his listeners.

A sparse-haired mustachioed six-footer with friendly eyes and a kindly smile, he had an imposing presence, a spic-and-span military air and a manner of speech suggesting a pontificating college professor. It is no wonder that during the 1920's he had no competition; but even so, not until that historic day of September 12, 1938, when Adolf Hitler addressed the Nazi Congress in Nuremberg, did Hans become for a brief span the most talked-about personality in American radio. It was then that the German Chancellor in one of the most frantic outbursts of modern times issued his ultimatum to Czechoslovakia and the entire jittery globe feared the outbreak of a new world war.

Now followed what, without question, was the most dramatic and hysterical period of American broadcasting. For beginning on that September 12th, through September 30th, when the Munich Pact was signed surrendering the Sudetenland to Germany, crisis followed crisis; emergency orders, mobilizations, fervent prayers, soaring hopes and bitter despondency. Over the air, Hitler, Chamberlain, Mussolini, Daladier, Beneš, Masaryk and the Pope himself were heard. Daytime and nighttime came the reports from Nuremberg, London, Paris, Berlin, Godesberg, Prague, Budapest and Rome; Murrow, Shirer, Jordan, Stephen King-Hall and dozens of others repeated bulletins, flashes, running stories, comments and analyses. But so far as the American listeners were concerned there was one voice which rose above the others—that of H. V. Kaltenborn.

For in Studio Nine of the Columbia Broadcasting System headquarters in New York, H.V. made eighty-five ad-lib broadcasts based on the news rushed to him from the four tickers just outside the studio and on the short-wave talks of the correspondents in Europe. For the first night, he did not sleep at all; for eighteen days and nights he did not leave the premises for more than an hour, eating, shaving, bathing there and cat-napping on an army cot. By the end of that time, not only was Kaltenborn famous, but all newscasters and commentators had acquired a new status. For the first time, news had outdrawn entertainment programs and within a few weeks, news periods, hitherto neglected by sponsors, had become salable commodities.

Kaltenborn, who since then has taken part in hundreds of notable broadcasts, shared for many years with Gabriel Heatter and Eleanor Roosevelt the distinction of being "the most mimicked" voice on American radio. He has been the source of thousands of jests by comedians and is certainly the only commentator who was ever "imitated" by a President of the United States. Millions still chuckle at the memory of Harry S. Truman's "take-off" on H.V. during a dinner in Kansas City, in 1948, when the Chief Executive gave his impressions of one of Kaltenborn's election broadcasts— the gist of which was that Truman could not win.

"But I don't mind being imitated," he once told me. "After all, they don't make fun of nonentities."

Most Americans do not realize it, but H.V. has another claim to fame, if it may be called that. He is the creator of the quiz show. During the 1920's, while still on the Brooklyn *Eagle*, he conducted over several New York stations a current-events "bee" or quiz for high-school students. This, so far as records show, was the first program of the type ever broadcast and attracted so much favorable comment that soon others were airing quizzes which were not quite so educational.

"Just think," he said to me one day, "what a wealthy man I'd be if I could have protected the idea and collected a royalty on every quiz show since then!"

"You wouldn't have had to continue commenting," I said.

"But I would have anyway," he laughed.

With Kaltenborn established as the pundit of the commentators, Floyd Gibbons, one of the most picturesque figures of the 1930's, swaggered across the radio news horizon as a swashbuckling character right out of Richard Harding Davis. Handsome and rugged, more than six feet tall, with a white patch over his left eye, which he had lost during the battle of Belleau Wood while a correspondent with the Marine Brigade during World War One, he wore a close-fitting trenchcoat and a rakish fedora. Floyd also had a hearty manner and a vibrant voice which, combined with boyish laughter, impressed men and captivated women—a fellow who in every outward aspect lived up to Hollywood's conception of a war correspondent.

Floyd, always a romantic and at times a lurid reporter rather than an interpreter, was primarily a teller of adventure stories in which he played the central role. But what stories he had to tell on his NBC series, "Headline Hunters!" Spraying words like a human machine gun, he painted stirring pictures of riding beside Pancho Villa in the Mexican revolution of 1915, his pursuit of the bandit hero with General Pershing and his exploits during World War One.

Fellow reporters sometimes waxed sarcastic over his yarns in which, seemingly, he was the axis on which all events revolved; but his valor was attested by the Croix de Guerre and the ribbon of a Chevalier of the Legion of Honor which France had conferred on him. The public, of course, accepted him wholeheartedly; to it he was the Three Musketeers merged into one heroic figure before the microphone.

I met him for the first time in 1929, when he came to the *News* office to chat with me regarding his radio series. I had already heard of him from friends on the Chicago *Tribune* who had told me of a memorable appearance by Floyd on that newspaper's station WGN on a Christmas Day a few years before.

Recently returned from a lengthy stay in foreign lands, he had made his radio debut in an almost deserted studio and gave an account of his adventures in so emotional a manner that even the hard-boiled engineers were reduced to tears. In words that sang, Gibbons told how he, a forlorn wanderer, had endured Christmases away from home . . . in drab French villages . . . in the muddy trenches . . . and in desolate faraway barbaric places. . . . How good after all these years to be home again, in Chicago, his own town, where, at last he could spend a quiet Yuletide with his kin, those he loved, by the family hearth!

"Why, that old son of a gun!" a member of his family exclaimed laughingly. "He hasn't even been around the house once since he's been here!"

One night I attended with him a performance of *Clear All Wires*, a Broadway comedy in which the hero, a foreign correspondent in Moscow, had been patterned on Floyd.

"It's you all right," I ventured, for Thomas Mitchell, who portrayed the character, not only wore the Gibbons style of trenchcoat but imitated his talk and mannerisms down to the slightest detail.

"It's no such thing!" Floyd said. "I've seen this show three times and still can't see the slightest resemblance."

Often, in the company of Larry Rue, now chief European correspondent of the Chicago *Tribune*, I used to visit with Floyd in his apartment in the Winthrop Hotel on Lexington Avenue. There he and Larry, who is a famous adventurer himself, engaged in friendly arguments on the merits of the factual versus the "romantic" school of foreign correspondence. Rue contended—rightly so—that the big stories were those concerned with economics and the behind-the-scenes diplomatic maneuvers rather than the battles.

"Maybe so," Floyd grinned, "but all I know is that if I were in a town where two armies had a fight, I wouldn't give a damn about the behind-the-scenes stuff. What I'd be interested in is the shooting."

Today it is quite commonplace for famous radio and TV speakers to employ "ghosts" for the writing of their scripts. Gibbons was one of the first to indulge in this luxury. When Rue kidded him about this, Gibbons gave a seemingly logical defense of this practice.

"After a man has proved his ability as a writer—and I have— he'd be a damned fool not to have a ghost," said Floyd. "When I want to write a book, sure, I do it myself; but radio's different. A star has so many things to do besides broadcasting that he really has no time for sitting down at a typewriter. So I provide the material and my ghost comes up with a script which copies my style so closely that even I couldn't tell the difference."

In this connection, it is interesting to record that Lowell Thomas, who eventually took over Gibbons' sponsored program in 1930, also has ghosts. But, unlike Floyd, he has not hesitated to let this be known. In fact, during a banquet at the Waldorf-Astoria given to him by his sponsors, he publicly introduced his two literary "haunts" and paid them tribute.

How Thomas inherited Gibbons' program, by the way, provides a sidelight on a truly bizarre period in broadcasting. Had it not been for Floyd's love of boyish pranks, Lowell might not have become one of our most celebrated radio newsmen.

Gibbons' series of daily newscasts had been sponsored by the now defunct *Literary Digest,* and the company official in direct charge of the program was one of the country's most ardent Prohibitionists.

One moonlit night during that Saharan era, Floyd, after a session with drinking companions in a Long Island roadhouse, had a sudden inspiration. "On the way back to town," he said, "let's serenade my sponsor."

A few minutes later, their car drove up a private roadway and halted beneath the bedroom windows of the man who was paying Gibbons a sum several times larger than a royal ransom. They gave forth with catcalls and other rude noises, and finally with "Sweet Adeline." The dignified and now irascible gentleman, awakened from his slumber, rushed to a window and immediately recognized Floyd as the most vociferous of the serenaders.

"Mr. Gibbons," he shouted. "I think you'd better go home."

The next day, those on Radio Row heard that, for some unexplained reason, the *Literary Digest* was in the market for a new newscaster. CBS immediately approached Thomas, at that time a foreign correspondent, author, explorer and lecturer. It was President William S. Paley's idea to offer Thomas as a candidate for the job and then, after clinching the deal, to move the program from NBC to his own network.

The CBS brass suggested to Thomas that, as he had no radio experience, he work with some men in the news department in the preparation of an audition script. There was an immediate disagreement over the format. So Thomas decided to bring in his own "brains," several friends from his publisher's office.

On the afternoon of the day set for the audition, which was to be piped over telephone lines to the *Digest* offices at 6 P.M., there still was no script. For a new argument had broken out among the two groups, with Thomas unhappily in the middle. Finally, about 4 P.M., with a plague-on-both-your-houses attitude, Thomas sat himself down in an empty office and pounded out a fifteen-minute news program, which he completed just a few minutes before zero hour.

Evidently, the gentleman who had fired Floyd was impressed with Thomas, a reticent man almost at the opposite pole from Gibbons in outlook, personality and temperament. He was undoubtedly also attracted by the baritone speaking voice and an enunciation so clear that recordings of Thomas' broadcasts are used today in speech classes of universities. For he signed Thomas immediately and, within a few days the latter began a newscast series carried by both NBC and CBS.

But before his departure Gibbons had a good-natured revenge. On his final program, he announced that the following week he would be succeeded by a man celebrated in the world of letters. "And I do hope you'll tune him in," said Floyd, "because he's a gentleman, a linguist and a scholar." And then to make it sound still drier, he added, "Lowell Thomas is one of the world's most profound students of archaeology, philosophy, zoology, and also one of our generation's greatest experts on the dead languages!"

Had Floyd Gibbons lived to play an active role as a reporter in World War Two and in the turbulent years thereafter, it would have been interesting to observe his impact on the listeners. For, although the public continued to be receptive to accounts of mere physical action, the emphasis soon shifted to the ideological and political phases of world events. The radio and TV audiences wanted to know not only what happened—but why. Whether Floyd could have adapted himself to the change must always remain a matter for conjecture.

Whatever the answer may be, in his day Floyd Gibbons was certainly one of the most colorful figures of American broadcasting.

The newscaster-commentator of this period who had the largest number of listeners, however, was neither Kaltenborn nor Gibbons. They were topped in ratings by Walter Winchell, a former vaudeville hoofer turned columnist. He brought to the microphones a type of material new to radio, a mélange of news, gossip and intimate revelations of Broadway, Hollywood and underworld magnificos. His staccato sentences, shrill tones and brash manner detonated in calm living rooms like a Roman candle set off at a meeting of the Ladies' Aid Society.

Conservative critics and some network executives were stunned, but Winchell, who made his air debut in 1929, already had two important sponsors by 1931 over two rival major networks. Within a few years, his Sunday-night show had become a must for millions. I recall strolling one Sabbath evening for six blocks through a residential section of Birmingham and scarcely losing a word of his broadcast as his voice came through a succession of open windows. Soon he became the highest-paid newsman on the air, signed by a sponsor at $12,500 for twelve and one-half minutes of chatter on a quarter-hour show—a thousand dollars a minute.

The world's greatest actors, musicians, orators, statesmen and editors did not and still do not earn regularly so great a sum for their broadcasting efforts. Therefore, some observers asked why the words uttered by one who had made his mark as a gossip columnist should have so high a value. The sponsors gave the only answer that counts in American radio: "He brings us a bigger audience than we could get anywhere else for our money."

As I sat with Winchell one night in Lindy's during his early years on the air, he suddenly remarked: "I'm branching out."

"How?" I asked.

The dapper, youngish man with the sharp clothes, whose every intonation echoed the rasping tones of Broadway, banged a fist on the table. "Lots of important things are happening today," he said. "I'm going to talk about them."

Not long thereafter, his original gossip format, which had countless imitators, underwent a radical change. Items about the loves, the marriages, the divorces and the imminent accouchements of the great and the merely notorious were interspersed with news and comments on national and international affairs. Sentences containing expressions he had coined, such as "making whoopee" and "middle-aisling," preceded or followed terse treatises on the world's sickly state.

Many intellectuals decried Winchell's loudness, his sensationalism and the air of excitement in which he held forth on the issues of the day. But most of them, being liberals, nevertheless applauded him as the most aggressive and hard-hitting advocate of Franklin D. Roosevelt and the New Deal. One of the first radio reporters to cry out against Nazism on the American air-waves, he also sounded the tocsin against Communism at a time when such talk was regarded as hysterical alarmism. His pipelines extended to almost every department of the Government, from J. Edgar Hoover's FBI to the White House itself. It was suspected that the Administration used his broadcasts as "trial balloons," and I questioned him about this.

"That's not so," he said, "save in one instance—and that was concerning F.D.R.'s third term."

One night, after Winchell had assumed the role of a commentator on world affairs, I advised him to "tone down," to speak in a calmer, more natural manner. "After all," I said, "you don't talk in that excited way when you're away from the mike."

"Sure, I don't," he said, "but while I'm on the air it's natural for me to be keyed up."

"But considering the important issues you discuss, don't you think your overemotional manner might irritate some people?"

Winchell stared at me in amazed silence. "Okay, so they're irritated," he said. "But you and all the other critics are wrong, because you fail to realize that this manner of talking is my trademark. And once a guy's got a trademark, he's set for life. Never forget that."

During the last decade, on the few occasions I have encountered Winchell he has been as courteous and friendly as ever, but recently his thoughts seemed to be far away, as he discoursed bitterly concerning his many personal feuds and "the ingratitude of heels."

On the air, he began to shift to the right with the advent of Truman, and during 1952 his news periods became campaign appeals for Eisenhower. Today, he is the idol of the conservatives just as he was the fair-haired boy of the liberals during the era of the New Deal.

Relentless in attack, Winchell is, at the same time, more sensitive to the reactions of radio and TV critics than any broadcasting personality I know. Seldom have I made a comment about him that he has not sent me a note—either a "thank you" or a "you're wrong" communication.

At this time, Winchell looms as a more controversial figure than ever. No one, however, disputes that he has had a major impact on broadcasting, especially during the heyday of radio.

Sensitive to critical barbs but seldom revealing it, is one of my favorite comedians, Bob Hope. And like Jack Benny he is one of the champion worriers of show business, although he covers his vexations with a coat of joviality.

In the 1930's Bob, an experienced trouper in musical comedy and vaudeville, was still unsuccessful on the radio. That was because he had come to the air in the most arduous form of comedy, as a rapid-fire gag man. When a comic is bolstered with a recognizable character and appropriate situations, as Freeman (Amos) Gosden said, every line does not have to be funny. The other elements carry him. But a teller of gags is only as good as his last one, and there simply are not enough writers capable of supplying a comedian with first-rate jokes for a forty-weeks-a-year broadcasting season.

As a consequence, Hope was forced to resort to the strategy of most gag comedians: "If the first ten won't kill 'em, maybe the last five will." Such a technique, however, is a severe drain on the nerves of any performer, and Hope showed evidence of this by repeatedly trying out cracks on friends at parties and in restaurants, anxiously observing their reactions. He would be thinking of his shows at all hours; spend days working with his writers (at times numbering almost a dozen) and sometimes call them at three or four in the morning to discuss with them over the phone some "punch line" that had just come to him.

It is, therefore, a tribute to the likable personality of the man and to his insouciance that he was able eventually to triumph over the handicap of his format. For, as all of the English-speaking world knows, he became one of the most popular of all radio and movie comedians. Today he is also one of the most successful of the television funnymen, an achievement due in considerable part to his increased stress on situation rather than mere verbal byplay.

In some ways, Hope is an Anglo-Saxon Milton Berle. Off-stage as well as on, he is a bubbling fountain of jocularity, one who is unhappy unless he be "always in the act."

One day in Hollywood, while on the Paramount movie lot, I saw him rehearsing a café scene with Doris Day and Mickey Rooney. For several hours he kept his director, his fellow players and even the usually dead-pan technicians laughing with his ad-lib gags.

On another occasion in the movie city, I visited him on the same lot while he was making a picture with Arlene Dahl. Bob, dressed as a flamboyant Turk in a harem, spent at least two hours practicing a strenuous dance before the scene was finally shot. Then he quickly changed into street clothes and, in company with his press agent, Mack Millar, we drove to the NBC studios at Sunset and Vine. There he rehearsed and then taped two of his morning shows. He then dashed over to another NBC studio to rehearse for his television program. That done, he rushed to downtown Los Angeles to appear at a benefit banquet for war orphans.

Hope is one of the wealthiest men of the entertainment industry. His holdings range from ownership of a radio-TV production company and of a radio-TV station to sizable interests in his motion pictures, oil wells and the Cleveland Indians baseball team. Certainly he is under no pressure to overexert himself.

"Why do you do it?" I asked. "You don't need the money. Your friend, Bing, doesn't knock himself out this way."

"Crosby's smart," said Hope, "but me—well, I'll tell you: I don't ever really feel good unless I'm exhausted."

The armed forces have reason to be grateful for Bob's seemingly inexhaustible energy. For this English-born former resident of Cleveland has devoted more time to entertaining our servicemen abroad than any other big-name performer. Literally millions of G.I.'s have laughed at and with him in Europe, Africa, Asia and the Pacific Islands. For years, even after World War Two, he did not have a Christmas with his family, as he usually spent the Yuletide trouping in some remote corner of the world. Recently, he announced that, come what may, he would spend at least that one holiday at home. The very next day, Air Force headquarters in Washington called him and asked that he give several Christmas shows at some remote bases in Alaska. Bob muttered beneath his breath, but accepted. Then, as an unexpected present, the A.F. transported his wife there, so that for the first time in many years the Hopes might have a holiday together.

Hope's strenuous life demands that he be in first-class physical condition; so he is the athletic type. His benefit golf matches with Crosby are famous; but he also devotes himself assiduously to other forms of exercise. If you are a friend, and he asks you to dinner in New York, Bob is likely to suggest that before dining you meet him in the gymnasium of Harold Reilly's health institute in Rockefeller Center.

"I once accepted such an invitation," Syd Eiges, NBC's vice-president in charge of press relations, confided to me, "and I'm still aching. Bob made his guests ride bicycles, punch bags and mount electric horses. By the time we were ready to eat, I was ready for bed!"

ELEVEN

Names are People

"The guy's so relaxed, he makes everyone else feel tired."

Frank Fay, the stage and radio comedian, made that remark about Bing Crosby, the Mr. Take-It-Easy of all time, the lazybones folk hero of the greatest up-and-at-'em country of the world.

When I met him for the first time in the early 1920's while he was still a member of the Paul Whiteman band vocal trio, The Rhythm Boys, neither Bing nor his friends had the vaguest notion that someday he would become an international institution. If you had mentioned such a possibility to him, he might have exerted himself sufficiently to chuckle right in your face. For then he was just an easygoing, somewhat colorless young man of medium height with blue eyes and brownish hair. Those in the Whiteman crew regarded him merely as a "nice guy," and if there was any comment at all about his singing, it resolved itself to the statement that the lad had "pretty good pipes."

It was not until Whiteman, during one of his engagements at the Paramount Theatre in New York, gave Bing an opportunity to do a solo that he attracted any attention. And then, as I have already told you, it was in the form of the caustic reaction of the house manager. But, in less than two years, Bing had his revenge, for he returned as the headliner at this theatre at $6,500 a week!

Since then, via radio, movies and recordings, Crosby has become one of that select list who need no other identification than their first names. The most durable of the crooner-personalities, he has outlasted Vallee and survived by many years his onetime greatest rival, Russ Columbo. Bing is the Number One best seller of all time in popular records, his version of Irving Berlin's "White Christmas" having attained a total sale of seven million copies; he

171

is the co-owner of every picture in which he appears; and he has millions in a gigantic investment corporation, real estate, baseball, horse racing, music publishing, a research enterprise, cattle ranches and the production of filmed television shows. Dozens of writers and Bing himself have already told the story of his fabulous success, so it would be pointless to recount again any of its details.

But despite this, many still do not know how Crosby came on his trademark, the famous "bub-bub-bub-boo" interpolation during his songs. It was this which first drew attention to him. During 1931, when Bing came to CBS, this "gimmick" was publicized as being the product of much planning. Actually, what happened was that during a broadcast a sheet of music fell off the stand and Bing could not retrieve it. So he substituted "bub-bub-bub-boo" for the missing words. Those in the studio liked it so well that he deliberately inserted these meaningless sounds during his next evening's broadcast and continued to do so thereafter.

Soon, millions throughout the country were imitating Bing's trademark, including President Franklin D. Roosevelt. Eddie Cantor once told me that while he was visiting F.D.R. at Warm Springs, Georgia, to do a "March of Dimes" broadcast, the Chief Executive tested the microphone before going on the air by crooning in a cracked baritone, "When the blue of the night . . . bub-bub-bub-boo!"

During the 1930's, when Crosby was a participant in the most highly publicized radio stunt of the day, "The Battle of the Baritones," a war of song between him on CBS and Russ Columbo on NBC, certain of his advisers frowned on his informality. A young man who "was going places," they argued, should conduct himself with more dignity. The very casualness which endeared him to his listeners was anathema to them.

One evening, while attending one of his rehearsals at CBS, I heard a director correct his pronunciation of the word "tomato" which Bing uttered as "tomayto."

"You should say 'tomahto,' " the director insisted. "It's got more class."

"Listen, you Bronx peasant," Bing laughed, "I ain't saying 'tomahto' until I got a million dollars."

But years later, after Crosby had many millions, I still heard him say "tomayto."

Even in those days, Bing was an informal dresser, given to sports jackets, slacks, loud shirts and ties, but he did not attain the heights in this line until he had taken up residence in Hollywood. Also, he was what is known as a "great joker."

On one occasion, while Bing was tape-recording a broadcast in a Hollywood studio, the audience was startled to hear him announce at the end of the program: "Our guests next week will be Joe Stalin and Hamilton Fish."

It often happened that, not knowing at the time who the guests would be, Bing would ad-lib any names that came to mind. When the recording was edited for airing, these names would, of course, be eliminated and the proper ones substituted.

One day, however, after Crosby had announced one "Rudolph Schmohoper" as the featured guest, through an oversight the name was not snipped from the tape. As a result, one week there appeared on the studio admission tickets: "Guest artist—Rudolph Schmohoper" and the line was carried in newspaper listings throughout the country.

There is something about the work of entertainers who play jesters to millions which compels them to surround themselves, in turn, with their own court jesters. Thus, it is difficult to name any big name comedian from Milton Berle to Fred Allen who is not the magnet for hangers-on, stooges and odd "characters."

Crosby, too, has had his full complement of these salty personalities. There is, for example, Barney Dean, a little fellow whose perpetual assaults on the English language keep Bing in a state of mirth. Crosby has such affection for him that when he was at Santa Monica Hospital a few years ago, Barney was the only one outside of the family circle admitted to Bing's room. Ukie Shurin, a balding graduate of the borscht circuit, is another personal comedian whose presence amuses the royal crooner. And in equally high favor is "Society Kid" Hogan, a former prize fighter of dry wit and dapper demeanor. During a Hollywood party, he attempted to sing but his voice broke on a high note. "What's the matter?" asked Crosby.

It was then that the Kid gave birth to that classic retort: "Once during a fight a guy socked me in the Adam's apple and hurt my voice. But, Bing, what's your excuse?"

Although Crosby is certainly the most successful and durable of all the singers who came out of radio, Frank Sinatra had a far more meteoric rise. Also, his career abounds in enough dramatic highlights to satisfy the most plot-hungry novelist.

In many ways he was, for a considerable period, a Latin Rudy Vallee. The Maine troubadour who used his nose as an instrument of song, and the New Jersey-born son of Italian parents who employed his diaphragm both had a hypnotic effect on the females of the land. Rudy won the flappers and Frankie the bobbysoxers; and these fans were almost equally fanatical in their devotion. A radio columnist could spoof Crosby, Russ Columbo or Morton Downey and the result would be a few chiding letters. But any reference to either Rudy or Frankie in terms less worshipful than that usually accorded by a Muslim to Mohammed would bring a Niagara of abusive mail, the mildest of which threatened immersion in boiling oil. These flappers and bobbysoxers, now mothers or grandmothers, are probably the ones who send scathing notes today to writers who wax sarcastic concerning Liberace.

During the early weeks of 1943, I had heard of strange goings-on at the Paramount Theatre. Word came that a new crooner who recently had been a low-salaried vocalist with Tommy Dorsey's band was causing hysterical commotion among the teen-age girls in the auditorium. They were indulging in frenzied outbursts which brought ecstasy to the management and delight to the heart of Sinatra's young press agent, the late George B. Evans. Despite the snide suggestions of certain cynics that the publicity genius was in great part responsible for this display, the applause, the sighing and the moaning continued day after day with increasing fury.

This was good enough so far as the plebian West Side was concerned; but to the fashionable East Side and its plush night clubs the new wonder boy was still an unknown quantity. Frankie was meat to the hoi polloi of the movie presentation house; would he be caviar to the war-boom splurgers of the expensive nightclubs?

Arthur Jarwood, the owner of a fashionable nightery, the Rio-bamba, was a despondent man at the time. Because of a wartime shortage of talent, which made it impossible for him to book "names," his place was on the verge of folding. Then the establishment's press agents, Gertrude Bayne and Irving Zussman, who had not been paid for several weeks, decided that if they were to collect their back salaries it was up to them to provide the club with a sure-fire attraction.

With Harry Kilby, an agent, they finally persuaded Jarwood to book the young singer who was disturbing the peace at the Paramount. The club man was still unconvinced, however, that the move was a wise one. But Bayne and Zussman, in collaboration with Evans, now began to pull every stop of the publicity organ.

"Our object was to make Sinatra as big a name as possible, so that the Riobamba could stay open and Gertrude and I could collect our back salaries," Zussman confided to me later.

I attended that opening on a night in spring and was astounded by the impact of this new singer who looked like a mischieveous but undernourished schoolboy awaiting a pat on the head from teacher. Some of the women at the ringside tables not only applauded but screamed, and in the rear an obese matron, affected by the close atmosphere, or perhaps by an attack of indigestion, actually collapsed in a faint. This phenomenon, naturally, did not escape the eyes of the press agents and the next day the papers abounded in stories about a voice so extraordinary that women actually "passed out" when it was lifted in song.

Gertrude Bayne, as a result of this, dubbed the crooner sensation "Swoonatra," which Earl Wilson popularized. The nickname caught on and thereafter Sinatra was publicized as the "swoon" singer.

The Riobamba turned away crowds, and during Frankie's eight-week run there his salary jumped from $850 to $1,500 a week. "Swoonatra" was made; he went to Hollywood to make a movie; returned to New York for an engagement in the aristocratic Wedgwood Room of the Waldorf-Astoria; he attained a five-figure weekly salary and was deluged with radio offers. For a while during the 1940's his popularity topped even Crosby's. But with the coming of a new decade his position as a crooner began to decline; his television shows were unsuccessful and, after a series of incidents leading to a divorce from his wife, Nancy, and his marriage to movie star

Ava Gardner, Sinatra became involved in a violent controversy with the press. His popularity sank to its nadir; but eventually he made a sensational comeback. In the movie version of *From Here to Eternity* the singer gave evidence of hitherto-unsuspected dramatic talent and to nationwide acclaim walked away with Academy Oscar.

The crooning vogue which had abated somewhat after the heydays of Vallee, Crosby and Columbo received its most powerful push from the Sinatra craze. He was directly responsible for the later popularity of Perry Como, Dick Haymes, Tony Martin, Eddie Fisher and the others who followed.

As Bing Crosby admits and Rudy Vallee does not, crooning at best is only mediocre singing. Some even go further and say it is a bastardization of the art. But Sinatra at least did bring an element that up to his time had been missing—a touch of Italian bel canto. And among his successors, Tony Martin and Eddie Fisher have this to a high degree.

One night while chatting with Sinatra, I remarked that if he had had training he might have become an opera or concert singer.

"I think you're right," he said. "Although I've grossed millions and made far more than any Metropolitan Opera star, I still can't read a note of music. But get this straight. I'm not untutored. I've studied with a great singing teacher."

"Tell me the truth, Frankie," I said, "wasn't that bobbysoxer hysteria during your first appearance at the Paramount pumped up by your press agent?"

The Voice became indignant. "That's a malicious rumor," he said. "The bobbysoxers went for me because my singing did something to them. And I want you to know that I have deep respect for those girls. Most of them are young, enthusiastic and sincere."

I, for one, could not share his regard for the bobbysoxers. To my mind they were frightening exhibits of juvenile deliquency. I do not refer to the normal female teen-agers who had or have crushes on entertainment idols. They are part of a commendable and great tradition. But I do mean the hordes of brawling loud-mouthed, pushing girls who all but committed mayhem in quest of autographs, made broadcasts horrendous with their hysterical screams, cluttered the entrances to stage doors and night clubs long after the midnight hour and often took part in barbaric demonstrations at the instigation of press agents.

One night, shortly following Sinatra's debut in the Wedgwood Room of the Waldorf-Astoria, I came into uncomfortable contact with this crew. After the singer had joined the party at our table, the maître d'hôtel at the door was unceremoniously pushed aside by a dozen or so unkempt girls. They rushed toward Frankie, but before they could snatch at his tuxedo buttons or pilfer his handkerchief a group of waiters converged and whisked them out of the room. One of the intruders, however, managed to elude them and soon returned to Sinatra's table.

"Could I see you alone a minute, Frankie?" said this girl who could not have been a day over fifteen.

"About what?" he asked.

"Listen," she said brazenly, "how about you and me being alone for five minutes—then you'll find out?"

Fortunately, the maître d'hôtel spotted her at that moment and she, too, was escorted from the room.

Some of these "kids" were potential blackmailers. Most of the male stars I know refuse to admit girls clamoring for autographs or having other "important business" to their dressing rooms unless a witness be present. For example, Tito Guizar, the Mexican singer who also has an ardent female following, makes it a practice to have his wife beside him during all such interviews.

On several occasions, Sinatra held forth to me about the newspaper attacks on him concerning his alleged friendship with gangsters, which he emphatically denied. He was also bitter over his temporary blacklisting by the Hearst papers after he had slugged Lee Mortimer, a New York *Mirror* columnist.

"I'll tell you what's behind some of these attacks," he said. "It's the fact that I believed in what Roosevelt was trying to do and I gave myself toward helping the underprivileged. Well, I'm not ashamed—I glory in it."

Following the break with his wife, Nancy, and his courtship of Ava Gardner, Sinatra again became a "bad boy" in the eyes of not only the Hearst papers but most of the American press. He resented "the invasion of his privacy," and on the day of his wedding in Philadelphia threatened to punch a photographer, called reporters "creeps," announced that he was "self-made" and that the newspapers had nothing to do with his fame as a singer.

The natural reaction of the columnists was: Sinatra for years had sought publicity via high-priced press agents and, now, having attained it, must abide by the penalty exacted of those whose every action and word is news.

Although I had the most cordial relations with him and had never written about his private life, a few months later Sinatra snubbed me at the Beachcomber restaurant in Hollywood. He sat at an adjoining table with Ava, stared at me and gave not the slightest sign of recognition. I was one of the hated tribe of newspapermen.

Although this snub failed to inspire within me any thoughts of suicide, Sinatra's press agent, Mack Millar, brought assurances later that it had not been intentional—the Voice had simply failed to see me. Soon thereafter, under Frankie's byline there appeared in Hearst's *American Weekly* an apology to the press. In it he attributed all of his rude actions to "emotional strain." Maybe this was so; anyway, I have far more respect for a performer such as Sinatra who openly proclaims his contempt of the press than for some stars who hide their scorn beneath a gloss of hypocritical flattery.

Frankie, however, could have avoided many a heartache had he schooled himself in the fine art of accepting unfavorable criticism. The entertainment figure who could have taught him more about this than any other is Guy Lombardo.

In the big time since 1929, Lombardo has been the target of more brickbats from jazz fanatics, "modernists" and other musical sophisticates than any other bandleader in the history of broadcasting. "Square," "cornball" and "strictly from hunger" are just a few of the milder insults tossed him. But Guy has been absolutely tone deaf to the sour notes of his critics. Smiling and suave, he has gone on for twenty-five years, leading what has been the world's most financially successful dance band.

"Those who don't like me have their fancy words, but I collect the money," Guy said to me with a laugh one evening at the Hotel Roosevelt Grill in New York, where he has been regularly featured for almost a quarter of a century. He could indeed afford this light-hearted attitude, for since opening there his band has made history in many ways.

For more times than any other band, Lombardo's "Royal Canadians" have been selected as the Number One dance orchestra in the national polls of radio-TV editors; they have grossed approximately twenty-five million dollars since 1929; and even today, when "name" bands are in a period of decline, they manage to earn a tidy million dollars a year. Also, even at the height of the swing craze, 1939–40, this ensemble snared higher Hooper ratings than Benny Goodman, Harry James, Gene Krupa and other top jive aggregations.

When Guy discusses his achievements, he does so modestly but analytically, in the manner of an industrial executive expounding the merits of his plant's production system. For although the audiences see a slender dark-haired youngish man gracefully swinging a baton, behind this façade is one of the keenest business minds in the country. This is augmented by an amazingly accurate knowledge of the musical taste of the average man.

Lombardo has had a detailed mental blueprint for his operations since 1915. At that time, with his brother in London, Ont., Canada, he launched himself as the leader of a three-piece amateur band.

He has explained this system of operation to me.

"First of all, our band is basically a family unit. My brothers Carmen, Leibert and Victor have played important roles in our success. My sister, Rosemarie, used to be our vocalist and now Kenny Gardner, married to another sister, Elaine, is our singer. As for the others, most of them have been with us for many years. That's why people in music business say that an engagement with Lombardo is not a job but a career. Just like a company of actors who have played together for a long time, our men co-operate musically in a way that you won't find in many bands," Guy continued. "But there are two things even more important—the type of music we play and the fact that we produce a distinctive sound.

"First of all, we have always specialized in what is known as 'sweet' music, performed with a strong dance rhythm. We have not changed our style. What does this mean? Two things: First, our music appeals to those millions who are merely listening over the radio, for you can't have it 'sweet' unless you have melody. Second, our strong rhythm caters to those who are dancing; either in the room where we play or in their homes. So we take care of both elements.

"You see, we have never tried to win the favor of the hot jive kids among the dancers or of the modernists who care only for intricate arrangements."

"But haven't these hot jive kids made some bands overnight?" I asked.

"Sure," said Guy, "But one season they made the Casa Loma boys. Then Benny Goodman was king, or Artie Shaw. They were great all right, but didn't last.

"But look at the 'sweet' music followers. Those who liked our band in 1929 still like it. However, the high-school and college kids of the 1930's and 1940's and the 'advanced' critics who called us 'corny' did not remain loyal to their idols. They switched year after year.

"And in the meanwhile, what has happened to our little outfit? Well, as you know, the youngsters who were more interested in dancing to hot music than in romancing became more sentimental as they grew older. At that point they turned into Lombardo fans. There were millions of them, and now their children are going through the same process.

"To put it as plainly as possible: The audience of the 'sweet' music man is replenished year after year. It's as simple as that.

In my view, and Lombardo agrees with me, one of the other basic elements in his success has been the simplicity of his arrangements. "I won't play one in which the tune has been changed so completely that you can't recognize it," he said.

"And there's something else," Guy added. "I never play a song that I myself don't like. An outsider doesn't realize the terrific pressure that is brought on bands and singers by music publishers and their song pluggers to perform certain numbers. Thousands of dollars are spent in entertainment, gifts, in cut-ins and sometimes in open bribery, or what is known as the 'payola.' This sort of thing may be difficult to resist if one is a struggling bandleader with a heavy payroll to meet. But if one succumbs, he will ruin his band by playing songs which either are inferior or not suitable to its style. I have seen many orchestras go down the drain that way. That is why I have never permitted a publisher to pick up my café check or even accepted a ticket to a ball game from one. And I have never had a cut in a song."

As to the "distinctive sound" the Lombardo band produces, there can be no doubt about the role this has played in its success. Along with Wayne King's, it has been for years one of the few units which one could tune in on the radio and recognize immediately. I've received scores of letters from readers who commented that Guy achieves his musical trademark by having his men deliberately play off-pitch.

"It's not so," Lombardo told me. "It just happens that my brothers and I studied music in Canada, where they teach you to use vibrato on the saxophones. Carmen mastered this and, as a result, he has a tone produced by no other saxophone player in the United States. We adopted this for our group and also blended the tuba with the saxes and added flutes and clarinets. So this 'off-pitch' business doesn't exist at all; it's just a different tone quality that has become the mark of our band."

Little ingenious touches such as this, Guy added, are necessary to achieve lasting success in the band field. He spoke not only as an orchestra leader but as a multimillionaire, the owner of real estate, stocks, a show producer and owner of a flourishing sea food restaurant on Long Island. And he insisted that any young musician of today with imagination, stubbornness and a knowledge of what the public wants could become the Lombardo of the next decade.

By the time Guy's "sweetest music this side of heaven" became a national rage, another figure had already dominated the air-waves for a number of years. A motion-picture exhibitor and producer of stage "presentations," he was idolized by millions of Americans who knew him only by his professional name of "Roxy."

Samuel L. Rothafel, the apostle of the rococo movie cathedral, who had been hailed as a "genius" for his elaborate stage shows at the Strand, the Capitol and then the Roxy Theatre in New York, became the father of the "group" type of entertainment on the air-waves. The "Roxy and His Gang" shows preceded by some three decades the repertory company which is known to TV fans today as "Arthur Godfrey and His Little Godfreys." As the producer and emcee of his weekly divertisement over NBC, Roxy established a rapport with his listeners achieved only by Godfrey since then. Members of his musical reportory company, such as Erno Rapee, leader of the symphony orchestra; James Melton, Wee Willy Robyn, Beatrice Belkin, Caroline Andrews, Doug Stanbury, singers; and above all, Maria (Gamby) Gambarelli, the ballerina, were well known throughout the country.

During the 1920's, Roxy's radio shows pioneered in the broadcasting of the "light classics." Through a judicious use of sentimentality and a homey type of intimacy, these programs complemented the work of Dr. Walter Damrosch in building audiences for a better type of music.

Often I used to sit with Roxy in his ornate private quarters atop the theatre named after him on New York's Seventh Avenue. At his enormous desk, in the midst of velvet and shining chrome, near a luxurious private dining room and a gleaming kitchen of enamel and stainless steel, he would lean forward in his high chair and transfix me with his shining eyes. A small man, with a countenance which he sometimes confessed resembled that of Napoleon, he said to me one day in 1931, "People think of me as a showman, which I am. But, also, I am an artist with visions for bringing beauty to the common man."

"Have you any plans to announce for putting these visions into effect?" I asked.

"No; but soon enough you'll see."

And that I did, on a hot summer's afternoon in 1932. At that time Samuel L. Rothafel conducted a small group of newspapermen through a maze of scaffoldings, exposed steel girders and the cement-splashed floors of what a few months later would be dedicated as the International Music Hall, now known as the Radio City Music Hall.

Although the country was in the slough of the Great Depression, Roxy glowed with enthusiasm. This was his "baby." He had conceived the notion of this gigantic structure built to house his own special brand of entertainment. With David Sarnoff, Merlin H. Aylesworth, John D. Rockefeller, Jr., and Owen D. Young, who had available more than two hundred million dollars of Rockefeller money for the creation of Rockefeller Center or Radio City, he had spent countless days and nights in planning the details of this gargantuan amusement temple. As President Aylesworth of NBC had told me, Roxy had provided the ideas for the stage, the lighting and all of the features which would set this picture palace apart from any other on the globe.

"Some say we are foolish to open such a place in times like these," Roxy said to us, "but this is my dream, gentlemen, and I say it cannot fail!"

Then came the tragic opening night of the Music Hall on December 27, 1932. None of the more than six thousand of us who attended can forget it—for its pathetic boredom still lingers in our memories.

An audience that outdid in finery and social distinction that of a Metropolitan Opera opening was not only awed but overwhelmed by the splendor and the vastness of the place. But the show! Roxy had tried to outdo himself. He presented fifteen acts, some of them enormous sprawling spectacles, with hundreds on the stage against stunning backgrounds. There were such stars as Weber and Fields, Martha Graham and her dancers, and Ray Bolger; also the corps de ballet, the breath-taking Rockettes, a gigantic chorus and a symphony orchestra directed by Erno Rapee. The performance ran for nearly five hours, with the final curtain falling at 1:15 A.M.

In a few hours, all of the town knew that the Music Hall was a flop. Roxy and Aylesworth made frantic efforts to cut the show, which now played to less than 3,000 spectators among the 6,200 seats. Within three weeks the house had lost $500,000, and finally the première stage show was eliminated. In its place the theatre offered a feature motion picture with a brief stage presentation.

For a week or so the life of Radio City Music Hall and, in fact, of Radio City itself hung in the balance. It was only through the cajolery of Owen D. Young and of Aylesworth, that Rockefeller, RCA, and General Electric and Westinghouse (which at the time controlled RCA) contributed another $500,000 to keep the project going. If the enormous theatre had closed its doors, it is doubtful that the other Rockefeller Center structures would have been completed in that time of despondency. There might have been no Associated Press, Time and Life, British, French, International and

RCA buildings, as we know them today. But this in-the-nick-of-time injection of financial plasma saved the enterprise, and the following year NBC moved into the towering RCA edifice which since then has been the broadcasting center of the Western world.

The Music Hall and Radio City survived but Roxy did not. A few days after the opening-night fiasco he collapsed. The financial powers behind the scene denounced him as an extravagant man. Soon he was out, and a new management had taken over.

From that moment on, the Music Hall has not had a losing week. Just like Radio City itself, it has become a "must" on the list of every New York sightseer. But this is the irony of it: the type of entertainment which has drawn millions of visitors throughout these years into the vast theatre was created by Roxy himself in his happier days before he came to Rockefeller Center.

A few weeks after Rothafel had removed his personal belongings from the modernistic office atop Radio City Music Hall, I attended a party there. "I wonder what Roxy's doing now?" I remarked.

An assistant manager gave me a scornful glance, which soon changed to a tolerant smile. "You know," he said, "we don't mention that name around here any more."

Roxy was an embittered man when he died. He did not recover from that first-night tragedy and his subsequent dismissal. But, sometimes, on a cold and rainy evening as I pass the Radio City Music Hall and see block-long lines of patrons snakewinding their way to the box office, I seem to hear his words again:

"This is my dream . . . it cannot fail!"

Just about the time this great showman was passing from the scene, a young red-haired announcer almost six feet tall, with blue eyes and a mellow voice, was causing talk in Washington. Samuel L. Rothafel did not know, and certainly neither did Arthur Godfrey, that within two decades the latter would become the new Roxy of the air-waves.

This statement of course must be qualified. For Godfrey, because of television, has achieved a renown and a following which even Roxy did not have.

In one sense, Arthur does not really belong in a book devoted to the old days of broadcasting. For it is only within the last six or seven years that he has achieved top prominence, first on the radio and then on TV with his two shows, "Talent Scouts" and "Godfrey and His Friends."

But the fact is that he has been around for a long time, having made his first appearance on radio in a Baltimore amateur hour as far back as 1929. Then twenty-six years old, this impoverished son of a New Jersey newspaper and magazine writer had already served in the Navy and the Coast Guard. He had also been a salesman for cemetery lots, which led him into show business after a customer had sold him a half interest in a vaudeville act.

In Baltimore, he snared a commercial program for a pet shop and was billed as "Red Godfrey, the Warbling Banjoist." But he did not begin to attract attention until, in 1934, he joined WTOP (then WJSV), the CBS station in Washington, as an announcer. Seven years passed before he became known in New York, where the Manhattan outlet of CBS was added to his hookup following intensive plugging by Walter Winchell.

About 1945, when he began broadcasting his popular radio series, "Arthur Godfrey Time," the performer became Columbia's "most valuable property." The reason for this, commercially, was self-evident. Save for Mary Margaret McBride, he had proved himself to be the most successful salesman of the air-waves.

Why has he acquired such phenomenal popularity as an entertainer? Examine Godfrey and you will find that he is a mediocre singer, a good ukelele player and no great shakes as a comedian. His humorous remarks are certainly not in themselves quotable or witty and his serious homilies and reflections, for the most part, if uttered by some other performer would be recognized as platitudes. Yet millions find him irresistible.

What's the explanation? Godfrey is handsome in a rugged athletic manner; the women tell me he has sex appeal; his voice, resonant and tinted with warm tones, conveys an inherent magnetism; he is capricious and unpredictable; he castigates unfriendly newspapermen and criticizes his sponsors' commercials on the air; and he has a boyish impertinence which his adorers describe as "Huck Finnish."

Hundreds of my readers once contributed to a symposium designed to explain Godfrey's popularity. The reasons they gave ranged from, "Arthur's got more sex appeal than any man in the world" to "He's a kind-hearted, God-fearing, religious man." After reading these varied and often contradictory responses, all I could contribute to the discussion was a safe generality: he owes his success to "some element 'X' in his personality, which must forever remain a mystery."

An analysis of Godfrey's technique discloses many similarities to that of the late Roxy. He, too, has a "gang": Frank Parker, Janette Davis, Marion Marlowe, Lu Ann Simms, and Haleoke, the Hawaiian singer. All of the "Little Godfreys" have become personalities and all are presented as being members of "one big happy family." And, in a sense, this "stock company" format is greatly responsible, too, for the success of the highly talented comedian Jackie Gleason's show.

This was also true of the late Roxy's troupe. His listeners gained a definite notion that Rothafel was a kindly man of generous disposition, motivated only by a desire to discover and encourage young talent. They were touched by his displays of fatherly solicitude for his performers. Godfrey consistently conveyed exactly the same impression until the autumn of 1953.

In discharging singer Julius La Rosa while he was on the air and in later excusing the rude action on the ground that Julius lacked "humility," Arthur perpetrated one of the poorest public-relations gestures imaginable. This impetuous act not only raised the singer to stardom but created deep resentment among countless Godfrey followers.

No one may dispute that the Redhead had a right to dispense with the services of anyone in his employ. Even the public firing of an "underdog" was not the core of scandal. What really mattered was that Godfrey had committed a sin of which Roxy would not have been guilty: he destroyed an illusion.

Unlike those in the "trade" who recognize a troupe such as Godfrey's for what it is—a purely commercial enterprise in which friendship and loyalty play minor roles—radio and TV fans have sentimental views of their air idols. It came as a shock to them that Arthur was not the benign paternal figure presiding over a contented family. The newspaper accounts depicted him as an autocratic egotist who resented too much talent on the part of his supporting cast; and the latter was portrayed as a group torn by jealousies, romantic intrigues and petty dissensions.

The immediate reaction astounded those who believed that a public idol can do no wrong. The mail count at newspapers and, no doubt, at his network (CBS), ran three to one against Godfrey— despite the outpouring of devotion to him just a few months before when he was in a Boston hospital for a hip operation. The bulletins, reports and feature stories of his progress there were front-page news, drawing more readers than items concerned with Russia or Korea.

But suddenly Arthur had become the whipping boy. It did no good that his friends argued he is a man of basically generous nature, a person of violent likes and dislikes, completely impulsive and unpredictable and, therefore, many times capable of kindness and displays of affection. The circle of Godfrey partisans learned to their dismay what already should have been obvious: the public, after a certain period of idolatry for the heroes it has created, secretly resents them, and will, at the first opportunity, topple them from their pedestals.

What ultimate effect the controversy over Godfrey will have on his career is as yet uncertain. At this writing the ratings of his shows are still high, although he has lost some of his former popularity. Not only Godfrey, but show-business experts, students of mass psychology and, of course, his network are all eagerly trying to read the signs. The network has an especially heavy stake in his success; after all, with his billings of some seventeen million dollars a year, he is CBS' most important and profitable property.

Godfrey has a busy schedule, with his five morning simulcasts and two evening TV shows. He spends Mondays through Wednesdays in New York rehearsing and engaging in countless conferences. On Thursdays, he usually flies to his 800-acre farm in Loudon County, Virginia, where he stays until Sunday evenings. His home there, equipped with full radio and TV studio facilities, is a refuge for himself and his family—his wife, Mary, a daughter, Pat, and two sons, Dick and Mike. Holding forth in it as a millionaire squire, his establishment, to gaping tourists and natives alike, is tangible proof of the miracles wrought by broadcasting—of what a man may achieve if he has a wonderful line of gab, plus that indefinable, mysterious element "X" of personality.

In this connection, have you noticed that every radio star who has been able to make a successful transfer to television has a full measure of this intangible—"personality"? There are, for example, Jack Benny, Bob Hope, Eddie Cantor, Gertrude Berg, Eve Arden, Burns and Allen, Fibber McGee and Molly, Garry Moore and Jimmy Durante. The same is true of singers Dinah Shore, Jane Pickens and Jane Froman. And when we come to Groucho Marx, we find that he is even more popular on TV than he ever was in the elder medium. The principle also applies to shows which have developed collective "personalities" of their own, such as Ted Mack's "Original Amateur Hour" and Don McNeill's "Breakfast Club."

Another "new" name in broadcasting who has been around since the pioneer days of radio is my New York *Daily News* colleague, Ed Sullivan. The emcee and co-producer, with Marlo Lewis, of the most popular TV variety show, CBS' "Toast of the Town," he came to television only six years ago. But he was on the air even before Godfrey, as far back as 1927. Many of the most famous stars of the entertainment world, including Jack Benny, Jimmy Durante and the late George M. Cohan, made their radio debuts on his programs.

I have known Sullivan since he was a columnist on the long-defunct *Graphic* and, of course, have come into repeated contact with him since he became Broadway columnist of the *News* more than twenty-three years ago. During his early days in broadcasting, I had regarded him as a nice, friendly, sentimental Irishman, but so cold in his personality, so utterly lacking in the exuberance commonly attributed to Gaels, that he would have been the last person I should have named as a future television star.

Worthington (Tony) Miner, the noted TV play producer, evidently did not share this viewpoint. For, in 1947, after seeing Sullivan emcee the *News'* annual Harvest Moon Ball in Madison Square Garden, which was televised by CBS, he was so impressed by his work that he recommended him for the post of emcee after that network had decided to telecast a Sunday variety show.

"Tony Miner said that I was relaxed," Ed told me recently. "But now I'll let you in on a little secret. The only reason I seemed relaxed that night was because I did not realize the event was being televised. If I'd known that, I'd have been nervous as hell."

For some months after the debut of "Toast of the Town" in June, 1948, it seemed as if those who had discounted Sullivan's abilities as an emcee had been eminently correct. For he appeared before the cameras cold, stiff and, above all, unsmiling. Although even the most caustic critics admitted that the talent on his shows was of high quality, he himself became the target of some of the most scathing words ever launched at a TV performer. His detractors said that a newspaperman had "no business trying to double as an entertainer," and that here was merely another instance of a columnist who had used the prestige of his position to "blackjack" his way into a job which scores of professionals could have filled more adequately.

But these critics did not know Ed Sullivan. They failed to realize that they had taken on a tough opponent who had written in his column that, although he had "missed the boat in radio," this was not going to happen in television. And it did not, for this Broadway columnist launched a series of counter-attacks that became the talk of the television industry. First, he swung back at his critics and pointed out that he did not pretend to be a professional emcee. He was not a gag man or a wisecracker; he was merely a newspaperman introducing various acts. Next, he dug into his pockets and spent thousands of his own dollars engaging the best talent available in order to make his show a standout. For a considerable period, far from making money, he was losing a goodly sum on the venture.

After the first year or so, this effort began to pay off. The jeers and the jibes began to subside; the program climbed to the top, eventually to be recognized as Number One among all the variety shows. And, then "Dead Pan" Sullivan, known for years as "The Unsmiling Irishman," actually smiled!

He told me how this came about.

"You see, I was born with a poker face," Ed said. "I am really a very emotional person, but always had great difficulty in showing what I felt. And the fact that during my early programs on TV I was always nervous didn't help matters.

"Well, one day I met an old friend, Stan Lee Broza of WCAU,

Philadelphia. He told me frankly that I wasn't as good in TV as I had been while doing personal appearances in vaudeville. Then he asked, 'Just how do you work when you're up there on that studio stage?'

"I answered that I worked to the cameras, of course.

"Stan paused for a moment and then he said: 'Did you ever think that it might be better if you forgot the cameras and worked to the studio audience instead?'

"I remembered his advice, and the next Sunday, I did exactly that. Naturally, I did keep an eye open for the cameras, but tried to put them out of my mind. I concentrated on the audience and just that simple act gave me a wonderfully easygoing and relaxed feeling. Before I myself recognized it, I was smiling—and that, mind you, without the slightest effort! Now they're beginning to call me 'Smiling Sullivan!' "

Today, with Marlo Lewis supervising and Johnny Wray directing, it requires a staff of 123 to put on this weekly one-hour presentation. Contrary to some reports, Sullivan himself chooses all of the performing talent and, in addition to emceeing, writes the scripts of the biographical programs, such as those devoted to lives of Oscar Hammerstein and Richard Rogers, which have become a feature of the show. He also routines the acts, on which he spends some $800,000 a year out of the sponsors' annual appropriation of $5,600,-000. Telecast coast to coast over 129 stations, the columnist's program is seen by between 35 and 50 millions every Sunday.

There is hardly a big name of the Broadway theatre who has not at one time or another appeared on "Toast of the Town." It was the first TV program on which major stars of Hollywood, including producers of the stature of Sam Goldwyn, made their television bows.

"It's not only the presentation of such names that makes a show," Ed explained to me, "but the way they're presented. And even at the risk of being called an egotist, I'll say this: the reason they have been presented so well is that I approached the problem not only as a showman but as a newspaperman. Anyone who has spent years reporting and being a columnist is certain to have a 'feel' for what is effective stagewise and also for what the public likes. That's why

I have said over and over again that television is missing a good bet by not bringing more newspapermen into the fold."

"What type of act has the greatest appeal to the TV audience?" I once asked Sullivan.

He said it is "one that touches the emotions," and cited Helen Hayes in scenes from *Victoria Regina* as an example. But, he pointed out, the performer does not always have to be a high-priced star. "Sometimes it may be a novelty turn, costing only four hundred dollars, with a dog or a monkey, that runs away with the show." And conversely, Ed said, excerpts from Shakespearean plays have seldom won the approval of his viewers, unless these were played by the most famous actors.

It is a revealing comment on the type of talent which, momentarily, draws the greatest returns, when I tell you that the highest fee ever paid to a performer on "Toast of the Town"—ten thousand dollars—went to the crying vocalist, Johnnie Ray.

"But we would have paid an equal amount to the movie star, Bette Davis, had she appeared on our show," Sullivan confided. "She was a sensation at the time in a revue on Broadway. In it she did a take-off on Tallulah Bankhead and we wanted her to repeat it on our program. But she balked and absolutely refused. And do you know what reason Bette gave? She said that Tallulah was merely a New York name and not well enough known nationally!"

Stories about the stars already mentioned in this chapter would fill volumes. But all of the legends and yarns concerning them, combined, would not equal in number those which are told about an eighty-seven-year-old musician of the radio. He is a genius who eats soup three times a day, imbibes red wine, champagne and vodka, and spends hours watching boxing bouts and wrestling matches on television. Also, he is a devotee of "The Lone Ranger," likes Mindy Carson, the Fred Waring chorus and dotes on the "Whiffenpoof Song" when it is done by Robert Merrill. I'm referring of course, to the world's greatest maestro, Arturo Toscanini, who retired in 1954.

Although he was signed by NBC to conduct its symphony orchestra in 1937, I have in all this time not had the privilege of an interview with the master. And neither, so far as I know, has any other writer about radio or TV. Toscanini has an aversion to newspapermen, especially photographers, which amounts to a phobia. During the many years he has been on the air, he has talked with only two or three of the journalistic tribe, and these were music critics.

But I have had many close-ups of the conductor under varied circumstances and, what is even better, have also observed him through the eyes of a man who has been his almost constant companion— a combination of secretary, valet, bodyguard, personal envoy, confidant and intimate friend. He probably knows more about the personal habits and idiosyncracies of the Maestro than anyone but the immediate members of the Toscanini family. His name is Al Walker, a dapper, wiry little former boxing instructor, who was assigned to double as NBC's director of transportation and to discharge the task of serving as the Maestro's alter ego.

Al used to tell me with great relish about the hours Toscanini devoted to radio and television in his Riverdale home. There, in a twenty-room brick and stucco house, the musician would seat himself on the couch of his study and listen to the recorded symphonies of WQXR.

"He is especially fond of Paul Whiteman's band playing Ferde Grofé's 'Grand Canyon Suite,' " said Al. "He also likes Gershwin's 'Rhapsody in Blue.' "

"What about television?"

"He seems to prefer music on the radio to anything else; but on TV, although the Maestro likes prize fights, he gets the biggest kick out of those hammy wrestling matches. You ought to see him get excited over those big fellows. He keeps crawling all over the couch, making gestures and shouting advice to the figures on the screen. Sometimes, when one of those bozos takes an especially hard fall, Toscanini will yell: 'Repose!' That's Italian, you know, for 'Take it easy!' "

The one fact about his idol that most amazes Walker is that he can conduct even the lengthiest and most complex works without a score.

"Why, do you know," Al said, "he memorized a new piece, Shostakovitch's Ninth Symphony, in just four weeks! By rehearsal time, he knew every note, every passage played by each of the 101 instruments. As great as he is in memorizing music, he is absent-minded about his personal affairs. That's why the big joke among the NBC Symphony boys was, 'The old man can remember everything, but don't ask him where his hat is.' "

For his weekly concerts Toscanini rehearsed the orchestra three afternoons, usually from 3:30 to 5:30, and occasionally longer if the scores demanded it. This was a rugged schedule for a man in his eighty-seventh year, but the amount of physical energy he lavished on these sessions would exhaust a conductor thirty years younger.

A few years ago, I watched Al performing some of his duties as Toscanini's all-around handyman. Prior to one of the rehearsals, he had received a detailed plan for the seating of the various instruments of the orchestra. After seeing to it that the chairs had been properly set up, he greeted the Maestro on his arrival at the NBC studios in Radio City, and accompanied him to his dressing room backstage of its biggest studio, 8-H. There he unpacked the conductor's bag and helped him to change clothes. During rehearsals Toscanini usually wore a black alpaca jacket with a white pique collar inset and light striped trousers.

Before the Maestro's arrival, however, Al had put the room in order. This meant, among other things, that neatly arranged on the dressing table were a cake of soap, a hairbrush, a comb, several towels and a number of silver-framed photographs of Toscanini's wife, his children and other members of the family. And most important, a perfume atomizer, as Toscanini is fond of delicate scents.

Al's own words describe what his other tasks were during a rehearsal or a broadcast. "Next, I go out on the stage, which is pretty noisy by this time, and tell the musicians to pipe down. That's because the Maestro's got to have absolute quiet when he enters. Now he begins working and I hang around until he comes back to the dressing room. Again, I help him to change clothes; his body is covered with perspiration; because he's had a tougher workout than a boxer who's gone fifteen rounds."

These rehearsals, incidentally, were about as closely guarded against intruders as a meeting of the Joint Chiefs of Staff in the

Pentagon. Save for a carefully screened few, outsiders were barred. Neither money nor influence was the open-sesame; there was, for instance, the wealthy society matron who offered a thousand dollars for the privilege of attending one of Toscanini's practice sessions, only to be turned down. But I managed to sneak past this Music Curtain on several occasions and observed the Maestro in action. I have in my possession a collector's item—a secret recording made during a Toscanini rehearsal. A microphone was hidden in the podium and every sound of this colorful session was preserved on plastic.

On this platter one may hear the orchestra repeating over and over again a few bars of music until perfection has been attained. There are repeated interruptions by the Maestro—rappings of the baton, hoarse shouts, yells and cuss words and, occasionally, the sound of Toscanini singing along with the ensemble in a horrendous quavering baritone.

As anyone who has attended a Toscanini rehearsal knows, two of his favorite expletives are *"Stupido"* and *"Vergogna!"* (Shame!) Now and then these are followed by a stream of words far more explicit and vivid than the unimaginative profanity of the Anglo-Saxons.

"But remember this," Al insists, "the Maestro's cussing isn't personal. He's bawling out the instrument, not the man. What makes him sore when he hears bad playing is that these instruments are insulting not him but Beethoven or Brahms."

Sometimes, Toscanini had a quaint manner of imparting his directions. During a rehearsal of a Mozart symphony, he asked the first violins to produce a faraway effect. They attempted it, but the Maestro was not satisfied. "Too far away," he said. They tried again and Toscanini rapped his baton. "Not far away enough," he commented.

"But, Maestro, will you please tell us just how far away you want it?" a fiddler asked.

"I want far away—but not too far away," said Toscanini. "Just far enough—you know, like Brooklyn."

Not long ago, Gian-Carlo Menotti, composer of *The Medium, The Consul* and other successful operas, told me a story of the "human" side of Toscanini. One night, after the Maestro had attended the double bill, *The Telephone* and *The Medium,* in a Broadway theatre, he came backstage to congratulate Menotti. He told him that he had been especially taken with *The Telephone,* a gay little curtain raiser depicting the adventures of a girl suffering from "telephonitis."

"I shall be back next Tuesday night, Carlo," said Toscanini, "And I shall bring with me an old friend, a lady who is a music teacher. Just like your heroine, she, too, is always busy on the phone whenever I call her. So, do me a favor, my boy. When the girl in your play sings out her telephone number, have her sing out this one." With a sly twinkle, he gave Menotti a slip of paper. "It's the number of my friend."

The performance the following Tuesday was interrupted by a loud explosion of laughter. Toscanini roared and clapped his hands as he watched the amazed expression of the lady seated beside him. "Why, that is my number!" she exclaimed.

One of the most complex of men, Toscanini is also one of the most naïve. He proved this one night after an NBC executive had suggested that perhaps the Maestro needed a bit of relaxation, and then escorted him to a garish Broadway night club. It was one of the most highly advertised and publicized places in town, known to every newspaper reader, and about as secret as Times Square itself.

At a ringside table, the great conductor, who in his eighties still has a keen eye for beauty, suddenly nudged his companion. "Look," he said, calling attention to the battalion of almost nude amazons who were parading, a few feet away, across the stage.

"Like it?" asked the radio man.

"Say!" Toscanini exclaimed with a chuckle, "how in the world did you ever find this place?"

Jan Peerce, the Metropolitan Opera tenor, once told me that not only instrumentalists but singers regarded an appearance with Toscanini as the ultimate test of artistry. "He has what so many conductors do not—the respect of those who work with him. And do you know why? Because the man knows his music."

Despite reports depicting Toscanini as a slave driver, Peerce said,

"I consider him to be the easiest man in the world to sing for—provided you know your business. It's a revelation to sing with him because Toscanini pays as much attention to the words as to the music. He has often told me that if the words weren't important, the composers would not bother to set them to melodies."

One day, while Peerce was rehearsing "Rodolfo" in *La Bohème* with the Maestro at the piano, he mispronounced one of the Italian words. Toscanini stopped playing and asked him to repeat the passage. Again Jan made the same mistake.

"I thought the heavens would fall! I braced myself against what I was sure would come," he said. "But all that happened was that Toscanini shook his head, looked up at me, and said plaintively: 'Peerce, you too?'"

Although Peerce was undoubtedly surprised by the Maestro's display of consideration, it is an old story to Al. On Christmas Day, 1946, Toscanini presented to him a gold medallion engraved with the head of the great musician. On it are the words: "To my friend, A. Walker."

TWELVE

How the Men from Mars Ruined a Quiet Evening

It was a pleasant little dinner with a few friends in a Tudor City apartment on a Sunday evening in October, 1938. "How about turning on Charlie McCarthy?" one of the guests said.

"Okay," I answered, "but do you mind if we first hear what Orson Welles is doing?"

Just a few days before, at CBS headquarters, I had asked one of the actors of Welles' "Mercury Theatre of the Air" about Sunday's show.

"Just between us," he had said, "it's lousy. Orson couldn't get ready the script he wanted, so he's run in a dramatization of that H. G. Wells chestnut, *The War of the Worlds.*"

"Oh, that," I said.

"Yeah, good old Sunday-supplement fantasy, but he's dressed it up. Anyway, don't bother to listen. Probably bore you to death."

His words had made me happy. There would not be too many programs worthy of comment on the radio the following Sunday, and instead of having to do an entirely new column of comment for the late editions, I should be able to get by merely with the re-writing of two or three brief paragraphs. It would be a quiet and restful Sabbath evening.

But Welles had staged some of the best experimental dramatic productions on the air during that period, and a sense of duty impelled me to eavesdrop on him for at least a few minutes. Even though he might be merely coasting along during this broadcast, if he displayed some ingenuity in dressing up the familiar fantasy, it might be worth a line or two for the Three Star.

The show began conventionally enough, with the announcer saying quite distinctly that the Columbia Broadcasting System and its affiliated stations were presenting Orson Welles and the "Mercury Theatre of the Air" in *The War of the Worlds* by H. G. Wells. Soon we heard a "news flash" which informed us that a tremendous explosion had taken place on the planet Mars.

Now came a veritable cascade of sensational "bulletins." A meteor had crashed near Grover's Mills, New Jersey. More than a thousand persons had been killed. Finally, an "on-the-spot" remote broadcast from the New Jersey countryside. The meteor was no meteor at all; it was a silver cylinder, a miraculous ship from outer space, and from it were streaming horrendous creatures, the like of which had not been seen on this globe before, men from Mars armed with disintegrating and incinerating death-ray guns. There was no defense against these; thousands who had rushed to the field where the craft had landed were being burned to cinders. The Martians had invaded the earth to exterminate its inhabitants!

We had not yet heard of flying saucers, artificial satellites and other such phenomena; but what came over the air was overwhelmingly terrifying. And the staccato "news reports" and pronouncements by "officials" which followed made it seem even more so. For the National Guard had been called out . . . the Secretary of War was issuing orders to the Army . . . a state of national emergency had been proclaimed . . . the State Department and even the White House were urging the people to keep calm. But what did these appeals matter? By now the Martians, with flame and terror, were marching on New York!

"You know," I remarked, arising from a half-consumed steak, "I think I'd better be getting back to the office. Some listeners might really believe this."

"How could they?" asked one of the guests. "They announced it was by H. G. Wells. That means it's fiction."

"But those who tuned in late didn't hear the announcement," another said.

It was lucky for me that I had returned to the nearby office. Passing through the city room, an assistant at the city desk yelled, "Hey! What the hell's going on?"

The switchboard was blazing; lines were jammed and phones rang all over the place. Rewrite men in booths tried desperately to reach CBS, but none of their calls got through; photographers with full equipment scurried toward the elevators.

"No, madam . . . no, sir . . . we don't know anything about an explosion in Jersey," the man at the switchboard was saying. "Men from Mars? . . . Yeah, I know it's on the radio . . . but it didn't happen. . . . Nothing's going on, I tell you. . . . No, madam . . . no, sir . . . there ain't no men from Mars."

A police official's call reached the city desk.

"It's just a phony, a radio play," the harassed assistant told him.

Then, shouting at me: "*You* try to get CBS. If you can't, go up there."

The two phones in the radio room were clanging wildly and I grabbed both receivers.

"Are they abandoning New York?" a hysterical woman asked over one.

"No, lady, it's just a play," I said.

"Oh, no!" she screamed and hung up.

A Red Cross man was on the other wire.

"I hear they're broadcasting about a terrible catastrophe in New Jersey," the man said. "Do you know where it is?"

"It's only Orson Welles," I explained. "He's on with a fantasy."

"But my wife just called me and said thousands have been killed," he said.

My assistant rushed in breathless with proofs from the composing room. The phones again. "My God! Those calls have been driving me crazy!" she said.

I made for the door. "You're not going to leave me all alone with these phones?" the distraught girl pleaded. I gave her no heed.

Downstairs, in the cab, the radio was tuned to WEAF. "Get WABC" (the CBS station), I said. The cabbie did, and we heard the calm voice of an announcer saying that this were merely an Orson Welles presentation of a story by H. G. Wells. A few seconds later the Martians were marching again. They had just destroyed Trenton and were, in fact, already on the Palisades, rushing with fiery death on to our metropolis. . . . Refugees were scurrying from the city in wild flight . . . but that wasn't all . . . some of the invaders, who had followed in other ships from outer space, had detoured to the Midwest and the South.

"God Almighty!" the cab driver exclaimed.

"It's just fiction," I assured him. "Didn't you hear the announcer?"

"No, I didn't hear no announcer," the chauffeur said. "You're sure?"

"You don't see any panic-stricken people running about the streets, do you?" I asked.

But just at that moment we passed a movie theatre on Third Avenue. A half-dozen women and children scurried from it as from nearby bars men dashed out to gaze at the sky. On Lexington Avenue and 51st Street a wailing woman sat on the curb and a policeman stood in the middle of the roadway surrounded by a crowd.

"There sure is something going on," my driver said.

And, indeed, there was, although one wouldn't have known it by the lack of turmoil in front of CBS. There were no more than the usual number of pedestrians going by and, showing my pass, I had no difficulty in gaining access to the seat of the hysteria which at that moment was sweeping most of the United States.

The broadcast had ended and the studio and corridors vibrated with chatter, as perturbed executives, attachés, officious page boys and annoyed cops rushed about. I was informed that during the latter portion of the program the policemen, in response to complaints, had marched into the glass-encased control room, and watched in disbelief as Orson and others of his Mercury troupe, in business and sports clothes, stood stoically before the microphones reading their scripts, ignorant of the havoc they were creating throughout the land.

When the executives and the law burst through the studio doors to confront him after the broadcast had come to its crashing finale, Welles was astounded to hear that listeners had taken his fantasy literally.

"How could they?" he said. "They were told several times it wasn't real."

"Have you any statement to make?" the newspapermen demanded.

"None whatsoever," he said, and ran with his cast from the studio down the corridor. The press followed, but before they could be intercepted, the Mercury troupe was downstairs and in the cabs that had been awaiting them. The reporters in other taxis pursued the fleeing performers, only to lose track of them in the maze of Times Square traffic. There, under the glow of sparkling lights, jittery thousands watched the *Times* electric sign for assurance that the "Martian invasion" had at last been repelled. The outwitted journalists then backtracked to CBS, where a "network spokesman" solemnly promised that "such a thing will not happen again." At the *News* office the phones were still ringing, although the radio was making repeated announcements (until midnight) that Americans positively were in no peril from the spacemen.

So, on this Sunday evening of October 30, 1938, which was anything but "quiet," I not only had to do a complete rewrite of the column but also give a hand in assembling items pouring in via telephones and teletypes. As these flooded the city and the telegraph desks, it became apparent that this was a startling story, with national and even international repercussions.

It had touched the movie theatre just around the corner, where scores had stampeded after a fear-crazed mother had pushed past the doorman to summon her husband and her child. "Get out! Get out!" she had screamed. "The city's on fire!" It had touched Harlem, where men and women had fallen to their knees in prayer . . . the Village, where crowds had converged on Washington Square . . . police stations throughout the city, besieged by frantic ones seeking refuge . . . upstate, Connecticut and, above all, New Jersey, where the "Martians" had landed. In that state's Trenton, Union City and other communities, thousands of fearful ones had taken to the streets and highways, and other foolhardy, curiosity-consumed hundreds in motor cars were still driving toward the spot where the "meteor" had crashed.

As the AP, UP and the Chicago *Tribune* News Service wires in our office gave evidence, the panic's coils had also clutched most of the cities, towns and hamlets from coast to coast and down south to the Mexican border. The people of the United States had succumbed to an unprecedented mass hysteria.

Immediately after the country had calmed its collective nerves, there were demands for government censorship of radio, but Washington wisely decided against such an un-American measure. After all, not only CBS but other networks had already decreed that thereafter no dramatic works should be broadcast which employed such realistic devices as news bulletins, flashes, or impersonations of public officials when these were of a kind to create uneasiness or panic.

It was said that this misstep would "ruin" Orson Welles; but, instead, it won him a profitable national sponsor, and lifted him from a theatrical "wonder boy," admired only by a narrow circle, to the status of a national celebrity. Even today, despite his many other achievements, his name is synonymous to millions with the great "Martian invasion."

Political pundits, psychologists, psychiatrists and other readers of the mass mind had a glorious time during the months that followed. The newspapers and the broadcasters of Hitler and Mussolini hailed the exhibition of hysteria as a sign of the decadence and cowardice of American democracy. Most of the native commentators attributed the incident to the climate of the times, which were truly hectic. That autumn of 1938 had witnessed one international crisis after another, and the world seemed to be on the verge of a mighty catastrophe.

"Is it surprising that this should have happened?" one analyst of public opinion asked. "Are not our imaginations so inflamed today that anything seems believable—no matter how fantastic?"

Those who gave serious thought to the episode also pointed out that broadcasting, improperly used by demagogues or dictators, could be one of the most dangerous weapons ever invented. And they called attention to a fact long recognized by the "trade": that a high percentage of those who tune in either do not listen attentively or do not hear accurately. Therefore, they said, major points must be repeated or emphasized several times. In other words, some of those obnoxious commercials which spell out each word and pound in their slogans are psychologically justifiable.

Three years after the Martians had made their foray against our planet, Pearl Harbor was bombed, but the excitement on that day did not approach the hysteria induced by Orson Welles. Observers explained that we had become so inured to tragedy it would be no longer possible to panic the American public. And, certainly, the stoical behavior of the British under the blitz gave them ground for such belief.

For a while, I agreed with them—but now I am not so sure. Just a few years ago, the Welles adaptation of *The War of the Worlds* was translated into Spanish and, with a few local touches added, broadcast over a Latin-American station. The reaction south of the border was even more violent than it had been in this country. The listeners not only gave way to hysteria but, in an outburst of fury over having been "hoaxed," burned down the radio station and killed some of the actors!

And what of the United States? Suppose today we heard over the radio a bulletin that a troop of little men with death-ray guns had come forth from a flying saucer on some sandy waste in Arizona —just how calm would we be?

Who can give an accurate answer? Frankly, all I know is that, back in 1938, Orson Welles and his "Men from Mars" ruined for one radio editor what might have been a quiet Sunday evening.

THIRTEEN

Via Camera and Mike in Politics

Most newspapermen pretend to be blasé characters, but I confess to having displayed an effervescent enthusiasm during the Democratic National Convention of 1924. It was the bitterest and lengthiest political powwow of this century.

A new reporter on the New York staff of the Associated Press, I was among those assigned to do menial tasks for the Washington bureau, which had moved *en masse* to the press box of the old Madison Square Garden. To work, ever so anonymously, in the same auditorium with Will Rogers, Mark Sullivan, Isaac Marcosson and other celebrated byliners congregated there was a privilege not to be taken lightly. To hear and see William Jennings Bryan and other political titans of the day engaged in rancorous combat gave one a sense of being a participant in the making of history.

Call such a reaction juvenile, but it is, in fact, one of the great fascinations of the newspaper profession. In some ways it is merely akin to the desire of a schoolboy to ride the fire engine or to that of an autograph hunter to come face to face with a movie star. Elderly newspapermen recognize this and shamefacedly hide their enthusiasm beneath a veneer of cynical "sophistication."

But, as yet, I was incapable of resorting to such pretense. To me, the recording of events was a noble pursuit and, save in rare instances (Caesar, Grant, etc.), one recalled that the significant events of the past had been preserved not by the principal actors but by the historians. And newspapermen, it was plain, were the true historians of the day, their eyes on the next edition instead of on posterity. Harried, underpaid and discontented as they may have appeared to be, they still had a basic love for their jobs which, regardless of recognition or financial return, sent them with fervent enthusiasm into the battle for a good story.

Because to me, in 1924, these reflections still had an aura of freshness, what took place in the Garden made a far more vivid impression than many dramatic events during the conventions of succeeding years. For one thing, I came into contact for the first time with one of the most colorful figures of radio—Graham Mc-Namee.

With his associate announcer, Phillips Carlin, Graham helped to make one of the most exciting episodes of American history understandable to millions of listeners. As one assigned to gather brief "human-interest" sidelights, I often visited Graham in his little glass-enclosed booth on the stage near the speaker's rostrum. With a switchboard, two telephones, a chair and a table with two microphones, it could scarcely hold two persons. Phil had even more cramped quarters in a birdcage-like contraption hanging high above the floor among the steel girders of the arena. In contrast with the dozens of microphones used today at such assemblies, the only others were on the rostrum, at the bandstand and organ and two or three more scattered about the auditorium to pick up crowd noises.

At Cleveland, where the Republicans had nominated Coolidge and Dawes a few weeks before, this duo had made a success of covering the proceedings for WEAF and connected stations with even less equipment. That Republican meeting of 1924, by the way, was the first national convention to be aired.

Nowadays, when hundreds of announcers, newscasters, commentators and technicians are assigned by the networks to conventions, it seems unbelievable that McNamee and Carlin, aided by a ridiculously small staff, could have dared to tackle such a task. From June 24th to 2:30 A.M., July 10th, often for twelve to sixteen hours at a time, the convention ground on and on, and Graham and Phil remained at their posts describing the commotion before them. And, day after day, while they rested their larynxes, the microphones picked up the frenzied speeches, the blaring music and the shouts, yells and catcalls that rose in hysterical waves from the floor and the galleries. For the battle between Governor Alfred E. Smith of New York and former Secretary of the Treasury William G. McAdoo for the Presidential nomination was more than a mere political contest. It was a dirty, loud, no-holds-barred battle to the death of the Catholic-hating Ku Klux Klan and allied "dry" elements against the liberal "wets" supporting the Governor of New York.

The bitterness had invaded even the press section. On the first day of the convention, a young Boston newspaperwoman asked, "Do you think Smith has a chance?"

"Yes," I said.

She turned on me angrily. "How can you think so? Why, he's Irish . . . he can't speak decent English . . . and . . . and . . ." she almost burst a blood vessel, "he's no gentleman!"

The lady must have had a difficult time restraining her temper during the next few days and nights while the committee on resolutions battled over the insertion into the platform of a plank denouncing the Klan. The Smith supporters favored this; those for McAdoo opposed the move.

One of McNamee's most vivid broadcasts described how at one of these sessions two committee members hurled themselves at each other, only to have William Jennings Bryan thrust himself between them, fall on his knees and utter a prayer. This prevented bloodshed but failed to allay the rancor which came to its full height when "The Great Commoner" faced the convention itself to plead against any mention of the Klan by name.

Beginning slowly, almost in a whisper, Bryan, "the silver-tongued orator," eventually attained a pitch of agonized frenzy. At the start, the audience sat silent; then his supporters broke into cheers. This was a taunt, an insult to the Smith followers, his delegates on the floor and the Tammany men and women in the galleries. The latter booed, whistled and stamped in uncontrolled anger. Bryan partisans rose and shook banners and fists at the galleries. The chairman pounded over and over again for order, but the uproar, resembling the bloodthirsty cries of two mobs bent on lynchings, continued, rising and falling to the very end of Bryan's address.

And later, after Smith's name had been placed in nomination, the loudest and probably the most terrifying sound in the history of political conventions was heard. It was compounded not only of the usual roar of organ and band music, plus the shrill whine of a siren that pierced the eardrums with stinging needles—there was also something else. It was a "something" fused out of blood-chilling cries, shrieks and yells so angry, so hysterical, that they seemed to explode from the depths of some mad animal. Delegates in the throes of a savage frenzy fought over state banners; knock-down fights erupted in every portion of the arena; on the floor and in the galleries, men and women stood on their chairs while others, swayed by an irresistible sweep of emotion, began jumping up and down like so many Indians in a war dance. Thousands of spectators tore newspapers into shreds of confetti, which drifted from the balconies onto the floor, while thousands of others, to the accompaniment of bands and the organ, chanted "The Sidewalks of New York" with a defiant pride. It continued for almost an hour and forty-five minutes.

But the drama was far from ended. In these times when conventions nominate after one or two roll calls, it is difficult to imagine the strain and the boredom that marked this assembly of 1924, when the delegates were deadlocked for 102 ballots. Only after the 103rd did they come up with a nominee—John W. Davis of New York.

But one reporter, who had come to New York from Alabama, was swayed by a certain provincial pride because each of these roll-calls was dominated by the chief executive of his native state. Over and over again, Governor Bill Brandon, in frock coat, gray trousers and shoestring tie, would rise from his chair and, with his walrus mustache quivering, shout in reverberating tones: "Ala-ba-mah casts twenty-four votes for Oscar W. Underwood!"

His sonorous baritone would literally ring among the rafters. After the first few ballots had been taken, his cry became a trademark of the convention itself, and not only the delegates but those in the galleries joined him in the chant. In front of thousands of radio shops and restaurants, crowds assembled throughout the days and the evenings to listen to the proceedings over the loud-speakers. They chimed in; schoolboys yelled the words in corridors and on playgrounds and vaudeville comedians won laughs with them.

Brandon, whom I had met while he was Probate Judge of Tuscaloosa County, told me some time later: "You know, I've done some mighty good things as Governor. But everywhere I go, all the people seem to remember is that I cast twenty-four votes for Underwood. Sometimes, I wish I had never said it."

The manner in which Brandon attained national fame was just one of the many odd facets of this convention. After the sessions had run past the twelfth day, newsmen noticed a number of delegates in rumpled clothes sleeping on cots in the basement of the Garden. They had exhausted their money and were unable to obtain more. Some of the luckier ones had been able to borrow from colleagues or political leaders and had moved from their hotels to rooming houses; but those less fortunate had arranged to occupy basement cots, subsisting on coffee, popcorn and sandwiches.

One of my AP colleagues was approached that day by a delegate from Arkansas who obtained a loan of two dollars.

"Ain't had no breakfast today," he explained. "I'll send you the money when I get home."

And much to the surprise of my friend, the man from Arkansas did.

It was also during this 1924 convention that, in company with Graham McNamee, I had my first talk with Will Rogers, whom I came to know later as a radio star. He was a bit miffed at the time, for, as he explained, a syndicate had signed him to write humorous observations about the Democrats. Will had agreed to do this for a lump sum, basing the amount on the supposition that the gathering would last no more than four or five days. But here he was already in his second week, and he felt that he had been "gypped."

On that occasion, the cowboy humorist also remarked that he believed radio would cause convention speakers to deliver better and briefer addresses.

"A fellow can get away with saying something foolish when he's talking to a thousand people in a hall," he said, "but it's going to be tougher when he's speaking to millions over the radio."

Of course, Rogers, a devastatingly sarcastic commentator on the political scene, was far too optimistic. Radio, like television, did affect campaign oratory somewhat but by no means eliminated the long-winded speeches and the asinine demonstrations at political conventions.

Certainly both were still in evidence sixteen years later at the Republican gathering in Philadelphia during the summer of 1940, the first national convention to be televised. The few hundred families who looked in via their old-fashioned mirror-reflector sets in New York and Philadelphia were as exhausted by the endless oratory as the radio listeners had been in 1924. But they did find a certain visual excitement in the "spontaneous" demonstration for Wendell Willkie which swept the galleries. They did not know, of course, that the rhythmic chanters of "We want Willkie!" were, in good part, employees in the banking, brokerage and business houses of the town who had been excused from work and dispatched to the convention hall. The "barefoot boy of Wall Street," supposedly representing the "plain people," had, in fact, the support of some of the mightiest financial groups of the country.

On TV, the man from Indiana projected the image of the idealistic country boy battling the big-city slickers. But, unfortunately —for him—there were only a few television stations at the time, so he had to make his appeal solely through the sound of radio. On this medium, however, Willkie's hoarse speechifying was no match for F.D.R.'s Groton enunciation, his epigrammatic sentences and, above all, the Great Mike Master's ability to convince each listener that he was speaking directly to him.

During this convention, I was one of the few newspapermen to appear on NBC's telecasts. Others had been invited to do so but most of them, on learning that their faces would have to be smeared with pancake makeup, indignantly declined. "Things have come to a hell of a pass when a reporter's got to be painted and powdered before he can tell his story!" a member of the News' Washington bureau remarked. This attitude prevailed among the majority of the politicians also.

Within the next four years there was a startling increase in the number of television stations, but in 1944 those of the East and of the Midwest were still unlinked. So during both the Republican and Democratic conventions of that year in Chicago, radio was still the major broadcasting medium.

For years I had been writing of radio as a sideline observer. Now, for the first time, save for a six months' stint as a news commentator on New York's WMCA, I was privileged to view broadcasting as a participant. NBC had engaged me as a "human-interest" reporter for both conventions, and I began to realize as never before the planning, the intense labor and the split-second timing that were involved in a network's coverage of a major event.

On the day prior to the opening of each gathering, the staff of commentators, reporters, publicity men and technicians assembled at NBC's headquarters in the Stevens (now the Conrad Hilton) Hotel. William F. Brooks, in charge of news and special events, presided over the group with the authoritative air of a college professor lecturing a class of freshmen. Seated before him like so many pupils, each faithfully transcribing instructions in loose-leaf notebooks, were some of the most celebrated commentators and newscasters of the country: H. V. Kaltenborn, Morgan Beatty, Bob Trout and Richard Harkness among them.

Brooks, a smooth and decisive executive, told of the months of preliminary liaison and technical effort preceding our arrival in Chicago. On his desk lay a gigantic chart with the position of every member of the news staff clearly shown. Some were assigned to microphones on the speakers' platform; others, with portable mikes, to various state delegations on the floor; and still others to the central glass-enclosed booth on the balcony facing the chairman's rostrum. Those who would be stationed in hotel lobbies, on streets with mobile units and at the headquarters of the candidates were also named and their positions indicated.

After a thorough explanation of the chart, Brooks briefed his crew on the meaning of certain signals and on the technique of transferring a pickup from one point to another.

"In this connection," Bill said, "let's suppose that a switch is made from Harkness to Kaltenborn. Remember, Hans, don't say, 'Thank you, Richard Harkness!' There are far too many 'thank you's' during these broadcasts.

"And another thing. Suppose you're interviewing Senator Blowhard and he becomes boresome. Try to switch as soon as possible to another point. But for heaven's sake, everybody, do it as diplomatically as possible."

"Who'll decide if he's a bore?" Beatty asked.

"Oh, I'll tell you, over the earphones," said Brooks. "On the other hand, if the Senator should prove to be more interesting than anticipated, we may keep him on."

During the Republican convention, which assembled the next day, many newspaper and broadcasting men, although wearing the proper badges, encountered considerable difficulty in gaining entrance to the press and radio sections. No one has ever been able to tell why, but it is a fact that reporters and newscasters usually have more obstacles to overcome at the GOP conclaves than at those of Democrats. The latter seem to be smarter at press relations.

During the two-week period of the conventions, the broadcasting activities were a mere sideline of my regular job, writing two columns a day for the *News*. After reporting to Richard Clarke, the amazingly energetic managing editor (now executive editor) of that daily's staff, at its Stevens and Convention Hall headquarters, I would check in with Bill Brooks. Often my assignment was to pick up some commentator during the morning hours and faithfully shadow him throughout most of the day and evening. In the company of Harkness or Beatty, for example, I would eavesdrop as the network reporter sought confidential information from the various candidates and their floor leaders. It was my function to observe their techniques as they got the "inside dope" on current and future developments. Then I would rush up to the air-conditioned central glass booth of NBC in the steaming Chicago Stadium, ready to go before the mike at any moment to do a "behind-the-scenes" broadcast. In this the radio editor was supposed to—and did—reveal how NBC's men obtained their stories.

Just like all other directors of news and special events, Brooks sat in this booth like a shirt-sleeved spider in an electronic net. With an ear receiver clamped on, and with a clear view of the proceedings on the speaker's platform and the floor, he manipulated a battery of telephones beside him. Through these he maintained contact with reporters and commentators in every portion of the vast structure, at candidates' headquarters and on mobile units cruising the streets.

The average listener or viewer cannot have the slightest conception of the strain endured by the man who co-ordinates and directs the broadcast or telecast of a national convention. It is a job with a thousand different facets, demanding not only knowledge of the personalities and the issues involved, but the ability to make instantaneous decisions. A nerve-searing task even for an iron man; but Brooks sat there chain-smoking, calmly uttering his commands in a bored monotone and seemingly paying not the slightest attention to Bob Trout in the next chair, who was giving the running story of what was taking place below.

So it went, day after day, from 8 A.M. until past midnight. Few news or radio men had more than three or four hours sleep; they griped, groused and grumbled, swearing that anyone who sought such an assignment should have his head examined. Yet they loved every minute of it and four years later were back at the old grind, still griping, grousing and grumbling and loving their backbreaking jobs all over again.

While seated in the press section of the Democratic convention of that year, I saw how scoops are born. Julia Shawell, now an eminently successful New York public-relations woman, but then the chief editorial and political writer of the Philadelphia *Daily News*, was arguing vehemently with her publisher, the late Lee Ellmaker, who was seated next to her. She was an ardent Democrat and he an equally fervent Republican; so heated discussions between them were no novelty. Nevertheless other newsmen nearby gasped as she committed the unprecedented lese majesty of "bawling out" her boss. Ellmaker, however, merely laughed; he respected her ability and valued her services to his paper.

So Julia, one of the most astute and keenest political writers in the country, now had an additional incentive to prove herself. Collaring one of the leaders of the Missouri delegation, she extracted from him an exclusive account of secret manuevers in high places. Many believed that Vice-President Henry Wallace still stood a chance of being renominated. Roosevelt's famous letter to Chairman Hannegan expressing a willingness to accept Truman, Byrnes or Douglas in place of Wallace had not as yet been made public. But now, before any other reporter, Julia not only knew that Truman would be the Vice-Presidential nominee but on which ballot the decision would be clinched.

Taking a long chance, with the consent of Ellmaker, she phoned the tip to her newspaper; but those in charge in Philadelphia refused to believe her. The publisher himself was forced to order the running of the story. Since the Philadelphia tabloid is an afternoon sheet, it beat every other daily in the country on the selection of Harry Truman. By the time the A.M. papers hit the street, the tip had become a reality.

Just after Truman's nomination had been announced, he could not be located and convention officials began a frantic search for him. The loudspeakers in the Stadium boomed with the chairman's plea: "Will the nominee for Vice-President kindly come to the platform!" Suddenly, a group of radio men turning a corner on the ground-floor corridor came on the future President of the United States at a sandwich stand. His lips smeared with mustard, he was leisurely munching a hot dog.

I recall vividly the impression Truman made on the press and radio corps during the informal conference he held in the convention hall immediately following that session. To most of us he seemed to be the personification of the average man, a likable little Midwestern small-towner whose chief attribute was humility. The cocky Presidential candidate of 1948 as yet was nowhere visible. To most questions he gave a set answer: "I shall place myself under the orders of my commander-in-chief."

Convention interviews with candidates—successful and unsuccessful—are fairly commonplace on radio and TV today. But so far only a scant attempt has been made to bring to the broadcasting audience a picture of one of the most colorful features of such pow-wows—the parties for the press and the politicians. Washington hostesses, official and social, descend on the convention cities; the Perle Mestas and the Gwen Cafritzes stage gigantic caviar and champagne bouts; national and local politicos and countless lobbyists, press agents and public-relations counsel preside over noisy wingdings which are attended by as many gate crashers as invited guests.

A newspaperman in his time attends many such affairs, but the party which made the most vivid impression on me was the one given for the press and the radio during this Democratic convention of 1944 by Mayor Kelly of Chicago. There must have been at least three or four thousand persons in the ballroom of the Drake Hotel and the streets and corridors converging on it. Most of those present, however, were definitely neither of the press nor of radio.

It seems that every district leader and ward heeler of the city had obtained scads of tickets which were duly distributed to their not-so-elegant constituents. From the North Side and the South Side, small merchants, butchers, bakers, housewives, saloon keepers and a considerable number of underworld habitués took advantage of the invitation to have eats and drinks on the house. Someone also had the bright notion of inviting dozens of lower-echelon call girls, and some young women who did not even wait to be called. Blowsy and blondined, in garish low-cut gowns and clanking with dime-store costume jewelry, they sent their shrill shouts and cackling laughter above the song of a trio around a portable piano, who were plugging the campaign ditty, "Don't Change Horses in the Middle of the Stream." In a whirling frenzy, this motley crowd charged against the buffet tables with their mountains of cold turkey and roast beef. It practically demolished the bars piled with hundreds of glasses of Scotch, rye and bottles of beer. Experienced as they are in maintaining contact with the sources of food and drink, most of the news and radio men failed utterly in their efforts to snare either a morsel or a swallow. By 10 P.M. they abjectly had surrendered and abandoned "their" party to the good Mayor Kelly's henchmen. They departed hungry and thirsty—but with an ample store of reflections on the odd folkways of politicians.

At the Philadelphia political conventions of 1948, I encountered many vivid characters who wrote both political and broadcasting history. For the first time, television made a major impact on both parties. A TV hookup of eastern and midwestern stations, plus non-connected video outlets using kinescopes, brought the sessions to a large portion of the country. And Philadelphia had been selected as the site of the meetings primarily because it was on the coaxial cable.

But despite the presence of television, one could detect few basic changes between the routines of 1924, 1944 and 1948. Here in Philadelphia it was Convention Hall instead of Madison Square Garden or the Stadium. The lobby of the Bellevue-Stratford was as jammed with sweating delegates as the Stevens, and the elevator service was much worse. There were the same hush-hush conferences, the same tips, the same rumors, the same pumped-up demonstrations, the same heavy consumption of indigestible food and alcoholic drinks . . . and in the headquarters of the News, on the second floor of the Bellevue, the same busy staff of Washington writers augmented by New York reporters, copyreaders and teletype operators.

This time, I reported to Robert Shand, the managing editor, who supervised the complex and utterly exhausting operations of convention coverage with the unruffled demeanor of a man about to enter a game of bridge. But just as in Chicago, four years before, here again I was a schizophrenic personality, split between newspaper work and broadcasting. For the News' TV station, WPIX, which had gone on the air just two weeks before the opening of the Republican conclave, was on the scene competing against the networks.

One of the eighteen video stations picking up the proceedings "live" (as against 1,500 radio outlets doing the same), we relied just as the others did, on the "pool" coverage of the floor sessions. All the networks had contributed their cameramen and technicians for this purpose, but the chains and the independent station augmented this with their own reporters, commentators and special features.

There we were, a tightly knit group of editorial workers under the direction of Carl Warren, who had made his reputation as editor of our paper's celebrated news broadcasts over New York's WNEW. Not one of us really knew anything about television, and our facilities were scanty beside those of NBC or CBS. Yet a few newsmen, with far more knowledge of the typewriter than of the TV camera, put on approximately twenty human-interest features, newscasts, and analytical commentaries each day. Lowell Limpus, head of our UN Bureau, Jimmy Jemail, The Inquiring Fotographer, Rex Marshall, a professional announcer and I made up the core of the station's staff. During the evenings, we received aid from John O'Donnell and Ruth Montgomery of the Washington Bureau and the New York political writers Dick Lee and John Crosson, with contributions by Broadway columnists Ed Sullivan and Danton Walker.

Yet this small, inexperienced group somehow managed to achieve a convention coverage that remained the talk of the telecasting industry. It was done through concentration on a few important news exclusives and on a great many human interest items.

We streamed from our studio atop the Bellevue through caucus and conference rooms, lobbies and in the convention hall itself, cajoling political leaders and assorted celebrities into appearing before our cameras. Sometimes we snared them in the hotel's corridors with portable mikes and cameras as they came out of caucuses. On one occasion, WPIX scooped its rivals by presenting the first Philadelphia interview with Governor Dewey of New York, who received the Republican nomination.

But by the time the Democratic convention had convened we had more guests than we could accommodate. Seemingly every press agent, public-relations counselor, lobbyist and spokesman for a politician, important or insignificant, tried to foist his client on us. Our two research men, Len Smith and Francis Stephenson, now of the Washington staff, were kept busy warding off dozens of groups, organizations, societies and scores of cranks who pressured them for a few minutes on the air.

Among the applicants was a woman who advocated that the President should be selected by the governors of the states. Another would-be speaker was a gentleman with a white beard, dressed in khaki and wearing sandals, who wished to abolish money and return to barter. And one of the most persistent of them all was "the man in armor," representing not a cause but a cigar. With the name of his stogie emblazoned on his suit of medieval metal, he would daily clank up many flights of stairs to our roof studio and plead for a chance to appear before the cameras.

In addition to these unorthodox personalities, some of our featured guests created a considerable stir with their unexpected remarks. Evie (Mrs. Chip) Robert, the Washington hostess, caused a great burning of ears with some brilliant but biting comments on the social game in the national capital. And the celebrated society writer, Austine Cassini, now Mrs. William Randolph Hearst, delivered a memorable comment on the attire of newspapermen during an interview with Jimmy Jemail.

"What is your outstanding impression of this convention?" Jimmy asked her one night during the Republican powwow. "Is it the fight between Dewey and Taft or . . ."

"Neither," she said. "It's the sloppy way most newspapermen dress!"

Thereupon the beauteous Austine, garbed in a ravishingly low-cut evening gown, explained: "It's terribly hot in the press section. Most of the men remove their coats and today I couldn't help notice that all of those directly in front of me wore belts instead of braces. That's inexcusable! In fact, during this entire convention, I've seen only one newspaperman sitting near me who dresses like a gentleman. It's Paul Gallico—he wears braces!"

I ran across Paul two weeks later during the Democratic gathering and told him of Austine's tribute to his elegance.

"Gosh!" he said gloomily. "That puts me on the spot. The suit she saw me in was made in London. Over there all trousers are tailored for suspenders. It's the only one of its kind I have and I've left it in New York."

He pointed sadly to the belt encircling his waist. "Now I won't be able to take off my coat. I just can't disillusion her!"

And for the remainder of that Democratic convention Paul Gallico suffered—a gallant gentleman who would not let a lady down!

But all such episodes, both important and picayune, were overshadowed by one of the most surprising developments in the history of American politics. It was that amazing shot of oratorical adrenalin injected into the veins of the dying Democratic donkey by President Truman. Those who were present in that Philadelphia auditorium will not forget it.

The bitter Dixiecrat revolt over civil rights had come to its climax with the walkout of some Southern delegations. An enraged Mississippian actually spat as he uttered the President's name.

Truman had arrived from Washington during that evening, expecting to address the convention by 11:30 at the latest. But when he appeared at the hall, to be ushered into a dingy waiting-room in the basement, the venomous fight between the North and South was still raging. The business of nominating a candidate had not been finished. And as the Chief Executive of the nation sat in his cramped quarters, the especially installed air-conditioning unit broke down. There, in the choking heat of a summer's night such as only Philadelphia or Washington can produce, the President in his shirt-sleeves, getting hotter and angrier by the minute, watched the proceedings upstairs on a TV set.

Finally, about 2 A.M., the party machine had triumphed. The President and Mrs. Truman, with Margaret, accompanied by military aide General Harry S. Vaughn, resplendent in uniform with decorations, made a grand entry onto the speaker's platform, as the band and the organ roared "Hail to the Chief."

In a bright cream suit, creased to a razor's edge, with a black handkerchief in his breast pocket, Truman was now the personification of self-confidence. He acknowledged the ovation which greeted him with relaxed smiles and bows, as Speaker Sam Rayburn, the permanent chairman, made a vain effort to stop the band.

At last, a representative of the Democratic women of Pennsylvania, accompanied by two uniformed pages carrying a gigantic liberty bell made of roses, appeared on the stage. This quieted the demonstration. She presented the flowery symbol to the President; but, just as he was about to speak his thanks, the lady gave a tug at a pink ribbon; an opening appeared in the floral bell and some two dozen white pigeons whirred into the air. Truman gasped; Rayburn almost expired; the birds, blinded by the lights and panic-stricken by the noise, frantically circled the speaker's platform at head level. The President and his entourage ducked again and again as the birds almost scraped their skulls. One of them actually landed on the Speaker's bald dome.

"Get that damned thing off!" he shouted. "Do something about these pigeons!"

Truman pounded his knees in laughter. General Vaughn almost rolled off his chair. For minute after minute, the birds caromed above the platform and then darted out onto the floor just a few feet above the dodging delegates, finally finding safe haven among the rafters.

The next day the ASPCA made an indignant protest. It despatched its agents to the convention hall, but a full week passed before all of the pigeons were caught.

It was after this hilarious and utterly ridiculous scene that Truman finally began addressing his audience. His pedestrian opening words won only faint applause. A group of newspapermen standing a few feet from him observed the President's taut manner, his realization that he was losing the crowd. Worried lines shadowed his eyes as he buried his head in the pages of the black loose-leaf notebook. The speech in it was typed in large-sized letters, only a few words to each line, written in uneven lengths to emphasize the rhythmic structure of the sentences.

Suddenly, with an emphatic gesture of disgust, he threw aside his notebook and made an ad-lib comment. The audience laughed; Truman smiled. He made another impromptu remark and it was followed by another wave of laughter.

From then on, the President began to talk "off the cuff." A remarkable change came over his listeners. They leaned forward, eager to catch every word; they applauded; they yelled; they cheered. At the climax of his oration, Truman announced he would "call the bluff" of the Republicans. They dominated the Congress. If they were sincere about their expressed determination to pass certain measures, he would give them that opportunity. Here and now, he notified them that he was going to call Congress into a special session. Let his opponents prove their sincerity!

The announcement astounded the audience. The stunned silence gave way to a roar; delegates waved their banners, yelled themselves hoarse, blew on horns and carried on as so many madmen.

It was an amazing transformation. An hour before, a deep, corroding despondency had engulfed the convention. Most delegates had believed and many had said openly that they would not "give five cents" for the chances of the Democratic Party in the coming election. But now, before one's eyes, one saw this hopeless mob electrified into a jubilant group.

It was perhaps the first time since he had entered the White House that Truman had dared to abandon a set speech and substitute for it an impromptu rambling, at times ungrammatical, "give-

'em-hell" oration. Those who were present in Philadelphia's convention hall that muggy morning witnessed a miracle—the metamorphosis of a dull speaker into a colloquial spellbinder who, during the campaign of 1948, made fools of the professional prophets and won an incredible victory.

Leaving the convention hall after that dramatic development, I was surprised to encounter Mary Margaret McBride, radio's foremost woman reporter-commentator, and her manager, Estella Karn. Surprised, because Mary Margaret had told me that she watched most of the proceedings on a TV set in her hotel suite.

"Had to go on the air from the studio out here. Otherwise I certainly shouldn't have left the hotel," she said. "One gets a much better idea of what's going on from television."

In 1948 such a statement by a commentator was still newsworthy enough to warrant a columnar mention. But by 1952 it had become a common practice for reporters assigned to conventions to tap TV for goodly portions of their running stories.

For, despite the importance of video at the 1948 conclaves, those of four years later in Chicago were truly the premier "TV Conventions." For the first time, the proceedings were telecast coast to coast via more than 100 stations to a nation equipped at the time with almost 17,000,000 television receivers. The combined radio-TV personnel, including reporters, commentators, publicity men, technicians, clerical help, etc., actually outnumbered the delegates. For example, at Republican sessions there were only 1,206 of the latter, compared with 1,300 on the broadcasting staffs!

The 1952 conventions gave birth to several significant features. One of these was the full-scale entry of big business as sponsors of the coverage of such events. For the first time these broadcasts on all networks—plus those of the November election returns—were done under commercial auspices. Westinghouse paid CBS some $3,000,000; Philco $2,400,000 to NBC and Admiral $2,000,000 to ABC. Nevertheless, the chains lost money on the deal, as their expenditures totalled almost $10,000,000.

Even the most virulent critics of the American system of broadcasting admitted that this commercialization had little, if any, effect, on the objectivity of the coverage. The reporting, with rare exceptions, was as unbiased as was humanly possible. The commentaries ranged from the liberal views of Elmer Davis to the extreme conservatism of Fulton Lewis, Jr., with such "anchor men" as Bill Henry, Walter Cronkite, and John Daly occupying middle-of-the-road vantage points.

But of far greater import to the listener and to the viewer was this fact: during 1952, radio and television established beyond argument the right of the public to know what occurred behind the scenes. No one is so naïve as to believe that all, or even most of the secret agreements and deals between politicos came to light via radio and TV. But a precedent of tremendous importance was established when cameras and microphones invaded the hitherto secret sessions of caucuses and committee meetings.

Old-school politicians shuddered when the Republican National Committee ruled that its proceedings could be both broadcast and telecast. Never before had there been so many witnesses to what went on in the "smoke-filled rooms," and political observers agree that the telecasting of the fight over the seating of the contested Eisenhower-Taft delegations played a major role in Eisenhower's nomination.

It became more and more apparent that a man sitting before a TV set in a Manhattan apartment or a Nevada ranch actually knew more of what was taking place than most of the delegates on the floor.

While the latter heard and saw only the action in the auditorium, viewers thousands of miles distant were whisked in seconds from the hall to the headquarters of the candidates, to committee meetings and conferences. Certainly, those in the Chicago Amphitheatre missed one of the most dramatic spectacles of recent political history. That was when the TV cameras flashed on the screen the image of President Truman, as he was departing from the Washington airport on his flight to Chicago, at the very moment the voice of his Missouri alternate was heard casting his chief's vote for Governor Adlai E. Stevenson.

The television coverage of the 1952 conclaves produced much pontificating on the future of such gatherings. Despite the fact that TV was on the scene to an extent not dreamt of before, no visible streamlining of procedures was noticeable. The delegates received printed admonitions telling them that "The eyes of television are on you" but they continued to chat, doze or read newspapers while speakers held forth on the platform. There were the same boresome speeches, the same time-consuming polls of state delegations, and the long-drawn, artifically pumped-up demonstrations differed little from those of twenty or thirty years before.

Now we hear once more that in 1956 the speeches will be shorter and demonstrations briefer. It is true that TV is outmoding the old style of oratory, but how many politicians are willing to abandon the flamboyance which arouses the convention crowds? And which candidate will be the first to surrender his right to as lengthy a demonstration as possible? Also, what state boss is going to deprive some small-town politician of the priceless opportunity to utter his name on a coast-to-coast hookup during a poll of his delegation?

Edward R. Murrow, the CBS commentator, believes that by 1956 the networks themselves will institute radical changes in convention broadcasting. "I think that in 1952 we saw the last of the gavel-to-gavel coverages," he says. "In the future, probably only the highlights will go over the air."

Let us hope that Murrow proves to be mistaken. Whatever their defects, these quadrennial gatherings are the means by which Americans select their Presidential nominees. Boresome or interesting, these sessions are of the utmost importance and the citizen has not only the right but the duty to hear and to see every possible moment of the proceedings. This is essential to his full understanding of the political processes of his country.

The year 1952 produced suggestions for the streamlining of not only the conventions but the Presidential campaigns. William S. Paley, chairman of the board of CBS, advocated that the political conclaves assemble about September 1st and thus reduce the electioneering period to two months. This would not only lessen the strain on the candidates—it is no secret that both General Eisenhower and Governor Stevenson were completely exhausted by November—but would eliminate major financial headaches for both parties.

Almost every political leader has bewailed the appalling cost of radio and television time. Eisenhower's first major speech at Abilene, Kansas, for example, set the Republicans back some $130,000, and the GOP's election-eve broadcast and telecast over all networks cost about $250,000. The national organization of this party spent approximately $2,083,000 for air facilities. As for the Democratic National Committee, its outlay for radio and TV on behalf of Stevenson totaled $1,428,000.

But these figures do not take into account the money expended for such purposes by the various state organizations, unions, clubs, associations, societies, committees and special groups functioning during a Presidential campaign. There is still no way of arriving at the exact total paid by them to the broadcasters.

Under the law, the national body of a political party may spend no more than $3,000,000 for all purposes during any one campaign. But Senator Douglas of Illinois was quoted in the newspapers recently as saying that during 1952 the combined Republican and Democratic expenditures amounted to $92,000,000!

This phase of the battle for the Presidency; the part played by the advertising agencies in the snaring of votes; the astounding rapidity of Adlai Stevenson's emergence as a popular television figure and the sensational impact of Vice-President Richard Nixon's video defense of his political funds helped to make 1952 the most significant year, politically, in the history of broadcasting. Each of these topics would require—and be worthy of—lengthy chapters in any comprehensive study of American radio and television.

Certainly these items are of far greater consequence than some of those recalled by the average viewer. Less than six months after the election, I asked twenty-five New Yorkers—policemen, taxicab drivers, elevator operators, small merchants and housewives— "What incident comes to your mind first when you think of the 1952 campaign?" Four said it was the comedy scene provided by that Puerto Rican delegate (Romani) at the Republican convention, and fifteen insisted it was Betty Furness' opening of iceboxes during her TV commercials!

No wonder that the most popular cartoon of 1952 was: "Pop, who's ahead? Ike, Taft or Betty Furness?"

FOURTEEN

That Fascinating Game

Al Smith was the first radio celebrity of national politics covered by me. He was one of the most picturesque players in what some observers still call "that fascinating game," but his early ventures into broadcasting were by no means successful.

Before the Madison Square Garden convention of 1924, he addressed a mass meeting in a public school on the lower East Side. The New York *American* had assigned me to attend this event, which had a special significance, having been advertised as one of the first political gatherings to be carried by radio.

In a brown suit, with his famous derby on a nearby table, Al began his talk several feet away from the old-fashioned carbon microphone in the center of the stage. After he had spoken only a few sentences, a worried-looking announcer stepped from the wings and pointed to the mike. Smith paid not the slightest attention. The announcer finally took hold of his arm and led him to the new-fangled gadget.

With a look of disdain, and with no regard for the listeners outside, the man who would later become the Presidential nominee of the Democratic Party said: "Leave me alone! I don't like these things!"

The few reporters present questioned Al about this incident. "When I talk to people, I want to see the whites of their eyes," he said. "I don't want 'em to be ten miles away."

Although eventually Governor Smith became one of the beloved personalities of American radio, throughout his career he showed a dislike of the medium. Some of his intimates professed to see evidence of this in his mispronounciation of the word as "rad-dio." He knew better; it was merely his way of hitting back at an unwelcome intruder.

Just like Willkie, Smith was never really at home before a micro-phone. His guttural voice and his "New Yorkese" accent—which, however, did not hide the natural warmth of a robust personality —became assets in the long run. But during his campaign for the Presidency in 1928, these offended many listeners. Merlin H. Ayles-worth, at the time president of NBC, often told me of the con-ferences he had with Owen D. Young, head of General Electric, and a devoted friend of Smith, about some method of improving the Governor's speech.

"We devised a plan," Aylesworth said, "but neither of us dared mention it to Al. He was too sensitive about such things and we did not want to offend him."

Smith's successful opponent in the 1928 campaign, Herbert Hoover, before and during his years in the White House was one of the dullest of all radio speakers. Only long after his exit from Washington did a touch of lightness appear in his well-written but ponderous addresses. Network executives, most of whom were Re-publicans and consequently favored his philosophy, shook their heads over Hoover's monotonous delivery. But they had respect for him because of the care he lavished on his campaign speeches. And he was a technical perfectionist who became indignant if his talks ran over even by the fraction of a second. In this he differed mark-edly from another Republican nominee, Wendell Willkie, who re-fused to do any rehearsing at all. When asked why, he explained:

"If I go over this stuff, I sound as if I weren't interested in what I'm saying."

But neither Smith, Hoover, Willkie, nor any other Presidential nominee since 1920, could approach the microphone mastery of Franklin D. Roosevelt. Adlai Stevenson is undoubtedly a brilliant speaker; Bryan was a great orator in the grand manner. But F.D.R. had a technique which was "made" for the electronic age.

As one professionally interested in such matters, I often tried to analyze his method on the many occasions he spoke over the radio. It was quite apparent that Roosevelt's speeches were oratorically impressive enough to sway the large groups he faced in auditoriums and open-air assemblies; but this quality never went to the extremes of the spread-eagle school. His addresses contained many warm appeals to the emotions and yet these were so deftly phrased as to give the illusion of cold logic.

Each word, each phrase, each sentence seemed to be built, whether by instinct or design, with the invisible audience in mind. Thus big issues were invested with a sense of intimacy. More than any other political speaker of his time, Roosevelt realized that although his radio listeners numbered millions this vast gathering was divided into small groups of individuals in homes, bars, restaurants and automobiles. So, while painting a verbal picture expansive enough for a museum mural, he reduced it to the proportions of a miniature hanging cozily on the wall of a living room.

Not wishing to rely solely on personal impressions gained through hearing and seeing F.D.R. many times, I obtained from Bryson Rash, the noted newscaster, his observations on the late President's oratorical technique. These were forwarded to me by Robert E. Kintner, president of the American Broadcasting Company, and once himself a celebrated Washington columnist.

"Mr. Roosevelt had the most accurate sense of crowd mood I have ever seen," says Rash, who for years covered F.D.R. in the White House and on his campaign tours. "He would open his speech as though he were feeling for the huge throng in the stadium or ball park, devoting his first few sentences merely to gauging its mood, watching for its reaction. Then, as soon as he had the crowd mood firmly in his mind, he would ram home the next sentence or thought with unerring instinct. The throng would roar its appreciation, because he had reached them."

Regarding the famous Fireside Chats, Rash confides that Roosevelt had such a "magnetic personality" that when he entered the broadcasting room of the White House, it seemed "as though the lights were suddenly turned on because of his cheerfulness and wit and tremendous love of banter."

The Fireside Chats marked the first time a President had ever reported to his people in a series of informal broadcasts. It was Merlin H. Aylesworth who had suggested these to Louis Howe, Roosevelt's secretary, a few months after the inauguration in 1933.

On such occasions, each of the four radio networks had an announcer present in a small booth made of dark blue velvet drapes with an isinglass window. Today, of course, television cameras are also on the scene in a room built especially for this purpose.

Although the chats were informal, there was strict protocol governing the broadcasts. The audience of about fifty radio and newsreel men, secret-service agents, White House attachés, members of the family, officials and a few privileged visitors maintained an attitude of cold formality as the President entered, preceded by an usher or a secretary. The mood of reserve was not broken until Roosevelt, usually with a smile, said, "Good evening."

During the few minutes before going on the air, the President would often jest with the radio announcers. One night he came into the room wearing a royal purple velvet smoking jacket with the initials F.D.R. embroidered on the breast pocket. "Holy smokes! Where'd you get it?" one of the broadcasters asked.

"Oh, I just whipped it up out of some old drapes we used to have around here," Roosevelt said, laughing.

Like Truman, he read his speeches from a loose-leaf notebook. One evening, as he reached the bottom of page 2, he inadvertently turned to page 4. Without the slightest hesitancy he read the first paragraph on that page, turned back to page 3, read it through, turned again to 4, skipped the first paragraph, and continued with the remainder of the address.

F.D.R. was a master of timing his speeches so that they would end "right on the nose," which made him a favorite of broadcasting networks. He had visible pride in this ability, and after a Fireside Chat would often hold aloft a watch, to which he would point proudly. Incidentally, until the last few years of his life the President did not carry his own timepiece for broadcasting purposes. Rash or one of the other radio men would usually provide him with one.

The sometimes high-schoolish sense of humor which caused Roosevelt to coin such nicknames as "Harry the Hop" for Harry Hopkins and "Sammy the Rose" for Justice Samuel I. Rosenman often manifested itself in his contacts with the broadcasters.

Following F.D.R.'s third election in 1940, an enthusiastic crowd greeted the Presidential train which had brought the Chief Executive's party to Washington's Union Station from Hyde Park. The network announcers were describing the scene from microphones set up beside Roosevelt's private car. But, instead of making an immediate appearance, the President remained in his lounge, chatting with old friends for more than twenty minutes.

Although there was absolutely nothing to describe, the unfortunate announcers had to continue talking all of this time. At last, the President and Mrs. Roosevelt appeared on the rear platform of his car to pose for pictures. Then, as he was waving his old campaign hat, F.D.R. spotted Rash directly beneath him.

"Look at that radio man!" he said in a magnified stage whisper, winking at Eleanor. "Talks constantly and doesn't know what he's talking about. He can't possibly remember anything he's said, but he keeps on talking just the same."

Instead of "breaking up," Rash calmly informed his listeners, "This is probably the first time, during a broadcast, that a radio announcer has ever been heckled by a President of the United States!"

Roosevelt's favorite broadcasting room was not the one in the White House, but his small, book-lined, memento-filled study in the mansion at Hyde Park. It was from there that he made his last campaign plea on the election eve of 1944. Immediately following the conclusion of his speech, his Republican opponent, Governor Thomas E. Dewey of New York, was scheduled to take the air. But F.D.R., strangely enough, on this occasion did not consume all of the time for which the Democrats had paid. So the interval was filled with organ music.

As the President leaned back in his chair, he smiled mischievously. "You know," he said, "a thought has just come to me. Most of the audience might tune out during this organ recital and not hear the Governor at all!"

Not only Governor Dewey, but President Hoover, Governor Landon of Kansas and Willkie, his other campaign opponents, were outdistanced by F.D.R. at the microphone. Landon was utterly inept as a radio speaker. But Willkie did have the advantages of a robust personality, a down-to-earth manner and a rugged voice which could have been developed into broadcasting assets.

However, he persistently ignored the demands of the mike. Not only did he refuse to rehearse his talks but he failed to take advantage of radio's amplifying power, shouting at top volume and straining his voice into a croaky hoarseness.

Charles C. Barry, later one of NBC's top program executives, was one of those assigned to the Willkie campaign in 1940. "I suffered with him through dozens of speeches," he says, "because of his failure to learn how to use his voice. Willkie had a bad throat most of the time. In Peoria, Illinois, for instance, the sounds he produced were so guttural and indistinct that the audience actually laughed. This was a great pity because Willkie actually was a fine man of exceptional ability."

Unlike Roosevelt, the GOP candidate had utter contempt for the time limitations of radio. Sometimes he would run over a scheduled period by as much as ten or fifteen minutes. On one occasion in Los Angeles, Willkie paid no heed to signals to bring his address to a close and set back the Republican National Committee ten thousand dollars for additional time.

Although not in the same oratorical league with Roosevelt, Dewey eventually became the most effective radio opponent the President faced. Prior to the campaign of 1944, the New York Governor's attitude toward the microphone was that of a district attorney shaking his finger in the face of a recalcitrant witness.

Then he was taken in hand by his Pawling, New York, neighbor, Lowell Thomas. The commentator's pointers were so effective that Dewey turned into a powerful rough-and-tumble orator. But he still is not at his best in the set type of speech. He comes into his own only in the give and take of debate or in the impromptu atmosphere of a question-and-answer session.

Television, not radio, is the ideal medium for this kind of political exercise, and it was via TV that Dewey brought a revolutionary innovation to American campaigning. During his 1950 race for the Governorship it seemed almost certain that he would be defeated by the heavy Democratic vote in New York City. So Dewey made an unprecedented maneuver. He bought time on WOR-TV and, facing the camera for hours at a time, sat at a desk or roamed about the room, as he pointed to charts and graphs to illustrate his arguments. Each point was made in response to some phone call from outside the studio.

This was a new form of vote-seeking, abandoning as it did, for the first time in broadcasting, the formal oration for the methods of the seminar. It brought the heckler within earshot of the television speaker. The technique requires a glib tongue and a mastery of facts and figures.

During the 1952 campaign one of Senator Joseph R. McCarthy's opponents in Wisconsin also used this method in a more highly developed form known as the "talkathon." But in his case it failed. This prevented its wider employment that year, but without a doubt this form of electioneering will become a fixture of American politics.

Even more adept, if possible, than Governor Dewey in his use of television as an intimate "off-the-cuff" medium is former President Truman, who certainly must be counted as one of the most effective political orators of this generation. This is undoubtedly a surprising statement to the millions who regard him as basically a poor speaker.

Academically, those who discount Truman's prowess in this field may be correct. The Missourian lacks polish; his delivery is pedestrian; his voice, at best, only average, and the content of his addresses devoid of those flashes of eloquence which mark the truly distinguished public speaker.

All of these defects were highlighted on the radio. In fact, it is safe to say that, without television, Truman might have been remembered as one of our duller political spellbinders. But with the camera added to the microphone, his speeches gained not only the added dimension of sight but also the more important one of person-to-person appeal—the attribute possessed in the highest degree by Franklin D. Roosevelt.

The ad-lib remarks, the colloquial turns of phrase, the flashes of temper, the down-to-earth vocabulary, and the commonplace hominess of manner were magically lifted from the realm of the lackluster. Under the eyes of the sensitive cameras, these became transformed into a vivid image of the "little fellow," the average man. But because of Truman's individual qualities, this picture of the average man was not projected on the grand scale of cold symbolism but in a warm, human and intimate manner. This did not prevent the 1952 electorate from repudiating his administration in a decisive manner; but the Missourian's TV know-how should not be discounted.

Truman's light, however, pales beside that of the candidate who suffered defeat in the 1952 campaign, Adlai E. Stevenson. As a speaker, he is to television what F.D.R. was to radio. The fact that, unlike Roosevelt, he lost the battle—because of resentments that no nominee could have overcome—does not reduce his stature as a broadcasting figure.

From the moment he began his acceptance speech at the Chicago convention until that fateful Tuesday in November, Stevenson proved himself to be one who could effectively address a vast visible audience and at the same time hold the attention of millions of others gathered in small groups about their radio or television sets. Truman had mastered the art of intimacy on TV, but not on radio; Roosevelt had done so on radio but not quite to the same degree on television. Stevenson achieved mastery of both media.

Although as yet none of his speeches has contained a sentence as vivid as F.D.R.'s on "fear itself," his addresses possess a literary quality, philosophical overtones, and a humorous touch unapproached in the utterances of any American political figure of to-day.

It was said during the last campaign that Stevenson's talks were appreciated only by the "egg-heads" and were far above the level of the general audiences. Some post-mortems emphasized that this "defect," plus his sense of humor, had been in considerable part responsible for his defeat. None the less, he polled more than twenty-seven million votes!

No Democrat—even one combining the oratorical virtues of Patrick Henry, Daniel Webster, Abraham Lincoln and Franklin D. Roosevelt—could have prevailed that year. As for the argument that Stevenson's propensity to indulge in jest prejudiced many voters against him—well, it is one that bears some examination.

True enough, Americans are reputed to be chary of "funny" men in public office. Yet Abraham Lincoln was known for his jokes and comic stories, and F.D.R.'s sense of humor was widely publicized. Also, there is the "Veep," former Vice-President Alben

Barkley, whose unending stream of anecdotes contributed probably more than anything else toward making him an affectionately regarded national figure.

Students of such matters, however, point out that the japes of these men were invested with a broadness which appealed to, and did not frighten, the man in the street. But Stevenson, some say, gave vent to his waggery on a higher plane. He chose to be witty rather than humorous—and that, so the argument runs, was fatal.

The fact is that a reading of Stevenson's campaign speeches will show a delightful and always literate sense of humor. But it is also a fact that, save on rare occasions, his "funny stuff" was not above the appreciation level of those who laugh at such comedians as Fred Allen, Herb Shriner, or Bob Hope.

Of course, even the broadest attempts at humor have their risks on the radio—as any speaker will tell you. Sometimes a considerable number of listeners do not differentiate between the "funny" and the serious portions of a speech. But this is not so on television. There the facial expressions of the man before the camera, if all else fails, will convey to the obtuse ones that they are hearing a jest.

No, I am not one of those who believe that Stevenson's humor contributed in any great degree to his failure at the polls. For he is one of those public speakers who knows just how far to go with his "comic relief." And immediately after uttering some drollery, the former Governor invariably follows through with a serious thought phrased in concise and cogent words. Oddly enough, this technique is reminiscent of that used by a distinguished Englishman, Malcolm Muggeridge, editor of *Punch*, whose address before the Overseas Press Club in New York during 1953 was hailed as one of the most brilliant speeches ever carried by American radio.

These qualities, potent as they are, could not have, in themselves, transformed Adlai Stevenson from a mere name into a familiar household figure from coast to coast within the span of just four months. But that is what television did in 1952. It is the most amazing example on record of its power.

General Dwight D. Eisenhower entered that campaign as a man

of worldwide fame, an advantage he sorely needed, as he was not so well equipped as Stevenson to meet the demands of radio and television. A blunt and occasionally a forceful speaker, he was nevertheless lacking in the verbal niceties and the gift of repartee possessed by his opponent. His was a broadsword wielded against a rapier. During the early phases of the battle, he apparently spoke under self-imposed wraps; his speeches had a muffled quality which, on the air, failed to convey either his dogged earnestness or his magnetic warmth.

"Eisenhower at the start of the campaign fought TV almost as hard as he fights an enemy in war." That is what David Schoenbrun, a CBS reporter who had been assigned to headquarters at SHAPE and also to his campaign trains, told the readers of my column.

"It was really tough working with him," Schoenbrun said. "He refused all makeup, ignored camera directions and wouldn't let anyone who wasn't on his personal staff advise him about TV."

When efforts were made to "tone down" via makeup the bald area on his head, the General protested indignantly: "It makes me feel like a ham actor!"

En route to the Chicago convention from Denver, those on Ike's special train heard that the Republican National Committee had decided to ban radio and TV from its hearings on contested delegations. One of the press-relations men aboard informed the correspondents that during a brief stopover at McCook, Nebraska, the General would make a speech in which he would say that this act reflected an "Iron Curtain mentality."

Eisenhower did refer to an "Iron Curtain mentality" but completely neglected to mention either radio or television in connection with it. The correspondents, who had already filed their stories highlighting this comment, were upset by this omission; so Ike agreed to use those words in another speech at Hastings, Nebraska. But again he failed to do so.

"Why?" Schoenbrun asked him.

"Oh, Dave," the General replied with genuine regret, "I always seem to forget!"

Recalling this incident, the network correspondent commented:

"I'm convinced that Ike's dislike of television was responsible for this. Psychologists say that when a person has an aversion to something, he is apt to show a lapse of memory regarding it."

Whether President Eisenhower has even today overcome his dislike of TV, I do not know. But one thing is certain: he has long since surrendered to the demands made on him by this medium. After his homecoming speech in Abilene, Kansas, the candidate was told in no uncertain terms that he had made a poor impression on television. Without his uniform, in a trench coat, with the thinning strands of his hair rumpled by a rainy wind, he was anything but a glamorous figure. And on several occasions during the campaign, his lack of makeup, plus the atrocious lighting, made him seem far older and much less vigorous than he really was.

But at last the experts of the big advertising agencies, which played such a prominent role in the last battle for the Presidency, took matters in hand. They reminded the General that in 1948, at the Philadelphia Republican Convention, even such a beauteous woman as Clare Boothe Luce had come a cropper when she had failed to adapt herself to video. That was the time when, after she had refused the services of a makeup man, Mrs. Luce's usually enticing image appeared on the home screens as one that might have belonged to a Salem dame about to mount a broomstick.

As a result of the hucksters' ministrations, Ike had shown a marked improvement by the time November had rolled around. Also, his addresses contained briefer sentences which were spoken in a more intimate manner. President Eisenhower, however, is still at his best not in a set speech but in the informal discussion or question-and-answer type of telecast. During his first year in the White House, discarding his unwillingness to adapt himself to the routines of TV showmanship, he placed himself under the tutelage of actor-producer Robert Montgomery who has become the official video impresario of the current administration.

Not only Ike, but all other candidates, regardless of personal inclination, were soon forced to accept the discipline of TV. During the 1952 campaign, CBS even conducted a heavily attended school for politicos of both parties in Washington.

There they were instructed to wear blue shirts instead of white before the camera; to eschew handpainted ties and to substitute Panamas for straw hats. As for the women, they were exhorted to pay attention to their "hair, faces and upper torsos" and cautioned to "avoid jewelry, frills and bows of every kind." Also, they were reminded that "simple fitted dresses come over better than those with ruffles and overelaborate details."

At the conventions, even the most aggressive politicians clamored for the services of the makeup men. Speaker Sam Rayburn had pancake makeup smeared on his bald head every day, and as Governor Devers of Massachusetts kept his daily rendezvous in the makeup chair his valet was standing by taking notes.

"I've merely come to observe, sir," he explained. "The Governor makes so many speeches on television and I want to know the right thing to do."

The element of theatricalism which TV has brought to campaigning was exemplified in the utmost degree by the address of Eisenhower's running mate, Senator Richard M. Nixon of California, in defense of the political funds which had been raised for him by some of his wealthy supporters.

The charges made against him were so serious that it seemed to many observers the Republicans might lose the campaign as a result of these. Friends and foes alike gave Nixon but the minutest of chances to extricate himself.

But he did it—through one of the most artfully contrived and spectacularly melodramatic television shows ever staged. Borrowing unashamedly from the techniques of the soap opera, he played on every sentimental chord known to the serial script writer: The clean young hero wrongfully accused by malevolent enemies; the kids, family puppy and loyal wife bravely facing adversity, etc. Judged purely as a histrionic effort, there are few stars of the theatre and of the movies today who could have equaled it.

The political sophisticates laughed at Nixon's performance, but they were fooled. What his critics called "blatant hokum" and "disgraceful ham acting" evidently swayed the majority of the viewers in his favor. This speech not only saved his place on the ticket but was credited with having been the final push needed by the Republicans.

Even before the campaign had ended, however, many were perturbed by the implications of the episode.

Disregarding the rightness or the wrongness of the charges made against Nixon, this incident raised a danger signal that must be heeded in all future campaigns. It proved conclusively that the impact of emotionalism is inestimably greater on television than on any other medium. And it must be remembered that emotionalism is the most valuable stock-in-trade of the demagogue. Hitler and Mussolini found radio to be a powerful weapon; it is almost inconceivable what they might have done with TV. In our country, if he had survived, Huey Long most likely would have propelled himself into the White House on the strength of his video appeal. No one who came into contact with him doubts that he possessed this in the highest degree.

Undisputed dictator of Louisiana, self-styled "kingfish," and the most successful American fascist of his day, he was a truly colorful figure on the radio of the New Deal era.

But it was not as a native fuehrer that I knew him; rather he came into view as a jovial, back-slapping, drink-dispensing aerial salesman of his slogans "Share the wealth!" and "Every man a king!"

On the morning of July 31, 1935, shortly before his assassination in Baton Rouge, Louisiana, there appeared in my "Listening In" column the following item:

"Tip to sponsors! Sign Huey P. Long! Grab the Kingfish for your commercials and you will have a comedian who will make Will Rogers, Ed Wynn or even Jack Benny turn green with professional envy. The Senator put on a show last night (WHN— 10:30 to 11:30)—and I mean a show!—that was far more entertaining than that of the professional funmakers. Here is proof:

"(a) Huey gave a lesson in the art of mixing Ramos gin fizzes. He denied that he advocated vanilla instead of orange and (b) he charged that reporters who had accused him of this sacrilege were drunk. (c) He asked his New York friends to call John D. Rockefeller and 'tell him to tune in my talk.' (d) He announced that, financially, under the guidance of President Roosevelt, the United States is 'going straight to hell.' "

It was one of the most remarkable broadcasts I have ever heard. He began it with the announcement: "This is Huey P. Long, Sena-

tor of the United States, from the sovereign state of Louisiana, talking to you." Then he added: "Now I want you to do me a favor. Go
to the phone and call up four or five of your friends and tell them
to tune in this station. They're going to hear something very important. In the meantime, I'll just be talking along to fill up time.
So go right ahead now and call your friends."

After a few minutes of earthy jokes and personal reminiscences,
Huey launched into one of the most violent attacks on Franklin D.
Roosevelt ever to go over the airwaves. He promised to do away
with the wicked New Deal and to substitute therefor his "plan
to guarantee every citizen at least $5,000 a year. . . . The rich
would become poorer but even the poorest would live like a king!"

Senator Long was bringing to the New York radio a campaign
that had resulted in the organization of "share-the-wealth" clubs
throughout the country, with a reputed membership of twenty-one
million.

A group of printers in my office, entranced by his tones, at times
mellow, at times harsh, listened intently to the radio. Under the
spell of his flamboyant hyperbole and homey man-to-man confi-
dences, one of them remarked, "He makes sense." Another added,
"He's got something." Huey's mastery of the microphone was second only to F.D.R.'s and he had something Roosevelt did not possess—an ability to seem even more common than the common
man. Wily and ruthless, he was also magnetic and likable.

He revealed himself as such to a group of radio editors and other
newspapermen whom he had invited to his suite at the Hotel New
Yorker, a few days before his address on WHN. While his guests
were imbibing Scotch, rye and bourbon, a reporter pointed to his
glass and said: "This ain't nothing like those Ramos gin fizzes you
get down in New Orleans."

"God damned right, it ain't!" Huey laughed. Then suddenly:
"Say! How many of you ever had a real Ramos fizz?"

The Senator looked disgusted when only a few admitted knowledge of this delight. Then he commanded one of the waiters behind the bar to "bring up a Ramos for everybody here." He explained that the New Yorker was only the place where "they're supposed to make 'em like they do in New Orleans."

When a few minutes later, two servitors appeared with trays of the creamy white drink, Huey snatched a glass, and took a sip. He spat it out with surprising violence. His face contorted in rage, he shouted: "What the hell do you call this?"

Then he announced: "You Yankees don't know what a Ramos gin fizz is. But, by God, you're going to find out!"

While the press delegation, not quite so finicky about its libations, proceeded to dispose of the stuff, the Senator picked up a telephone and put in a long-distance call to a bartender at the hostelry of his political henchman, Seymour Weiss, the Roosevelt in New Orleans.

"Charlie," he said. "This is Senator Long. I want you to charter a plane and be up here in New York by tomorrow night. And I want you to bring enough stuff with you to mix several hundred Ramos gin fizzes. . . . We're going to show these ignorant bastards up here what a real drink is like!"

Late during the evening of the following day, newspapermen assembled again in Huey's suite. Charlie, a jovial, chubby little man, was there with all of the ingredients, including the essential Florida water. With these he had been rushed from the airport, accompanied by a police motorcycle escort, directly to the hotel. After all, he was a personage on an important mission, in the service of a member of the "greatest deliberative body on earth."

The drinks were now made to the satisfaction not only of the guests, but of the host himself. The session ended in song, and by the time the party had come to its close more than one easygoing newspaperman was heard to observe, "You know, he's not a bad guy." But there were others who, viewing Huey Long through more somber spectacles, ventured: "He's a dangerous man."

That certainly was also the opinion of another firebrand of radio, General Hugh S. Johnson, head of Roosevelt's ill-fated NRA. During a year of intense verbal violence—1935—over Station WNEW of New York he referred to the Senator and his followers as a "plague of lice." And later that evening, Huey appeared on the air to call the General a "dirty liar."

Such mud-slinging was the essence of life to Long in his advocacy of national socialism without the racial elements. But his language became the most torrid when speaking of his arch-hate, President

Roosevelt. On his frequent visits to Merlin H. Aylesworth, president of NBC, in his Radio City headquarters, he seldom referred to F.D.R. without prefacing the name with the words, "that sonofabitch anarchist."

His visits to NBC, however, were not purely social. For months he had been trying to persuade Aylesworth to recommend to John D. Rockefeller, Jr., that the latter sponsor Huey on a gasoline program. Deac had refused to do so and that explained Long's request to his radio audience to telephone the oil magnate.

But even the Louisiana Senator lacked the emotional hold on listeners possessed by that other prime rabblerouser of the day, Father Charles E. Coughlin, "the radio priest." I had no personal contact with him, but for a brief time had been impressed with the eloquence on his early broadcasts, devoted solely to religious topics. Like other radio editors throughout the country, however, I soon was affected personally after his talks had turned into a violent form of political propaganda.

Originally one of the most ardent supporters of Roosevelt, Father Coughlin began his attacks by denouncing the fiscal policies of the New Deal. Then his talks came to be tinged with anti-Semitic overtones, and by 1937 the priest was advocating a form of the fascistic "corporate state" and, later, openly calling on his supporters to "fight the Franco way." Hundreds of letters poured into my office weekly demanding favorable reviews for his speeches, most of them accompanied with threats of boycott, followed later by missives so obscene that they could not be published in a newspaper. Other writers about radio, from coast to coast, reported similar experiences.

In the meantime, bitter waves of controversy raged in broadcasting circles. The question was: How far should a speaker over the air be permitted to go in attacking religious or racial minorities? There was considerable fear that the Government itself would be forced to clamp down a stringent form of censorship. But, in 1939, the National Association of Broadcasters adopted a code of practices which forestalled such a calamity.

Eventually, more and more radio stations throughout the country refused to carry Father Coughlin's addresses. After WMCA of New

York did so, it was subjected to months of turbulent picketing, but the new code of the broadcasters prevailed, and today there are few, if any, stations in the United States which would dare to air a speech denouncing any racial or religious group.

By 1940, the "radio priest" of Royal Oak, Michigan, was off the channels. Some said it was because of government pressure; others that the Church had intervened, and still others that Father Coughlin himself had decided to retire from active combat.

Whatever the reason, this fact remains: broadcasting can be a mighty weapon for good, but at the disposal of those appealing to the base emotions of prejudice, it could become one of the most powerful media for evil ever devised.

Coughlin, Long and Johnson, each known for his verbal pyrotechnics, were characteristic of the Roosevelt era. Radio during this period was given over to fiery debates over the repeal of Prohibition, the economic issues flowing out of the 1929 crash, isolationism and our entanglement in the crises of Europe and the Orient. It soon became apparent that there was a need on the air for a type of program as yet nonexistent, one which would present both sides of the great controversies then raging. This need was met by the creation of discussion periods, the first of which to be established on a national basis was Theodore Granik's "American Forum of the Air."

It came into being more or less accidentally. Granik, in 1928, while still a student in the law school of St. John's University, was conducting a feature known as "Law for the Layman" over WOR, in New York. He had invited Congressman Emanuel Celler of Brooklyn to discuss the legal aspects of Prohibition repeal; and Mrs. Ella Boole, president of the Women's Christian Temperance Union, reading of this, demanded equal air time to answer the legislator. So Granik booked both for the same broadcast and suggested that the program be turned into an ad-lib debate. This rough-and-tumble affair took place one night before an eager audience of newspapermen assembled in the studio.

Mrs. Boole, known as a vitriolic speaker, grew angrier and angrier by the second. She became so excited that when she reached for a glass of water its contents were spilled down her bosom. Enraged by the razzing laughter of the studio audience, she now let go with an astounding accusation. Certain Government officials in Washington, she said, had such contempt for the law that they actually had constructed subterranean passages between their offices and nearby speakeasies! The story made the front pages and it also made Granik's radio forum.

Since that time, this public-service program, like so many others, has contributed some exciting moments to radio and television. On one occasion, while appearing on Ted's show, U.S. Supreme Court Justice Sherman Minton, then a Senator from Indiana, became so enraged at Congressman Clare Hoffman of Michigan that he lifted his opponent from the floor and was about to hurl him into the audience! Only Granik's quick intervention prevented this. It was also on this program that General Johnson, no longer relying on his sulphurous vocabulary, seized a table microphone and attempted to bop Senator Claude Pepper of Florida over the head. And, one evening, Congresswoman Clare Boothe Luce, now our Ambassador to Italy, displayed such fury discussing "Communism vs. Democracy" with William Z. Foster, Communist leader, that the moderator was forced to seize her flaying arms in order to restrain her.

Since the days of Hoover, Presidents (but not Eisenhower) before entering the White House, Vice-Presidents, cabinet members, admirals, generals, and leading members of both houses of Congress have appeared either on "American Forum of the Air" or on the more recent "Meet the Press." The latter has the distinction of having brought the Washington press conference to radio and TV for the first time.

Sometimes these programs not only discuss but make news. For example, one day Marvin McIntyre, President Roosevelt's secretary, phoned Granik to suggest that "it might make an interesting show" to discuss the possibility of swapping some old U.S. destroyers for certain British bases. The mail reaction to that program gave assurance to the White House that it could safely proceed to negotiate such an exchange.

The "public affairs" show which has most consistently made the headlines during recent years is "Meet the Press," created by Martha Rountree and Larry Spivak. During one of its broadcasts Whittaker Chambers charged, without benefit of Congressional immunity, that Alger Hiss "was and still may be a Communist." As a result, Hiss sued Chambers for libel, and it was during the proceedings which followed that Chambers produced those celebrated "pumpkin papers" which eventually led to Hiss' conviction as a perjurer.

"Meet the Press" also created sensational news when the late Theodore Bilbo, Mississippi's bellicose white-supremacy advocate, openly admitted that he was a member of the Ku Klux Klan. "Once a Kluxer, always a Kluxer," he said. This broadcast brought about an official investigation which resulted in Bilbo absenting himself permanently from his Senate seat.

These programs, along with "Man of the Week" and others of their type, have had a major effect on political life in Washington. Their conductors wield considerable unofficial power. Congressmen and Senators vie for the privilege of appearing on shows, as more and more their constituents judge their importance by the number of times they are seen on television. Even "Meet the Press," whose expert reporters, led by the incisive Spivak, pull no punches in their questions, has had no difficulty in obtaining guests.

Although, unlike Granik's "American Forum," "Meet the Press," up to this writing, has not produced any instances of physical violence, I do recall several of its "interesting" moments. There was the night when, after the announcer had said: "Our next week's guest will be Senator Claude Pepper of Florida," Congressman Harold Knutsen of Minnesota, the interviewee of the evening, thinking he was off the air, remarked: "That's going from the sublime to the ridiculous!" And also there was the time when a reporter asked Mrs. Martha Taft if she thought her husband, the Senator, had enough political "sex appeal." Her answer was an explosive "Pooh!"

Almost as marked as its effect on political discussion has been broadcasting's revolutionary impact on that old American custom— the election-night celebration. By 1952, the gay crowds on the streets watching bulletin boards in front of newspaper offices and the raucous jubilations in cafés and night clubs had all but vanished.

The "smallest election-night turnout in its long existence," Meyer Berger wrote in the New York *Times* of the sparse groups strolling in Times Square during the evening of the Eisenhower victory. Up to 1944, there had never been fewer than 250,000 on such occasions and sometimes at least 1,000,000 New Yorkers had been crowded into the area between 42nd and 50th streets. Now, at the peak hour, there were fewer than 25,000.

Television was responsible, of course. Anyone intent on getting the latest figures, analyses of trends and first-hand glimpses of party headquarters would be foolish to leave his TV receiver to go wandering around the town. Yet some of a reporter's most vivid memories are those gleaned during excursions out of his office on election nights. They gave him close-ups of celebrated political figures both under the depression of defeat and the elation of victory.

The Republican leaders were in a jubilant mood that memorable Tuesday of 1952; but they were a melancholy lot on November evenings in 1944 and 1948.

I recall visiting both the crowded and exuberant Democratic headquarters and the almost deserted rooms of the Republican National Committee on the election night of '44. In the grand ballroom of the Hotel Roosevelt, the operating center of the GOP, only a few photographers, reporters, newsreel and radio men, along with a half-dozen weary cops, awaited the arrival of Governor Thomas E. Dewey. It was 2:30 A.M. and, an hour before, Dewey's national chairman had refused to concede Roosevelt's fourth victory.

A long wait, then a sudden clapping of hands, as the Governor finally entered with Mrs. Dewey and Herbert Brownell. Flanked on either side by policemen, smiling wanly and appearing to be utterly exhausted, he walked with seeming effort to a table banked with microphones. Several strands of his black hair were out of place and a lingering sadness clouded his eyes.

Cutting short the shooting of the cameramen with "Hold it! I'll give you all you want after I finish," the Republican nominee faced the microphones at exactly 3:14 A.M. and began reading in a resonant voice from the typed sheet in front of him. He conceded the election and congratulated F.D.R.

Now, off the air, he read his brief statement twice again for the benefit of the reporters who complained that he had spoken too rapidly in front of the microphones. More and more pictures, until at last with unusual joviality Dewey bantered, "Remember boys, I've got to do this all over again for the newsreels."

On the way out, he shook hands with several news and radio men who had covered his unsuccessful campaign. As he reached a side door, someone shouted, "How about 1948?"

"I'm not even thinking of that," Dewey answered.

A cop munching a ham sandwich said, "Too bad. Must be awf'lly disappointed."

A minute later, only an announcer, Ann Gillis, a radio reporter, and I were left in the vast ballroom. Overturned chairs, newspapers, Dixie cups and sandwich wrappers littered the floor. In one corner, a red-lettered sign, "Win with Dewey," provided an ironic footnote to the desolate scene. Leaving, we passed in the corridor a young woman campaign worker wiping away her tears.

It was the finale of a drama which had begun in a triumphant moment one hot day of the preceding summer, during the Republican National Convention in Chicago, when the New York Governor had accepted the nomination for the Presidency. Bands had blared, banners had waved and thousands had cheered. And now all that remained was a deserted room and, outside, a woman quietly weeping.

Although television had played a political role as early as 1940, the election of 1944 was still a major radio event. Not until four years later did TV take the center of the stage.

On the election night of that year, the commentators, the analysts and the opinion expounders of the air-waves, of whom I happened to be one, learned a lesson in humility. The developments of that evening produced more breathless drama and greater surprise than any like event since the beginning of broadcasting. Practically everyone save Harry S. Truman had predicted an overwhelming victory for Dewey, who, despite his 1944 statement, evidently had been thinking of 1948. All that remained was the counting of the ballots, a mere cumbersome formality.

Under the supervision of Carl Warren, head of the WPIX news department, a group of New York *News* men had been chosen to telecast the returns. Lowell Limpus, UN bureau chief, Jimmy Jemail, Inquiring Fotographer, and John Tillman, an announcer, served as newscasters, and I as the analyst of trends. We were supplemented by a group of political writers—John O'Donnell, Ruth

Montgomery, Ted Lewis, John Crosson and Dick Lee among them.

Almost during the first hour it was evident that something had gone wrong. Truman was ahead. Then, returns from the Midwest and the Pacific Coast began to echo the same story.

"It can't be!" I remarked. "Is it possible that Truman's winning?"

"Seems so, but you'd better not commit yourself too strongly as yet," advised a puzzled Carl Warren.

"The whole world's gone crazy," Limpus whispered to his colleagues.

"We haven't yet heard sufficiently from the Midwestern farm belt," O'Donnell told his audience. "When we do, the picture may be changed."

It was the same on every other station—radio and TV. H. V. Kaltenborn, Bob Trout, Quincy Howe and even ardent New Dealer Elmer Davis were still advising caution. In fact, into the early morning hours many of them, notably Kaltenborn, were arguing, or at least indicating, that some miracle would occur which, at the last moment, would change the outcome. But it wasn't changed; Truman won a colossal and completely unexpected victory. The stations had planned to remain on the air no later than 1 A.M. By that time, they were certain Dewey would be in. But when they signed off two and three hours later, along with the poll conductors, the most deflated group of men in the United States were the political prognosticators of radio and television.

And, while all this was happening, on the seventh-floor city room of the News, from where WPIX held forth in a corner cubicle, scores and scores of reporters, rewrite men, feature writers, copy readers, editors and others labored on the election story for the printed page. Glancing beyond our studio confines, one could see the great room lined with long pine tables and, bending over these, tabulators compiling figures beside the political writers gathering data on the national, state, Congressional and Senatorial contests. Copy boys tore tapes from tickers, carried these to city and telegraph desks and distributed them to those at the tables. With earphones clamped on, rewrite men pounded their typewriters; others sitting in booths scribbled on copy paper columns of figures phoned from every quarter of the city; they worked quietly, smoothly, each man

a gear in a vast machine. And, over them all, directing and co-ordi-
nating the multiform activities, the managing editor, Robert Shand,
sat at his desk, while Richard Clarke, the paper's executive editor,
strolled calmly from table to table glancing at the figures.

Movies and television plays of newspaper life to the contrary not-
withstanding, there is surprisingly little excitement in a city room
during the coverage of a big story. The accurate reporting of a Presidential election requires a plan of organization almost as detailed as
the orders for the conduct of a major battle. Every contingency is
provided for; every source, ranging from national to precinct levels,
is covered; leg men, telegraph, telephone, press-association tickers,
radio and TV are all utilized.

Evolved through many years, the newspaper plan of organization
has been adopted by the broadcasters. It enabled them on November 4, 1952 to air the most accurate and speediest election returns of
history. This was truly a TV night, as it was the first time that the
returns were telecast from coast to coast.

Making the rounds of the studios that evening, a reporter saw
them transformed into vast factories for the processing of tens of
thousands of figures. In NBC's gigantic Studio H, Radio City, in the
cavernous quarters of CBS in the Grand Central Terminal Building,
and in ABC's sprawling plant on West 66th Street, the setups were
much the same: long rows of tables with tabulators, both human
and mechanical, and desks in charge of newscasters and commentators concerned with the Presidential, Senatorial and Congressional,
and local contests. But at NBC and CBS, in addition to these, there
were also, for the first time, the so-called electronic brains—"Mike
Monrobot" at the former, and "Univac" at the latter.

These are machines of unbelievable complexity which were designed to handle figures in the billions and more, and to forecast
trends and the probable outcome of all the contests. Their operators
fed them problems such as these: "As of now, the vote for Eisenhower is such-and-such, and for Stevenson so-and-so, from twenty-
four states. Projecting this on a national basis, what will the outcome be?"

To the vast amusement of the human tabulators and prognosticators, these electronic marvels did not fare too well. At CBS, for

example, late in the night while Eisenhower was apparently the winner by a landslide, the "electronic brain" was still predicting that although Ike would be the victor in the electoral count, Stevenson would have a million more popular votes. Then, just twenty minutes later, it announced that Eisenhower was "100 to 1" to win.

But Charles Collingwood, the CBS commentator, explained to me that this was not really the fault of the machine. Those operating it did not pose the problem correctly, he said. Also, one of the men in charge of "Univac" revealed that, as early as 8 P.M., it had predicted a thumping Eisenhower victory, "but its operator had simply refused to believe it. So he changed his queries to conform more to his opinion of what was probable."

Despite this explanation, Lowell Thomas commented, "I'll still bet on the human brain," and Ed Murrow added, "The trouble with machines is people."

Over at NBC, practically no one was paying any attention to the miraculous "electronic brain." The invited, full-dress audience of big business men and social registerites who filled the studios were too busy celebrating. All save a solemn-faced Jim Farley. But even he did not seem too perturbed, although earlier that evening, on "Meet the Press," he had predicted a Stevenson victory.

An entirely different atmosphere prevailed at ABC. There it was strictly business; no social frills and no magical machines. John Daly, the anchor-man commentator of the evening, insisted: "The old-fashioned pencil and paper, plus political know-how, are still the best equipment of the political pundit." Walter Winchell, in shirt-sleeves, after reading a staccato statement proclaiming Ike's victory into the mike, looked down at me from his perch on the dais and exclaimed: "It's wonderful!"

Although an Eisenhower landslide was evident during the early hours of the evening, the shock of it was still too intense. Never before have I seen losers more profoundly affected, or quite so despondent, as on this election night. This emotion reached its high point when Governor Stevenson faced the cameras and the microphones in Springfield to concede the election. Even die-hard Republicans were moved by his speech.

But it was different at the Commodore Hotel headquarters of

General Eisenhower. What a contrast to the scenes of Dewey's defeat in 1944! As Ike and Mamie, he in a tuxedo and she in an evening gown with a white ermine stole and a corsage of white orchids, entered the grand ballroom and mounted the dais, the 1,500 men and women there almost went wild in an uncontrolled outburst of ecstasy. They laughed and cheered and stamped without restraint. For twenty years they had longed for this moment—and now it was here.

"I can't believe it! . . . No, no, I still can't!" a white-haired woman beside me said to her companion.

Millions of Americans who had voted for Stevenson shared her disbelief. Those trite words, "the end of an era," truly meant something that night. The time of Roosevelt and of Truman, too, with its two decades of events which will affect the destiny of the United States and of the world for centuries to come, had at last reached its finale.

And in carrying to the four corners of the land the sights and sounds attendant on the falling of the curtain, broadcasting had played a significant role. It had its birth during the last days of Woodrow Wilson, the Democrat; it came of age as a political instrument with the entrance on the scene of a Republican who had just divested himself of a five-star uniform.

FIFTEEN

The Drum Beaters

"Brother, will you join me in a bit of genooine Hoboken Scotch?"

The bald, stoutish fellow in a frock coat extended the invitation to me in his office at Madison Square Garden during the Radio World's Fair of 1928. The publicity man of a set manufacturer, Heber McDonald, better known as the "Bishop," thrust into my hand a Dixie cup filled with Prohibition hooch.

"Well, here's to you," I said.

"Ah-ah!" He waved an admonitory finger. "You, Brother, are too precipitate. First, we'll say grace."

Bowing his head, the "Bishop" gave brief thanks to the Almighty and then curtly added: "Brother, down the hatch!"

There are only a few such characters as the "Bishop" among radio and television press agents today. Most of the flamboyant adjective-concocters and imaginative stunt men of the 1920's and 1930's have long passed from the scene. They have been replaced by more hum-drum and practical devotees of the art of snaring free space.

The drum beaters of broadcasting have adjusted themselves to these days when most publicity men are, or at least pretend to be, "public-relations counselors." No longer the picturesque and com-pletely unconventional characters of two or three decades ago, they keep regular office hours, wear Brooks Brothers clothes and turn out copy dull enough to be classified as "institutional."

Press agentry used to be an adventure; today it is a profession, with charts, graphs and surveys. This is especially so at the networks and the advertising agencies. Such publicity directors as Syd Eiges at NBC, George Crandall and Dave Jacobson at CBS and Jack Pacey at ABC, for example, aid in the formulation of policies in addition to publicizing performers. Mike Foster, also of CBS, played a role in the FFC's approval of his network's incompatible color television system. And in the field of independent radio and TV press agentry, Jack Perlis has been in good part responsible for the influence exerted on American life by such public-service programs as "Omnibus" and "Meet the Press."

The writing shills of earlier days would have scorned such distinctions. Consuming smoked salmon and cream cheese on bagels between sips of celery tonic at Lindy's, they prided themselves on "dreaming up" stories and indulging in hilarious personal idiosyncracies.

It is not because the modern crop of drum beaters are less imaginative than those of two or three decades ago. But times have changed and so have the techniques of publicity. With news of world and national importance flooding editorial rooms, there is no longer space, save on rare occasions, for the fripperies of days gone by.

Because of this, among other reasons, some columnists pretend a disdain of press agents and all of their works. I do not share this attitude. Publicity men who are honest and industrious can be and are of inestimable help to newspapermen. Those who incline to laziness and purvey misinformation are soon unmasked and disappear from the scene.

Years ago, colleges and universities began recognizing the function of the publicity man in modern civilization. It did not surprise me, therefore, when one afternoon an eager youth in collegiate clothes, a beginner in the profession, asked permission to sit beside my desk in order to observe the "contact" techniques of radio press agents.

First, an elderly fellow limped in with a cane. "Broke my leg," he announced woefully, depositing a release before me. "Just outa the hospital. Doctors' bills something awful. Please use this if you can, old pal."

No sooner had he hobbled out of sight than a harassed-looking man with the saddest countenance I have ever seen entered. "I got only a few clients left. This one says if I don't get an item in tomorrow's *News*, I'm through," he wailed. "If I lose him, God knows what will become of the wife and kids." With a leaden sigh, he, too, made his way out, a woe-burdened Job on the verge of tears.

By now I detected a puzzled look in my young visitor's eyes. But before he had a chance to make some comment, the third caller appeared. A pale, shrunken little man, he was coughing louder and longer than a Broadway first-nighter.

"Got T.B.," he wheezed. "Need fare to Arizona. Help me out, friend." He handed me a few typewritten notes on onion-skin paper and, like a Camille in tweeds, he staggered through the door.

I turned to the youth, now himself ghostly pale, as he rose from his chair. "This is no business for me," gasped Irving Mansfield, today a successful TV producer, "I'm healthy!" and rushed from the room.

Had he only paused in his flight I should have informed him that not all publicity men are the victims of such misfortunes. Could this boy have met G. W. (Johnnie) Johnstone, first press-relations director of NBC, for example, he would have quickly perceived that the profession also has its lighter moods.

Although given to flights of imagination, Johnnie was the precursor of today's efficient, institutional-minded broadcasting publicists. I met him while he was drumming the praises of WEAF, on downtown Broadway, and became his friend shortly thereafter, when the first network came into existence. After he had brought in an assistant, my column commented in amazement: "My, how radio is growing! NBC now has two press agents. . . . Will there be enough work for both?" (Today, NBC employs 90 publicity men.)

One of the men who proved there was more than "enough work" for the broadcasting publicist of those days is Alfred J. ("Hollywood") McCosker, at that time on the staff of WOR. Now living in retirement after having become president and then chairman of the board of the Mutual Broadcasting System, he was the first to bring razzle-dazzle showmanship to radio press-agentry. Within a few years he had become a legend, which he still is today, for he combined stunts with a nose for news which resulted not only in newspaper stories but also in scores of novel human-interest broadcasts. "Hollywood" had acquired his flair while serving as Arthur Brisbane's office boy, and had developed it as a movie publicity man.

A tall, black-haired man with flashing eyes and the warmest of smiles, he was one of New York's fashion plates. With gloves, cane, spates, and white carnation in his coat lapel, McCosker might have easily passed as an ambassador.

During the 1920's, in his quest for the unusual, "Hollywood" rushed to the WOR microphone a woman piano-player in a Brooklyn movie house just after she had inherited a million dollars. This was the predecessor of "We, the People" and similar shows of later years. He also staged one of the earliest of the giveway programs when, in 1925, he offered the "sensational" prize of ten dollars to the winner of a music "memory contest." Then, two years later, McCosker put on the first "Mr. and Mrs." offering, presenting John B. Gambling and an actress, who pretended to be the latter's wife, in a chatter period. And, as far back as 1930, he had persuaded his station to broadcast transcribed shows. "If listeners approve, WOR may set up a network specializing in electrically recorded 'package' programs," read an announcement sent by him to the newspapers. This was the first faint sound made by what has since become a gigantic industry.

About that time an inventor made it known that he had perfected a new bullet-proof vest. So "Hollywood" won headlines for WOR by having Supreme Court Justice Cotillo fire a pistol point-blank at a human target beside a studio microphone. And it was this publicity genius who persuaded Thomas A. Edison and Charlie Chaplin to appear on radio for the first time.

Chaplin was more difficult to persuade than Edison. "I don't want to deliver a talk or be interviewed," he said. "I've got to have an act that will be 'different.'" Thereupon "Hollywood" wrote him one.

"You will probably be surprised to hear that I am a pianist," Chaplin told the listeners, following which they heard a brilliantly played solo. Then, in quick succession, Charlie asked for a violin, a clarinet and a cello, on each of which he displayed amazing virtuosity. "And now I shall play them all together," he said. And they were played in unison—by the studio orchestra.

Luring celebrities to the microphone, "Hollywood" had the difficult task of cajoling them into making a trip from New York to the station in Newark. His bosses had refused to rent space in Manhattan; so, without consulting them, the daring press agent opened the first New York studios of WOR in the metropolis' Chickering Hall. His superiors were stunned by his brazen impudence, but later, when this action resulted in filling the station's schedules with dozens of big-name personalities, they agreed that a New York branch was not such a bad idea after all.

There was one slight difficulty. Adjoining the chamber in Chickering Hall was the studio of the celebrated concert pianist, Josef Lhevinne. Thus, listeners tuned in on the reminiscences of a visiting movie star might also hear strains of Chopin and Liszt. Soon, however, "Hollywood" exerted his diplomatic charm and Lhevinne agreed to refrain from practicing during broadcasting hours.

A few months before the opening of this New York studio, a temperamental Russian actress created one of the stormiest scenes in the history of radio. With her leading man, the fiery lady was transported to Newark in a Rolls Royce limousine reserved for such purposes, a gargantuan vehicle of royal purple with salmon-pink upholstery. It was equipped with a uniformed chauffeur and a liveried footman and bore a placard announcing that its passengers were stars en route to a broadcast over WOR.

At the studio in Bamberger's department store, the dazzling actress was greeted with awe by all the upper-echelon executives, including Mr. Bamberger himself. It was truly a gala occasion, and after the announcer had informed listeners that the Madame and her leading man would enact a scene from her current Broadway success, dowagers of an East Orange women's club in the studio applauded with fervor. The artist gave such an exhibition of scenery chewing that at the end the hand-clapping gave way to cheers.

The announcer expressed his thanks and added that the station was honored by her presence.

"I have been honored, too," said the Madame to the surprise of the mike man, who was not accustomed to back talk from a guest who had already done her stint. Then, elbowing the amazed fellow aside, she continued: "But you would have honored me still more had you permitted me to do the really important scene of our play, instead of this innocuous one. It's important because it deals with our theme. And what is our theme? That I shall tell you. It is free love!"

The combined gasps of the aging ladies in the studio sounded like the exhaust of a locomotive on a frosty morning.

No WOR man would ever discuss what followed. But for many years thereafter, Radio Row chuckled over the oft-repeated and, no doubt, amplified story.

"Now, ladies and gentlemen," the actress went on, "you may ask what do I think of free love. That also I shall tell you. I like it!"

A lady in the front row began fanning herself, and kindly Mr. Bamberger, hand clasped to forehead, muttered to a nearby station attaché: "Do you think this is nice?"

Before the latter could venture an opinion, an engineer rushed from the control booth to Mr. Bamberger's side and whispered loudly, "Don't worry, they didn't hear it. I cut her off the air."

Unfortunately, the Madame overheard this. Turning a ghostly white and a gory red at the same time, she plunged a long thin forefinger under the engineer's nose. "You beast! You dog!" she screamed. Then, facing the studio audience, she gave a display of "emotional drama" that was better than any of her paid performances

"You ask me out here . . . me, one of the world's greatest artists . . . I leave New York for you . . . I come to this unspeakable place . . . and you cut me off the air! It is an insult I shall never forgive!"

Bamberger tried to pacify her.

"Do not speak to me!" she cried. And then, addressing the studio audience: "And just for that I shall take to tube back to New York. . . . I shall not ride in his lousy limousine!"

Turning majestically, accompanied by her leading man, she stamped out of the studio. Followed by entreating executives and stunned clubwomen, Madame rushed through the store and into the street, where she hailed a passing taxi.

The next day, there appeared this notice on the bulletin board of WOR:

"After this—positively no more free love!"

"Hollywood" McCosker, as his career proved, combined executive ability and a shrewd business sense with his flair for ballyhoo. So did the first and one of the most successful independent broadcasting press-agents, the late George D. Lottman. A man of slight stature with a bald head, keen eyes, a rosy face and a puckish smile, he was a pixie, and a sardonic one. At times moody, at times jovial, imbibing Canadian Club from a silver hip flask at ten-minute intervals, a lively conversationalist forever spouting wisecracks and mordant comments, he personified the fiction and the movie writer's conception of press agents.

Addicted to working from midnight to 3 or 4 A.M. in his cramped offices in a building high above Broadway, across the street from the Capitol Theatre, he represented more important stars at one time than any drum beater in the history of broadcasting. Rudy Vallee, Vaughn de Leath, Paul Whiteman, Kate Smith, Morton Downey, Amos 'n' Andy, Bing Crosby, Russ Columbo and Richard Himber were among his clients. He pounded out copy on their behalf on a rickety typewriter, while a bootblack shined his shoes and assorted Broadway characters in the room ate, drank, chattered, rolled dice and played hot jazz records on a portable phonograph.

Between takes of copy, "The King," as he referred to himself, gulped swigs from his flask, ate sandwiches and discoursed on topics ranging from Baudelaire to Tin Pan Alley. He spoke sarcastically of editors and of his hired help, inevitably concluding his diatribes concerning the latter with "I think I'll give 'em all a raise." Sometimes he insisted on his wage slaves reporting to the office on bright summer Sunday afternoons to "dream up stories." As the grousing crew hunched over their typewriters, Lottman with his gray fedora slanted over his left eyebrow would pace the room and wax oratorical:

"What fortunate lads you are! Think of all those poor people out there on those Long Island beaches, dousing themselves in salt water (ugh!) and getting those painful sunburns. The flies, the mosquitoes, the noise, the crowds . . . and you sitting here in a nice, cool, quiet office on Broadway in the ecstasy of creation! . . . Oh, you just don't know what lucky bastards you really are!"

Lottman was known for the zaniest of feats. It was he who introduced a goodly segment of the British aristocracy to the joys of kosher delicatessen.

Roger Wolfe Kahn, son of Otto, the millionaire financier and

Maecenas of the Metropolitan Opera, had organized a dance band and had engaged George to accompany the crew to Europe. "I was the official money handler of the safari," he used to tell me. "Never had less than ten thousand dollars in cash on me and Roger didn't care how the dough went. He believed in buying whatever hit my fancy.

"Well, one day we attended a garden party at his father's estate in England. There were more earls and dukes than bookies on Broadway and 49th. The elegant flunkies served lots of tea and gobs of caviar, but I don't happen to like the stuff. I'm strictly a Lindy's boy myself. I was longing for some marinated herring and other real delicacies. So I made a few discreet inquiries, and some fellow, probably one of the lower classes, told me about a certain delicatessen in Soho. I got into Roger's car, drove into London and returned with an enormous hamper of herring in sour cream, pastrami and salami and other stuff."

George then ordered a protesting servitor to clear one of the tables on the lawn of such fodder as pâté de fois gras and pickled artichokes, and replaced these with his own items.

Then, in the manner of a Coney Island barker, Lottman began to cry his wares. "Ladies and gents! Here yez are! Try 'em! Try 'em! . . . Real Yank goodies imported directly from the good old U.S.A."

A blueblooded guest ventured to sample the pastrami; another took a nibble on a bagel, and soon, amid joyous exclamations over this "delightful native American food," George disposed of his entire stock of merchandise.

"If Lindy only knew it," he said to me drily, "he'd find his best customers in Burke's Peerage or the Almanach de Gotha."

It was in Lindy's, incidentally, that George introduced one of his new employees to the mysteries of expensive food. His cousin, George B. Evans, who later became famous as the press agent who "made Frank Sinatra," like dozens of other radio publicity men served his apprenticeship in the Lottman office. At lunch time during his first day there, he accompanied his boss to the colorful Broadway restaurant.

An uptown boy who until then had patronized only eateries with comparatively limited offerings, Evans was confused by the gigantic menu card. Therefore, he eagerly accepted Lottman's suggestion that he order a sandwich of smoked Nova Scotia salmon, an expensive tidbit known for its delicate flavor.

Evans took his first bite and frowned. Accustomed as he was to the much cheaper and saltier variety of smoked salmon known as "lox," the blandness of the fish disappointed him. Lifting a glass shaker, he doused his order with salt.

"You damned fool!" Lottman screamed. "You have just succeeded in converting a $1.50 Nova Scotia salmon into a 15-cent lox sandwich!"

Lottman had an unconventional manner of dealing with his employees. One of them, a fellow famed for the gags he contributed to Broadway columns, was as heavy an imbiber as his boss. Periodically he would ask for and win a raise, and George would faithfully pay the augmented salary to the man's wife.

"How can I live, when you don't give me the money?" the man complained one day. "What am I going to do?"

"What are you complaining about?" said George. "You know damned well I always leave my stamp box open!"

Just as this employee eventually did, other youthful press agents in George's office, including Tim Marks, the humorist, and Milton Josefsberg, now one of Jack Benny's principal script writers, learned not to take literally the advice he offered.

One of the firm's clients was an amiable and popular bandleader named Anson Weeks. For some mysterious reason, Lottman had extreme difficulty in planting items about him. So when a tyro entered into his employ, George would test him by ordering a newsworthy story on the musician.

One such lad asked, "Where can I find this fellow Weeks?"

"Try Denver," said Lottman.

Seven days later, George received a collect telegram from the youth announcing that he was in Denver but Weeks was not. "An amusement editor tells me he is playing in San Francisco. Shall I go there to interview him? What shall I do?" the message concluded.

Lottman promptly answered: "Try sliding up Pike's Peak and

credit Weeks with the feat." He also wired the fare back to New York.

Once at 2 A.M. I was sitting in George's office when through the open window we heard a yell from Broadway below.

"Hey, Lottman! . . . Hey, Lottman!"

We recognized the shrill voice of one of his clients, Richard Himber, the orchestra leader.

As we leaned out of the window, Himber shouted, "I don't see anything about me in the *News* and *Mirror*."

"Listen, you bastard," Lottman called back. "You're fired. I don't want your account!"

The next night, however, Himber was back again beneath the window. He was too lazy to come upstairs and insisted on conducting business with his press agent in this unconventional manner at the top of his voice from the sidewalks of Broadway.

An individualist, Lottman could not work in tandem. One day he would announce the formation of a partnership, and within a week he would send out an announcement that it had been dissolved. But for a much longer time than usual he worked in collaboration with Earle Ferris, another of broadcasting's fabulous press agents. During this brief association their client Russ Columbo, the crooner, Bing Crosby's great rival, was drawing thousands to a roadhouse, Woodmansten Inn, near New York City.

Lottman had the idea that Russ must have a great romance with Pola Negri, at that time the *femme fatale* of the films. One Sunday night, he rushed her out to the club and seated her at a table near the bandstand. Then, as Russ was singing "Paradise," the lamps dimmed and an amber spotlight played on Pola staring pensively at the singer.

Columnists' pencils flew and the next day, as Earle says, "the romance was hotter than Fibber McGee and Molly's Hooper." Did Russ love Pola? Did Pola love Russ? Millions concerned themselves with the answer.

Some time later, just before Russ left New York, he was strolling along Broadway with Lottman and Ferris to lunch at Dave's Blue Room. There was a crowd in front of the restaurant, gaping not at the crooner but at a beautiful woman.

"Who's the dame?" Russ asked.

"Why, you tortured tonsil agitator," said Lottman, "that's the woman you have been in love with for the past four months!"

Lottman, so far as I know, is the only press agent ever to have called a conference of rival publicists to divide among themselves the free plugs available in a newspaper. A certain carefree amusement editor of a New York morning daily did not read, much less write, the night club and radio items appearing on his page. He was so generous in publishing "puffs" of the most blatant kind that even the drum beaters shuddered.

One night George assembled his competitors in his office and said, "Listen, fellows. Our friend's a good guy, but some day they're going to clamp down on him, maybe fire him. And then where'll we be? So let's not overdo it. How about making an iron-clad agreement? I'll take him Mondays, some one else on Tuesdays, and so on. . . ."

"Okay! That's fine!" They agreed unanimously. But the pact was as well observed as one of Stalin's. In less than a week that amusement page had again become the press agent's gravy train. Then, a few days later, the sword fell. The jovial editor, having one column to fill with type, waved cavalierly to the makeup man and said, "Put in some overset." ["Overset" is type omitted for lack of space.]

This was done, and not until the early edition had rolled from the presses did he discover that the entire column was made up of a half-dozen separate items, each informing the world that one of Lottman's clients, Lee Wiley, was the world's greatest blues singer! Unfortunately, the publisher made a like discovery, and the next day the press agents' Santa Claus was without portfolio.

As the years rolled on, past the Twenties and through the Thirties, George began to wither. The Broadway scene was changing; and so was radio, as he dwelt more and more on his triumphs of other days. He was an ill man and, during the last months of his life, a bedridden and shrunken figure.

But when I called on him one afternoon, there was still a smile on his lips and the same sardonic glint in his eyes. "How's the King?" I asked, and for an answer he drew a hidden flask from beneath his pillow.

"You know," he said with amused unconcern, "the doctor says if I take another drink I'll pop right off." Then glancing about the bedroom of his apartment, he lifted the flask. "Here's to a merry popping off!" he said.

"Maybe I've wasted my life," he commented as he returned the flask beneath the pillow, "and maybe I haven't; because I've got a son—and he's not a Broadway guy, but a brilliant student, a scholar, and he's going to show the world what Old Man Lottman didn't. . . . Oh, what the hell! I had my cards and I played the way I wanted to."

Then, he clutched my hand. "Do me a favor, will you?"

"Sure," I said.

"The obit column will call me George D. Lottman. But the next time you use my name, will you write beside it in parentheses (The King)? And please, old friend, don't have any quotes around The King."

I promised. And two days later, after his death, there were no quotation marks in my column around the words, The King.

One Lottman associate, Earle Ferris, was himself one of the most colorful radio publicity men of the 1930's. A former Mobilian, who had served as sports editor of a Cleveland daily and as editor of the United Features Syndicate, he had both newspaper know-how and showmanship.

On one occasion the Gillette Safety Razor Company, sponsoring a radio series starring Max Baer, the prize fighter, sent word that unless the pug landed on the front pages Earle would lose the account. During a rehearsal, Max, whom Ferris describes as "the best actor who ever fought Joe Louis," was shot at by a fellow player with blank cartridges, and a young actress, Peg La Centra, sustained powder burns about the eyes. The story produced thirty-one volumes of press clippings, which were promptly forwarded to the head of the Gillette advertising department. This worthy, no believer in overpraising the hired help, then dispatched the following note:

"Dear Ferris: I have checked the scrapbooks, and I believe they are adequate. —Charles Pritzger."

In his later years, Earle gave up the representation of individual performers in favor of agencies and sponsors. But his most interesting adventures involved his activities on behalf of those unpredictable clients—the stars. The latter he classifies simply as "bright or dumb; grateful or ungrateful."

"Not too many of them are bright," he once told me. "But it just so happens that some of the dumbest ones have the cleverest press agents. These boys work overtime to atone for their clients' deficiencies by planting in the columns all kinds of gags, puns and funny stories which they attribute to their employers. Then you meet these alleged founts of humor and you wonder how such dumb clucks could give birth to such witty sayings.

"I have been fortunate, however, in representing a few who talk good newspaper copy: Frank Black, Meredith Willson and B. A. Rolfe, conductors; Bess Johnson ("Lady Esther") and Virginia Payne, the actress known to millions as 'Ma Perkins.' They, however, are the rare exceptions. Frank Black has perhaps the driest humor of any man I've ever known."

Earle recalls the time Black was escorting Helen Hayes from a broadcasting rehearsal at NBC. They were immediately surrounded by young autograph-hunters. After Helen had signed their books, a boy shoved his volume at Frank and said, "You, too!" The latter calmly wrote, "Franz Liszt."

"You ought to have seen the look of disgust on that kid's face," says Ferris.

"Come on, let's scram," the boy called to his companions. "We don't want this guy—he's a long-hair!"

Fred Allen is the client who caught Ferris' especial fancy. Like Irving Mansfield, the TV producer who also served as the nasal comedian's press agent at one time, Earle considers Allen to be "the most charitable person in broadcasting." But Fred insists on dispensing his largess in his own way—in countless handouts to broken-down actors and actresses, and in defraying their hospital expenses.

Some years ago, every Wednesday night Earle used to walk with Allen and the latter's assistant, "Uncle Jim" Harkins, from the Dorset Hotel to the NBC studios. Fred carried a coat pocket stuffed with two-dollar bills. This was at a time when two bucks bought something more than a headwaiter's glare. "In front of the studio, there was an inevitable line-up of old performers and hangers-on, many of whom did not even know Fred," says Ferris.

But all they had to do was to call, "Hiya, John," and Allen shook hands with them, thus passing a two-dollar bill. (His legal name is John Florence Sullivan, and the greeting implied that they knew him in the days when he was a juggler.) One night, as Fred was shaking hands with one of his regulars, the latter asked, "Johnny, couldn't you make it three bucks tonight?"

"What are you trying to do," said Allen, "start an inflation?"

"Well, I tell you," the fellow explained, "I pawned my teeth for three bucks and now that I got a chance to play a split week in Jersey, I'm in a tough spot."

Fred made it three. "What good is an emcee without teeth?" he said.

Ferris, like other press agents, could tell many a tale of a performer's ingratitude toward his drum beater. This story is almost a regulation item in the entertainment business. It goes something like this:

A struggling young comedian or singer hires an even more struggling young publicity man. The latter attends to his press chores, serves as confidant and chaperon, and even obtains bookings. For this he collects perhaps twenty-five dollars a week. "But don't worry," says the performer. "When I come into the big dough, so will you. I'll take care of you. We're partners, pal."

Then comes the day when the fellow actually lands in the big time; he's making records, he's booked at the Paramount, has his own TV show, and MCA or William Morris is handling him. Then what?

"Listen, Joe," says the big man to his p.a., "my agent says I'm big now and what I got to have is an important publicity man. You know, somebody with lots of prestige."

So he hires one of those ultra-expensive and fashionable public-relations counselors, who thereupon turns over the account to one of his $75-a-week assistants.

A certain press agent, Sid Ascher, who organized the Society for the Prevention of Derogatory Remarks About Brooklyn, could illuminate this point. When Vic Damone, the singer, was holding forth years ago on WHN for about twenty-five dollars a program, Ascher did valiant service for him for little pay. He was one of the "brain trust" behind the campaign to place Damone into the ranks of those who earn thousands of dollars a week. However, as soon as the crooner attained this goal, Sid was dropped.

He was less fortunate than Ed Dukoff, who began sending out items about an obscure borscht-circuit comedian named Danny Kaye at ridiculously low pay. Danny made the usual promises and Ed "played along" with him. Kaye eventually became an internationally celebrated star and Dukoff accompanied him up the ladder. Today, still with Danny, he is one of the highest paid and most successful publicists and personal managers in the country.

On one occasion, Ferris sent one of his assistants to accompany a notoriously difficult singer on his road tour.

"And no matter what the circumstances, I want you to stand up for this man," he instructed his employee. "Your first duty is loyalty to our client." Not long thereafter, the youthful press agent heard someone at an adjoining table in a restaurant denouncing the singer in the most scathing terms. "Look, I work for him," said the youngster, "and nobody in my hearing can talk about him that way." The vitriolic critic, a hulking fellow, repeated his ill opinion; whereupon the publicity man knocked him down.

What he didn't know was that this man was a friend of the singer who had decided to "test" the press agent. The loyal reaction of the latter, however, did not improve his standing. The next day, the star greeted him abusively:

"You got some nerve socking my best pal. Get the hell out of here! You're fired!"

Jack Perlis, who long ago ceased handling individuals and devotes himself to the press relations of such shows as "Omnibus" and "Meet the Press," can also tell of the cavalier attitude of certain clients. During his tyro days, after weeks of persuasion he finally succeeded in placing a "lead" with a picture in my column about a then obscure actress in a soap opera. This was a considerable feat. So, about an hour after the Pink Edition of the News had appeared on the streets and the girl called him on the phone, he was prepared to bow gracefully under a barrage of honeyed words.

"Jack," she said, "I'm in the News tonight, but in the copy I bought my picture's all smeared with horrible black ink. Can't you do something about it?"

"What do you expect me to do, go down to the press room and wipe off the plates?" Perlis asked after he had recovered his breath.

"Well, couldn't you do that?" the actress said coyly.

Jack's answer would not have been approved by Emily Post. It ended with: "And, as of now, you may consider me to be your express agent!"

Another of Perlis' early clients, an actor with literary ambitions, had a yearning to have his byline appear over an article concerned with the radio drama in the pages of the august New York *Times*. Jack wrote such an article, credited it to the actor, and placed it with Jack Gould, the erudite TV-Radio editor of that sheet. Here was a publicity break for which most performers would have given a month's salary.

But a few days after the piece had appeared and the actor had taken bows for his literary effort, Gould was amazed to receive a call from him demanding that he be paid for the contribution. A few days later, there was even the threat of a law suit!

The *Times* paid, but thereafter displayed a most remarkable lack of interest in that performer's broadcasting activities. Also, Perlis "fired" another client.

Jack, by the way, is one of the few modern press agents who can get away with space-winning "stunts," even though city editors frown on such antics these days. During the summer of 1949, for example, he was handling a young soprano, Cathy Mastice. However, there were thousands of other young sopranos with equally good voices trying desperately to make a mark in the entertainment world. But these girls lacked the services of an ingenious publicity man. During a post-midnight joke session with Milton Berle at Lindy's, Perlis convinced the comedian that what his TV program needed was a girl who could sing "high-class stuff."

So she appeared on the show in costume singing *"Sempre Libera"* from *La Traviata*, an aria with which Dorothy Kirsten, the Metropolitan Opera soprano, had long been identified. The following week, Dorothy, who evidently had not seen the program, announced that she was suing Berle for $100,000, because the comedian had presented a "horrible-sounding mess, with a long chin, big mouth and pointed nose," whom he had "passed off as me," and that, at the very least, the girl "had burlesqued me."

An average press agent would have merely issued a statement expressing Miss Mastice' indignation over these charges. He might even have called a conventional press-conference. Not Perlis. He dispatched telegrams to all news media announcing that Cathy would hold, at the Biltmore Hotel the next day, "the first musical press-conference in history." There would be songs instead of harsh words. The outraged artist would appear in costume and sing the aria she did on the Berle show and let the press decide whether Dorothy's sour comments were justified.

The result, on June 7, 1949, was one of the most unusual press-conferences New York has ever known. Reporters, feature writers and photographers from the newspapers and wire services, plus news-reel cameramen, were on hand. CBS' special events department even sent a crew to tape a sound-record of the proceedings. Cathy sang her number and the applause was so enthusiastic that she responded with several encores. Then she announced that she was filing a $100,000 libel action against Dorothy Kirsten.

Needless to tell you, neither action ever came to court, but the next day millions read the story, saw cheesecake pictures of the young singer in newspapers throughout the country, and many more heard excerpts of this novel conference broadcast over the radio. Cathy was immediately bombarded with offers of theatre, night-club and TV appearances, made the "big time," and held the spotlight for a brief period. Then she turned her back on it all, left the entertainment world and married a millionaire.

Although, like Perlis, publicity men often put on shows for the press, I once turned the tables by staging an entertainment for a press agent—right in Alimony Jail.

More than two decades ago, Jay Faggen, another former partner of George Lottman, was one of radio's most famous drum beaters. A stout, balding man with a mournful face, a kindly fellow of many ideas, he had a "different" approach. Whereas some of his competitors resorted to cajolery and flattery, Jay's specialty was the sob story. Although many of his items had exceptional merit, he seldom presented a story unaccompanied by some such remark as "If you fail to run this, I'll lose my client". . . or "If you don't do this, I just don't know what will happen!"

One day his plea had a truly novel "twist." "I'm behind in my alimony," he said, "and if I don't produce, I'll land in jail."

Dismissing this perhaps as just another dire prediction of a calamity which would not materialize, I did not use his story. A few days later, I received a phone call from Jay and he sounded even more melancholy than usual.

"You didn't believe me," he sighed. "But here I am, in Alimony Jail."

After he had received my sympathies, Jay's voice brightened. "And while you're on the phone, here are a few items for you."

"But if you're in jail, how can you be telephoning items?" I asked.

"Oh, the warden's a swell guy," he said. "I'm using the phone in his office."

For some time, Jay conducted his business amidst such unorthodox surroundings. One day he remarked in the most forlorn of tones: "I'm awf'lly lonesome here. No theatre, no nightclubs, no radio studios, no Lindy's."

"I can see you miss Broadway," I said. "So how about bringing Broadway to you? We'll get together some acts and put 'em on over there."

Jay laughed for the first time in all the years I had known him, and promised to consult the warden. Soon he was back on the phone; that gentleman thought a show in Alimony Jail, given especially for Jay Faggen, was a swell idea.

So on February 20, 1936, a group of performers, led by a radio editor, appeared there. Even if I do say it, it was a good show. Certainly Jay and the other "boys" gave evidence of their enjoyment. A rising young comedian, one Bob Hope, was among the entertainers, and the troupe included, among others, George Hall, orchestra leader, and his vocalist, Dolly Dawn, bandleader Red Nichols, singers Toya Sasabe, the Rhythm Boys, Chris Fahey, the Landt Trio and White, The Cruising Troubadour, and other famous radio names of that day.

We gave our show on an upper-floor hall of what appeared to be an ancient mansion; only the bars on the windows suggested a prison. The inmates, civil prisoners, rather than criminals, in this aristocrat of bastilles dwelt in rooms instead of cells; some of these cubicles had homelike touches: family pictures, calendars, books, musical instruments and flowers in porcelain vases.

News of the highjinks in Alimony Jail, including a songfest and a party with cake and soft drinks, reached the ears of a prisoner's wife, and a few days later that indignant lady petitioned the Supreme Court for a ban against any such didoes by their errant husbands.

Even on this merry occasion, Jay did not neglect his business. As our troupe took its leave, he drew a typed sheet from his pocket. "A couple of client notes," he said.

Strangely enough, after his release from durance vile, Jay radically altered his technique. He had a carefree approach and indulged in many a jest and jape. But even if he hadn't, I, for one, would never again have doubted any dire prediction he might have cared to make.

Neither would I, of course, give anything less than the utmost credence to anything Eddie Jaffe might tell me. One of the few stunt men surviving in this era, he is a master of ballyhoo, plus a solid human-interest technique. Holding forth in a fantastic office-apartment right off Times Square on West 48th Street, he is a homely, magnetic little fellow who takes pride in his nickname, "The Monster," and publicizes himself as "the world's ugliest press agent."

Many of his Hollywood and Broadway antics have set the nation laughing. And so have some of his efforts on behalf of radio and television personalities.

Jaffe, for example, as a publicity gesture, suggested that Jimmy Davis, the hillbilly singer, run for Governor of Louisiana. It proved to be more than a stunt, for Davis was elected by a big plurality. Eddie, on behalf of the radio comedian, Eddie Garr, organized with another p.a., Noel Meadow, the "National Order of Screwballs." They created an emblem, a screw upon a ball, which some interloper copyrighted and made thousands from, through its sale as a lapel decoration. And in preparation for the air appearances of Margie Hart, the stripper, Jaffee organized the "Society of Redheads of America," with Margie as president. She demanded that the post-office department change the color of George Washington's hair on the stamp from white to the more accurate red.

Sometimes, the best-laid plans of press agents misfire, as Eddie will freely inform you. He knew that two of his colleagues, Larry Gore and Lee Solters, had won considerable space for a hairdresser by having him style the manes of Gene Autry's horses, the resultant pictures being published with the caption: "Which pony has the Toni?" So Jaffe was gleeful when he had a chance to make a tie-up with a Rhode Island race track on behalf of Marlene Dietrich. Employed by the press agent of the movie star to publicize her radio shows, he arranged for a Marlene Dietrich award for "the horse with the most beautiful legs."

"Neither the Hollywood press agent nor I had anticipated the enormous number of clippings—each paid for by the client—which a sports story, carried by all the wire services, would return," Jaffe said. "After thousands had come in, the movie p.a. was so disgusted that he fired me!"

But Eddie's favorite story concerning himself is about the time he escorted one of his clients, Zorita, the snake charmer, to a psychiatrist. "Doctor, can you find out what's wrong with this girl?" he asked. "She's in love with her snakes."

But after brief interviews with both, the specialist gave this verdict: "This girl is perfectly sane; but you, sir, are completely crazy!"

Just as Jaffe would wax indignant if you did not refer to him as a "character," so would another press agent known as "Genial" Joe Morgen. A solid, shaggy man with the physique of a truck driver and the countenance of a lovable prize fighter in an old Warner Brothers movie, he first attracted attention by preceding every mention of his client, John Popkin of the Hickory House, with the adjective, "Genial."

Perpetually complaining about a score of maladies, which do not, however, prevent him from lounging about Lindy's all night, Joe has an exaggerated concern for the physical well-being of the columnists with whom he deals. Let one of them so much as remark that he has a slight headache, and during a span of a few hours he will receive several phone calls from Morgen: "How's your health?" That some of these inquiries may arouse the recipients from their slumbers at five or six in the morning does not in any way lessen their appreciation of this tender solicitude.

A big-hearted and basically a lonesome fellow, Joe is a hero-worshipper and his idols are the columnists and the byliners of the press. He will discourse on the state of the world, politics and theology with uninhibited enthusiasm. He will regale his listeners for hours with what Louis Sobol or Earl Wilson said, but his favorite topic is his ulcers.

One night, while he was consuming an order of marinated herring with onions in Reuben's, I said to him, "Isn't spicy food like this bad for ulcers?"

"Yeah," said Joe, "but I happen to like it."

After enduring a diet of bland food at Johns Hopkins hospital, Morgen checked out one day and hailed a taxicab. "Drive me to the station; I'm taking a train back to New York," he said to the chauffeur. But a few blocks away, Joe disembarked. They had just passed a delicatessen. He went in and bought a pastrami sandwich.

Violating every conception of what a Broadway or broadcasting press agent should be, in appearance, manner, speech and approach, Morgen for a time was the object of his colleagues' ridicule. Today this is no longer true, for he has won some astounding breaks for his clients, including Popkin, Duke Ellington and Elliot Roosevelt.

But his methods are still a bit unconventional. One night at Lindy's, after he had helped Bob Sylvester, the *News'* drama and entertainment editor, into his overcoat, the latter felt a strange hand in his left pocket. He clutched it and asked, "Whatya doing, Joe?"

"Oh," said Morgen, "I was going to come by your office with a release tomorrow; but I figure I might as well save time. You'll find it in your pocket in the morning."

On another occasion, Joe was sharing a taxicab with the same Sylvester. "Boy, have I got a story for you!" he said. "Don't tell anyone where you got it." Thereupon he proceeded to glance about the cab as if suspecting the presence of an unseen eavesdropper and whispered his item into Bob's ear.

Shortly thereafter, Sylvester, who was on his deadline, received an urgent phone call from Joe. "Boy, is this a story! It'll knock your eyes out!"

"Okay, hurry and let's have it," said Bob.

Morgen at considerable length then gave the editor an item of sensational news value.

"Say, this *is* a good story!" Bob exclaimed minutes later. "I'm going to use it."

"But you can't," said Joe. "I just gave it to Louis Sobol—exclusive!"

Joe's idiosyncracies also amazed another columnist on an afternoon newspaper. He had agreed to use one of the press agent's items on Duke Ellington the next day but, unfortunately, it landed in the overset.

The following noon, which is midnight to most Broadway pillar conductors, Morgen called his friend's apartment. "You promised to run my story," he said plaintively. The newspaperman protested violently against being aroused from his slumbers, but assured Joe that the item would positively appear the next day. "And don't you ever again call me so early!" he added.

The next day the item landed once more in the overset and the following morning Joe was on the phone. "You again!" the columnist shouted. "I told that damned makeup man, whatever he did, to get that item in. Now, I'll tell you what I'll do, Joe. Tonight, instead of sending my column to the office by messenger, I'll go down myself and hang around the composing room until the page is made up." And he did just that, until 4 A.M.

Not so many hours thereafter, a bellboy delivered a copy of the paper to Morgen's room in the Capitol Hotel. There, at last, was that item in type! A minute later, the ringing of his bedside phone awoke the columnist again. What he said this time made the dialogue in *From Here to Eternity* seem like prattle in a home for retired Charleston gentlewomen.

"Here I've done for you what no other guy in the world would do," he added. "And now, for the third day, you've ruined my sleep!"

"Yeah, I know," said Joe in teary tones. "Call me all the names you want . . . but when I looked at the column just now, I got to thinking that this was the nicest, sweetest thing a fellow ever did for anybody. Believe me, I just couldn't help it. I just had to call and *thank you!*"

The columnist said, "You're welcome," and like most of his colleagues he still continues to use the items of a press agent who is truly different—"Genial" Joe Morgen.

By no means a "character" like Joe, David O. Alber is a publicity man on the more conventional side. But, like Irving Zussman and Gertrude Bayne, whose activities have already been mentioned in connection with Frank Sinatra, he was involved in dozens of "stunts" during his early days. As the representative of Ralph Edwards, this was only to be expected.

One day he arranged with the New York Port Authority to have his client, Morton Downey, greeted as the 50,000th user of the Henry Hudson Bridge. The singer was so eager to get to the ceremonies—and to the photographers—that on the way he was detained and received a ticket for speeding! Then, for the opening of the Jack Denny Orchestra at the Waldorf-Astoria, Alber suggested that a song titled "Champagne Waltz" be written for that occasion. Denny plugged the number until it became a hit and also the title of a movie, and Dave collected healthy royalties on the song for years.

But another of his brain waves backfired. At a time when he was representing Dinah Shore, he arranged for her to be photographed leading a goat down Fifth Avenue. "Why couldn't you have my picture taken with some animal?" another of his singer clients asked. So she was lensed in a racing stable. But the girl was allergic to horses, began sneezing and had to cancel her radio program for an entire week.

Irving Cahn, a studious publicity man who doubles as drama critic for a weekly, also has many a story to tell—especially about that odd tribe who persist in crashing the dressing rooms of stars. One of his clients, Louis Prima, was having his handwriting analyzed one afternoon backstage of New York's Strand Theatre, when a doorman brought up a card on which was this message: "I am the author of *Handwriting of the Stars* published by ——— Co. I want a sample of your handwriting for my new book."

Cahn suspected a hoax, called the publishers and was told that it had heard neither of the book nor the author. For a lark, Irving brought the girl up to Prima's dressing room and had the handwriting expert, who knew nothing about the imposter, analyze her chirography. "My dear lady," he said in shocked tones, "I hate to say this, but you'd make a whale of a forger!"

Most press agents face the problem of attracting fans—even pestiferous ones—rather than discouraging them. And in the formative days of broadcasting their ingenuity was boundless. Fred Waring's hired Boswell, for example, one day decided there was nothing to the simile, "Like a bull in a china shop," so he persuaded Fred to lead one into a Fifth Avenue establishment and made his point. There was no damage done.

Then there was another space-hungry fellow, Eddie Lee, who represented Dave Ellman's radio show, "Auction." He visited a remote section of Kentucky and while there prevailed on a mountaineer named Orville Tuttle to write Dave a letter, offering to put up his daughter for sale to the highest bidder.

Still another Machiavelli of press agentry, Milton Berger, found it difficult to gain attention for a toupee maker who provided hair for many a balding radio star. So one day the papers carried stories about a suit against an Eighth Avenue barber. The latter, while giving a dozing customer a haircut, had snipped off some of the curly locks of his wig. The plaintiff, introducing in evidence a canceled check to the toupee maker, said he had suffered considerable financial loss. But the barber pleaded, "Your Honor, that wig looked so natural I thought it was his own hair."

John Irving Fields, also an imaginative radio-TV drum beater, representing a Masillon, Ohio, manufacturer, wished to dramatize the need for more industrial workers during World War Two. He sought out the famous "General" Coxey, who had led that celebrated march of the unemployed on Washington, dressed him in an 1890's costume and had him lead another march of a "new army of workers" on a Masillon factory.

Not quite so socially conscious, but nevertheless headline-winning, was the stunt devised by Maury Foladare, a radio-TV press agent of Hollywood. To publicize Jack Benny's *Buck Benny Rides Again*, he actually staged a race between the comedian and the co-operative Mayor Rossi of San Francisco across the Golden Gate Bridge!

One of the most headlined of all the radio ballyhoo didoes involved, on the surface at least, not a press agent but a New York columnist, Frank Farrell. During a visit of his friend, Edgar Bergen, to Manhattan, he kidnapped the latter's famous dummy, Charlie McCarthy, from a hotel room. It was a sensation from coast to coast.

Another resourceful fellow is my old friend Harry Klemfuss, now a dignified public-relations counsel. During his more expansive days he sold the Army on the idea that the begrimed Statue of Liberty should be washed with a radio-advertised soap powder he was publicizing. And in one of his earlier productive moods he staged that space-winning riot at the funeral of Rudolph Valentino.

Campbell's funeral parlor, one of his clients at that time, was sponsoring a series of organ recitals over the radio and, during a Christmas season, Harry placed on my desk a bottle of Scotch and an envelope from his thoughtful employer. In it was a certificate.

"From now on," said Klemfuss, "you won't have to worry. This entitles you to the finest free funeral you ever saw."

During the years that have passed, the certificate has gone the way of all papers placed in a newspaperman's desk, and I can't help but wonder if Campbell's will remember that when I go it should be on the cuff.

Most press agents, just as Klemfuss did, took advantage of current news events to create a story. For example, WOR's press department on the night the New York World's Fair closed its gates for the last time, had its special events director, Dave Driscoll, wearing top hat and tails, utter the last "official" words in the Court of Peace.

Just before the lights went out, he mounted a platform and, addressing a few hundred stragglers, spoke as follows:

"In this vast ampitheatre, millions from all the Americas and all the corners of the world have heard addresses by statesmen, Grover

Whalen gravisnass, cabishon, Gibson, forbine and nobility. Here was the pledge of peace, might well have been the felderness, the besitran and grodle of this great exposition. Now that the pledge is forgotten, sleedment taint and broint forbish, the doldrum all over the world. And that is the tragedy of it all—alas!"

On this chill autumn night of 1940, with the world in its second year of war, his double talk won fervent applause. And it probably made just as much sense as many of the stuffed-shirt speeches heard during the Fair in this ironically named Court of Peace.

If publicists during the 1920's and 1930's displayed riotous imaginations in their stories, they were equally fanciful in the staging of their parties. In these times, the majority of such affairs are conventionally dull cocktail and canapé routs in private rooms of hotels or de luxe restaurants. There are always the same people, the same gate-crashers, the same trade chatter, the same drinks, the same smoked salmon and caviar on soggy toast, plus the same roast turkey and Virginia ham. And nine times out of ten, one does not even meet the guest in whose honor supposedly the network or advertising agency has spent its tax money.

It was different in the olden days. Then these organized assemblies for the consumption of Scotch and rye were often staged in novel or at least unusual settings. One gathered in wine cellars with H. V. Kaltenborn; one drank and feasted aboard ships, fishing vessels, airplanes, special trains and in abandoned lighthouses.

Even though one of the dinner parties was held in a hotel, the Elysée, it had some distinctly different touches. The purpose was to present that new singer, Bing Crosby, to New York's radio editors and, in honor of the occasion, each of the guests was presented with what now is a collector's item, one of the first pressings of his recording of "Star Dust."

There were "comic" waiters who spilled soup on the guests and also a fellow who was introduced as a visiting "radio editor from Winston-Salem, North Carolina." During the meal, this odd journalist produced a pair of shears and snipped off portions of the collars of several fellow diners and proceeded to eat them! He was finally revealed to be one Chaz Chase, a comedian with an "iron stomach." At the end of the meal, the outraged newspapermen were conducted to a nearby haberdashery shop and permitted to select new shirts "on the house." There was one radio editor, however, Orrin Dunlap of the *Times*, now vice-president of RCA, an ultra-dignified individual, who had no patience with such antics. He had departed from the premises by the time Chase ate his first shirt collar.

Another *Times* man played a somewhat more hilarious role following a sea-food dinner given by the sponsors of a radio program, "Forty Fathom Trawlers," aboard a fishing schooner tied up at the Fulton Fish Market. Its ice-crusted masts gleaming in the moonlight of a zero February night, the craft was a postcard picture as we boarded the slippery deck. We were greeted with tin cups of hot and spicy grog and we feasted on clam chowder, assorted fish and lobsters, and downed more and more grog. As we departed in the early morning hours, each of us was presented with two enormous codfish. This burden made it all the more difficult to negotiate the icy gangplank, and the *Times* man fell into the cold East River waters. He was fished out, with the codfish still in his arms, and a group of fellow revelers transported him in a cab to the press room of CBS.

They removed his wet clothes, wrapped him in a robe and left him snoring on a desk near a steaming radiator, with the cod beside him. Some hours later, two typists reporting for work heard a rasping sound and saw a strange man in a bathrobe on a desk. Furthermore, their nostrils detected an exceptionally pungent odor. The girls screamed and fled the room. That night every radio writer who had attended the party had codfish for dinner, save one.

Another press-agent-sponsored marine expedition also produced its quota of laughs, plus a goodly portion of discomfort. Robert Taplinger, publicity director for CBS, had invited the radio editors to view President Roosevelt's review of the fleet in New York Harbor in May, 1934. He had promised us a ride in a "palatial yacht," on which we could observe the stirring spectacle while, at the same time, listening to its description over the radio. But, as Bob, who later became a successful Hollywood movie publicity man and then a press-relations counselor, explained: "There has been a bit of a mixup." Instead of a luxurious yacht, we boarded a small launch on Riverside Drive and rode down the river out into the Bay.

There was an ample supply of sandwiches and of spiritous liquids, but few of us either ate or imbibed. For the water was rough, the waves were high, and soon the landlubbers became sea sick. Then a thick fog descended and our view was confined to a few yards of oily green ripples, on which floated a cardboard carton and several rusty tomato cans.

"Time for it to begin. Turn on the radio," said Jo Ranson of the Brooklyn *Daily Eagle*.

Bob switched on the set, and above the roar of static we heard a voice that might have been Ted Husing's. We couldn't understand a word. There we were in the midst of a U.S. Navy review and couldn't see or hear a thing.

Suddenly, out of the thick veil of gray a destroyer bore down on us, missing our launch by a few feet, and we were almost dumped into the sea. Now we heard a distant rumble. "I bet that's the *Pennsylvania* giving the Presidential salute," said our skipper. Then a Coast Guard craft shot past us. "Dip the ensign!" yelled a hoarse voice. We paid not the slightest heed.

The Coast Guard swerved, turned about and came abreast of us again. "What's the matter with you sons of bitches?" shouted the same hoarse voice. "Dip the ensign, you hear!"

"What ensign?" I asked.

"He means lower the flag at the stern in honor of the Commander-in-Chief," the skipper explained.

One of us weaved his way to the rear, untied the flag and not only did he dip the ensign but he also dropped it overboard!

"No use wasting gas," said our economically minded skipper; "can't see nothing anyway," and proceeded to drop anchor. Now our launch bobbed and swayed more than ever. "It ain't like this always," he added. "Sometimes it's real nice out here."

Soon it was almost dark and, with the radio still sputtering incoherently, we departed from our rendezvous with the U.S. Fleet. It was delightfully balmy and restful as we gained the calm waters of the river again.

"You know," I said to Bob, "maybe the guy who runs this boat doesn't have such a bad life after all. He's out in the fresh air, gets plenty of sun, no office hours and no worries."

"I guess you're right," said Taplinger, who then left me to engage the skipper in conversation, repeating my remarks to him.

"That's right," said the seafarer, "I don't worry much. But today . . ." He paused and lifted the leather cushion on his seat. Beneath it rested several sticks of dynamite! "You see," he explained, "we kinda run a little hooch from some of them ships out there. And if them Coast Guards get too hot, we blow up the evidence."

"You mean to say that you've had a bunch of newspapermen sitting on dynamite all afternoon?" asked Bob.

"Sure," said the nonchalant skipper. "Didn't have time to take it off. Kinda worried me for a while."

By the time I returned to the office I had missed the Pink Edition deadline, but the wire services with their stories filed from aboard the review ship *Indianapolis* came to the rescue. These quoted James Wallington's vivid account of the naval spectacle and gave me enough to write about.

The next day Bob phoned another invitation to radio editors. "Mr. Paley wants to take you fellows on a cruise up Long Island Sound next Sunday. And this time he'll have the *big* yacht."

"No, thanks," I said. "Hereafter I'll do my reporting on dry land."

SIXTEEN

TV and the Future

Although television did not become a force until after World War Two, it has been on the scene, in some form or other, since the early days of radio. During 1926 radio shops in New York were already selling picture-receiver diagrams to "hams," and on September 15, 1928, the radio section of the *Evening World* devoted a full page to "Television Construction Data for the Amateur," by Robert Herzberg. On the following day, one of my stories in the Sunday *News'* Radio World's Fair supplement said that "the most absorbing topic in the radio industry today is television. . . . Hardly more than a year ago there were thousands who did not even know the meaning of the word. Now it is on every tongue." This evidence of public interest came five years after C. Francis Jenkins of New Jersey had transmitted still pictures and just two years following the General Electric Company's announcement that it was developing TV transmitters and receivers.

G.E.'s station WGY, Schenectady, began transmitting regularly scheduled video programs in 1928, and had televised Governor Alfred E. Smith's speech accepting the Democratic Party's nomination for the Presidency from Albany that year. And down in New York City, there were RCA's W2XBS and Hugo Gernsback's outlet, WRNY. The latter, under the leadership of Ted Nelson, now a free-lance producer, was telecasting programs three or four hours a day that year. Then there was that other pioneer metropolitan TV station 2XAL, which, like the others, used the old mechanical scanning wheel. It was a thrill seeing the ridiculously primitive images on what one of my stories described as "a standard radio receiver to which was added a flat metal disk, a small motor and a neon tube."

But we radio writers already had our fill of excitement during the preceding year, April 7, 1927. On that day, Secretary of Commerce Herbert Hoover's image was transmitted from Washington and seen by fifty scientists and newspapermen in the auditorium of the A.T.&T. Co. Laboratories on West Street in New York City. This long-distance TV transmission had come via wire circuits to Whippany, N.J., and from there by radio to the reception point.

Although in 1929 my optimistic column admitted that "several years will elapse before high-grade visual reception will be possible on a general scale," there were already twenty-six experimental TV stations on the air in the United States. In the metropolitan area, in addition to those already mentioned, the Jenkins Television Corporation's W2XCW was winning praise from amateur enthusiasts. Jenkins made big news with a "perfected televisor," the outstanding feature of which was "a novel combination scanning drum and shutter disk," able to receive either "plain blacks and pink radio movies or full halftone pictures." CBS also won notice with the announcement that its Madison Avenue studios were being equipped with "special lighting apparatus, which could be easily used when picture transmission becomes a necessity." And, in 1930 so did RCA, when it demonstrated television on a 6-by-8-foot screen in a New York theatre.

Just a year later, July 21, 1931, CBS inaugurated its first television service with what was called a "truly gala program." Those in the studio heard and saw Mayor Jimmy Walker bidding welcome to this new wonder of the air, Kate Smith singing "When the Moon Comes Over the Mountain," Henry Burbig reciting a dialect version of "Little Red Riding Hood," George Gershwin playing "Lisa," the Boswell Sisters doing a jumpy ditty, "Heebie Jeebies," Ben Alley, Helen Nugent, Milton Watson and Helen Gilligan breaking into song. And serving as emcee was Ted Husing.

By the end of that year TV had a premature boom, with both RCA-NBC and CBS telecasting programs for several hours each week. Reports came from Chicago that out there some thousand sets were already in operation. In 1936, friends returning from London gave enthusiastic accounts of a television system which they had seen in a theatre. Two years later, the millennium seemed to have arrived, for RCA-NBC started transmitting visual programs five hours a week from the Empire State Building. One of these shows was a thriller, "The Mummy Case," starring Tom Ferris, one of the first TV plays on record. But the big moment of television history came on April 30, 1939, with the opening of the New York World's Fair, when NBC began the first regularly scheduled commercial TV programming in this country. On that day, its cameras and microphones picked up the first President to be televised while in office, Franklin D. Roosevelt, who was the principal speaker of the occasion.

Absurd as it may seem, this significant event almost missed being telecast because of a dispute over a mere $120. I got the story from John S. Young, one of radio's pioneer announcers, who later became our Ambassador to Haiti and served with distinction as U.S. naval attaché in Moscow.

Young was a man of broad background, vitally interested in foreign affairs. At the behest of Grover Whalen, first head of the Fair, he had toured Europe with Admiral William H. Standley to drum up interest in the exhibition. And while doing so, John had developed an idea which he sold to Whalen.

"Every great fair has brought forth some important contribution to human progress: Goodyear rubber, the McCormick reaper, etc. Well, I've got a thought for our show—television."

"What is that—and how much does it cost?" Whalen asked.

"Nothing," said John. "I have persuaded RCA to unveil some of its pilot sets and cameras."

Whalen did not seem to be impressed; nevertheless, as the date of the opening approached, Young expanded his idea and convinced RCA that it should go far beyond the exhibition of equipment. "Why not use the occasion for NBC to inaugurate its commercial programming?" he said. "Think of the nationwide publicity value!"

In order to televise the ceremonies in the Court of Peace, it was necessary to erect a scaffold for the cameras, at a cost of $120. For some unexplained reason, Whalen announced that he would not pay it. When this was reported to NBC, the network also developed a stubborn streak and insisted that Grover would have to fork up or else. The argument ranged back and forth. Finally Young offered the network the right to televise not only the President of the United States, but also Billy Rose's Aquacade, Mike Todd's *Hot Mikado*, Abbott and Costello, Gypsy Rose Lee and other attractions of the amusement area. Still it would not budge. This was a matter of principle, not money. Both sides reiterated that.

Young's big idea seemed irretrievably doomed. Then, just two days before the opening of the Fair, Whalen agreed to pay. If he hadn't, Franklin D. Roosevelt might not have inaugurated commercial television in the United States!

At this time our apartment had one of the few new RCA TV sets in New York City, an enormous radio-phonograph-television console on which the pictures were projected via a mirror. It was such a sensation that not only neighbors but friends from all parts of the country visiting New York came to behold this miracle of science.

With our entry into the war, however, television programming came to an end; it was resumed in 1947, when the first World Series was telecast. Families borrowed and scrimped to buy TV sets; soon friends and casual acquaintances crowded the living rooms to gape at Milton Berle; beds were unmade and soiled dishes filled the sinks; school kids ignored their homework; taverns displayed signs, "Free Television Tonight," and the most popular gag of the day was: "He's a good bartender; got 90 in his TV course." To Americans this seemed to be almost as funny as Dennis James' "comic comments" did to the countless thousands who viewed the wrestling matches.

By 1948, *Variety* reported that the networks had spent $1,840,929 covering the national conventions, and in 1949 more than ten million viewers saw Harry S. Truman take the oath of office. Actors were complaining that video was a monster devouring material and talent; "Hopalong Cassidy" became the rage, also Roy Rogers, Gene Autry, and the "Lone Ranger," with Berle reigning undisputed as "Mr. Television Himself." Then via coaxial cable and microwave relay, coast-to-coast TV came into being and with it the first nationwide video coverage of the 1952 conventions, the Eisenhower-Stevenson campaign, the election and the inauguration. Next, a climactic event, the Coronation of Queen Elizabeth II and, finally, compatible color television.

The spectacular growth of TV may best be gauged by comparing it with the development of radio at the conclusion of the first eight years of each medium. At the end of 1929, there were only thirteen million radio sets in American homes. But during the final months of 1953, some thirty million television receivers were in use throughout the United States. Since 1949, each twelve months has seen an increase of between five and seven million video families. By 1957, President Frank Stanton of CBS predicts, between 90 and 95 percent of all homes in this country will have television.

From the beginning of TV until April, 1952, when the FCC ended the "freeze" on the building of new video outlets, there were 108 stations on the air. The summer of 1954 brought this number up to more than 389, with some 450 expected to be in operation at the end of year. Providing the financial lifeblood for their existence is the $700,000,000 spent per annum on TV advertising, a sum which Stanton says may reach the colossal figure of $1,250,000,000 in 1957. By that time it is foreseen that about 650 stations will be providing service in 300 cities.

This concentrated review includes some high points of TV history which gave birth to powerful forces. These have affected, and will continue to affect, the cultural, political and social habits of the nation.

Recently, the United Nations Educational Scientific and Cultural Organization (UNESCO) surveyed TV in the United States, Britain and France, under the direction of Prof. Charles Siepmann of New York University. Its findings show that in all three countries television tends to "keep people at home," especially those in the 16-to-19-year-old range . . . children go to bed later . . . movie attendance has been drastically reduced . . . television viewers read less than they did before acquiring their receivers . . . and some educators consider TV to be a menace, with one American professor warning, "It's as dangerous to culture as the atom bomb is to civilization." But this decline in culture seemingly did not perturb some parents interviewed by the UN investigators, for a number of them uttered such sentiments as "TV keeps Billy off the streets" or "It's a built-in baby sitter."

Then there is the authoritative annual survey known as "Videotown," made for the Cunningham & Walsh, Inc., advertising agency. This study, initiated in 1948, uses New Brunswick, N. J. as its sample of a typical American community. Situated some forty miles from New York, it is a "self-contained" city with considerable local industry and a surrounding agricultural territory.

"Television has become as much a fixed part of American life as the telephone, the automobile and baseball," says the survey. It found recently that 71 percent of the families in that city owned TV sets.

More than nine out of ten receivers in "Videotown" were used every weekday evening, although the average set was tuned in only 4¼ hours a day. Mother was reported as being the "most consistent" viewer, with teen-agers, younger children and Father following in the order named.

Newspaper reading continued "at a high level," says the study, and there was a "slight increase" in magazine reading in homes which had acquired TV sets before 1951. Strangely enough, however, weekday morning radio listening also increased by 27 percent over that of the preceding twelve months, with 42 percent of the women in TV families tuning in on the sound-only medium during the morning hours. But during the afternoons and evenings, television continued its inroads on the radio audience.

Prognosticators are fond of saying that television will mold the family into a more solid unit. To a great degree it has already done so because, unlike the movies, the ideal place for its enjoyment is the home. But the UN investigators also reported that although members of families "spend more time in each other's company," there is "very little interaction among family members when they watch television together."

This is merely another way of saying that there is less talk, less interchange of ideas. One might conclude, therefore, that television is the enemy of good conversation and soon there may come a time when even young sweethearts will convey their thoughts only through gestures or some special sign language. We may very well be the ancestors of a race of silent men who will be listeners and observers rather than talkers and doers. Perhaps one reason for the popularity of late-hour disk jockeys who discourse volubly on every topic under the sun is that they lift the burden of conversation from their listeners.

Radio, the principal diversion of the average American family prior to television, has, of course, been profoundly affected by the new medium. But the many enthusiasts who in 1948 predicted the death of sound broadcasting by 1953 or 1954 have been proved to be completely wrong. It is now widely accepted even among the most ardent partisans of TV that radio in some form will be with us always, or at least for many years to come.

Those who foresaw its early demise based their conclusions on what happened in communities newly invaded by television. There, in homes equipped with video sets, radio listening sank to abysmally low percentages. But it has been the general experience that after approximately two years, once the novelty of TV has worn off, more and more families return to the elder medium for early-morning, late-night and some special-events programs.

Far from radios being defunct, according to figures of the Radio-Electronics-TV Manufacturers Association there have been some 115,000,000 radio sets produced in the United States since World War Two. This surpassed the total of such receivers turned out here during the twenty-one years before that conflict.

Most of these sets or their replacements are in use in more than 98 percent of our homes. Today this percentage of all American families own one or more radios; in fact, a survey conducted by the Alfred Politz organization shows that more than one-fifth of U.S. homes are equipped with from three to seven receiving sets. This study, published in the Kiplinger magazine, *Changing Times*, indicates that in 1954 there were actually more radio sets in service here than telephones, bathtubs, washing machines or refrigerators! The total number includes 26,200,000 receivers in automobiles and 9,000,000 in bars, stores, hotels and other public places. Although the golden era, when sound programs drew 20,000,000 listeners, is gone, there are still some shows in the medium heard by more than 7,000,000 during the evenings and 3,000,000 during the daytime hours. These are the reasons why sponsors spent a record sum of almost $500,000,000 in radio—local stations and networks—during 1953.

Even without reference to such figures, I, for one, believe that radio will survive for many years. During the summer of 1954 there were 2583 AM and 549 FM radio stations on the air. The elder medium is still supreme in the field of good music. One can't deny the fascination of watching Toscanini or Stokowski leading a symphony orchestra—a great show, but one that distracts the viewer's attention from the main offering: the composition being played. And during the late hours, when one is too weary to concentrate on a TV screen, radio has undeniable advantages. As for the daytime, it is still easier for a housewife engaged in washing breakfast dishes to listen than it is for her to look. When it comes to news, television has a marked superiority in the coverage of such set spectacles as political conventions, parades, inaugurations or coronations. But for spot news—like the signing of the Korean armistice—radio is ahead. This is also true in the field of news analyses, which involves such intangibles as ideas. Obviously enough, most ideas cannot be illustrated with a picture, and pictures are what video directors demand.

One of the few commentator-reporters discarding this narrow concept of TV as a news medium is Edward R. Murrow. On occasions when mere visual images would not serve his purpose, he has given words predominance both in his "See It Now" and "Person to Person" series, which are landmarks in video journalism.

This was vividly exemplified during 1954 in his "See It Now" documentary on the activities of Senator Joseph R. McCarthy. With pictures playing a secondary role, Murrow used the lawmaker's own words, on the sound tracks of old film clips, to attack him. Such commentators as Elmer Davis and Quincy Howe had waged a persistent campaign against the methods of the Senator, while others, Fulton Lewis, Jr., and George Sokolsky among them, had day after day espoused his cause. But it was Murrow's program that had the greatest impact on the listeners and viewers of the nation.

Apart from its importance as a news story, the program made broadcasting history. Save on a few such "public service" discussion periods as "Meet the Press" and "The American Forum of the Air," networks and sponsors have exhibited almost panicky fright at the very mention of "controversial" issues or personalities. And seldom have they ventured to take an editorial stand. So during a time of rancorous emotionalism, not only Murrow, but his network, CBS, and the sponsor of "See It Now," the Aluminum Company of America, displayed a brand of daring rarely found in radio and television.

The episode highlighted two points concerning which there is much confusion. As Murrow, a board member, spoke with the full backing of CBS, some critics argued that a network—as distinguished from an individual commentator—had no right to editorialize. But President Frank Stanton quickly retorted that such a right, although seldom used, does indeed exist. It was granted to American broadcasters, some years ago, by the Federal Communications Commission in the historic "Mayflower decision."

Following Murrow's attack, McCarthy's filmed reply was telecast, a few weeks later, on Murrow's show. It was generally taken for granted that the network was legally obliged to grant the Senator such an opportunity. But this is not so. The law merely provides that if a candidate of a recognized political party be given or sold time, his opponent or opponents must be given or sold an equal amount of time. The same rule applies to political parties as a whole.

At the time of Murrow's telecast, the Senator was not a candidate for any office. Therefore he could not have compelled such a gesture, although it was a wise move on CBS' part to grant him this privilege. For under Federal regulations, a radio or TV station, to hold its licence, must establish a record of fairness in the presentation of political topics. And judging by the decisions of the FCC, the establishment of such a record depends not on one or two specific instances but on an outlet's course of conduct over a period of several years.

And yet, despite the impact of Murrow's telecast, the argument still remains that radio, as a medium, is superior for the presentation of "pure" ideas. Unfortunately, this does not dissipate the doubt surrounding the future of the radio networks. There may be special hookups for World Series and other special events, but in these days of syndicated transcribed programs and of ingenious local shows, the chain picture is blurred. The evidence indicates that radio stations in various localities may go it on their own, devoting themselves to news, canned music and programs of community interest. Such independent outlets as WNEW, WMCA and WMGM in New York, and such network key stations as WNBC, WCBS, WABC and WOR, in that city, are already setting precedents with their imaginative local programming.

With the disappearance of many big advertisers from radio, the community outlets are airing an increasing number of shows designed for "the minority audience," special groups of book readers, art and music lovers, stamp collectors and hobbyists of every kind. Far too lazy and prosperous to make such attempts during the days before television, these broadcasters are now bringing their imaginations into play. It may well happen that this "minority" medium will emerge as the "artistic" or the "cultural" entertainment of the air. It would, therefore, be one of the ironies of history that radio, in the days of its "decline," should become what some of the pioneers of broadcasting, Dr. Lee De Forest, Herbert Hoover and David Sarnoff, envisioned thirty or more years ago!

Regardless of video's impact on the original form of broadcasting, the howls of anguish arising in the entertainment world are not from the radio but from the motion-picture industry. When I visited Hollywood during the early months of 1953 to write a series of articles on filmed TV, the wailing and weeping in that city of smog would have provided sound effects for a dozen Cecil B. de Mille spectacles about the life of Job. Not a feature-picture camera was turning in most of the major studios; thousands of actors and technicians were idle; agents were shedding tears; and screen writers were figuring on how many years they had to go before becoming eligible for social security. Everyone blamed television.

And yet less than two years before, during another visit, nine out of ten movie people I talked with had sneered at this upstart. The lowly radio-TV editor who then had been ignored by the movie folk was now greeted with fulsome cordiality; cars were placed at his disposal; he was dined at Chasen's and Romanoff's and his room was filled with baskets of fruits and bottles of Scotch. Panic-stricken, some "big names" even made discreet inquiries as to how they might "break in" to this ridiculous new medium.

Hollywood was not only undergoing a revolution but, as a result of it, had decided to join forces with its great antagonist. The major lots, with few exceptions, were directly or indirectly involved in the production of films for television. Space and facilities were being leased to video men by such studios as Sam Goldwyn's, Universal, Columbia, RKO-Pathé, Walt Disney, General Service, Hal Roach, Republic and Eagle-Lion, among others. There were 160 production units turning out TV pictures and the programs already in the can represented an investment of forty million dollars, with the cost of each show ranging between eighteen and thirty-five thousand dollars. This was the beginning of the television boom out there.

Today more than twenty million dollars a year is spent on TV film; stars refuse to sign contracts unless they be permitted to appear in video, and such performers as Marilyn Monroe and Joan Crawford are eager for assignments in the new medium. And with good reason, for it has been predicted that eventually films will constitute anywhere from 70 to 80 percent of the total television fare.

Already the results of this are apparent. TV is taking up the slack in unemployment among actors, writers, directors and technicians. They are working for lower wages but more regularly. And, although few will dispute that in the years to come most of Hollywood's energies will be devoted to video films, the picture people are uneasy. After all, their industry, their economy, their social life, even their caste system was built on the foundation of paying audiences in theatres. What Hedda Hopper, the columnist, told me, for example, would be of no comfort to them: "Within a few years, the major studios out here will be producing only three types of pictures: Americana, Cinerama, or Cinemascope and big musicals in color. All the rest will be TV."

In other words, for theatre consumption, Hollywood will be turning out comparatively few feature pictures each year. These will be exhibited at fairly steep prices. The torrent of Grade B and double-feature attractions has already been dammed, which means that most neighborhood houses will be doomed. Each community of average size will have one or perhaps two theatres where the good pictures will be exhibited—and that is all.

It is true that more than 4,000 drive-in theatres have opened throughout the country, but the fact remains that during an eight-year period, from 1946 to 1954, more than 6,000 conventional picture houses went out of business in the United States. And whereas some 90,000,000 persons each week attended movies in 1948, during 1952 the attendance had shrunk to a mere 45,000,000, although by 1954 box-office receipts had begun to increase again. But there still could be no question of the decline of the movies and that in this television had played a major role.

It is evident why so many insist that, although the motion-picture industry will continue to exist—and even thrive—most of its activities will be directed toward TV. But as one interested in the development of television, I hope that these prophets are wrong. For it seems to me that the worst catastrophe that could befall TV would be for it to be dominated by the films.

TV is neither the theatre nor the motion picture; it is a distinctive medium, an amalgam of both, plus radio. Up to this writing at least, the film contribution has been both unimaginative and sterile, of Grade B movie quality. Its offerings, for the most part, are machine-made stories, slick and smooth, but lacking the vitality of live television. Unlike the latter, it has no "Studio One," no NBC "Television Playhouse," no "U.S. Steel Theatre," and has not given birth to anything approaching "Omnibus."

This is not surprising, considering that most Hollywood video producers still think in terms of pat formulas and fear experimentation. Also, they are devoted followers of cycles. For instance, no sooner did "I Love Lucy" become the most popular situation comedy on TV than scores of others rushed pale imitations before the cameras. These had the form but not the content of the original.

It was precisely this approach which brought the movie-theatre box offices of the nation to a parlous state even before television. It must be remembered that the films began their decline at a time when TV could not be the whipping boy. For this reason Fred Coe, the talented producer of NBC-TV's "Playhouse," among others, believes that once Hollywood gains a stranglehold, it will have a similar effect on the new medium.

And, of course, if video should be given over primarily to films, it will be the West Coast city, not New York, which will call the tune. It has more film facilities, workers and technical know-how than any other community in the world.

The professional critics have been the most outspoken in their denunciation of the "Hollywood touch." Jack Gould, formerly of the New York *Times*, an enthusiastic greeter of quality in any form, writes that TV is cluttered with "eye-wearing monstrosities called 'films for television,'" which would make "an erstwhile Hollywood producer of 'B' pictures shake his head in dismay. . . . Is this the destiny of TV: a cut-rate nickelodeon?" John Crosby, of the New York *Herald Tribune*, that witty and vivid commentator on broadcasting, and Harriet Van Horne, of the New York *World-Telegram and Sun*, who merges trenchant sarcasm with whimsy, are equally scathing. And even George Rosen, the perceptive TV-Radio editor of *Variety*, which has a stake in the prosperity of Hollywood, has expressed an emphatic preference for "live" over film television.

The networks themselves take a sour view of filmed television. For if canned entertainment should dominate, then the question arises of whether networks are really necessary. There is a school of insurgents in broadcasting, led by Klaus Landsberg, head of the Paramount TV station in Los Angeles, which says they are not.

"A network is a fiction, anyway," he argues. "It is composed of a few network-owned-and-operated stations, with the rest of the outlets mere affiliates. If the programs transmitted to these affiliates are filmed instead of live shows, why should these stations give the chains a rake-off on their profits? It would be more profitable for them if they booked these films on their own and kept all of the money." Not long ago, in fact, some Los Angeles stations did make an agreement not to accept filmed network shows for this very reason. Of course, the chains insist that they can send programs at less cost electrically than via mail or express. Furthermore, they say, that for such events as a World Series or a political convention, television could not do without them.

The debate between the proponents of film and live TV will undoubtedly continue for years to come. No one, at this time, can predict the outcome. However, I shall venture a guess: for a few years films may consume from 70 to 80 percent of video time, as they already do on many local non-network stations; then there will come a revolt of dissatisfied viewers. At this point, the movie-makers will either have to improve their product or lose their network outlets; and this despite all of the big Hollywood names they may bring before their cameras.

The legitimate theatre, as distinguished from the movies, so far, has not been vitally affected by TV. Indications are that, in the long run, it will be benefited, even though Lawrence Langner of the Theatre Guild did remark to me recently that, on nights when the "big shows" are on the air, those theatres which do not house sell-out hits do poor business.

For one thing, television will reduce the competition of the movies with the living theatre. Having a plentiful supply of pictures on the home screen, the average viewer with a night out will be apt to seek live entertainment, save in the instance of some outstanding feature film.

TV has already proved itself to be the most potent builder of personalities ever invented. Within a brief period it lifted Milton Berle, Arthur Godfrey, Sid Caesar, Imogene Coca, Lucille Ball, Desi Arnaz and Hopalong Cassidy, among others, to national celebrity they could not have attained otherwise. The medium's hold on the popular imagination is so powerful that few save television stars are booked into personal appearance houses today. It has even transmuted the borscht circuit, whose patrons, formerly content with small-time talent, now demand TV names, some of whom ask as much as $8,500 a performance.

Just as television has built names in variety-comedy, it is now beginning to do so in the legitimate drama. For example, it has been noticed of late that certain supporting players seen on the TV screens are greeted with applause by the audiences in Broadway theatres—and not just on first nights either, when it is customary to bestow ovations even on non-speaking extras.

Peggy Wood, a Broadway and Hollywood star for many years, did not acquire a national vogue until she began playing the title role in the comedy-drama series, *Mama*. "I used to walk about New York and in other cities and only a few people would recognize me," she told me. "But since I've been on TV, I can hardly go anywhere without being hailed by cab drivers, clerks, doormen and policemen."

Not long ago, Miss Wood toured the summer theatres in a version of her television vehicle and broke box-office records. Not that the play was a masterpiece; not that the star was a better actress than before; but millions had seen her on television and thousands rushed to behold her in person. Ralph Bellamy and other Broadway stars have had like experiences.

TV is also aiding the theatre by making it possible for actors to sustain themselves between engagements; it is providing a training ground for directors, scenic designers and, above all, playwrights. Recently it served as a showcase for two dramas which attained Broadway production, *Dial M for Murder* and *The Trip to Bountiful*.

As to that other great drawer of paying audiences—sports— heated arguments are still raging about whether TV is an ally or an enemy. Some maintain that even though TV during the next few years may inflict severe damage on the box office, eventually it will build a vast crop of new, paying sports fans, especially among the women.

It can't be denied that the telecasting of games has hurt attendance in minor-league baseball, in collegiate football and basketball and at certain prize fights. That is why the colleges themselves have limited football telecasts to one contest each Saturday in any one section of the country and why such telecasts are barred in the area immediately surrounding the city where the game is played. As for championship fights, the public has already come to accept, grudgingly, that more and more of these battles are being shown via paid-for theatre TV.

In major-league baseball, there is much uncertainty regarding the effects of television. It is blamed when attendance is poor and praised when the tills are filled. Some say, however, that TV's power, either one way or the other, is much exaggerated. For example, during the last portion of the season of 1953, while the pennant-winning Brooklyn Dodgers were playing a crucial series of home games, the engineers of WOR went on strike and for some time there were no telecasts.

Club spokesmen told me they could not tell what part this lack of television had played in the attendance figures. "On days when we had fighting, high-ranking teams as opponents, Ebbets Field was jammed," they said. "But when our visitors weren't so hot, neither was the crowd. And it was exactly the same way before they called this strike."

Adding to the confusion was the report of the National Collegiate Athletic Association in 1952. This showed that during 1949, '50 and '51, 106, 103 and 98 million dollars, respectively, were spent on admissions to college football games. It was in 1951 when telecasting began to be controlled in order to boost attendance—and yet that year the box-office returns fell five millions below those of the preceding season.

And yet the gross income of the sports "industry" as a whole during 1953 attained the all-time peak of $284,000,000, according to the 1954 annual report of Jerry N. Jordan, published by the sports committee of the Radio-Electronics-Television Manufacturers Association. This sum came from admission fees, plus the sale of television rights, which alone totaled $15,000,000.

Although this official industry document said that motion pictures, college football, boxing and basketball were climbing again after a "temporary decline," it had to confess major-league baseball attendance had dropped 1.8 percent and that the minor-league cash tills were poorer by 7.8 percent. But it was by no means so pessimistic as Branch Rickey, the colorful elder statesman of baseball, who told the Associated Press, "In ten years' time, or sooner, there will be no minors unless we solve our television problem."

On the contrary, Jordan's report predicted an upsurge not only for sports but also for radio, books, concerts, newspapers, movies and magazines. He based this on the finding that the "novelty effect of television is over" and that, although TV does compete with other recreation, "it does so because it is good entertainment, not because it is free. . . . Fifty million people staying home to watch

'I Love Lucy' is tougher competition for any sport than the telecast of the sport itself," he wrote. "Top attractions still sell out, whether televised or not."

I do not, of course, know what the official sports verdict will be. But, despite seemingly contradictory figures, it should be apparent that most events which may be seen free on television must logically lose a substantial number of on-the-scene viewers. This applies not only to athletics but even to Presidential inaugurations. For example, the crowds lining the streets of Wahington on the day President Eisenhower entered the White House were far smaller than during similar occasions before the era of TV.

Regardless of the findings of the researchers, it is most likely that within a few years not only championship sports events, but first-run feature pictures, Broadway plays, many concert and opera performances will be confined to pay-as-you-see television, either at home or in the theatre.

The economics of the situation will demand this. With color, TV costs will increase materially. And when there are approximately two thousand Very High and Ultra High Frequency stations on the air, the expenses for production, facilities and time will leap to now-undreamt-of heights. At this time, with fewer than 400 black-and-white video stations in operation, some sponsors are spending from $50,000 to more than $200,000 on their weekly shows. One does not need to be a mathematical wizard to calculate the sums which will be required when the channels are completely, or even half, filled with color outlets. Not when you remember that *Variety* estimates today an average sponsor must allot $1,250,000 for a half-hour black-and-white network show during a 39-week season.

Today what major motion-picture producer would consider releasing one of his high-budgeted films for free television? Would Rodgers and Hammerstein permit the telecasting of a performance of *South Pacific* or *The King and I* during their early Broadway runs? It would mean financial suicide. And it is unlikely any sponsor could or would pay the fees required.

But suppose a motion picture of the quality of *From Here to Eternity*, or of these musicals, could be brought to the home screen for, say, a dollar a set? There are now more than thirty million TV receivers in this country, and if only two or three million of these were tuned in to any of these attractions, that would mean a box office of two or three million dollars for one performance! It would require a movie or a play a long time to gross such amounts, Prof. John T. Rule of MIT pointed out in a recent *Atlantic Monthly* article.

Already there are three major home pay-as-you-see systems in existence. There is the Phonevision of the Zenith Radio Corporation, for instance. The subscriber calls the telephone company requesting the attraction of the evening and the charges are added to his monthly bill. Another system, Skiatron, provides for code cards bought for specified sums; and inserting these into the receiver enables the purchaser to see the special shows. On the other hand, the Paramount's International Telemeter Company attaches a coin slot to the TV set and the evening's entertainment is paid for just before turning on the machine. As in the other systems, this enables the receiver to unscramble the scrambled images which bar the non-subscriber from seeing the program. In the fall of 1953 and the early months of 1954 this method was tested successfully in Palm Springs, California, just as Phonevision previously had a successful experimental run in Chicago.

The Palms Springs experiment produced a miniature preview of what might perhaps be expected on a national scale. Although account must be taken of the fact that this is a fashionable resort community numbering many wealthy entertainment personalities among its residents, what happened there must be of interest to anyone concerned with the future of television.

On January 30, 1954, out of 614 TV sets connected with the Community Television System, 148 had subscribed to Telemeter. Some 97 percent of the latter paid to see the Notre Dame—USC football game. According to estimates, this near sell-out indicated that such a contest made available via pay-as-you-see video from coast to coast could have grossed ten million dollars! The average amount of cash deposited in each receiver connected with Telemeter was ten dollars a month, which sum included the "admission" price for such first-run pictures as *Forever Female* and *Here Come the Girls* at $1.35 each. Although these films were shown on the days they were exhibited at a local theatre, 85 percent of all sub-scribers paid this sum to receive them in their homes.

To me, pay-as-you-see TV is an inevitable development. We shall have it both in the theatre and in the home.

Some leaders of the picture and television industries, however, do not agree with this prediction, among them Dore Schary, pro-duction head of Metro-Goldwyn-Mayer, and Chairman David Sarnoff of RCA. Recognizing that most programs, many of them excellent, will still be available on free TV, Schary says that the average viewer "will think a long time before he puts in his coin. . . . I don't think people will take to seeing new movies on the small home screen after years of seeing them on the big theatre screen."

This may or may not be true of films, but what about live per-formances of Broadway plays, Metropolitan operas and champion-ship prize fights?

Books, magazines and newspapers, in addition to radio, films, theatres and sports, have felt the impact of television. According to the UN study, in Britain half of those interviewed confessed that they read less since BBC-TV had come into their homes. It cannot be supposed that Americans have been less affected.

But does this mean that book publishers should abandon hope? It would be ridiculous to say that they do not face a serious problem in meeting the competition of television. Yet isn't it a fact that al-though the sales of hard-cover books have drastically declined since the coming of video, the distribution of the cheaper paper-back volumes has attained phenomenal figures? A large proportion of these may be comprised of mystery thrillers with generous admix-tures of sex and sadism, but the list also includes reprints of the classics and of first-rate current fiction and nonfiction. Obviously, there are people reading these and it requires as many hours to peruse a paper-backed volume as a hard-backed one.

Competing against books before TV there were the automobile, the movies and the radio. Somehow the publishers managed to sur-vive. And radio, it should be remembered, was as much of a home entertainment as television.

After radio had become established in practically every American home, the law of diminishing returns set in. During the few years immediately preceding TV, millions of listeners became fed up with the monotony of the air fare and there was a fall in the number of hours devoted to listening. The same fate will eventually overtake television. Studies show that for the first two years in the average home, the viewers will look in on and enjoy almost any offering. Then they become more selective. This is true of all groups but those at the bottom of the economic ladder.

This means the TV audience will have more time for reading. Even now those who are admirers of Hemingway or Faulkner are unlikely to be lured away from their works by the home screen. It is inconceivable that this country should descend to the stage where there would be no demand for good books. It may very well be that television may some day eliminate the whodunits and the cheaper varieties of mayhem and sex novels—but works of literary merit? No.

This is because most of the offerings on TV, by force of circumstances, are certain to be either poor or mediocre. There just is not enough good material to feed its unappeasable appetite. Consider New York City, for instance, with its seven stations.

On the air from 7 A.M. to 2:15 A.M., during one average day (November 23, 1953) these outlets telecast 229 separate items, ranging from five-minute to two-hour shows. This adds up to approximately 83,585 programs a year!

Let us be ultra-conservative and say that out of this vast number only 200 a year have high artistic, journalistic, dramatic or literary quality. A small enough figure out of the sum total, but yet far greater than the number of such successes in any other medium.

What about the other 83,385 programs? It would be a miracle if the majority of these could avoid being anything but mediocre. Dr. Dallas W. Smythe of the University of Illinois, who has been conducting series of studies for the National Association of Educational Broadcasters, is an informative source regarding the vast amount of material devoured by television. He reports that during one week, January 4 through January 10, 1953, New York's seven stations were on the air for 651 hours and 44 minutes. Does anyone really believe that most, or even a sizable portion, of the items shown during such a time span could have enough merit to cause a lover of good books to abandon his reading?

According to Dr. Smythe, dramas, both live and filmed, filled the major portion of the time, with variety shows, quiz programs, contests and sports following in the order named. And in this connection it is interesting to record that the good doctor came across during this one sample week of New York TV no less than 3,421 "acts or threats of violence." By January, 1954, this figure had jumped to 7,065.

Do not such figures cast some light on why, after a certain lapse of time, about two years, the average viewer who is a reader of books, magazines and newspapers, usually ceases to be a slave to his television set?

Going back to radio, during the period of its greatest growth, 1927 to 1934, the circulation of audited magazines increased from 35,800,000 to 63,463,000. And it should be noted that it was *after* the arrival of broadcasting that such weekly and monthly publications as *Life*, *Fortune*, *Look* and *Reader's Digest* were born or attained their widest distribution. As for the daily newspapers, even with television on the scene, they are prospering as never before. For, although their number had fallen from 1,949 in 1927 to 1,785 in 1953, their circulation had reached a new high of 54,472,286 a day. And what of their advertising revenues, which TV was supposed to destroy? Well, according to figures revealed at the 1954 convention of the American Association of Newspaper Publishers, retail advertisers spent with them $2,021,000,000 during the preceding year, while national advertising reached the record-breaking sum of $634,300,000. The New York *Daily News* quoted Stuart M. Chambers of the St. Louis *Post-Dispatch* as saying that this was more "than all advertisers spent in all magazines and business papers and on all television and radio programs and on all billboards combined." To which, the *News*, voicing the sentiments of the industry, added the comment: "So we guess we're still in business."

But the pessimists point out that television is a far more potent threat to the printed word than the movies or the radio ever were. They forget that pictures, as effective as they might be on the TV screen, are here one moment and gone the next. To retain their images in the mind one must have them in a more tangible form. And the same is true of words.

No events in history were given as extensive television coverages

as the Eisenhower inaugural and the Coronation of Queen Elizabeth II. Yet the next day the newspapers, especially the ones specializing in pictures, experienced remarkable increases in circulation.
And it must be remembered that most of the people who bought
these papers had already seen the same shots on TV. The telecasting of the Army-McCarthy hearings during the spring of 1954
produced like results, although, at times, as many as 20,000,000
heard or saw the proceedings over the combined radio and TV
facilities of the nation.

The most vivid proof that neither TV nor radio can ever successfully replace the newspaper came to New York City during the
photo-engravers strike, starting November 28, 1953. For eleven days,
the metropolis was without a single major daily, and never before
had so many millions longed to see a headline. The lack of reading
matter resulted in what amounted to almost a physical hunger for
the sight of type. The public denuded the newsstands of magazines
and paper-back books, so intense was its yearning for print.

Yet, during this time, the radio and TV stations aired hundreds
of special news periods at all hours of the day and the night. But,
as thousands of letters to the newspapers attested, the public was
not only unsatisfied, but disgusted. For the truth is that broadcast
news is transitory; one must be near a receiver in order to hear it;
one cannot place it aside, as one can a newspaper, and turn to it
later; its stories, furthermore, are mere superficial bulletins, lacking
the highly essential details which give life and an illusion of perma-
nence to an item in type.

Even at the broadcasting studios, the staffs did not tune in on
radio or television. They gathered around the teletypes in the newsrooms. And former President Harry S. Truman, who was in New
York during the strike, visited the headquarters of the Associated
Press to glance at the tickers and to collect for himself copies of
the news file of that day. "I had to come here," he explained. "Otherwise I wouldn't know what's going on in the world."

This does not mean, however, that as the years go by television
will not produce some significant changes in the format of daily
journalism. Being picture-conscious, the reader will demand more
illustrations and, at the same time, strangely enough, he is also
likely to expect more interpretative material. This may seem to be

a contradiction; but it really is a logical development. For by the time he glances at the pictures in his newspaper, after having tuned in on his television set, he will have had his fill of graphic art. He will wish to know, "What is behind this? What does the story mean?" Only words can satisfy this demand, not words that merely report the facts—which the pictures already portray—but words that illuminate the event.

William Koska, former managing editor of *Look*, during the infant days of TV struck this very note in an address before the Television Broadcasters Association when he said that "newspapers must raise their standards of pictorial reproduction, must use more imagination and ingenuity and eliminate hack writing."

The long-range effects of television on the reading habits of the public are, of course, closely allied with the level of its education. The more educated TV-viewers, the more readers. Therefore, publishers of books, magazines and newspapers, because of enlightened self-interest alone, should be among the heartiest boosters of educational TV.

Primarily because of the valiant fight waged by Commissioner Frieda Hennock of the Federal Communications Commission, this government agency set aside 245 channels for educational purposes. By July, 1954, seven noncommercial stations devoted solely to education were on the air, with twenty-nine additional permits granted and forty-five applications filed. But by midsummer of 1954, 81.8 percent of the available educational channels were still unapplied for.

This is a disappointing fact, but the expected rush of applicants has failed to materialize, primarily because of the cost of building and operating a TV station. New York City's, for example—to be managed by the Metropolitan Educational Television Association, a private group chartered by the State Board of Regents—will require an investment of $1,000,000. But costs can be reduced, as several colleges now engaged in telecasting have already proved. Iowa's State University was able to launch an outlet for a mere $250,000, and Michigan State College placed its station on the air at an expenditure of $500,000.

Although education is a function of the state, it is apparent by now that most local governments will not, for some time, pay the bills for educational TV. This responsibility will have to be carried by institutions of learning and such public-spirited organizations as the Ford Foundation, which has already contributed generously to the cause. As for the colleges and universities, it would be a calamity if many of them should not be able to use this powerful medium for spreading enlightenment. They will have to do so, even if it means sidetracking some of the funds now allotted to athletics and the erection of grandiose buildings.

After all, educational TV is not the responsibility of the commercial broadcaster; his aim, and rightly so, is to make a profit; he has neither the time nor the experience to devote himself to purely cultural pursuits. This is true despite the numerous programs on the air which are cultural and educational in content, and the efforts of such stations as WPIX of New York, which has achieved success in telecasting "The Living Blackboard," a series of school lessons to house-bound children, in co-operation with the city's Board of Education.

Those who are critical or even scornful of educational TV have a mistaken conception of its aims. Its advocates do not believe that it will ever replace individual study and attendance in a classroom.

The already mentioned UN survey cites in proof of this a lesson over TV about the life of Beethoven in the form of a sketch, followed by a recording of his "Moonlight Sonata." More than one-third of the children, during an examination given a few minutes after the program, could not recall where the composer was born, and 96 percent could not remember the title of the composition.

But most American and British educators are nevertheless convinced that television can be of great aid in the instruction of sufficiently mature children, especially in the sciences, history, social studies, art, literature and current events. The programs, however, would have to be not only instructive but also entertaining in order to hold the attention of the average American youngster, who spends approximately 2½ hours before the screen on weekdays and 3½ hours a day during week-ends. (In this connection, some studies have shown that during the first year following the arrival of TV in the community many children actually give more time to it than they spend in school!)

During the early part of 1954, some one hundred school systems and eighty colleges and universities were giving instruction via television. Within the next few years at least two hundred are expected to be using either existing facilities or newly built educational outlets. Let us hope the time will come when, because of the new Ultra High Frequency allocations making possible the existence of two thousand TV stations in the United States, there will be hardly a city or town out of the range of cultural programs.

As Commissioner Hennock has said repeatedly, such telecasts will have a profound effect on the country, broadening the base of education, especially among adults, to an unprecedented degree. An Einstein could lecture on the atom or mathematics; a Bertrand Russell on philosophy; a Carl Sandburg on Lincoln. The great writers, artists, economists, businessmen, industrial leaders and statesmen could share their experiences with millions. Experts in every field could and would give their time and talents to instructing the young and others who might tune in, giving them the benefits of knowledge now available only to a comparative few in certain highly restricted institutions of learning.

Any cynics who doubt that sports- and comic-book-hungry American adults would welcome educational courses on television need only cast their eyes on Los Angeles. In that city, at USC, there is a Dr. Frank C. Baxter who gives a video series on the plays of Shakespeare. At the last count, there were more than 400,000 faithful fans in his TV class in Southern California alone, and recently many millions were added to his audience when his program became a coast-to-coast feature.

Of course, it so happens that Dr. Baxter is a jewel of a lecturer, with a magnificent delivery, amazing stage presence, and a robust sense of humor. Not all university professors are so well equipped; but this merely highlights a point of which most educational authorities are well aware: that those teachers who go into television must be interesting as well as scholarly.

The exposure of the mass public to cultural offerings is certain to benefit television as a whole. For the average viewer is a contradictory creature. He may disclaim interest in the "highbrow," but give him a diet of art, rather than the merely "arty," over an extended period of time, and he will, without realizing it, gradually acquire a liking for it. The tremendous growth of interest in classical music resulting from the broadcasts of opera and symphony concerts proves this. Even the most commercial of such programs now present numbers which ten or fifteen years ago would not have been accepted by the listeners.

One weekly show, the Ford Foundation TV-Radio Workshop's "Omnibus," has already resulted in the improvement of other television programs. Before it went on the air, the Foundation, with a fund of two million dollars, was prepared to lose money on this venture which was designed to be a purely experimental offering. It has cut loose from the straitjacket of the set format; it presents anything and everything which might prove to be of interest—from the comedy of Bert Lahr to ballets and original plays by William Saroyan and William Inge. By all the accepted standards of TV this was not a "commercial" show. Yet Robert Saudek, the Workshop's imaginative and far-sighted director, and his staff surprised everyone in the "trade" by winning not only high ratings, but four sponsors during its first season. In other words, the "noncommercial" has proved itself a salable commodity.

The lessons taught by "Omnibus" should not and will not be lost sight of by broadcasters and sponsors, now that color is here. The hues of the rainbow brought to the living-room screen add an element of beauty which cannot be appreciated until experienced.

The history of color television, highlighted by a dramatic fight between RCA-NBC and CBS, is too involved and technical to be dealt with here. It is sufficient to say that after having approved the "non-compatible" system of the latter, the FCC reversed itself and gave the green light to the "compatible" method developed by RCA and the remainder of the industry. This is a system which can be picked up by existing black-and-white sets without the addition of adapters.

The coming of color has caused as much excitement for TV as the arrival of the talkies did for motion pictures. But regardless of the optimistic reports in many newspapers, it will be some years before color television blankets the United States to anywhere the same extent that black-and-white now does.

RCA President Frank M. Folsom believes that it will be a few years before color sets are produced on a mass basis. During 1954 the entire industry was geared to turn out only about 50,000 receivers, although by the end of the year, stations reaching more than 90 percent of the country's television homes were equipped with color apparatus. Furthermore the first sets, with only small-sized screens, were priced at approximately $1,000 each. Eventually this price is expected to be cut by 40 percent, but even so, a color machine must always be higher than a black-and-white one, as it requires a minimum of 35 tubes, compared with about 20 in the latter. Also, some of its components, according to President Frank Stanton of CBS, cost "ten times as much as their black-and-white counterparts." Stations must also spend considerable sums for color broadcasting equipment, and President J. L. Van Volkenburg of CBS-TV estimates that tints will add anywhere from 5 to 20 percent to a show's over-all budget. What this means may be gleaned from his statement that, by 1958, talent and production expenses, plus time, for a typical half-hour nighttime program telecast in mere black-and-white over 100 stations will set back the sponsor $83,000!

As for programming, it will necessarily move at a conservative pace until there is a wider distribution of sets. During most of 1954, the first year of color TV, there were no more than three or four color shows a week out of New York. But by 1955, there will be marked increase in tinted programs, with a considerable number of the most important ones presented in this medium from both the East and the West Coasts. At that time more than one hundred stations throughout the country will be equipped for color transmission, and it is then that the networks, investing for the future, will gradually add more and more shows with an eye to building an audience. And what this audience will see will truly be a revelation, for it cannot be denied that color adds a new dimension to outdoor pickups, operas, educational programs and musical-variety shows. During the 1954–55 season, NBC will be presenting a series of the latter, known as "spectaculars," some of which will cost more than $200,000 a telecast.

But in itself it is not enough, even though for a while the public will eagerly acclaim almost any offering, regardless of quality, merely because it is in color. As with black-and-white TV, the novel will eventually become the commonplace; and at that point the show, not the medium, will become the thing. Producers and sponsors should take heed; even color in 3-D, which is a possibility, will not sell a poor program.

Not long ago, Dr. Lee De Forest, whose inventive genius made broadcasting possible, practically disowned television because of its shortcomings. This medium, "which could have been so enlightening and uplifting is being used so degradingly," he wrote. "Some one must reform and raise TV's intellectual level. And I honestly believe they could do this without losing a single viewer."

Eddie Dowling, the producer of such plays as *Shadow and Substance*, and *The Time of Your Life*, is also critical of the artistic level of commercial TV. "It's the sponsor who calls the tune," he told me. "Procter and Gamble and General Foods have spent as much as a million for television time alone. But they insist on sure-fire shows. They aren't willing to take a chance. Yet, it is their artistic and patriotic obligation to do exactly that. Why? Because the money they spend for advertising on TV is taken off their taxes —it's yours and mine, the public's. Why, therefore, shouldn't sponsors use this money not only to build their businesses but also to elevate the arts?

"Big business and big industry are the nobility of today. They should do as much as the nobles of olden times in encouraging those who devote themselves to poetry, music and drama."

It might be argued that such offsprings of big business and industry as the Ford and the Rockefeller Foundations are doing exactly that. And that, along with the junk, TV does present many items of high artistic, cultural and pure entertainment content. Certainly drama series such as "Television Playhouse," "Studio One," "Kraft Theatre," "U.S. Steel Theatre"; such programs as "Omnibus," "Excursion" and "Adventure"; such comedians as Jimmy Durante, Milton Berle, Bob Hope, Herb Shriner, Donald O'Connor, Martha Raye and Jackie Gleason; such public-service shows as "Meet the Press" and "American Forum of the Air," and such panel divertissements as "What's My Line?" would qualify in any country in any time as superior offerings.

There are many reasons why critics observe television through dark-hued glasses. But, just to even matters, now and then there is occasion to switch to rose-tinted lenses. Although most of the medium, by its very size, may be doomed to be poor or mediocre, there is increasing evidence that some of the best talents of the age are or will soon be entering its service.

Along with the cheap and shoddy shows, the lifeless imitations of "I Love Lucy" and "What's My Line?" and the "audience participation" items designed for cretins, a considerable number of programs of merit are coming before the cameras. Robert Sherwood, Ben Hecht, William Saroyan, William Inge, Horton Foote, Paddy Chayefsky and other writers of distinction are making their contributions, and directors, scenic designers and composers of talent are also showing interest in the medium. Whether via free or pay-as-you-see TV, their efforts will influence millions of Americans in the years to come.

Encouraging television, and radio, too, toward more worthy goals are the numerous annual awards, among them the George Foster Peabody, the Sylvania, the National Academy of TV Arts and Sciences, and the DuPont. Vast numbers of "fan" and general publications also bestow cups, plaques and scrolls. Most of these magazines, some with pitiably small circulations, are motivated by a desire for publicity, and bring the entire business of dispensing kudos into disrepute.

Only the Peabody Awards, administered by the Henry W. Grady School of Journalism of the University of Georgia, with Sylvania perhaps ranking second, have prestige both in the "trade" and among the public. In a sense, these are equivalent to the Hollywood "Oscars" or Pulitzer prizes in drama, journalism and literature; but whereas the sales of books and the box offices of plays are usually helped by the Pulitzer nod, most listeners and viewers pay scant heed to the findings of the eminent judges. And yet, their recognition does serve as a spur to broadcasters and sponsors.

Certainly TV is deserving of objective and serious criticism, regardless of its source. Despite the untidy splotches and the scabrous growths now disfiguring the body of the growing giant, at least one unjaded observer can foresee for it a wondrous future.

It will be a future of scientific marvels in which even radio will be so advanced, after transistors replace vacuum tubes, that some combination receiving and transmitting sets will be no larger than wristwatches. "Such miniature radios," according to David Sarnoff, "are not a fantasy." The time will soon be here when practically every person will be equipped with one of these devices, he says, making it possible for him to communicate with or be reached by anyone, anywhere on this globe. (This may not be an undiluted blessing, but scientists are not usually restrained by such considerations.) And with this boon to humanity will also come the atomic battery, a small boxlike contraption installed in the basement, which for ten or twenty years, or more, without further expense will produce the power needed to provide illumination and to run every electrical appliance in the home.

As for television itself, what prophecy concerning it could be considered too far-fetched? A century ago would not its very existence have been regarded as one of the major miracles since the Creation?

One does not merely parrot the visionary imaginings of science fiction when one ventures that TV a hundred years from now will indeed be an "unbelievable" medium. The small screens of today will be nonexistent. Pictures will be received on the glass walls of houses, with a mere turn of a dial producing an image ranging from a few to a hundred feet in size. Television in the mid twenty-first century will be more than a device of sight and sound. It will transmit odors (the fragrance of perfume and of sizzling bacon will be quite commonplace on certain commercial programs). Each receiver will also serve as a maid of all work. Connected with a central wireless system, of which every household gadget will be a part, it will set into motion machinery to boil the coffee, fry the ham and eggs and draw the bath of its fortunate master, the moment he arises from bed. And later it will start the dishwasher going and, without human aid, propel the vacuum sweeper across the floors. I don't say that it will go so far as to make the beds; but television will eventually transport material objects. A housewife seeing a demonstration of some product in a department store will merely press a button on her receiver and a few minutes later will find a parcel reposing in a special TV package receptacle on the roof of the building.

By this time, video will have developed another much-needed apparatus—an attachment enabling the viewer to express his approval or scorn of what he sees on the screen. He may applaud, cheer, hiss or boo, and these outbursts will be audible in the studio where the program originates. Furthermore, he may talk back to and heckle political speakers with whose sentiments he disagrees. This neat little invention will, of course, eliminate the need for professional critics, for a raucous razz of a certain number of decibels will speak ever so much more loudly than a column of inert newspaper type. Most of those in my craft, by the year 2954, will have to be seeking other jobs—the thought of which does not exactly perturb me today.

On what are the above predictions based? Scientific knowledge, research, intuition or occult powers? On none of these. But there is a solid foundation for such flights of fancy—the boundless enthusiasm of an ardent television fan.

POSTSCRIPT

A SCRAPBOOK

When the broadcaster's time is up, he usually thinks of all he might have said before the inexorable clock forced him off the air. The reporter, restricted by space if not by time, indulges in the same kind of afterthought. This section, a repository for odds and ends of radio and newspaper lore, contains a miscellany of information, anecdotes and items remembered after the word "finis" was written the first time. It is a scrapbook that gives shelter to stray offspring which could find no home elsewhere in the book.

Jack Snow, a writer who did research on the works of Frank L. Baum, creator of the *Wizard of Oz*, came across this story in the October 2, 1908, issue of the Chicago *Daily Journal*:

"Chicago found out last night about the radio play. Frank L. Baum, who admits he discovered the Land of Oz . . . revealed the novelty at Orchestra Hall.

"A radio play is a moving picture . . . thrown upon a screen set in a great red plush frame, besides which stands Baum, who repeated the fairy stories he has written. The pictures illustrated the tales."

Baum exhibited his "radio play" throughout the United States during 1908 and 1909 and made a valiant effort to popularize the term in connection with what we now know as motion pictures. He was backed by the authority of some of the dictionaries of the day, which defined "radio" as "emanating on a beam or ray of light." At that time, of course, the film entertainments were called "cinema," "cinematograph," "kinetoscope," etc.

Then, Snow's research reveals, the U.S. Navy in 1912 formally decreed that its "wireless' should be known as "radio telegraphy." Because of the widespread interest in this novel means of communication, the Navy's edict received national attention. More and more newspapers and speakers used the word "radio"—but not for films—and Hollywood eventually became the "movie" instead of the "radio" capital of the world.

During pioneer days, Vaughn de Leath, "the original radio girl," in 1921 created the style of singing known as "crooning," not because she was an innovator but because of technical necessity. During those primitive days of broadcasting, the high notes of sopranos often "blew out" the delicate tubes of the transmitters. Therefore, in an effort to hold her voice within the proper range, Vaughn sang in a low-pitched throaty manner. After her first broadcast, more than thirty-three years ago, Vaughn received one of the first radio fan letters ever written. It read: "You have inaugurated a new form of song which, no doubt, will become very popular."

When Gracie Allen and George Burns auditioned at NBC in 1930, an important executive turned them down. "From my knowledge of what the public wants, I can tell you that it would not accept you as a regular feature. For one thing, Gracie's voice is too squeaky—absolutely unfitted for radio," he said. But two years later, Eddie Cantor gave them a chance to appear on his show and since then their combined salary has reached sixteen thousand dollars a week and they have grossed more than seven million dollars.

Years before that, in vaudeville, strangely enough George was the comedian of the team, with Gracie "feeding" him as the "straight" girl.

"But soon we had to switch our routines," George told me, "because they laughed more at Gracie's 'straight' stuff than at my jokes."

Speaking of Burns and Allen, it is ironic to recall that, long before they became famous on the air, another comedy team, Jesse Block and Eve Sully, featuring a similar dumb girl and a straight man act, were celebrated headliners in vaudeville. But George and Gracie beat them to radio. As a result, when Jesse and Eve finally went on the air, the critics accused them of imitating Burns and Allen!

Jack Pearl, the beloved Baron Munchausen of the air-waves, has always been an exponent of the broadest type of comedy. So I was surprised when he told me his favorite story, far more subtle than his usual material.

An old man placed a glass of tea on the dining room table one day and called in his family to view it.

"This glass of tea is just like life," he said.

"Why is it like life?" one of his children asked.

"How should I know," said the old man. "After all, am I a philosopher?"

Listeners and viewers during broadcasts of collegiate football games have been startled by some odd sounds of late. Between the halves devoted to the usual highjinks, the bands have been tooting and the crowds in the grandstands singing not only songs of alma mater, but also those commercial jingles popularized by radio and television. After this, could anyone still doubt the mesmerizing power of advertising set to music?

Singing commercials such as "How Are Ya Fixed For Blades?", "Be Happy—Go Lucky," "Chiquita Banana" and "Pepsi Cola Hits the Spot" have become folk songs. Even those who can't go beyond the opening lines of "The Star-Spangled Banner" can reel off their words and hum their tunes. Alan Bradley Kent, Austen Croom-Johnson, Garth Montgomery, Len Mackenzie and other writers have made big sums by creating these melodic plugs. Kent and Croom-Johnson's "Just the Other Day," and Montgomery and Mackenzie's "Chiquita Banana," among others, were best sellers in sheet music, on records and in juke boxes. One of the "Chiquita Bananas," in the person of its singer, actually made appearances as a guest star on the Fred Allen, Edgar Bergen and Alec Templeton shows. Also, she appeared—no, this is not a typographical error—with the Boston Symphony and at Ohio State University's Institute of Education by Radio!

These ditties are "big business." One titled, "Ah Come from Carolina," according to *Sponsor Magazine*, built a certain brand of rice "from a modest position to overwhelming sales leadership in the nation's toughest market—New York." And "Chiquita Banana" was thought of so highly by its sponsor that more than a million dollars was appropriated in one year to air it on some four hundred United States and Canadian stations. Countless conferences by advertising, sales and other high-priced executives are devoted to weighing the form, the content and, in fact, each word of the roundelays devised by the minnesingers of the market place. Sometimes more man-hours are spent on perfecting the sales appeal of a jingle than on the production of a Broadway play!

For it seems that the creation of a musical commercial involves many elements. According to *Sponsor*, it must "command attention; establish emotional acceptance; get over the sales message; have high remembrance value and it must sing."

So here, for your amusement—and perhaps amazement—are a few of the jingles which have added millions to the coffers of American industry and captured the favor of listeners from coast to coast:

> "Pepsi-Cola hits the spot!
> Twelve full ounces, that's a lot.
> Twice as much for a nickel, too,
> Pepsi-Cola is the drink for you.

> "Nickel, nickel, nickel, nickel
> Trickle, trickle, trickle, trickle" *
> (Fade out)
> —Writers: ALAN BRADLEY KENT and
> AUSTEN CROOM-JOHNSON.

> "I'm Chiquita Banana and I've come to say,
> Bananas have to ripen in a certain way.
> When they are fleck'd with brown and have a golden hue
> Bananas taste the best and are the best for you.
> You can put them in a salad, you can put them in a pie—
> Aye!
> Any way you want to eat them, it's impossible to beat them;

* Reproduced by permission of Pepsi-Cola Company—all rights reserved.

But bananas like the climate of the very very tropical equator
So you should never put bananas in the refrigerator." *

Words by: GARTH MONTGOMERY.
Music by: LEN MACKENZIE.

"Barbasol, Barbasol!
No brush, no lather, no rub-in
Wet your razor, then begin.
Barbasol, Barbasol—" †
(Fade out)
—Sung by "Singing Sam" during
early days of radio.

"How are ya fixed for blades: Do you have plenty?
How are ya fixed for blades? You'd better look.
Please make sure you have enough,
'Cause worn out blades make shavin' mighty rough.
How are ya fixed for blades? You'd better look:
Gillette Blue Blades, of course," **

"(First line whistled)
First you learn the whistle
(Short whistle)
Then you sing it
Dentyne Chewing Gum.
(One phrase whistled)
Dentyne, delicious, refreshing
Put the two together, then you swing it . . .
Dentyne Chewing Gum
Buy, try Dentyne!" **

"Be happy—go lucky,
Be happy—go Lucky Strike;

* (Copyright, 1945, by Maxwell-Wirges Publications, Inc.)
† Reprinted by permission of Erwin, Wasey & Company, Inc.
** Reprinted by permission of Maxon, Inc.
** Reprinted by permission of the American Chicle Company.

Be happy—go Lucky
Go Lucky Strike today.

"A flying saucer came to earth
So ends a mystery;
'Cause out jumped twenty men who said,
'Smoke L.S.M.F.T.!'

"Now Venus is a gorgeous girl
But life for her is rough.
A statue simply cannot smoke,
A Lucky, puff by puff!

"Said Sandy to the lass,
'My gurrl, have you no kiss for me?'
She said, 'I've something *milder*, lad—
It's L.S.M.F.T.!' " *

Policemen and private detectives have sour opinions of most of the detective-story shows on radio and TV. John Scott Tobin, for twenty-three years a detective on the New York police force and then a successful private investigator, is no exception.

"In all my years of police work, I've never heard a fellow cop refer to a private detective as a 'private eye' or a 'shamus,' " he says. "We call 'em just plain investigators or detectives. It always gets me sore when I see one of those TV guys solve a case in a few minutes, when I know that most of the time it takes days, weeks, months or even years. And also, I have come across only one private detective who has a secretary that could be called sexy.

"But, despite such foolishness, we policemen do tune in on these crime shows. And now I'll tell you why. It's because these detective-story writers do think up some damned clever ways of outwitting the law. Sometimes, but not often, a fellow will actually try to follow the blueprint for a crime which is set out in one of these stories. So we keep on looking or listening in. We're always hoping that some day we'll come across a case that follows the pattern of a radio or TV show. And if we do, that puts us one jump ahead of the criminal."

There is hardly a youngster in the country who does not know the names of Gene Autry, Bill (Hopalong Cassidy) Boyd, Roy Rogers and the other cowboy heroes of radio, movies and TV. But try to find one who can identify the actor who portrays "The Lone Ranger"!

Since this almost legendary character burst on the American scene more than twenty years ago, he has not appeared before the cameras or in public without a mask. Also, he has been played by a number of actors whose identities have not been publicized.

In collaboration with Fran Striker, a script writer, "The Lone Ranger" was created by George W. Trendle, a Detroit movie-theatre operator who acquired a radio station. "I'm no writer," the latter once told me, "but I'm responsible for having given this character those qualities which have made him popular. How was this done? By studying systematically the likes and dislikes of American kids and analyzing carefully the stories which have appealed to younsters throughout history."

What is this formula? A great deal of physical action, of course, plus suspense, plus the never-failing triumph of virtue over villainy. But this is only the bare framework. Superimposed on this structure are such elements as the appeal of an almost human horse, "Silver," and the staunch loyalty of an Indian friend, "Tonto." And even more important are the character traits of the masked hero which were established in the first broadcast and not deviated from since.

"First of all," Trendle said, "our man is a clean fighter. He never attacks from behind. Then, he is tolerant, completely without racial prejudices—just look at the way he treats Tonto. He is kind to animals—why, he'd give his life for Silver. He respects womanhood and also he's religious—but without indicating that he belongs to any special church. As for smoking, drinking and using profanity, they're completely out. Of course, it goes without saying that he never makes love, and certainly he doesn't ever kiss a girl—not on radio or TV. The kids, you see, don't go for mushy stuff."

"Is it true," I asked, "that one reason so many schoolteachers approve of the Ranger is that he doesn't use slang?"

"That's right," said Trendle, "and, even more important, our hero is a bug on good grammar. When he says 'who' or 'whom' or 'shall' or 'will,' you can bet your boots that he uses these properly."

Perhaps you will argue that there "ain't no such animal" as this highly antiseptic hero, and that the space-cadet-conscious kids of today are too sophisticated to be taken in by such hocus-pocus. But before you utter such treasonable sentiments, pause for a moment and consider the appeal of this multi-million-dollar property:

"The Lone Ranger" plays to an audience of five million each week via television and to more than twelve million a week on the radio. Some seventy-one million people follow his adventures in cartoon form in newspapers; he is the hero of many books; you may hear him on records and there are any number of products which bear his seal of approval.

As Trendle told me, he is no writer, but he certainly could give some authors a few lessons in what the public wants!

"New York's Cradle of Jazz" is what jive men call the Hickory House, a famous steak eatery on West 52nd Street. It was from there, in 1935, that its co-owner John Popkin broadcast some of the earliest "jam sessions" held in Manhattan. Behind its circular bar such notables of jazz as Louis Prima, Wingy Manone, Jack and Charlie Teagarden, Hazel Scott, Marian McPartland, Buddy Rich, Frances Faye, Joe Gluskin and many others came to fame.

"What great bands we used to have in those days!" Popkin reminisced one night. "For example, Joe Marsala's crew played here during 1935 and 1936. His sidemen included: Marsala, clarinet; Buddy Rich, drums; Joey Bushkin, piano; Adele Girard, harp; Bobby Hackett, guitar and trumpet, and Artie Shapiro, bass. Each of these is a recognized master. At that time the whole outfit cost me only $450 a week. Today, I couldn't get this combination for $10,000."

Duke Ellington, the son of a former White House equerry, is entirely self-educated musically, except for a few piano lessons during his childhood. Yet he is not only among the top ranks of American band leaders but is also a composer who has won an international reputation. His "Mood Indigo," "Sophisticated Lady" and "Solitude" are popular classics and he has composed such ambitious symphonic works as "Liberian Suite" and "Black and Tan Fantasy." Since he led his first jazz band, in 1923, his gross at the box office has exceeded twenty million dollars.

Although many critics say that he is the greatest of living Negro composers, he told me one day that actually there is no such thing as Negro music. Not in America, that is.

"Yes, fifty years ago, some of our music was basically Negro," he said. "But now there is no essential difference between the numbers composed and played by whites or Negroes. Consider jazz. We Negroes have made some great contributions, of course—but what about the whites: the Original Dixieland Band, George Gershwin, Benny Goodman, Gene Krupa and all the others? I do admit, however, that among the great jazz pieces written in this country—and there are ever so many of them—the one that stands out above all the others was composed by a Negro: W. C. Handy's 'St. Louis Blues.' "

Without a doubt, "Senator" Ed Ford, Harry Hershfield, once teamed with the late Joe Laurie, Jr., know more anecdotes, gags, or jokes than any other performers on the air. For years they amazed those who tuned in "Can You Top This?" with their ability to dredge up funny stories fit for any and all occasions. Each insisted that there is no such thing as a "new" joke. Even the most recent "funnies," they would tell you, are hoary ones with a "different twist."

"Some of the so-called Joe Millers of today can be traced directly back to the ancient Greeks," Ford once told me. For example, according to Aristotle, you'll find that this story was told on the public square of Athens:

"A man, after beholding his reflection in a pool, said to his wife,

'I have just seen the image of my dead father.' His wife thereupon glanced into the pool and, seeing herself, said to her husband, 'It's not your father. It's that old hag you've been running around with.'

"Do you know, the other night I heard this very story, with a new twist, on television!"

And, speaking of "twists," Laurie informed me that there are almost a thousand of them on that classic, "Who was that lady I seen you with last night?" . . . "That was no lady, that was my wife." One of the corniest of them all, says Hershfield, goes like this: "Who was that ladle I saw you with in the restaurant last night?" . . . "That was no ladle. That was my knife."

According to Ford, the first compilation of jests ever made was that of a Greek named Hiericles in the fifth century A.D.

"Yes," Laurie added, "and you can find in this collection some gags which would be no strangers to Milton Berle."

"That's right," said Ford. "One of these reads: A man remarks to a surviving twin: 'I heard one of you died last week. Which one was it?' "

Gabriel Heatter, who for a considerable period earned as much as $400,000 a year as a radio commentator, made his reputation on the night Bruno Richard Hauptmann, kidnapper of the Lindbergh baby, was electrocuted in the New Jersey State prison in Trenton. On that occasion he ad-libbed in melodramatic fashion for forty-five minutes without a pause, drawing more than fifty thousand letters from listeners.

But he became even more widely known for his trademark, "There's good news tonight." Heatter originated this expression during World War Two while broadcasting nightly from the private studio in his Long Island home.

"And I did it more or less without design," he once told me. "Even during the darkest days of the war, I was certain of our victory over the Nazis. My optimism caused me, almost unwittingly, to look for at least one item favorable to our side for each of my broadcasts. So no matter how dreary the outlook, I'd play up this item and preface it with 'There's good news tonight.' "

One night with Samuel Phoenix Morse, the Merlin of WOR-Mutual's sound technicians, I was discussing which was the most difficult sound effect to produce on the air. Morse, who is the great-grandnephew of Samuel B. Morse, inventor of the telegraph, insisted it was that of a ground hog's hissing and teeth chattering.

"As a matter of fact, no one has ever been able to produce this sound in an accurate manner mechanically," he said. "We had to get an actual recording of it, and our crew was forced to spend ten weeks in the Bronx zoo before it succeeded.

"Other sound effects are tough too. Once our problem was to make a man talk like a goat for a play called 'The Sea Hound.' It required 160 hours of experimenting with sound boxes, oscillators, spark gaps and a secret short-circuit gimmick. We finally found what we were looking for by using a 'flutter box' and an electronic interrupter.

"One of our problems is that certain sounds, when recorded, do not seem to be the real thing. A fall of rain, for instance. To make it sound real we run water under pressure through straw and then down a drain pipe. If you put on a live or a recorded rattlesnake's hiss, what you'd hear would be something like escaping steam. But remove the shell from a doorbell; attach the buzzer to a cellophane bag and then activate the buzzer; and what you'll have is a reptile hiss that will make you jump right out of your chair!"

Recently, I asked this question of the readers of the *News:* "If radio had existed since the dawn of time, and it had been possible to broadcast and record the great events of history, which of these would you like to hear today?"

In the order named, my correspondents chose the following: The Sermon on the Mount; The Three Wise Men as they followed the star; Moses proclaiming the Ten Commandments; The Creation; The Flood; George Washington praying at Valley Forge; the remarks of the Pilgrims as they landed at Plymouth; the words of Christopher Columbus on sighting the New World; Socrates as he drank the hemlock; and William Jennings Bryan delivering his "Cross of Gold" speech.

It was in 1949 that Mel Allen, a Birmingham, Alabama, lad, created a slogan that swept the country. The sportscaster of the New York Yankee games, who has been heard and seen during many World Series, told the story.

"Do you recall the thrilling baseball season of that year?" he asked me one day. "Joe DiMaggio, after missing sixty-five games, came back to the Yankee lineup and hit four home runs in three days. The fans were hysterical and I myself, as the voice of the Yankees, couldn't help showing enthusiasm as they began to climb. It was during those exciting afternoons that, after every spectacular play on the part of the home team, I'd cry, 'How about that?'

"I did this without the slightest premeditation. It was just a natural impulse. I had occasion to repeat it many times. Then, a few days later, as I was describing a particularly spectacular put-out, I said, 'How—' and then I suddenly stopped, because at the moment I heard thousands of fans in the grandstands and in the bleachers yelling. They were chanting, 'How about that?' Ever since then, this question has been my trademark and I couldn't do my job without those words."

"You say that you betrayed your enthusiasm for the Yankees during those broadcasts," I asked. "Doesn't that mean a lack of objectivity on your part? Aren't sportscasters like you and Red Barber supposed to maintain impartiality?"

"As a matter of fact, we do," Mel assured me. "One may be enthusiastic for the home team and factual at the same time. One must be accurate and, of course, fair. No sportscaster could last five minutes in organized baseball today if he weren't. I do admit, however, that there is a great difference in the techniques one uses in broadcasting a game during the regular season and during a World Series.

"This difference has nothing to do with accuracy or with fairness. Rather it concerns the control of one's emotions. One must not show such great enthusiasm for the good plays of the home team during a series."

Jimmy Melton, the tenor who rose from Roxy's Gang to the memorable Revellers Quartet and finally to the Metropolitan Opera

House, is what the boys at the Elks Club down in his home town of Moultrie, Georgia, would call a "card." For, in addition to devoting his spare time to antique automobiles (his collection is worth more than $300,000) he is one of the most successful practitioners of the practical joke. On one occasion he was invited to a post-concert party at the home of a leading Cincinnati citizen. Late that night, a screeching ambulance halted before the host's mansion; eight attendants stepped from the vehicle and lifted therefrom four stretchers, on each a man swathed in mummy-like bandages.

Brushing past an outraged butler at the front door, they deposited their cargoes in a drawing room filled with astounded guests. The bandaged individuals—Melton, his manager, his accompanist and a friend—promptly jumped from their stretchers.

Jimmy grasped the hand of his petrified host and announced: "Hi! It's good to be here!"

Ralph Edwards, who brought the practical joke to its zenith on his "Truth or Consequences," has created in his time some of the most amusing, ingenious, and embarrassing tricks ever perpetrated on the public. Examples: A New Jersey housewife who couldn't play a note appeared under the billing of "Madame Yifnif" in New York's Town Hall to give a violin recital; a Los Angeles man raced an airplane by bobbing up and down on a pogo stick.

I once asked him why otherwise sane Americans permitted themselves to engage in such outlandish antics on his programs.

"Very simple," he said. "Americans more than any other people like broad gags and practical jokes. Call it juvenile if you wish, but it's true. Also, we have a fear of being regarded as 'poor sports.' Consequently, most of us are willing to 'try anything once.' It is this urge which in great part, is responsible for the popularity of lodges whose initiation ceremonies feature all kinds of horseplay.

"A program such as 'Truth or Consequences' would be absolutely impossible in such a country as France or Germany. They go heavily for personal 'dignity' over there. Before I even finished with my first stunt, I'd be challenged to a duel or killed on the spot. Unlike Americans, Europeans take themselves so seriously that they lack the ability to act in a childish manner.'

John Royal, a former Cleveland theatre manager, NBC's first vice-president in charge of programs, wielded a wider influence on the country's tastes in entertainment than probably any other program man during the early years of radio. So, on the night of December 7, 1935, when his network dedicated its Hollywood studios, he was eager to demonstrate that the movies had at last extended a welcoming hand to that upstart—broadcasting.

But at that time the film magnates were even more hostile—and contemptuous—of radio than two decades later they became toward television. John, with President Aylesworth of NBC, had planned a dazzling inaugural broadcast and exerted every effort to pack the studio with the most famous stars of the movie capital.

They had engaged Al Jolson as the emcee and persuaded the head of the Motion Picture Producers' Association, Will Hays, to deliver a talk. This was a triumph indeed. It was in the bag.

Then came the big night. An expectant audience filled the studios. They had heard that dozens of the most celebrated actors and actresses of Hollywood would be there. So had the millions who tuned in from coast to coast. But when Jolson took the mike, he noticed with horror the empty chairs which were to have been occupied by his fellow stars. Without exception, they had stayed away.

As the program, which included songs by a rising radio singer named Bing Crosby, ran its course, Al was haunted by the gloomy look of John Royal. At the end of the broadcast, however, he came to the succor of his friend.

"This has been a great show," said Jolson, "so I hope you'll realize, ladies and gentlemen, that it is only the lack of time which has prevented me from calling on the dozens of great picture stars who are here tonight."

I don't know about the reaction of that studio audience, but for years thereafter millions of listeners firmly believed that the NBC opening in Hollywood was one of the starriest events of history. And, strangely enough, so did the movie people themselves! Listening to Jolson's voice over the loud-speaker, they were convinced that their rivals had capitulated to the enemy and, fearful of being left behind, many of them phoned the network the next day, offering their services!

Royal's difficulties with Hollywood were over. He soon was able to present most of the glamorous personalities of the film factories to the radio listeners, just as he eventually placed on the air many of the outstanding entertainment programs of broadcasting.

Those who tuned in radio station WQAO, New York, more than 30 years ago heard then, and later over WHN until 1929, a powerful voice denouncing divorce, evolution, atheism, corrupt politicians and every aspect of "modernism." It was that of the famous fundamentalist pastor of the Calvary Baptist Church, the Rev. Dr. John Roach Straton. It was he who initiated the "world's oldest radio gospel service," which first attracted listeners because of his salty castigations of the shimmy, the "orgies" in Broadway cabarets, the Elwell murder mystery and those who devoted themselves to the ouija board.

If you have ever wondered what Heaven is like, you should have heard the good doctor's description of it in a radio sermon delivered during the early 1920's:

"Think what Heaven will be! . . . Stand below the Arch of Triumph on Fifth Avenue. Instead of that graceful arch of man's plaster, think of it as carved from one perfect opal, fairly stabbing the eyes with the dazzling beauty of a million rays of light. See the Avenue paved with pure gold, so rare that it shines like transparent glass and, as far as our wondering eyes can see, behold mansions of glory, built of opals and sapphires. Add to that a thousandfold increase in beauty and sweetness, and let the city stretch out and out with its jeweled walls fifteen miles in each direction, and its exquisite beauties piled plain on plain, soaring up toward the eternal blue!"

One of the press giants of the age, Captain Joseph Medill Patterson, gave me a lesson in writing one afternoon. The man under whose leadership the New York *Daily News* attained the largest circulation in America asked why I had used the words *faux pas* in the radio column. "Why not plain English?" he said.

I explained that everyone undoubtedly understood at least that much French.

"All right," the Captain said, "go out on the street and ask the first ten persons you meet whether they know the meaning of *faux pas*. Give me your report tomorrow."

The next day I had to confess that only two out of the ten had come up with the right answer.

The Captain smiled and shook his head. "You know," he said, "you fellows could learn a lot if you talked more with truck drivers."

Then, after a pause, he added, "Remember this: Anyone who uses foreign words when there are good English ones to express the same thought is either a show-off or doesn't know his own language."

A colorful personality in the *News* legends of early days was Gene McHugh, the present night managing editor. Just as certain attorneys are lawyers' lawyers, or certain physicians doctors' doctors, so Gene is the newspapermen's newspaperman. Now a tall, gray-haired veteran with kindly eyes, a musical voice and typical Irish wit, he once served as the press agent of Billy Sunday, the evangelist. A master craftsman in every phase of editorial work, his contacts range from the highest political circles through the environs of Broadway to the nether depths of the underworld. Governors, senators, authors, stars, columnists, policemen, truck drivers and gangsters confide in him. His deeds have been celebrated in fictional form more than those of any newspaperman I know; Paul Gallico, in fact, won a considerable portion of his early fame with a series of short stories about an editor who was but a thinly disguised portrait of Gene McHugh.

Oldtimers are still fond of recalling one of the most celebrated of his exploits—how at nine o'clock on the morning of December 18, 1931, with the aid of a handful of stragglers, he got out an extra edition which scooped the town on the slaying of the notorious gangster, Jack (Legs) Diamond. On that day the annual Christmas bonus was to be distributed to the *News'* employees and Gene, among other night workers, had remained in the neighborhood of the office after the last edition was in, to await the opening of the cashier's window at 9 A.M. This edition, it so happened, carried a front-page headline about the acquittal of the said Mr. Diamond in a Troy, New York, court of certain "unpleasant" charges. But even as he walked, a free man, from the presence of the judge, certain determined gentlemen were bent on spelling out with bullets the finale of the mobster's story. They succeeded in their flaming literary endeavors some time after 4 A.M.

Shortly after 7:30, McHugh had returned to the editorial room and was there when news of the end of "Legs" flashed into the office at 8:03. By that time the staff was gone and the presses were silent. Then at 8:06 and 8:12 more details came in.

Here was one of the most sensational stories of many years. Diamond's standing in the hierarchy of crime during the Prohibition period was such that even his most insignificant activities were news. Furthermore, any story mentioning his name sold countless newspapers.

But there was McHugh in a deserted city room at an hour which is the most forlorn one in the cycle of a morning daily. The night men had departed; those on the day shift had not yet reported. The News had an explosive exclusive, but what good was it if it couldn't be got out on the street?

Some editors would have regarded the situation as an ironic jest, and let it go at that. But Gene got on the phone, called nearby coffee pots, lunchrooms and speakeasies; then he dispatched one or two sleepy messengers to these hangouts and in a few minutes had rounded up an improvised crew of linotypers, stereotypers and pressroom men. He wrote a vivid story of Diamond's demise, adding colorful touches gleaned from his knowledge of the gangster's bullet-dodging career. Also he wrote heads, selected pictures, did the captions, rushed the copy to the composing room in takes, supervised the setting of the type and the making of the mats. All of this in less than one hour's time! Just fifty-seven minutes after the first flash had been received, the News' late EXTRA was on the street —the only newspaper in New York with the story. Thus, as a house ad in Printers' Ink had it, from the 9 P.M. issue, when the front page had read: "Jack Diamond Acquitted," to the 9 A.M. paper, which proclaimed "Diamond Slain," Legs had gone from a "Great Victory to the Great Beyond—in five editions." And Gene McHugh was responsible.

It seemed as if every man, woman and child in the land who could get near a radio was listening to the race between War Admiral and Seabiscuit on a November day in 1938. The sports world had talked of nothing else for days; business came to a standstill; the interest was so intense that President Roosevelt in the White House cut short a press conference to tune in on Pimlico.

Clem McCarthy, the NBC sportscaster, attained the heights that afternoon, and for years afterward fans spoke of his vivid description as "the most exciting race report ever heard." And yet, through a fluke, this memorable broadcast almost failed to get on the air.

Clem himself told me of it one day while recalling the high points of his picturesque career.

"Abe Schechter, the special events and news director of NBC, and I were sitting in our broadcasting booth, high in the grandstand," he said. "While waiting for the big event, I strolled down the stairs to the paddock, expecting to return to our microphone within a few minutes. But I couldn't make it. The crowd was so great that it was impossible for me to push through.

"I just can't describe my panicky feeling as I glanced at my watch and saw there were less than four minutes to air time. I elbowed, fought and pleaded, but there was a solid wall of humanity before, behind and all about me.

"What could I do? Every network had fought for the right to broadcast this historic race and NBC had an exclusive. The whole world would be listening, and if the broadcast failed to go on the air because of my mistake I could never live it down.

"I pushed and pleaded some more; but it did no good. Then, looking up at our booth, which now seemed miles and miles away, I saw Abe waving his handkerchief at me. Through his glasses he had picked me out of that crowd. He was gesticulating wildly, trying to tell me something—just what, I didn't know. It was plain that he realized I couldn't get up there in time for the broadcast, but he was conveying instructions. Then suddenly I realized what

—for, by luck, I was standing against the rail, at the very spot where Abe had installed a second microphone which would later be used to put on the air the jockey and the owner of the winning horse (Seabiscuit). He was telling me to take that mike.

"That was a great piece of quick thinking on his part and I couldn't let him down. So I jumped up on the rail and, with the mike in one hand and my glasses in the other, began talking when Abe gave me the go-ahead by lowering his handkerchief."

From the moment Clem sounded his famous "They're off!" until the horses thundered over the line, he spoke with breathless intensity. Many consider it to have been the Number One horse race description of all time—this broadcast which Clem almost failed to make.

Many of my former and current assistants have achieved celebrity: Danton Walker, the Broadway columnist; Sid Shalit, the radio-TV editor; Doug Watt, the music critic; Robert Wahls, drama writer, Jack Doherty, White House correspondent, and Nick Kenny, the song writer-versifier-radio-TV editor of the New York *Daily Mirror*. But the departmental worker who had the greatest impact was a New Jersey housewife who temporarily displaced me as radio editor of the *News*. During the 1930's someone sold management on the following idea:

"Who is the most powerful factor in the radio audience? Who spends more time listening to programs than any member of the family? The housewife, of course! Why not, then, have a typical married woman of average intelligence write the radio column, instead of a blasé newspaperman?"

Some time before, another tabloid, the *Graphic*, had assigned an amateur critic to accompany its professional play reviewer to Broadway first nights. The result was not too successful; but the *News* had succeeded in many an enterprise in which others had failed. So our paper launched a contest, offering big cash prizes for the best radio columns submitted by its readers, with the writer of the Number One entry to be awarded a job as radio critic. There were thousands of contributions.

The winner, an attractive young woman married to a jovial chain-store manager in a suburban town, was surely a "typical housewife." She doted on radio, worshipped its stars, was an ardent soap-opera devotee and knew by heart the romantic details concerning every popular bandleader and crooner as embellished by their imaginative publicity men.

A few days later, we established contact with each other via a two-way teletype system which had been installed in her home and in my office. One moved the "Send" switch and typed a message; then turned the "Receive" key, and on a thin roll of tape words began miraculously to appear. Such a contraption, no novelty in a newspaper office, created a sensation in the living room of a New Jersey suburban home. Acquaintances and friends came from miles to view the wondrous gadget.

"Now that you're using this housewife column, does that mean I'm fired?" I had asked Colonel Hause, the managing editor, while the electricians were still tinkering with the machine.

"No," he said. "You make up the program listings; and twice a night you turn the switch. Snip off the paper ribbon, copy the words on it; take them to the composing room and then make up the column for the early and the late editions. . . . And remember this: let her copy ride as is; don't change a word or even a comma. What we want is real housewife stuff."

With hurt pride and deflated ego, I suddenly found myself with only about three hours a day of actual work. My byline was gone.

Promptly at 4 and 10 P.M. every day we followed a routine. I turned on the machine, pressed a signal bell button and then typed: "Hello. Are you ready?" Back came the message: "Hiya! Feeling fine today. Let's go." Before we went, however, there were minutes of chatter with the housewife (whom I shall call Helen). She would tell me of herself, her husband, her children and the state of their health. Often she would add: "There's quite a gang here in the living room watching me send this stuff."

There was quite a gang, indeed. For within a few days Helen had become a town celebrity. At the A&P, shoppers pointed to her as probably the only woman in the world with a teletype right in her front parlor, and at the neighborhood movie house she was besieged by autograph hunters.

But, despite this sudden fame, Helen's columns during the early weeks lived up to every expectation. Wholesome and sentimental, salted here and there with acute down-to-earth observations, hers was a typical outpouring of the suburban housewife.

"She's damned good," Hause said to me one day. And he was right. Letters expressing approval of her column flooded the "Voice of the People," and a network executive added to the chorus of acclaim with the comment: "At last we have a radio critic who represents the average listener!"

As time passed, Helen's writing began to reflect a subtle change. A serpent in the guise of the press agents of Manhattan had slithered into paradise. For a reason I had no difficulty in fathoming, only a few of this gentry still continued to cultivate me; instead of ten or twelve invitations a week to cocktail parties, dinners or night-club openings, there were only one or two. Now it was the Jersey housewife who was bombarded with press releases, phone calls and flattery.

"You're big time, kid," is what they told her. "You shouldn't bury yourself in that tank town. Come on in; meet the people; make the rounds; we'll show you the ropes."

Where her copy had been refreshingly naïve, it now gradually became "sophisticated." The housewife's space was an echo chamber of a half-dozen Broadway columnists.

One afternoon, after Helen had teletyped her column for the Pink Edition, she added: "Wish you were here tonight. It's our wedding anniversary and we're having a swell party."

A few hours later, Colonel Hause said to me: "Do a column and have it in the Two Star. And you'd better open your machine now and tell Helen not to send any more stuff."

I told him of the wedding-anniversary party. Wouldn't it be kinda tough on a gal to receive word that she was through while her family and friends were celebrating her happiness, many of them probably crowded around the teletype as the keys spelled out the fateful words?

"Okay," said the Colonel, really an old sentimentalist at heart. "Just let her send her stuff and don't use it. She'll get a letter in the morning."

At ten o'clock the bell rang and I opened the machine.

"Hiya, Ben," Helen typed.

"Hiya, Helen, how's the party?" I asked.

"Great," she wrote. "Big jam, swell time. Everybody's peering over my shoulder as I'm sending this. Why don't you come on over?"

"Sorry; wish I could. Jimmy Jemail, our Inquiring Fotographer, who is standing beside me, joins me in wishing you a happy anniversary," I replied.

"Okay. See you this night next year. Have some champagne for you," came her words. Then the column: brittle, crackling, "sophisticated." She must have had a good time writing it; but the copy did not go to the composing room. It was impaled on the spike.

And while the feast continued across the Hudson, the Two, Three and Four Star editions carried again my once-familiar byline. A few days later, a crew of mechanics removed the marvelous teletype machine from the living room of the little suburban home.

Since then there have been no more "housewife" radio or television critics in New York.

Depressed by the defects of our television, some Americans are lured by the apparently greener grass in the British backyard. "Look at the BBC!" they exclaim.

Well, let's look at it. Even a glance will demonstrate that the British system—a monopoly under government control—would produce a revolt among viewers in this country. A lengthy book could be devoted to the differences in the American and the British set-ups. But here let us consider only two important points: the compulsory license fee levied on each TV set and the autocratic control exercised by the BBC hierarchy over the programs the public is permitted to see.

The license fee is, of course, a necessity in any national system in which the sponsor does not pay the bill. Although many Americans might willingly subscribe for pay-as-you-see TV for special programs, it is safe to say that the majority, long accustomed to free entertainment on the air, would not submit to licensing. If a law requiring all viewers to do so were enacted, there would not be sufficient jails to hold the violators!

And what of the protests that would sweep this country if the choice of programs were left solely to a few broadcasting officials, no matter how high-minded? The British Broadcasting Corporation presents many offerings of outstanding merit; but too often the selection of shows is guided by the idiosyncracies and prejudices of the few men in control.

This, of course, also is true of any American network or station. But here we are not dependent on one company for our radio or TV fare. There is intense competition and any program rejected by a broadcaster may land on a rival outlet.

Only a fool would deny the high quality of many BBC presentations. In some instances its dramatic shows are superior to anything heard or seen in America; there are also a considerable number of first-rate talks on science, literature and international affairs, and some excellent music. Also, the air-waves are uncorrupted by horrendous crime shows and tastless types of "giveaways." But it is nevertheless true that the public is forced to accept many dull speeches, poor comedy and variety programs; and, furthermore, there is a lack of that rough-and-tumble discussion of domestic issues which marks American broadcasting.

Proof that thousands of British listeners and viewers are dissatisfied with the programs of the BBC may be found almost any day in the letters-to-the-editor columns of the London newspapers. These outbursts are even more scathing than those of our disgusted fans. Most of these assiduous correspondents demand a greater variety in the air menu—which is exactly what we have in the United States. They also want more and better comedy, less stodginess and complacency.

The answer to this widespread discontent is that the British themselves are adopting commercial television. By 1955, it is expected, stations accepting advertising will be operating in London, Birmingham and in the North. Although Government-controlled, these outlets will compete with the noncommercial BBC.

There will be one vital difference, however, between the American and the British commercialism. Over there, although advertising will be sold, there will be *no* sponsors. This means that the advertiser may purchase time for his announcements, but will have no control over the content or the personnel of the programs. That will be the responsibility of a private corporation accountable only to the Government. Assurances have already been given that sensational crime shows and other tasteless attractions will not be tolerated and also that the commercial copy will be held within "proper" bounds. Americans will observe this venture with interest; for, should it succeed, it may have important repercussions in this country. But let us be more specific. Suppose you had been in London on a typical broadcasting day—Tuesday, April 20, 1954. According to the listings in the *Daily Express* here is what you would have seen on BBC television:

London Daily Express—Tuesday, April 20/54

3.15	For Women: Meet Ninette Jeanty; Career, New interests, Alan Loveday, violin.
4—4.15	Andy Pandy.
5—5.30	Children: The Wide, Wide World: serial.
7.30	Newsreel; Weather.
7.50	Teleclub: magazine for under 21's.
8.50	The Name's the Same.
9.20	Six Characters in Search of an Author: play, Mary Morris, Ralph Michael.
10.50	News.

However, if the same day you had been in New York, according to the schedules of the New York *Daily News,* here are the programs you might have tuned in:

N. Y. Daily News—Tuesday, April 20/54

Television Features

1:25 P.M.—11	Giants-Pirates.
7:00 P.M.— 2	Gov. Thomas E. Dewey, talk.
7:30 P.M.—11	First Show—Film; "Twice Upon A Time."
7:30 P.M.— 7	Cavalcade of America.
8:00 P.M.— 4	Milton Berle Show; Steve Allen, Janet Blair, Ezzard Charles.
8:00 P.M.— 5	The Goldbergs.
8:30 P.M.— 2	Red Skelton Show.
8:30 P.M.— 5	Love Story (Premiere).

9:00 **P.M.—11** **Trotting from Yonkers Raceway.**
9:00 **P.M.— 4** **Fireside Theatre.**
9:00 **P.M.— 7** **Danny Thomas Show.**
9:30 **P.M.— 2** **Suspense; Art Carney.**
9:30 **P.M.— 4** **Circle Theatre; Gene Lockhart, Mildred Dunnock, Wallace Ford.**
9:30 **P.M.— 7** **TV Hour; Judith Anderson, Sir Cedric Hardwicke, Martyn Green in "Black Chiffon."**
10:00 **P.M.— 4** **Fred Allen Show.**
10:30 **P.M.— 2** **See It Now; Ed Murrow.**

7:00—**2.** Morning Show.
4. Today.
9:00—**2.** George Skinner.
4. Herb Sheldon.
7. Breakfast Club.
10:00—**2.** Arthur Godfrey.
4. Ding Dong Sch'l.
7. Honeymoon.
10:30—**4.** Man's Family.
7. Your Show.
10:45—**4.** Steps to Heaven.
11:00—**4.** Home.
11:30—**2.** Strike It Rich.
5. Kitchen Fare.
7. Comedy Film.
12:00—**2.** Valiant Lady.
4. Bride and Groom.
7. Time for Fun.
13. News; Club.
12:15—**2.** Love of Life.
4. Hawkins Falls.
12:30—**2.** For Tomorrow.
4. Betty White.
5. News.
7. Ern Westmore.
13. Feature Film.
12:45—**11.** **Go Places.**
2. Guiding Light.
5. Chapel.
1:00—**11.** **Your Figure.**
2. Brighter Day.

4. M. Amsterdam.
5. Claire Mann.
1:10—**11.** **Frankie Frisch.**
1:15—**2.** Portia's Life.
5. Walter King.
1:25—**11.** **Giants-Pirates.**
1:30—**2.** Garry Moore.
4. Richard Willis.
5. Movie Quiz.
7. Maggi McNellis.
13. Ruth Bean.
2:00—**4.** Tex and Jinx.
5. Lee Graham.
7. Stories.
13. Feature Film.
2:30—**2.** House Party.
5. News.
2:45—**5.** Ted Straeter.
3:00—**2.** Big Payoff.
4. Kate Smith.
5. Paul Dixon.
7. Nancy Craig.
3:30—**2.** Bob Crosby.
7. Joe Franklin.
13. Comedy Film.
3:50—**11.** **Frankie Frisch.**
4:00—**11.** **Ted Steele.**
2. Woman's Past.
4. Travelers.
5. Robert Dana.
7. Jerry Lester.
13. Western Film.
4:15—**2.** Secret Storm.
5. Feature Film.
4:30—**2.** Robt.Q. Lewis.

4. Your Account.
9. News.
5:35—**9.** Aunt Jean.
5:00—**11.** **Dance Time.**
2. Film.
4. Pinky Lee.
7. Bar 7.
9. Col. Venture.
13. Junior Frolics.
5:15—**5.** Roy Doty.
5:30—**11.** **Kartoon Klub.**
4. Howdy Doody.
5. Funny Bunny.
13. Fun Time.
5:55—**11.** **News.**
6:00—**11.** **Film.**
2. News: Sports.
4. Western Tales.
5. Magic Cottage.
7. Kazootie.
9. Merry Mailman.
13. Western Film.
6:15—**2.** Feature Film.
7. Jolly Gene.
6:30—**4.** Faye and Skitch.
5. Mr. Adventure.
7. Film.
6:45—**4.** News.
7. Bob and Ray.
9. News: Sports.
7:00—**11.** **News.**
2. Gov. Dewey.
4. Reg. Nurse.
5. Capt. Video.
7. Bill Tabbert.

334

9. Feature Film.
13. Feature Film.
7:10–11. **Bolton, Weather.**
7. Roger Price.
7:15–11. **Jimmy Powers.**
5. Marge and Jeff.
7. John Daly, news.
7:25–11. **Telepix News.**
7:30–11. **First Show.**
2. News.
4. Dinah Shore.
5. Weather; News.
7. Cavalcade.
9. Big Picture.
7:45—2. Jo Stafford.
4. News.
5. Sports News.
8:00—2. Gene Autry.
4. Milton Berle.
5. The Goldbergs.
7. The Mask.
9. Spotlight.
13. Your State.
8:30—2. Red Skelton.
5. Love Story.

13. Rutgers Report.
9:00–11. **Trotters.**
2. Meet Millie.
4. Fireside Theatre.
5. Film.
7. Danny Thomas.
9. This Is Your Life.
13. Political Talk.
9:30—2. Suspense.
4. Circle Theatre.
7. TV Hour.
9. Feature Film.
13. Western Film.
10:00—2. Danger.
4. Fred Allen.
5. Assignment.
10:30—2. See It Now.
4. The Norths.
5. Death Valley.
7. Name's the Same.
9. High Tension.
13. Feature Film.

11:00–11. **Telepix News.**
2. News; Sports.
4. News; Weather.
5. Barry Gray.
7. News; Talk.
9. Art Ford.
11:10–11. **Bolton, Weather.**
11:15–11. **Sport Spotlight.**
2. Feature Film.
4. Sports News.
5. Ernie Kovacs.
7. Film.
11:20—4. Steve Allen.
11:30–11. **Film.**
13. Feature Film.
12:00—4. News; Film.
12:15—5. News.
2. Feature Film.
1:45—2. News.

CHANNEL NUMBERS
WCBS—2   WNBT—4
WABD—5   WABC—7
WOR—9   WPIX—11
WATV—13

PPS

A question mark, a colon or a dash instead of a period should have followed those fateful words, "The End," on the last page of this book's manuscript, typed on a late summer day in 1954. Far from being the end, the succeeding years marked only the beginning of a new and significant chapter in the continuing story of broadcasting.

Although devoid of the fervent enthusiasm and the zeal of radio and TV's early years, what has happened since then has left its imprint on every phase of American life: the politics, the entertainment, the education, the news events and the social customs of our time.

Both radio and TV have undergone revolutionary changes. The intent of this new chapter is to mention some of the highlights of this transformation.

Television, for instance, is no longer merely a major part of the American scene; often it actually makes that scene. As an example, nowadays, it plays a vital role in political campaigns and national conventions. It is because of TV that the nominating speeches, the balloting and the acceptance addresses are scheduled for prime time. Sports, especially pro football games, are so planned that the climactic plays will not blank out the commercials. Motion-picture producers, who once regarded the living room tube as a menace, now welcome it as a rich source of income.

Along with the migration of the middle classes from the cities to the suburbs, TV has cut down attendance at theatres, neighborhood movie houses and night clubs. And such interview and discussion programs as "Meet the Press," "Face the Nation," David Susskind's Show and the roundtable periods of the National Education Television Network, among others, have become prime forums for the airing of political and social problems. Also, through televised press conferences, so deftly employed in recent years by Presidents Eisenhower, Kennedy, Johnson and Nixon, the White House has been brought closer to the people than ever before. It was no accident that President Johnson's announcement that he would not seek his office again came first over TV.

Radio, too, has undergone radical changes. Once the nation's prime source of entertainment, today it is devoted basically to canned music and news. This, despite the fact that in metropolitan centers there are a considerable number of talk and interview shows such as Long John Nebel's (WNBC), Barry Farber's (WOR) and Barry Gray's (WMCA) of New York.

But although even then radio was fighting a losing battle, during the early 1950's the sound medium was still holding millions of listeners, with "Amos 'n' Andy," Jack Benny, "People Are Funny," the "Lux Radio Theatre," "My Little Margie" and "Our Miss Brooks" among the leaders in popularity.

Despite the disappearance of such shows from the kilocycles, radio did not die; in fact, it is more prosperous than ever before, with a larger number of stations and listeners than in the past. The transistor receiving sets, the increasing popularity of FM stations and wide distribution of automobile radios are responsible for this.

And yet, the sound medium long ago gave up its attempts to compete with the one that has the additional dimension of sight. Not only has TV a monopoly on most of the world's great entertainers, it has literally become "a window on the world." With the gory battling in Vietnam, a war was for the first time being fought in the living rooms of the land. Every home by now is an arena wherein the most controversial and dramatic problems of the day come to their climax.

This was partly so in the 1950's even before TV came into its full flowering. Who can forget the sight of gangster Costello's twitching fingers as he testified before the Senate subcommittee investigating the underworld? What stage drama has produced more gripping scenes than the confrontation between the late Senator Joseph McCarthy and the late attorney Joseph Welch during the Army–McCarthy hearings? It was the nationwide exposure of these episodes that eventually led to the Wisconsin solon's censure and his elimination from public life.

Television also played an overwhelmingly important role in the public affairs of the 1960's. The televising of the John F. Kennedy–Richard M. Nixon debates was in great part responsible for the latter's defeat in 1960. And it is widely recognized that TV's recording of the bitter conflict and riotous scenes in Chicago during the Democratic convention of 1968 dealt a decisive blow to the Presidential aspirations of Hubert H. Humphrey.

Although TV programming as a whole in recent years has undergone a transformation, one important segment of it still maintains its overwhelming popularity. It is—

Comedy. . . . The comedians and the situation comedies continue to be major audience–drawers of the medium. The former, as in the past, are in two categories: the rapid–fire deliverers of one–liners, represented by such stars as Bob Hope, Milton Berle and Henny Youngman, and the creators of comic characters such as those projected by Lucille Ball, Jack Benny, Jackie Gleason, Red Skelton and also Hope.

But even the one–liners, as a rule, no longer confine themselves to a series of mere unrelated jokes or wisecracks. These flip fellows often tinge their humor with topical satirical comments, as exemplified by the material of Hope, Mort Sahl, Dick Cavett and Woody Allen.

Perhaps the greatest of these would have been that outstanding wit, the late Fred Allen. Unfortunately, he was never permitted to rise to his full stature in the medium, primarily because his talent was mired in too elaborate productions and artificial gimmickry.

In contrast to the increasing number of funny men and women, commentators on the follies of the day, there are now fewer clowns and jesters who step before the cameras in guises other than their own. Formerly, TV abounded in these multi–talented performers who created laughable fictitious characters.

One still recalls fondly the late Bert Lahr, Ed Wynn, "The Perfect Fool," and Amos 'n' Andy, among others. Today, however, we still have such veterans as Jack Benny (the tightwad), Red Skelton (the clown), the cyclonic Lucille Ball, the rarely seen Martha Raye, who has been devoting most of her energies to entertaining our troops in Vietnam, Jackie Gleason (the bus driver), Art Carney (the king of the sewers), Sid Caesar and Carol Burnett.

As for situation comedies, only a few entries in this field since the first publication of this book have captured the secret of longevity. "Father Knows Best" is one notable exception, and, of course, there is that undisputed champion, the weekly Lucille Ball show. But long run or short run, there can be no denying the popularity of this genre.

Indicative of the changes that have come to TV comedy is the fact that last season Rowan and Martin's "Laugh–In" on NBC was the Number One show in popularity. A series of kaleidoscopic blackouts, some bordering on the line of old time burlesque, and some with a definite touch of irreverence, it captures the questioning and often scoffing mood of the younger generation.

Just as marked, and perhaps even more so, have been the changes in the realm of—

Drama. . . . During the 1950's, television became the heir to the rich dramatic tradition of radio. The imaginative plays of such writers as Arch Oboler and Norman Corwin were still fresh in the memories of millions.

So for several years, TV offered original scripts that comprised the body of what is still referred to as its "golden age of drama." Series such as those of the "Philco Playhouse," "Studio One," and "Playhouse 90" made a number of distinguished contributions. Paddy Chayefsky's *Marty* and Rod Serling's *Requiem for a Heavyweight* were among the classics of this period. And so were a number of outstanding items seen on that memorable experimental program, "Omnibus," supported by the Ford Foundation.

But with the amazing increase in the cost of television program production, more and more sponsors, and also the networks, began to frown on downbeat, realistic plays. They shied away from dramas concerned with the important issues of the day—war, poverty, civil rights, etc. So, avoiding controversial topics, guided by a desire to offend no one, the producers devoted themselves, with few exceptions, to bland exercises in escapism.

Therefore, it's not surprising that most of the major dramatists of the channels deserted the medium to write for the motion pictures and the theatre, where they found greater freedom and also more lucrative financial returns.

During the last few years, however, a few fairly successful attempts, mostly experimental, have been made to restore original drama to its former position of importance. CBS' "Playhouse" and NBC's "Prudential On Stage" have led in this endeavor, along with the National Educational Television Network. They have brought before the cameras scripts by young writers who dare to face up to the realities of these times.

In one sense, the ground was laid for these experiments by the tremendous success scored on the channels by the televising of Arthur Miller's grim stage tragedy, *Death of a Salesman*. It proved that there is a definite hunger for plays of meaning and substance. And additional proof of this is found in the long life of the Hallmark Hall of Fame series, one that specializes in the revival of famed dramas of the present and of the past.

The hesitant and often downright fearful attitude of the advertisers who provide the money for both radio and TV leads us to a word or two, not from, but about the—

Sponsors. . . . The purveyors of detergents, autos, toothpastes, deodorants, foods and other mass–consumed products, for the most part, aim their shows at the lowest common denominator. But with the increasing number of college graduates in this country and the wider distribution of information, they often underestimate the intelligence levels of the viewers.

Of course, there are some exceptions, including the already mentioned Hallmark Company, makers of greeting cards. In the forefront for many years—on radio as well as TV—has been the American Telephone and Telegraph Company, the world's largest corporation, with its offerings of top quality musical programs and its recent documentaries on the urban crisis, over NBC. Also, there is the Xerox Corporation, which has presented over all three of the networks top-notch dramas and vital documentaries, among them *The Rise and Fall of the Third Reich*.

However, if one takes into consideration that commercial TV is primarily an advertising medium rather than an art form, the typical sponsor's approach to broadcasting becomes understandable.

A decade or so ago, it was still possible to produce a 30–minute situation comedy for $40,000 or $50,000. Today, this has jumped to somewhere between $75,000 to $100,000. As an example, in 1964, Lucille Ball's Lucy show called for an expenditure of $70,000 for each episode. Now, it's $115,000. The price tag on some hour presentations nowadays is around $150,000, and a 90–minute offering such as NBC's "The Virginian" or "The Name of the Game" will set the producer back about $175,000. These sums do not include the sums paid for network facilities.

Multiply these weekly costs by a full season of telecasting and it's easy to understand why any series is a venture involving millions. It is, of course, the sponsor who pays—to a medium on which a one–minute network commercial during prime time may draw $30,000 or more.

As it is, it isn't surprising that the commercial backer of shows, who must pay the fiddler, often lavishes his princely sums on—

Music. . . . There are a greater number of symphony orchestras and local opera companies in the United States than ever before and yet there has been a decline in the presentation of so–called classic music on TV. In recent years, only Leonard Bernstein's "N.Y. Philharmonic Young People's Concerts" on CBS have been nationally featured. But the demand for the works of the masters was vividly demonstrated in 1968, when Vladimir Horowitz's brilliant piano recital over CBS not only won rhapsodic critical acclaim but also drew millions of viewers.

It's a different story on radio, especially FM, which has carried live concerts of such orchestras as the Philadelphia and the Boston Symphony and also the Saturday afternoon performances of the Metropolitan Opera. The best in recordings—classic, popular, jazz, rock, country and folk—continues to be heard on the kilocycles.

Only a handful of the "big bands" survive on the air and the same is true of "straight" stylists of pop songs. Such artists as Robert Goulet, Dean Martin, Vikki Carr, Steve Lawrence and Eydie Gorme, to mention only a few, are highly successful. However, they do not tower over their rivals as did the giants during the heyday of radio, Frank Sinatra, Bing Crosby, Perry Como, Dinah Shore, Kate Smith and others of their school, who are still with us on TV.

With the coming of the "new sound," the insistent beat of rock, the plaintive tones of folk and the social significance of protest songs, a startling revolution in popular music has taken place. It all started on a large scale with Elvis Presley in the 1950's, and, powerfully boosted by the influence of the Beatles, television nowadays has been taken over by scores of shaggy, unkempt groups. At one time, they scored as mere noisemakers singing off–color and, at times, unintelligible lyrics. Now their material has evolved into what is known as rock–folk.

And with the transformation, there has risen a different breed of singers worshipped by the younger generation. Bob Dylan, Joan Baez, and Johnny Cash, among many others, are new idols of the collegiates.

Almost simultaneously with the emergence of these figures, another type of entertainment has come to full flowering on television—the late-hour—

Talk-Variety Show. . . . It really began during the salad days of TV when comedian Jerry Lester and sexy Dagmar entertained viewers over NBC. Later Steve Allen successfully offered a night owl divertissement; but the format established itself permanently when Jack Paar came onto the scene via the same network. Charming, witty, irascible, controversial and, above all, unpredictable, he made the "desk–and–sofa show" a national institution.

His successor, Johnny Carson, who is a combination of small town "cutup" and big city sophisticate, has gained even wider popularity. So it was inevitable that rivals should appear on the channels. Now we have the Merv Griffin (CBS), the Dick Cavett (ABC), the Mike Douglas (CBS), and the David Frost series (the last two being Group Westinghouse productions). Although not all of these are confined to the late hours, each caters to a loyal following and features conversation and some form of theatrical entertainment. One element of these programs rarely seen on TV before the 1960's is—

Satire. . . . The late playwright George S. Kaufman once remarked, "Satire is something that closes Saturday night." If that was true of Broadway, it was doubly so of TV. Save for the contributions of the late Fred Allen, Robert Benchley and a few others, the tongue–in–cheek approach was absent from the air.

Robert Blake, the perceptive public–relations chief of Group W productions, put it well when he said, "Although satire may be the caviar of the entertainment world, the fact is that more places today serve ham and eggs than the delectable roe of the sturgeon." But, he added, more and more Americans are acquiring a taste for it. And as proof he could have cited the popularity of such performers as Henry Morgan, Woody Allen, Mort Sahl and Dick Cavett.

Too, it will be recalled that the British–originated satirical series, "That Was the Week That Was," had a successful run on NBC until it became more pretentious than funny. As for the Smothers Brothers show, although it aroused furious protests from the conservative–minded, which resulted in its cancellation by CBS in 1969, its jibes at politicians and the Establishment, plus its irreverence, won the enthusiastic approval of the under–30 crowd.

Along with proof that there is a place for satirical funning, came renewed evidence of the current popularity of—

Conversation Shows. . . . During the pioneering period of video, when millions were content to gape at the tube regardless of what was on it, some observers feared that the box in the living room would destroy the art of conversation in the American home. This parlous objective may already have been achieved, but the fact is that a goodly number of TV programs do feature literate talk today.

In this connection, it should be remembered that television is merely treading the path long ago carved out by radio. At this time the sound medium, whatever its artistic or intellectual deficiencies, offers many verbal prestidigitators, including Long John Nebel, Barry Farber, Barry Gray, Martha Deane, Bill Mazer, Brad Crandall, Jack O'Brian, Arlene Francis, and others.

The continuing popularity of such programs contradicts the idea that "talk is cheap." In reality, it's one of the most valuable commodities on the air. Many sponsors and their ad agencies now acknowledge this, just as more and more of them realize the artistic and commercial importance of—

The Negro in TV. . . . Within the last five years, members of the black minority have won new stature as performers. Formerly, the majority of them were confined to music, solo comedy or to the roles of menials in drama. It was regarded as a truism that the average viewer would refuse to accept the Negro as an announcer, a newscaster or as a participant in a commercial. An Afro-American starring in a weekly drama or comedy series was unheard of.

However, the racial barrier was crossed suddenly and without commotion when Bill Cosby won praise and also an Emmy as the co-star of Robert Culp in the NBC espionage series, "I Spy." Then, during the 1968–69 season, also on this network, Diahann Carroll scored as heroine of the series, "Julia." There were only a few protests.

Result: The producers, convinced that racial liberalism would not damage their bank accounts, have joined the ride on the equality bandwagon. So for the 1969–70 season, they have signed black stars or featured players for 14 weekly series.

Among these you will find not only "Julia" and a new Bill Cosby show on NBC, but also the Leslie Uggams show on CBS, and on ABC, "Room 222," about a black high school teacher, with Lloyd Hanes in the principal role.

Of course, Negro musicians—giants in their field—such as Duke Ellington and Count Basie and comedians of the importance of Sammy Davis, Jr. have long been accorded honored positions on TV. But they have been the exceptions.

However, the TV audience now takes for granted the rapidly growing number of blacks among the ranks of actors, newsmen, masters of ceremonies, moderators and interviewers. And it is a rare day when one does not see Negroes in what was formerly an ultra-exclusive white domain—the commercials.

When one beholds what is happening on the living room screen today, one may marvel at the racial progress that has been achieved since the film makers turned out those stereotypes still seen occasionally on the late-late shows of—

The TV Movies. . . . Shortly after World War Two, during a party given in my honor by the Young and Rubicam ad agency in the Victorian Room of Hollywood's Brown Derby, Bob Hope introduced me to an M–G–M executive. While discussing TV, the latter remarked, "You can bet on it, our studio will never lower itself by making pictures for that miserable little peep show."

Today, there is not a major lot in Hollywood that is not reaping fortunes through the making of films for that very "miserable little peep show." In addition to providing action–adventure series, situation comedies and documentaries, the motion–picture companies are making vast sums by selling the TV rights to their feature theatre films. Their products are shown not only during the daytime and the early evening hours, but during network prime time every night of the week. Belying the predictions of some West Coast Cassandras that television would deliver a fatal blow to the movies, it has instead proved to be a lifesaver.

Consider a few items: Ten years ago NBC paid $800,000 for the privilege of screening several times the *Wizard of Oz*, and more recently CBS handed over to M–G–M more than $1 million for the same rights, bringing the cost of each showing to about $200,000.

But by TV standards, even these are picayune sums. For NBC not long ago bought the rights to 94 United Artists films for $116 million; CBS spent $800,000 for each of 30 features, with the privilege of showing them twice; and ABC enriched 20th Century–Fox's treasury by $20 million for 23 movies to be seen on the living room sets during the 1969–70 season.

TV's movie gold rush had its start a few years ago when *The Bridge on the River Kwai* drew an estimated audience of 60 million. For a while it seemed that a program specifically made for television could not compete with an outstanding motion picture. However, during the latter part of 1968, no theatre feature film landed among the "top ten" attractions. The reason? Too many complaints from the public about the too frequent interruptions for commercials.

Even so, the TV demand for movies is so great that many producers have about reached the bottom of their barrels. As a result, some of their pictures have actually been seen as many as 30 times on independent stations in one city.

So now, with NBC as the pioneer, networks are producing some of their own feature films. One of these, "The Name of the Game," became the basis of a successful weekly drama series.

Rivaling or perhaps even exceeding the importance of the movies to TV programming is—

Pro Football. . . . Sparked by the legends created by the New York Jets and their sensationally unpredictable quarterback "Broadway Joe" Namath—and before that by the N.Y. Giants and the Green Bay Packers—pro football has become TV's Number One igniter of popular frenzy.

This means that as far as television is concerned, the professional pigskin game is "big business." For the 1968–69 time span, the networks spent $110 million for football broadcast rights. In addition to the sums paid for the regular season gridiron battles, the 1968 Super Bowl Game sold its airing privileges for $2.5 million. However, this income was justified by the fact that the contest attracted 70 million TV–viewers.

Because of the size of the audience and the gargantuan costs, sponsors pay hefty sums for the chance to air their "messages." The NFL games on CBS are reported to have brought in as much as $70,000 for a one–minute commercial and the AFL contests on NBC $40,000 for a sales spiel of similar length.

Commenting on the role played by pro football in TV, the *Wall Street Journal,* a publication not unaccustomed to dealing with figures, reports the opinions of some observers who say that the sport is "overexposed." Maybe so. But nevertheless, many may recall what happened on Nov. 17, 1968. Some employee of NBC cut off the Jets–Raiders game in order to put on that children's classic, *Heidi* (which was scheduled to be telecast at that time), and what followed was a national furor of such intensity that it rocked the broadcasting world. You would have thought that the network was guilty of mayhem, murder and high treason.

College football? It's still around. In fact, ABC has bought the games of the National Collegiate Athletic Association (1970–71 season) for a tidy annual sum of $12 million. But it can't be denied that the rah–rah circuit is overshadowed by the pros—a far cry from those ancient days when the gridiron season began in September and officially ended on Thanksgiving Day, with a Bowl game or two thrown in January 1 as lagniappe.

But if the interest in our institutions of higher learning has declined as far as TV sports are concerned, the contrary is true when it comes to—

Educational Television. . . . Known as ETV, a term embracing not only classroom types of instruction periods, but also forums, discussions, drama, music and even comedy, for years it lagged behind commercial TV. But today, the National Educational Television Network (NET), which provides programs for stations throughout the country, has become a vital force.

Non–commercial TV, in fact, is now on the verge of a most promising future. At this writing, there are 159 educational outlets on the air in the United States and many of their offerings prove that "culture" need not be synonymous with dullness.

This, because ETV is at last the inheritor of generous funds supplied by what is known as—

Public Television. . . . Unlike commercial TV, which is sustained by the dollars of sponsors, this form of telecasting gains its support from foundations, the government itself and the contributions of the viewers.

The Ford Foundation, a major backer of ETV, has provided so far approximately $181 million for the raising of the cultural level of the channels. One of its recent grants—of $7,463,000— was donated for a year of "supplementary general support."

Ford recently served as the "angel" of the now defunct Public Broadcast Laboratory (PBL), an experimental series which failed to live up to expectations. The Carnegie Commission on Educational Television has also played an influential role in this field.

But from a long–range point of view, perhaps the most significant factor of all has been the creation of the Corporation for Public Broadcasting (CPB). This is an agency chartered by the Federal Government, launched by an act of Congress in 1968, "to encourage the growth and development of non–commercial radio and television."

CPB has already made an initial allocation of $5 million for a comprehensive study of the entire field of educational broadcasting. This will eventually provide the guidelines for the nationwide setup. Today only a minute portion of the public has even heard of this agency's activities, but during the years to come it may affect the entire programming structure of both radio and TV in the United States.

But regardless of the quality of a program, its effectiveness depends on how well it is received on the set of the viewer. The improvement of reception is the prime objective of—

Cable TV. . . . During recent years, especially in metropolitan centers with highrise buildings and in certain remote rural areas, the pictures on the screen in too many instances have been marred by "ghosts" and a grainy fuzziness.

So a new industry has come into being—Community Antenna Television (CATV), known to most persons as Cable TV. Its basic function is to give the viewer pictures of clarity and high definition.

It originated about 20 years ago in the little town of Lansford, Pa., a community surrounded by high hills, which made good television reception almost impossible. Robert J. Tarlton, an ingenious technician, built a community antenna on one of the heights and fed the signals thus received to some 3,000 homes by means of cable, with each home paying a small fee for the service.

That was the beginning of it all. During the autumn of 1969 some 2,300 CATV systems were in operation throughout this country, with about 4.5 million subscribers, who were assessed sums averaging from $4.00 to $7.50 a month.

Originally conceived as a mere deliverer of already existing network and local programs, CATV now is also creating some of its own features, with emphasis on community affairs.

Frederick W. Ford, president of the National Cable Television Association, has proposed that the industry employ satellites to bring in distant programs and use its channels for the distribution of educational and agricultural material, weather reports, medical information for physicians, pickups of Congressional hearings and repeats of outstanding public service specials. According to Ford's plan, some 36 key distribution points from coast to coast would receive these features from the satellites.

The final status of CATV is yet to be settled by the Federal Communications Commission and the courts. But one thing is certain: although those in the industry carefully avoid the use of the words, what some of them are already providing the public is—

Pay TV. . . . As already mentioned, CATV is originating a considerable number of programs, and a portion of the monthly fees received reimburses the CATV systems for these.

As for toll or pay television, presented without disguise, it has been the victim of a number of setbacks during the last few years. Experimental operations such as those in Connecticut, Oklahoma and California suffered because of local conditions, economics and free TV.

And yet, despite the furious campaigns waged against it by theatre owners and station operators, many astute broadcasters believe that the day of pay television will soon be here. They regard it as almost certain that such events as the Super Bowl, the World Series and championship fights, in addition to operas, symphony concerts, ballets and Broadway plays, will be seen exclusively by this means.

As for the motion–picture studios, it is believed that they too will eventually welcome it as a profitable market for their films. So will the Broadway theatrical producers who, it is pointed out, might regain the entire cost of a production through a one night telecast. The network? Well, it's a safe bet that, already in possession of facilities and talent under contract, they will not remain aloof. It is no secret that their plans are already drawn up, ready to be put into effect at a moment's notice.

But even if toll TV should blanket the land, that would not doom free television, for the latter would still have available to it most of the entertainment programs and also the telecasts of—

News, Documentaries and Special Events. . . . It is these that give the medium its true importance, even though on a day–to–

day basis the comedians and singers draw the largest number of viewers. Each of the aforementioned categories is based on what is happening in the world, and when the three networks cover live such an occurence as the *Apollo 11* moon walk, for example, the make–believe of the studios is completely overshadowed by reality.

As a matter of fact, according to a recent study made by the most important of the rating services—Nielsen—a number of "real life" telecasts have won the largest number of viewers in the history of television. This survey shows that 53.5 million television households (93.9% of all U.S. TV homes) "viewed at least a part of the sponsored network coverage of *Apollo 11* from July 14–27, 1969."

And in 1963, the network coverage of the events following the assassination of President Kennedy was "viewed, at least in part, by 49.4 million television households (96.1%)." Too, tremendous audiences tuned in on Colonel John Glenn's (1962) and other space flights, the funerals of Senator Robert F. Kennedy and Dr. Martin Luther King, Jr., the turbulent 1968 Chicago Democratic National Convention and President Johnson's State of the Union Address (1967). Also, more persons than ever before saw the Presidential election returns on their home screens, Nov. 6, 1968, when Nixon triumphed over Humphrey.

Although the networks gain their basic incomes from entertainment, it is the "actuality" features that give them their greatest prestige and their most valuable publicity. This is so not only because more events of world-shaking importance than ever before are taking place today, but because TV at this time, unlike its first two decades, has few new dominating personalities. How many new stars are there now who have the impact of such personalities as Milton Berle, Lucille Ball, Arthur Godfrey, Jackie Gleason, Bob Hope, Red Skelton, the late Ed Murrow, David Brinkley, Chet Huntley and Walter Cronkite during their early years on the channels?

All of the above (save Murrow) continue to maintain their popularity. So does the Ed Sullivan variety hour (now in its 22nd year) and ditto the shows of Skelton and Ball (both in their 18th year), "Lassie" (in its 15th), Lawrence Welk and "Gunsmoke" (in their 14th year), and "Bonanza," which recently observed its 10th anniversary.

But the truth is that most of the younger stars seen in purely escapist entertainment have a difficult time competing against the front pages of the newspapers. More and more of the increasing number of young college graduates are demanding that even programs of pure entertainment help television fulfill its function as "a window on the world." For after all, Vietnam, racial turmoil, ghetto and campus riots are on tap by the mere twist of the dials.

Jack Perlis, the astute TV and radio public–relations man of A.T.&T., the world's largest corporation, makes this point: "The business and industrial giants of America are beginning to realize that when they go into TV, they must show some social responsibility and offer more than time-killing folderol. And this some of them do by sponsoring specials—entertainments or documentaries—that appeal to the intelligent young and to the older opinion makers. Their first consideration is not high ratings but quality."

And the mention of specials, which in the primitive times of TV used to be known as "spectaculars," reminds one that the networks can no longer depend on the regularly scheduled weekly situation comedies, Westerns and action–adventure series to carry them to victory in the battle for ratings. During the 1969–70 season, approximately 300 of such shows will be seen, with NBC alone preparing 100 such offerings, starring among others Jack Benny, Julie Andrews, Jack Paar, Rowan and Martin, Debbie Reynolds and Diana Ross and the Supremes. Most of such productions will cost anywhere from $150,000 to $300,000.

And now . . . having concluded the aforegoing cursory notes on the development of broadcasting during the last decade and a half, we come to the story's—

Epilogue. . . . the net result of all that has gone before. Toward the end of 1969, there were 497 Very High Frequency and 126 Ultra High Frequency commercial TV stations on the air in the United States, and also 71 Educational Very High Frequency and 88 Educational Ultra High Frequency outlets in operation.

The number of commercial AM radio stations had jumped to 4,246 and commercial FM broadcasters to 1,976. There were also 365 educational FM outlets.

Almost one–third of all U.S. households had color TV sets, according to the U.S. Bureau of the Census, and 55 percent had receivers capable of bringing in Ultra High Frequency telecasts.

NBC's research department estimated that 20,560,000 color TV receivers were in use, and the Nielsen rating service reported that the country's television audience, excluding Alaska and Hawaii, numbered around 184,230,000 persons in almost 95 percent of all American homes.

And that, my readers, I'm certain you will agree amounts to a lot of LOOKING and LISTENING.

For the benefit of those who would like to be reminded of the development of TV during the years since the first publication of this volume, herewith is presented a list of some of the high-light attractions, innovations and personalities of that period.

Although radio was still playing to enthusiastic listeners in 1955, with such shows as those of Jack Benny and "Amos 'n' Andy", television was rapidly becoming the major medium. "I Love Lucy," Ed Sullivan, Jackie Gleason, and Arthur Godfrey's "Talent Scouts," among others, were top successes.

1956

The 90–minute entertainment specials, known as "spectaculars," came into vogue. . . . "Gunsmoke" and "Wyatt Earp" scored among the Westerns. . . . "The Show of Shows," starring Sid Caesar and Imogene Coca, was a comedy sensation. . . . One of the big money quiz shows, "The $64,000 Question," ignited a national frenzy. . . . Frank Sinatra, Eddie Fisher and Patti Page rode high in public esteem. . . . Mary Martin in *Peter Pan* was the top–rated special. . . . News period gained new importance with Edward R. Murrow an almost sacrosanct figure. . . . NBC introduced new techniques, with live cameras wandering from coast to coast, in a show titled "Wide World."

1957

More and more specials appeared. . . . Video tape was introduced, doing away with the necessity of telecasting a program live. . . . Several systems of pay TV appeared on an experimental basis but failed to achieve success financially. . . . Among the high rated shows: "I Love Lucy," Ed Sullivan, "Disneyland," Perry Como, "I've Got a Secret," "Talent Scouts" and "$64,000 Question."

Annie Get Your Gun, with Mary Martin; *Green Pastures*, with William Warfield; the Old Vic and the Royal Ballet of Great Britain; *Kiss Me Kate*, with Alfred Drake, and *The Great Sebastian*, with Alfred Lunt and Lynn Fontanne were among the year's distinguished specials. Danny Thomas, and that long–

running Western, "Maverick," also came to the home screen. The inauguration of President Eisenhower and the visit of Queen Elizabeth II to the United States led the list of special event features.

1958

The quiz show scandal raged and eventually drove the big money giveaways from the air. . . . Most of the top shows of the preceding year retained their popularity, with the addition of "Have Gun, Will Travel," Danny Thomas, Alfred Hitchcock and Dinah Shore. The Miss America Pageant, as always, drew a tremendous audience.

"Omnibus," the best of all TV's experimental series, won acclaim and many awards. The death and funeral of Pope Pius XII provided the news highlight of the year.

1959

Among the series, "Rifleman," "Perry Mason" and "The Desilu Playhouse" were added to the top popular shows. . . . The Emmy winners included, among others, "Playhouse 90," the "Alcoa–Goodyear Theatre," "Omnibus," the "Huntley–Brinkley Report," Edward R. Murrow, Perry Como, Dinah Shore, Jack Benny and Fred Astaire. . . . A news sensation: The broadcast from a satellite over the Atlantic of President Eisenhower's Christmas message to the world.

1960

Politics of the Presidential campaign dominated the air. As already pointed out, the John F. Kennedy and Richard M. Nixon debates played a decisive role in the election of President Kennedy.

The decline of soap opera reached its final phase on radio, with the cliffhangers transferring to TV. . . . Outstanding series: "Twilight Zone," "The Untouchables," and "77 Sunset Strip." . . . Award–bedecked entries: Sir Laurence Olivier in "The Moon and Sixpence," the Leonard Bernstein "N.Y. Philharmonic Young People's Concerts"; the "Huntley–Brinkley Report" and "Tonight with Harry Belafonte."

1961

FCC Chairman Newton Minow accused TV of being a "vast wasteland." . . . Some 30 million viewers (the largest TV day-time audience up to that time) saw astronaut Alan Shephard's 15–minute rocket flight launched at Cape Canaveral, Florida. . . . and from then on, year after year, the Mercury, Gemini and Apollo space shots attracted record–breaking numbers of viewers. . . . President Kennedy's inauguration, the first live TV coverage of a White House press conference, and the President's journey abroad to confer with de Gaulle and Khrushchev made this a headline–winning news year. . . . Educational TV was formally launched, and "The Defenders," "Rawhide," and the Dick Van Dyke series stood out among the successful shows. Among the appealing specials: *Victoria Regina,* with Julie Harris, *The Teahouse of the August Moon,* with David Wayne, and "The Broadway of Lerner and Loewe," with Maurice Chevalier, Richard Burton and Julie Andrews.

1962

Another big TV news period: 135 million saw Col. John H. Glenn Jr.'s first U.S. manned orbital flight, according to NBC. . . . and 80 million tuned in Mrs. John F. Kennedy's White House tour. . . . The first U.S.–European transatlantic exchange of live TV programming came this year. . . . So did the dramatic network coverage of the University of Mississippi race riots and the suspenseful reports on the Cuban crisis.

Among the top popular shows: Bob Hope's Christmas entertainment in Vietnam, "Hazel," Red Skelton, the "Luci–Desi Hour," "Wagon Train," Garry Moore, "Perry Mason," and the two medical fiction series: "Dr. Kildare" and "Ben Casey."

1963

This was perhaps the biggest news and special events period in the history of television. . . . The dramatic and shocking incidents that followed the assassination of President Kennedy, including the murder of the accused assassin, Lee Harvey Oswald, by Jack Ruby, in the sight of millions of viewers, stunned the nation.

. . . The funeral of Pope John and the coronation of Pope Paul, the first Town Meeting of the World, each feature transmitted via satellite, and the showing for the first time by means of a live telecast of an astronaut, Gordon Cooper, in the interior of his spacecraft were among the truly notable features of the 12–month period.

"The Beverly Hillbillies" and the Andy Griffith series joined the top ten. . . . "Bonanza" and "Gunsmoke" exemplified the staying power of Westerns, and among the game shows, "What's My Line?" continued to be the most enduring. . . . The British satirical import, "That Was the Week That Was," "East Side, West Side," "My Favorite Martian," the Judy Garland, Jimmy Dean, and Patty Duke shows won popular approval.

1964

For the first time, both the Democratic and Republican National Conventions were streamlined so that the most important segments would come during prime TV time. . . . "Peyton Place," the sex saturnalia, achieved such popularity during the night hours that ABC scheduled two installments a week instead of the usual one. . . . James Nabors' hillbilly U.S. Marine character, "Gomer Pyle," captured the fancy of the viewers. . . . And among the most important specials were the opening of the New York World's Fair, the Presidential campaign periods, and the election night coverage, marking the landslide victory of Lyndon B. Johnson over Senator Barry Goldwater.

1965

The inauguration of President Johnson was seen by 50 million TV-watchers . . . the state funeral of Sir Winston Churchill and the visit of Pope Paul to New York City . . . the documentaries dealing with Vietnam . . . and the civil rights demonstrations again emphasized that the recording of reality was television's most important function. . . . NBC was so engrossed in public affairs that it devoted three and a half hours of an evening to U.S. foreign policy. . . . The Smothers Brothers show (CBS), the spoof on espionage stories, "Get Smart" (NBC), and the

Barbra Streisand special, "My Name is Barbra," created an unusual amount of comment.

1966

The color year, with the three networks telecasting their entire evening schedules in "rainbow hues." . . . Movies became top channel attractions, *The Bridge on the River Kwai* (ABC) playing to an estimated audience of 60 million. . . . The Broadway theatre was the source of the best entertainment specials—*Brigadoon, Guys and Dolls, Porgy and Bess, The Glass Menagerie,* and *The Death of a Salesman.* It was the revival of the latter on CBS that gave a new spurt to quality plays on TV. . . . Among the series, "Mission: Impossible" won unanimous praise, "That Girl" impressed the public with its youthful zest, and "Batman" created a veritable craze for "camp" on the living room set.

1967

The Arab–Israeli war and President Johnson's "summit" conference with Soviet leader Aleksei Kosygin at Glassboro, N.J., provided the material for two of TV's noteworthy factual reports. . . . More and more viewers showed signs of boredom when confronted with the conventional weekly items; so the networks in an effort to revive interest, offered almost 300 specials—big name entertainment, documentaries and news features. . . . Movies attained new heights of popularity and some of the broadcasting companies began to produce feature pictures of their own. . . . With the telecasting by ABC of a four–hour documentary about Africa during one night of prime time, the informational special won new prestige. . . . The Winter Olympics, the "Ice Follies" and "Rudolph the Red–Nosed Reindeer" gained wide approval. . . . And among the successful weekly programs were "Bonanza," Dean Martin, Walt Disney, "Tarzan," "I Spy," "Star Trek," "The Man from U.N.C.L.E.," "Run for Your Life," the Andy Williams show, the Smothers Brothers, Carol Burnett, "The Flying Nun," "Judd for the Defense." . . . Joey Bishop, in an attempt to give NBC's Johnny Carson competition, entered the late–hour show field over at ABC.

1968

By the end of this year, NBC had gone 100 percent to color. . . . CATV systems had increased to 1,800. . . . Educational TV was booming. . . . The assassinations of Dr. Martin Luther King, Jr., the civil rights leader, and of Senator Robert F. Kennedy were responsible for the most moving radio and TV coverage of 1968. . . . The big stories, politically, of course, were the national conventions, the Presidential campaign, and the election of Richard M. Nixon. . . . The network coverage of the Democratic Convention in Chicago, violent demonstrations, and brutal battles between Vietnam war protesters and the police aroused heated controversy.

As a result of the violence that marked the year, producers announced they would reduce the ratio of murder and mayhem in their shows. For a while, they did; but by December the old law of the gun and the fist prevailed again.

Rowan and Martin's "Laugh–In" on NBC became the Number One show in ratings, with such old reliables as "Bonanza," Dean Martin, "The Virginian" and Walt Disney's "Wonderful World of Color" also in the upper ranks. . . . "Julia," "Ironside," "Dragnet," "The Ghost and Mrs. Muir," "Here's Lucy," "Mayberry RFD," "Hawaii Five–O," and "The Good Guys" also brought in cash and kudos.

Among the specials, the experimental dramas of the "CBS Playhouse" and of NBC's "Prudential On Stage," the TV essay, "Don't Count the Candles" by Lord Snowdon, "Sol Hurok Presents," Vladimir Horowitz's piano recital and "He's Your Dog, Charlie Brown" were standouts.

1969

When TV and radio fans, for decades to come, speak of this year, there can be no doubt whatsoever that they will recall it as the time of the most sensational, dramatic, gripping and suspenseful series of telecasts (up to now) in the history of broadcasting. The eight–day TV coverage of the *Apollo 11* journey, climaxed by the landing of astronauts Neil Armstrong and Edwin (Buzz) Aldrin on the moon (July 20) thrilled (and that word is advisedly used) a global audience of more than 500 million—the largest ever gathered to witness a television feature.

Those now living will never forget what they saw on their screens that memorable Sunday night. From the moment of the liftoff at Cape Kennedy (July 16) until the splashdown, the networks gave their viewers magnificent coverage. The events abroad the U.S. *Hornet,* the recovery ship, where Armstrong, Aldrin and their companion Michael Collins, were greeted by President Nixon, the ticker tape parades and the state banquet given them by the President in Los Angeles merged into an epic tapestry of sight and sound.

There will be other landings on the moon, but the one in July was the first, and, therefore, the most significant.

As in other years, the events of the world outside of the studios again exceeded in interest the entertainment offerings. Among these: President Nixon's two visits abroad, including his stopover in Communist Romania, and Senator Edward M. Kennedy's TV address to the nation, explaining his involvement in an auto accident that resulted in the drowning of his companion, Mary Jo Kopechne.

The inauguration of President Nixon and the state funeral of former President Eisenhower also received first–rate coverage. . . . The music of the shaggy long–haired rock groups flourished all over the channels. . . . In Glenn Campbell and Johnny Cash, the "country" style of song received a hefty boost. . . . The "conversation" shows of Dick Cavett and David Frost made most favorable impressions. . . . Merv Griffin, with heavy emphasis on boyish charm, transferred from Group W. Westinghouse to CBS in order to combat Johnny Carson and Joey Bishop during the late hours. . . . The long–running shows of TV maintained their popularity. . . . Of the newer laugh periods only "Laugh-In" gave evidence of staying power. . . . And the often entertaining Smothers Brothers divertissement was thrown off the channels by CBS because of its controversial material.

As this is being written, a new season is about to begin—that of 1969–70. What will it be like? Good, poor or mediocre? Memorable or easily forgotten?

Well, as always, you will find the answer by watching that tube in the living room. . . . Do that, and you'll know more than any critic can tell you.

Index